Sustainable Solutions for Water Resources

Policies, Planning, Design, and Implementation

James Sipes

WILEY

John Wiley & Sons, Inc.

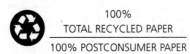
Library of Congress Cataloging-in-Publication Data:

Sipes, James L.

    Sustainable solutions for water resources : policies, planning, design, and implementation / James Sipes.

      p. cm.

    Includes bibliographical references and index.

    ISBN 978-0-470-52962-1 (cloth)

      1. Water resources development—Planning. 2. Water-supply. 3. Water—Law and legislation. 4. Water resources development—United States—Planning. 5. Water-supply—United States. 6. Water—Law and legislation—United States. I. Title.

  HD1691.S617 2010

  363.6'10973—dc22

                                          2009043687

Contents

Acknowledgments

Writing acknowledgments is the best part of writing a book, because it means you made it! You finished. You turned everything in . . . and you had to have met at least one or two deadlines. Yes!

Special thanks to Margaret Cummins, Leslie Saxman, and all of the talented people at John Wiley & Sons for putting my words together so they make sense. A writer could not survey without good editors and a good publisher.

To all the people who shared their thoughts, projects, photographs, and advice, thank you. I particularly appreciate the kind folks at EDAW.

I owe a lot to my three kids, because they inspire me and help me understand what is important in life. Matt is one of the enlightened engineers, and when he graduates from the University of Kentucky I am confident he will help us find sustainable solutions to addressing our water resource concerns. Sara and Alexandra encouraged me and offered advice, and they gave me the confidence to keep writing. Sara is my talented musician, and one day I want to be there when she receives her Grammy. Ally is already a tough-nosed but beautiful lawyer, and you had better not mess with her in court.

To the Sipes family, thank you for your continued support. I love you guys.

And finally, to Angie Bowen Sipes . . . yes, this is your book, too. Thank you for completing the captions for me when I didn't like the ones I wrote. Now that this book is done I will work on taking you to Bora Bora like I promised.

And to Oprah, yes, I would love to be the first nonfiction book in your book club. I promise to jump up and down on the couch if you have me on your show.

1.0 OVERVIEW

1.1 THE IMPORTANCE OF WATER RESOURCES

Is it really necessary to have a chapter on the importance of water resources? How about I simplify this section and get to the point: Without water, there would be no life on this planet. Water is *the* major environmental issue of the 21st century; all other concerns pale in comparison.

We think of Earth as a water world, and it certainly is, with ocean waters covering nearly 71% of Earth's surface.

Ninety-eight percent of the water on the planet is in the oceans and therefore unusable for drinking. Of the 2% of the fresh water, the majority is in glaciers and the polar ice caps. Approximately 0.36% is in underground aquifers, and about the same amount makes up our lakes and rivers. (See Figure 1.1.)

But although there is plenty of water on Earth, it is not always in the right place, and it is not always there when we need it. The world's population is expected to expand to over 9.4 billion people by 2050, and scientists are concerned that our water resources will not be able to

Figure 1.1 *Water is the most important environmental issue of this or any other century. Image courtesy NRCS.*

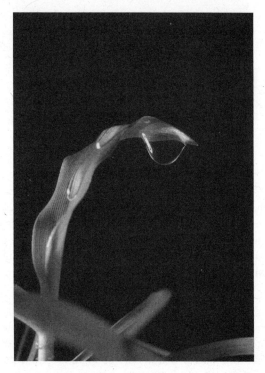

Figure 1.2 *Water is essential for life on this planet. The question is how to protect existing water resources while meeting all the demands for water. Image courtesy NRCS.*

accommodate this mass of people. According to the Stockholm International Water Institute, more than 1 billion people worldwide do not have adequate clean drinking water, and 2.5 billion lack safe sanitation (U.S. Census Bureau).

In most parts of the United States, people take for granted that cheap, clean water will always be available to us. In other parts of the world, tens of millions of people do not have access to safe water. The United Nations calls it a crisis of epic proportion. According to the U.S. Census Bureau, at the beginning of 2000, one-sixth (1.1 billion people) of the world's population was without access to improved water supply and two-fifths (2.4 billion people) lacked access to improved sanitation. The majority of these people live in Africa and Asia.

In recent years, though, even the United States has experienced severe droughts that rival the dust bowl days of the Great Depression. Water is a natural resource that is

already in short supply in many parts of the nation, and the situation is only going to get worse. As the population continues to grow, demands for water increase, and climate change mucks up the hydrologic cycle, water will become even scarcer. (See Figure 1.2.)

For example, the state of Georgia is one of the fastest-growing states in the United States. In the past two decades, however, Georgia has experienced the two worst droughts on record. According to the U.S. Army Corps of Engineers, on August 14, 2008, Lake Lanier, which supplies most of the water for the Atlanta metropolitan area, had fallen to 16 feet below full pool. This is a full 9 feet lower than the lake level during the droughts of 2007. Within a matter of days, Atlanta was running out of water.

It is important to point out, though, that the issue is not just about water availability. Water quality is increasingly becoming a major concern. Poor water supply and sanitation have a high health toll. Much of our water is polluted to the point where it is no longer safe for human use. One of the keys to ensuring we have sufficient water for the future is our ability to use small amounts of clean water to bring large productivity gains.

Since this book is about "sustainable" solutions to water resources, I would be remiss if I did not talk about the amount of energy it takes to meet water demands and the environmental impact of our actions. According to the National Resources Defense Council (2009), the collection, distribution, and treatment of drinking water and wastewater nationwide produce as much carbon dioxide each year as would 10 million cars on the road (www.nrdc.org/water/energywater.asp). We need to develop sustainable water resource policies that allow us to meet all of our needs.

The 1987 Bruntland report from the World Commission on Environment and Development defined sustainable development as development that "meets the needs of the present generation without compromising the ability of future generations to meet their needs." One objective of the Commission is to find the right balance between society's needs for economic growth, protection from floods, and affordable power, with environmental concerns such as water quality, the preservation of wetlands, and the protection of threatened or endangered species. (See Figure 1.3.)

Figure 1.3 *The Yolo Bypass Wildlife Area is a 3,700-acre restoration project that opened in 1997 near Sacramento and Davis, California. It is part of the 59,000-acre Yolo Bypass, which provides flood control for the cities in the area. Image courtesy NRCS.*

1.2 OVERVIEW OF WATER RESOURCES

Water resources involve surface water, water below ground, and water that falls from the sky. Most cities meet their needs for water by withdrawing it from the nearest river, lakes, reservoir, or aquifer. In some parts of the United States, precipitation is considered to be public domain because it is such a valuable resource.

One thing discovered over the years is that groundwater and surface water are fundamentally interconnected and are integral components of the hydrologic cycle. They have to be thought of as one cohesive system.

The United States Geological Survey (USGS) compiled estimates of surface-water and groundwater withdrawals for the nation at five-year intervals since 1950. The data are compiled at the county, state, and national levels for eight categories of water use. These include:

1. Public supply
2. Domestic
3. Irrigation
4. Livestock
5. Aquaculture
6. Self-supplied industrial
7. Mining
8. Thermoelectric power

1.2.1 Rivers and Streams

When we talk about water resources, most people probably think of rivers and streams. The United States has more than 250,000 rivers that collectively make up 3.7 million river miles in length. The longest river in the United States is the Missouri, which is approximately 2,500 miles in length, and the largest is the Mississippi, which has a flow volume of 593,000 cubic feet per second at its mouth (www.americanrivers.org/library/river-facts/river-facts.html). (See Figure 1.4.)

Figure 1.4 *The NRCS in Idaho has developed the Conservation Stewardship Program, which encourages producers to adopt new conservation practices and improve or maintain existing conservation practices that address resource concerns. The program has had a significant impact on water quality in the state. Image courtesy NRCS.*

Of the country's rivers and streams, 45% were reported as impaired according to the 2002 National Assessment Database. Sediment, pathogens, and habitat alterations are the biggest problems associated with the nation's rivers and streams. This fact obviously raises some big concerns.

The 2002 National Assessment Database includes water quality information for all states as well as the District of Columbia and the U.S. Virgin Islands. Alabama, North Carolina, Washington, Puerto Rico, the tribal nations, and the island territories of the Pacific did not provide data electronically in 2002.

A *watershed* is defined by the U.S. Environmental Protection Agency (EPA) as "the geographic region within which water drains into a particular river, stream, or body of water" (www.epa.gov/adopt/defn.html). Watershed drainage areas are large, ranging from 20 to 100 square miles or more. Each watershed is composed of a number of smaller "subwatersheds," which typically range from 5 to 10 square miles in size.

Rivers have had a major impact on settlement patterns in the United States. Most of the nation's major cities in the eastern part of the country were built along rivers. Rivers provide water needed for drinking, sanitation, growing crops, and even navigation.

Unfortunately, many rivers and streams have been seriously impacted by human activities. The EPA considers urban runoff and pollution from other diffuse sources the greatest contaminant threat to the nation's waters. More than 235,000 river miles in the United States have been channelized, 25,000 river miles have been dredged, and another 600,000 river miles are impounded behind dams. Nearly 40% of the rivers and streams in the United States are too polluted for fishing and swimming. Thirty percent of the native freshwater fish species in North America are threatened, endangered, or of special concern (www.americanrivers.org/library/river-facts/river-facts.html).

Floodplains

Floodplains are areas along rivers, streams, or creeks that may be inundated with water following storms. Floodplains help reduce the number and severity of floods, filter stormwater, and minimize nonpoint source pollution. Water expands into the floodplain areas and infiltrates into the ground, slowing water flow and allowing groundwater recharge. Floodplains also provide habitat for both flora and fauna. One significant problem, though, is that human activities have had significant adverse impacts on the effectiveness of a stream's floodplain to convey and store floodwater.

Riparian Corridors

Riparian corridors include grass, trees, shrubs, and a combination of natural features along the banks of rivers and streams. Protecting these corridors is critical for preserving water quality. Riparian zones also harbor a disproportionately high number of wildlife species and perform a disparate number of ecological functions compared to most plant habitats (Fischer and Fischenich, April 2000). Riparian corridors often are considered to coincide with the 100-year floodplain.

Impaired Rivers and Streams Database

Information on state-reported causes and sources of impairment is available from the National Assessment Database at www.epa.gov/waters/305b.

Environmental Protection Agency, *Handbook for Developing Watershed Plans to Restore and Protect Our Waters.*

1.2.2 Groundwater and Aquifers

Groundwater is one of the world's most critical natural resources. It is vital to most nations, and worldwide more than 2 billion people depend on groundwater for their water needs. It provides half the drinking water in the United States and is essential for maintaining the hydrologic balance of surface streams, springs, lakes, wetlands, and marshes around the world.

Groundwater is the largest source of usable water storage in the United States, containing more water than all of the reservoirs and lakes combined, excluding the Great Lakes. According to scientists, an estimated 1 million cubic miles of groundwater is located within one-half mile of the land surface. Only a very small percentage of groundwater is accessible and can be used for human activities (http://pubs.usgs.gov/gip/gw/gw_a.html).

Groundwater is stored in an underground aquifer as a geologic formation, group of formations, or part of a formation that contains sufficient saturated, permeable material to yield significant quantities of water to wells and springs (www.nationalatlas.gov/mld/aquifrp.html). The top of the zone of saturation is known as the *water table*, and it varies significantly in depth from one region to the next. The water table can rise in wet years and fall in dry years. All aquifers have an impermeable layer beneath that stops groundwater from penetrating farther.

The area over which water infiltrates into an aquifer is known as the *recharge zone*. Rainwater that falls in the recharge zone typically makes its way into the aquifer below. Rates of recharge for many aquifers can be very slow because water has to infiltrate through layers of soil and rocks. Preservation of the water resources requires protection of groundwater quality and recharge capacity. Recharge to shallow, unconfined aquifers can be preserved by restricting the amount of impervious areas. Some aquifers were formed a long time ago and are no longer actively recharged. If water is pulled from these aquifers, eventually they will become empty.

Most cities meet their water needs by withdrawing it from the nearest river, lake, or reservoir, but many depend on groundwater as well. Water is already in short supply in many parts of the world, and the situation is only going to get worse. According to USGS, groundwater is the source of about 40% of the water used for public supply and provides drinking water for more than 97% of the rural population in the United States. Between 30% and 40% of the water used for the agricultural industry comes from groundwater. An understanding of groundwater is important if we are going to continue to make good decisions about sustainable resources.

In recent years we have learned that groundwater and surface water are fundamentally interconnected and are integral components of the hydrologic cycle. Interestingly enough, most laws governing groundwater issues are based on the notion that groundwater and surface water have nothing to do with each other. In most parts of the United States, surface water is governed by doctrines of riparian law or prior appropriation. Groundwater traditionally has been treated as a common resource, with virtually no restrictions on accessing it. If you can afford to pay someone to drill a well and you happen to hit water, you can do whatever you want with it.

Today, the unregulated pumping of groundwater is no longer a viable option. In many parts of the United States, groundwater is being withdrawn at rates that are not sustainable, and the result is a degradation of water quality and quantity. The water level in aquifers is being lowered, and because people keep digging deeper and deeper wells in order to access the water, the water quantity is depleted even more. In coastal areas, intensive pumping of fresh groundwater has caused salt water to seep into fresh-water aquifers. Groundwater is also critical for the environmental health of rivers, wetlands, and estuaries. Groundwater withdrawals can result in reduced flows to streams and alter wetland hydrology. Changes in stream flow have important implications for water and flood management, irrigation, and planning.

Data about groundwater has been collected worldwide for decades. The Worldwide Groundwater Organization was formed in 1956, and it is just one organization involved in collecting such data. Worldwide maps of groundwater resources are available, and most countries produce their own maps. In the United States, one responsibility of the U.S. Geological Survey is to assess the quantity and quality of the nation's water supplies. On a national scale, quite a bit is known about groundwater resources, but most of that information is very general in nature. The USGS National Water Information System (NWIS) contains water data for the nation. USGS has offices around the country that collect local data and conduct studies as part of NWIS. The groundwater database contains records from about 850,000 wells, and data have been collected for more than 100 years. Measurements are commonly recorded at 5- to 60-minute intervals and transmitted to the NWIS database every 1 to 4 hours. The Ground-Water Database includes more than 850,000 records of wells, springs, test holes, tunnels, drains, and excavations. Each well location includes information such as latitude and longitude, well depth, and aquifer. This information is available online through USGS's NWISWeb, the National Water Information System Web Interface (http://waterdata.usgs.gov/nwis). (See Figure 1.5.)

The Regional Aquifer-System Analysis Program was initiated in 1977 as a response to droughts during that year. Computer models were used to develop estimates of current and future water availability for aquifers and to provide a baseline for future studies. The National Water-Quality Assessment Program was developed by the USGS in 1991 to determine the condition of the nation's streams, rivers, and groundwater.

The location, hydrologic characteristics, and geologic characteristics of the principal aquifers throughout the 50 states, Puerto Rico, and the U.S. Virgin Islands are described in the Ground Water Atlas of the United States (Miller, 2000; http://capp.water.usgs.gov/gwa/). The atlas consists of an introductory chapter and 13 descriptive chapters, each covering a multistate region of the country. The atlas provides useful information in a regional and national context, but it is not useful for design or planning projects. The information summarized in the atlas has been collected over many years by the USGS with state and local agencies as well as other partner agencies (USGS; Reilly, Dennehy, Alley, and Cunningham, 2008).

In the United States, groundwater management decisions are made at a local level, not at the federal level. State and local agencies manage water resources and collect and analyze local data. Each state produces a report about groundwater within its borders. For landscape architects,

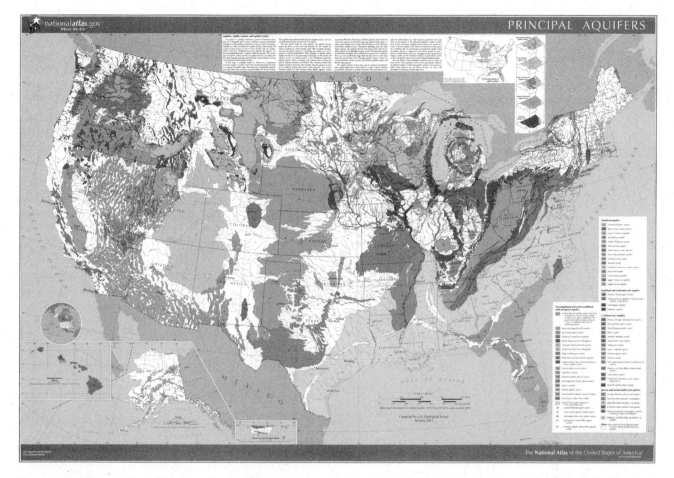

Figure 1.5 *The U.S. Geological Survey produces geospatial data for water resources. This map shows the major aquifers in the United States. Image courtesy USGS.*

the best source of groundwater information is from state, counties, or regional water districts.

Many states are using interactive maps for sharing groundwater information (see Figure 1.6). For example, the Kentucky Geological Survey (KGS) Interactive Groundwater-Quality Data Map displays groundwater-quality data for Kentucky. Users can choose from a list of 32 layers to display including geology, watershed boundaries, roads, orthophotography, and sinkholes. There are seven types of information about groundwater, including:

1. Water well and spring record search

2. Water well and spring location map service

3. Groundwater-quality data search

4. Graphical groundwater-quality comparison service

5. Groundwater-quality data map service

6. Karst potential index map service

7. KGS water research home page (www.uky.edu/KGS/water/research)

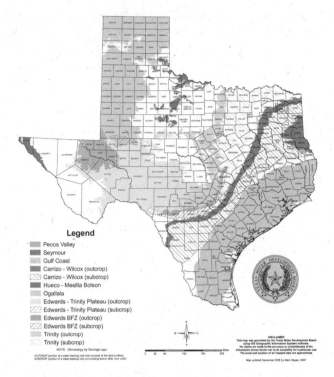

Legend
- Pecos Valley
- Seymour
- Gulf Coast
- Carrizo - Wilcox (outcrop)
- Carrizo - Wilcox (subcrop)
- Hueco - Mesilla Bolson
- Ogallala
- Edwards - Trinity Plateau (outcrop)
- Edwards - Trinity Plateau (subcrop)
- Edwards BFZ (outcrop)
- Edwards BFZ (subcrop)
- Trinity (outcrop)
- Trinity (subcrop)

NOTE: Chronology by Geologic age.

OUTCROP (portion of a water-bearing rock unit exposed at the land surface)
SUBCROP (portion of a water-bearing rock unit existing below other rock units)

DISCLAIMER
This map was generated by the Texas Water Development Board using GIS (Geographic Information System) software. No claims are made to the accuracy or completeness of the information shown herein nor to its suitability for a particular use. The scale and location of all mapped data are approximate.

Map updated December 2008 by Mark Hayes, GISP

Figure 1.6 *This map shows the major aquifers in the State of Texas. Most states collect data on groundwater and utilize this information to augment national water resource data. Image courtesy USGS.*

Counties across the United States are also implementing their own groundwater policies. For example, in 2001, the King County (WA) Council created the Groundwater Protection Program to provide management, policy, and technical expertise to help protect the quality and quantity of the groundwater resources in the county. One objective of the program is to help local communities identify groundwater protection needs and to integrate groundwater issues with other local planning efforts, such as growth management plans. King County uses an interactive map that enables visitors to select and query groundwater information through Web-based maps and geographically based software.

USGS also has geospatial information on aquifers and other water resources for use with Geographic Information Systems (GIS) programs. GIS are used to capture, store, retrieve, analyze, and display geospatial data. GIS and data management technologies allow users to manage the complexity of information needed on many design and planning projects. The power of today's GIS programs and the use of open GIS standards, combined with the vast array of digital data available via the Web, makes it easier than ever before to ask "what if" questions about a site, regardless of how large or small it is. The GIS data include information on:

- Aquifers
- Dams
- Groundwater climate response network
- Hydrologic units
- Surface-water sampling sites
- Stream-flow stations
- Water use
- General hydrography data

Groundwater maps show several types of data, including:

- Expected yield of a particular drilled well
- Well depth
- Aquifer type
- Depth to bedrock
- Naturally occurring, inorganic chemicals
- Groundwater geology

Groundwater maps are defined primarily using geologic contacts and hydrogeologic divides. These maps typically use USGS topographic maps as a base and include significant natural and man-made features, such as roads, streams and rivers, lakes, and buildings. The maps are generated from well log and drilling reports, bedrock information, and geologic and hydrogeologic data.

The volume of groundwater is decreasing in many areas of the world because of large-scale development of groundwater resources and a significant increase in withdrawals. Many people are concerned that if this trend continues, nations will not be able to meet domestic, agricultural, industrial, and environmental needs (USGS; Reilly, Dennehy, Alley, and Cunningham, 2008).

One positive sign is that groundwater withdrawals for irrigation decreased in the western United States in recent decades as a result of expanding urban areas, an increase in dry-land farming, and increased efficiencies of application. In contrast, groundwater withdrawals for irrigation in the eastern half of the country increased steadily over the same period, in part as a supplemental source of water to protect

Aquifers

The Ogallala Aquifer is one of the largest underground sources of water in the world. It covers around 174,000 square miles of the Great Plains and includes parts of eight U.S. states. The amount of water in the aquifer varies from region to region but is typically between 100 to 300 feet below ground. Most of the water in the aquifer comes from the last Ice Age. If irrigation demands continue at their current rate, there is a real chance that the Ogallala Aquifer will eventually run dry.

Despite its size, the Ogallala does not compare in size to the Guaraní Aquifer, which lies under Argentina, Brazil, Paraguay, and Uruguay, and covers 1,200,000 square kilometers. In places this aquifer is more than 1,800 meters in depth. Like the Ogallala, there are concerns that increased demand on the waters of the Guarani will have a negative impact on water quality and availability.

against dry periods (USGS, 1960–2000; Hutson, Barber, Kenny, Linsey, Lumia, and Maupin, 2005).

1.2.3 Lakes and Reservoirs

Did you know that other than Earth, the only planetary body that we know that has lakes is Titan, Saturn's largest moon? On our planet, most of the lakes are freshwater and most are in the northern hemisphere. Canada has 60% of the world's lakes. Worldwide, estimates are that there are more than 304 million standing water bodies, but the vast majority are small ponds, not lakes.

There are more than 39.9 million acres of lakes and reservoirs in the United States. Freshwater inland lakes and reservoirs provide 70% of the nation's drinking water (www.epa.gov/owow/lakes/lakessurvey). (See Figures 1.7 and 1.8.)

Freshwater lakes and rivers contain less than 0.01% of all water on Earth (USGS. The Water Cycle: Freshwater Storage. http://ga.water.usgs.gov/edu/watercyclefreshstorage.html), but they are an important water resource in many parts of the country. They are a major source of recreation, provide drinking water to many cities and rural developments, and are a major attraction for people seeking to build vacation homes. Most man-made lakes are created by constructing dams in river or stream valleys. These lakes and reservoirs typically are constructed for purposes of power generation, flood control, navigation, water supply, and recreation.

There are some major fundamental differences between natural lakes and man-made lakes, or reservoirs. The drainage basins of natural lakes typically are much smaller than are the basins of man-made lakes. In contrast, reservoir basins tend to be narrow and elongated, with dendritic branching, because they are most commonly formed in river valleys. Reservoirs receive runoff from large streams and rivers, and are not typically intercepted by wetlands or shallow interface regions.

Natural lakes tend to be located at the headwaters of rivers or streams, and the water levels are fairly consistent. Man-made lakes tend to be closer to the mouth of a river or stream.

Natural lakes tend to have lower nutrient and sediment concentrations than those in man-made systems. Small man-made lakes frequently have no outflow point, so they accumulate sediments and nutrients much faster than do natural lakes.

The water levels in natural lakes are fairly constant, while those in reservoirs fluctuate because typically they are managed for flood control, hydropower production, and/or navigation. Water released from reservoirs frequently comes from the bottom of the dam pool; as a result, it contains little dissolved oxygen. This may impact water quality downstream. Natural lakes, in contrast, typically release water from the surface of the lake, and it is well aerated.

One of the biggest benefits of reservoirs is that they provide a reliable source of water for human use. Water released downstream from reservoirs is regulated according to water use. Smaller man-made lakes may be constructed for agricultural irrigation, recreation, or aesthetic purposes. Deciding how much water to release and how much to store depends on the time of year, flow predictions for the next several months, and the needs for residential and commercial uses.

Figure 1.7 *Lake Tahoe is a large freshwater lake in the Sierra Nevada mountains on the California/Nevada border. The lake is a major tourism destination in all seasons. Image courtesy J. Sipes.*

1.2.4 Wetlands

In the United States, *wetlands* are defined in federal regulations as "those areas that are inundated or saturated by surface or ground water at a frequency and duration sufficient to support, and that under normal circumstances do support, a prevalence of vegetation typically adapted for life in saturated soil conditions. Wetlands generally include swamps, marshes, bogs and similar areas" (EPA, Manual Constructed Wetlands Treatment of Municipal Wastewaters, September 1999). (See Figure 1.9.)

The U.S. Army Corps of Engineers uses three characteristics when making wetland determinations: vegetation, soil, and hydrology. Unless an area has been altered or is a rare natural situation, indicators of all three characteristics must be present during some portion of the growing season for an area to be a wetland.

Figure 1.8 *Lake Tahoe is the second deepest lake in the United States. The depth of the water helps create the deep, rich blue that is visually so attractive. Image courtesy J. Sipes.*

Wetland hydrology refers to the presence of water at or above the soil surface for a sufficient period of the year. It is not always possible to identify a wetland during a field review because water is not always present. A more reliable approach is to measure the amount of water with a gauging station, but that is not always a viable option.

Wetlands serve as filters that minimize the amount of nutrients and sediments that drain into a lake. Bogs, marshes, ponds, estuaries and wet meadows, bottomland forests, mudflats, and wooded swamps are all different types of wetlands. Wetlands can range from small marshes to massive ecosystems such as the Everglades, which cover thousands of square miles. The Everglades National Park is 2,357 square miles in size, making it by far the largest national park east of the Mississippi River.

Wetlands are among the most productive ecosystems in the world; most environmental experts consider wetlands to be second only to rain forests in terms of environmental importance. But only in recent years have we begun to recognize the value of these resources. Historically, wetlands

Figure 1.9 *This open-water wetland is located in Newago County, Michigan. This type of wetland typically is located in shallow basins and includes shallow ponds and reservoirs. Image courtesy NRCS.*

were considered wastelands with little if any economic value. "Progress" was when we filled wetlands to create developable land. As a result, more than half of the wetlands in the United States have been destroyed by filling and draining. (See Figure 1.10.)

Wetlands provide a number of benefits, including improving water quality, reducing pollution, providing sediment filtration, reducing potential flood damage, producing oxygen, providing temporary water storage, and impacting nutrient recycling.

Worldwide, we have lost over half of our wetlands in the last 100 years. In New Zealand, for example, only 8% of the original wetlands remain. In Alberta, Canada, more than 60% of the wetlands have been lost. Since the 1600s, the United States has lost more than half of its native wetlands. Today, the United States has adopted a national policy of "no net loss" of wetlands and a goal of a net gain.

1.2.5 Coastal Zones

Population growth along the world's shorelines continues at a rapid pace, threatening coastal resources, global fisheries, and biodiversity. Two categories of coastal resources are identified in the U.S. National Assessment Database:

1. Coastal shorelines—the water immediately off shore, reported in miles

2. Ocean/near-coastal waters—the area of water extending into the ocean or gulf, range not specified, in square miles

A total of 27 states in the United States have coastal shorelines. Collectively there are a total of 58,618 miles of shoreline. The National Assessment Database assessed 2,571 miles of coastal shorelines, or about 4% of the nation's total. More than 83% of these shorelines were considered to be supportive of their anticipated use. The other 17%

Figure 1.10 *The state of Louisiana has lost up to 40 square miles of marshes and wetlands a year for the last several decades. Extensive renovation efforts are being undertaken to restore many of its wetlands and barrier islands. Image courtesy USGS.*

of shoreline miles were negatively impacted by pollutants, stormwater runoff, and industrial discharge.

There are also more than 54,120 square miles of oceans and near-coastal waters in the United States, but of the 5,000 square miles that have been assessed, 87% were identified as impaired. For example, it has been estimated that virtually all of Texas's coastal waters are impaired due to mercury contamination.

Data on Coastal Areas

In the last couple of decades, we have come to realize how little we actually know about coastal areas, so there has been a concentrated effort to collect more information and expand our knowledge base. In the United States,

the Coastal Zone Act Reauthorization Amendments of 1990 (CZARA) mandated that the EPA develop the Coastal Management Measures Guidance, which functions as a blueprint for coastal states and territories in putting together Nonpoint Source Pollution control programs. Under CZARA, states are required to develop management measures to address nonpoint source pollution, land use conflicts, and other issues that may have an adverse impact on coastal areas. The Coastal Management Measures Guidance includes management measures for urban areas, agriculture, silviculture, marinas, hydromodification, wetlands and riparian areas protection, and constructed wetlands. State Coastal Zone Management Programs address nonpoint source pollution under Section 6217 CZARA. These programs can provide the basis for developing or consolidating watershed plans in coastal areas. Coastal zone management measures guidance documents are available at www.epa.gov/owow/nps/pubs.html.

In the United States, the National Coastal Assessment addresses the condition of the nation's coastal resources. The results of these surveys are compiled periodically into a *National Coastal Condition Report*. EPA, the National Oceanic and Atmospheric Administration (NOAA), USGS, the U.S. Fish and Wildlife Service, and the states with coastal areas are all involved with developing the report. The *National Coastal Condition Report II*, which was published by NOAA in 2005, found that 35% of U.S. coastal resources were in poor condition, 21% were in good condition, and 44% were threatened. (See Figure 1.11.)

Under the Beaches Environmental Assessment and Coastal Health (BEACH) Act of 2000, EPA is working on addressing contaminants and pollutants in recreational waters. Detailed information on U.S. coastal condition trends are also available in the series of *National Coastal Condition Reports*, which includes information collected by the states, EPA, and other federal agencies to characterize the condition of the nation's coastal resources.

Figure 1.11 *This satellite image shows the extent of siltation along the Louisiana coast. Image courtesy USGS.*

The National Estuary Program (NEP) was established in 1987 by amendments to the Clean Water Act. The intent of NEP is to identify, restore, and protect nationally significant estuaries in the United States. Under NEP, states work together to evaluate water quality problems and their sources, collect and compile water quality data, and integrate management efforts to improve conditions in estuaries. There are currently 28 active NEPs along the nation's coasts.

Coastal Issues

Coastal zones have their own unique issues. Alternative water supply projects, such as desalination, aquifer storage and recovery, and reclaimed water use, are all being explored in coastal areas. Desalination is a process that removes salt and other minerals from brackish water and seawater to produce high-quality drinking water. There are more than 12,500 desalination plants worldwide, and that number is growing. Currently, about 60% of these plants are located in the Middle East. Although there is some discussion in the southern United States about utilizing seawater treated through desalination, the process is very expensive and currently is not affordable. It is much less expensive to treat and transport river water or to build a new reservoir than to treat seawater.

One concern along the Atlantic and the Gulf coasts is that drawing too much water from freshwater aquifers will result in "saltwater intrusion." Saltwater intrusion is a natural process that occurs in virtually all coastal areas and involves the encroachment of saltwater from the sea flowing inland into freshwater aquifers. In particular, the Floridan aquifer, which lies beneath Florida, southern Georgia, and parts of South Carolina and Alabama, is being threatened by saltwater intrusion in places. Some public wells on the northern end of Hilton Head Island, South Carolina, were closed after saltwater started seeping into the source there about 20 years ago.

In many coastal areas, aquifers are critical for supplying a substantial portion of water. The easiest way to avoid saltwater intrusion is to maintain an adequate level of freshwater in the aquifers. That is easier said than done, though. For example, currently more than 7 million people live in South Florida, and the result is a huge demand on the region's water resources.

There is also concern about the vulnerability of coastal areas, especially after Hurricanes Rita, Katrina, and Ike. Along the East and Gulf coasts, more than $3 trillion in infrastructure adjacent to shorelines is susceptible to erosion from flooding and other natural hazards. In the next few decades, these issues will have to be addressed. (See Figure 1.12.)

1.2.6 Precipitation

The term *precipitation* includes rain and snow that falls to the ground. In most of the United States, there is sufficient rain to grow crops and maintain rivers and lakes. According to USGS, the continental United States receives enough precipitation in one year to cover the land to a depth of 30 inches (http://ga.water.usgs.gov/edu/earthrain.html). One inch of rain falling on 1 acre of land is equal to about 27,154 gallons of water, so that is a lot of water, isn't it?

The amount of precipitation that falls varies considerably worldwide. London, England, receives 29.6 inches of rain per year and Rome, Italy, receives 2 inches more. Sydney, Australia, receives 48.1 inches and Tokyo, Japan, receives 60 inches per year. In Egypt, Cairo receives just 1 inch per year.

Across the United States, Savannah (GA) receives 129 inches of rain per year, while Los Angeles (CA) gets 12

Figure 1.12 *When Hurricane Katrina hit the Gulf Coast in 2005, it devastated much of New Orleans. Stormwaters that breached a levee flooded most of the Ninth Ward. Image courtesy FEMA.*

inches a year, and Las Vegas receives 4 inches of rain per year. Houston (TX) receives 46 inches; Knoxville (TN), 47 inches; Philadelphia (PA) 41 inches. It may surprise many who believe that it always rains in Seattle (WA), but the city only receives an average of 38 inches of rain per year, and Portland (OR) receives 36 inches. (See Figure 1.13.)

According to the National Weather Service, more than 50 trillion gallons of water fall over Georgia each year. If the State of Georgia was able to manage a major portion of this rainfall, it would have sufficient water to accommodate any future needs (Bazemore, 2007). Unfortunately, approximately 70% of Georgia precipitation is lost as evapotranspiration, while the other 30% runs into rivers, streams, and lakes. The state experiences little monthly or seasonal variations in rainfall, so there is a relatively uniform distribution of precipitation throughout the year.

In many southern states of the United States, tropical depressions, tropical storms, and hurricanes can result in long-duration rainfall of moderate to high intensity over large areas, and this can restore lake levels very quickly. Most of these types of events occur between June and November.

Much of the precipitation from rainstorms is absorbed back into the ground close to where it falls as long as there is sufficient pervious surface to allow this to happen. In urban areas, though, where the percentage of paved, impervious surfaces is much greater, much of the precipitation that falls runs off.

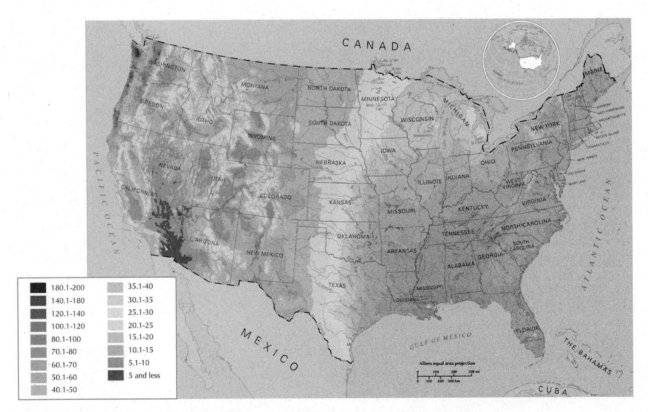

Figure 1.13 *The National Weather Service produces precipitation maps at both the national and local level. Image courtesy National Weather Service.*

Rainfall per City

City	Amount of water received when an inch of rain occurs	
	Area (square miles)	Amount of water (million gallons)
Atlanta, GA	131.7	2,289
Baltimore, MD	80.8	1,404
Chicago, IL	227.1	3,947
Cincinnati, OH	78.0	1,356
Denver, CO	153.4	2,666
Detroit, MI	138.8	2,412
Honolulu, HI	85.7	1,489
Houston, TX	579.4	10,069
Jacksonville, FL	757.7	13,168
Louisville, KY	62.1	1,079
Milwaukee, WI	96.1	1,670
New Orleans, LA	180.6	3,139
New York, NY	303.3	5,271
Philadelphia, PA	135.1	2,348
Salt Lake City, UT	109.1	1,906
Seattle, WA	83.9	1,458
Washington, DC	61.4	1,067

Note: 1 inch of rain falling on 1 acre is equal to about 27,154 gallons of water, and there are 640 acres in a square mile.
Source: http://ga.water.usgs.gov/edu/earthrain.html.

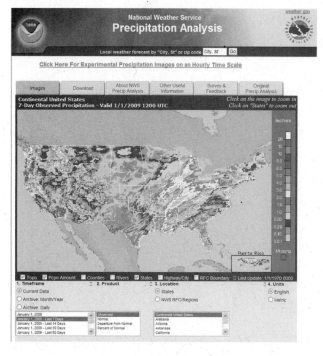

Figure 1.14 *The National Weather Service produces maps that show precipitation patterns for a specific period of time. This map shows the amount of precipitation in the United States for a 7-day period. Image courtesy National Weather Service.*

1.2.7 Sources of Information

Changes in precipitation patterns have significant impacts on our water resources. Developing a better understanding of precipitation and drought—regardless of whether it is for a national, state, or local level—will enable us to make better decisions about how to protect water resources. This knowledge will also help government agencies, private institutions, and stakeholders make more informed decisions about risk-based policies and actions to mitigate the dangers posed by floods and droughts. We may not be able to prevent droughts, but we can certainly help develop alternative water sources, introduce water-efficient planning approaches, and help establish effective and affordable redundancy in water systems.

It is difficult to predict future changes in regional precipitation patterns and to identify areas where drought is a priority, but there are digital tools that realistically generate forecasts across the United States with seasons and geographic area. For example, continuous, national-scale precipitation estimates are available through the Advanced Hydrologic Prediction Service (AHPS), a Web-based suite of forecast tools that are part of the National Weather Service's Climate, Water, and Weather Services. AHPS products are developed using sophisticated computer models and large amounts of data from multiple sources, including automated gauges, geostationary satellites, Doppler radars, weather observation stations, and the Advanced Weather Interactive Processing System. (See Figures 1.14, 1.15, and 1.16.)

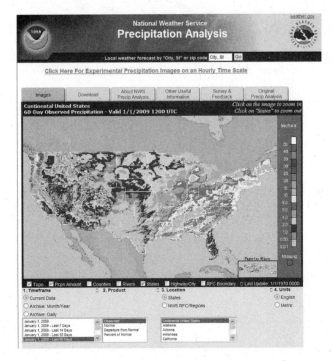

Figure 1.15 *This map shows the amount of precipitation in the United States for a 60-day period. Image courtesy National Weather Service.*

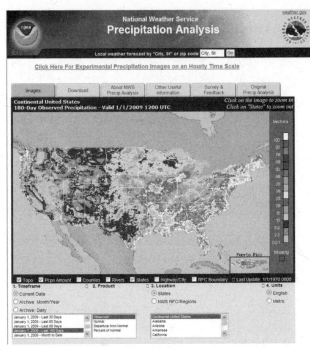

Figure 1.16 *This map shows the amount of precipitation in the United States for a 180-day period. Image courtesy National Weather Service.*

AHPS allows users to view a national composite map or to zoom into regions, states, and county-level areas over multiple time periods, including for the previous day and precipitation totals over the past 7, 14, 30, or 60 days. Archived data are available back to 2005 with monthly estimates of departure from normal and percent of normal precipitation. There are also links to historic data going back decades.

U.S. Snowfall Maps are Web-based products available from the National Climatic Data Center (NCDC). The data are extracted from a meteorological database from the U.S. Cooperative Observer Network (COOP). COOP consists of about 8,000 stations operated by state universities, state or federal agencies, and private organizations. The earliest data are from 1886, and they are organized by month. Data on snow are available from the National Operational Hydrologic Remote Sensing Center, which provides information on snow cover, snow depth, average snowfall, snowfall total the past 24 hours, and more. Information from radars, gauges, and satellites is combined to provide fairly accurate estimates of precipitation. According to the National Weather Service, the data set is one of the best sources of timely, high-resolution precipitation information available.

2.0 ISSUES INVOLVING WATER RESOURCES IN THE UNITED STATES

2.1 GLOBAL WARMING AND CLIMATE CHANGE

In the 2000 presidential debate, President George W. Bush was asked about global warming. He commented, "I don't think we know the solution to global warming yet and I don't think we've got all the facts before we make decisions." He then added, "Some of the scientists, I believe, haven't they been changing their opinion a little bit on global warming? There's a lot of differing opinions and before we react I think it's best to have the full accounting, full understanding of what's taking place."

These days, George W. may still not believe in global warming, but he is in a very small minority. There is universal agreement among scientists that global warming is occurring, except now we refer to it as "climate change." It is pretty hard to disagree with the concept that the climate is changing, isn't it?

The Kyoto Accord is an international treaty that calls for participating countries to reduce the amount of greenhouse gases they emit. As of 2006, 164 countries had agreed to participate. The United States and Australia both refused to ratify the treaty. The accord set a goal of reducing greenhouse gases by an average of 5% against 1990 levels over the five-year period 2008 to 2012.

Some scientists believe that climate change is inevitable to some degree, but others believe we can significantly reduce the amount of change by reducing greenhouse gas emissions. All agree that much of the warming in recent decades is most likely the result of human activities.

According to National Oceanic and Atmospheric Administration (NOAA) and National Aeronautics and Space Administration (NASA) data, the eight warmest years on record have all occurred since 1998, with the warmest year being 2005. Scientists predict that the most likely scenario for the continental United States is an increase in temperature by 5 to 10 degrees Fahrenheit by the end of this century.

2.1.1 Impacts of Climate Change

There is no question that climate change is having an impact on the availability of water worldwide, and these changes are expected to increase over time. Due to rising global temperatures, rainfall is expected to drop by 20% across much of the West and even more in the arid Southwest.

The Intergovernmental Panel on Climate Change projects that sea level will rise by 7 to 23 inches by 2100, and other studies predict that the increase will be far greater than that (www.ipcc.ch). Even at the more conservative estimates, the impacts will be devastating. (See Figures 2.1 and 2.2.) Communities along the coasts will be flooded, wetlands will erode, barrier islands and other natural protection will disappear, and the coasts will be more susceptible to hurricanes and storm surges than ever before. Levees in New Orleans, San Francisco Bay, and other parts of the country will collapse, because they were not designed to handle the added pressure.

The rising sea level will impact how rivers discharge their water into the ocean, which could significantly increase

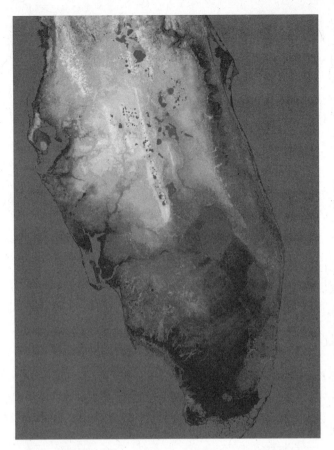

Figure 2.1 *Areas such as the Florida Panhandle are susceptible to changes associated with climate change, such as a rise in sea level. Image courtesy NOAA.*

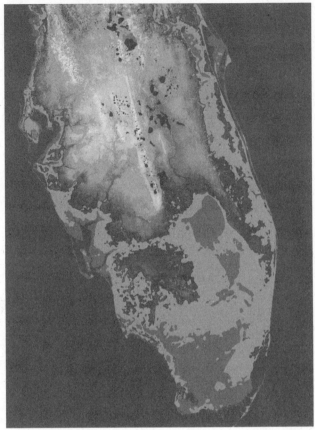

Figure 2.2 *If the sea level rises even a couple of feet, the impact on the Florida Panhandle will be significant. Many of the coastal areas will be inundated, and a new Florida coastline will be established. Image courtesy NOAA.*

the risk of flooding. The rising seawater will also push saltwater farther inland, and the result could be contamination of many existing water sources. Net losses of more than 402,000 acres of coastal wetlands are expected to occur in the next 50 years just in Louisiana.

Scientists predict that warmer temperatures will lead to more stormwater runoff, less snowpack, larger winter stream flows, and hotter, drier summers. It is feasible that much of the mountain snowpack in the continental United States will be gone by the end of the century. In the West, this would be disastrous because mountain snowpack is

a primary source of water. There is a greater likelihood of earlier spring flows, higher peak flows, and longer, drier summers.

Increased air temperature will result in a loss of moisture from lakes, rivers, and the oceans because of evaporation and transpiration. Scientists predict increased precipitation and evaporation and drier soil in the Midwest.

There will be a fundamental change in the nation's rivers and creeks, which will have a major impact on fish and wildlife species. For example, scientists estimate that up to

38% of locations currently suitable for coldwater fish could become too warm to provide habitat by 2090 (www.nrdc .org/globalWarming/hotwater/hotwater.pdf).

2.1.2 Addressing Climate Change

The future effects of climate change on water resources in the United States will depend in large part on the policies established to help protect these resources.

The U.S. government has established a comprehensive policy to address climate change. This policy has three basic components:

1. Slowing the growth of emissions

2. Strengthening science, technology, and institutions

3. Enhancing international cooperation

In the United States, energy-related activities account for three-quarters of the human-generated greenhouse gas emissions. The biggest culprit is carbon dioxide emissions that result from burning fossil fuels. In February 2002, the United States announced a comprehensive strategy to reduce greenhouse gas by 18% over a 10-year period.

Traditional planning processes are inadequate for dealing with the upcoming changes associated with global warming. Many of the laws that control water use were created many years ago and do not have the flexibility needed to address recent trends. Innovative planning approaches that promote sustainability and flexibility could significantly reduce the severity of impacts associated with climate change.

Most water experts say that one of the most important goals for water utilities and water resource managers is to increase cooperation and collaboration and minimize the competition for limited resources.

The Natural Resources Defense Council (NRDC), an international, nonprofit organization of scientists, lawyers, and environmental specialists, created a blueprint for action to address the impact of climate change on water resources. This blueprint includes four action items:

Action 1. Evaluate the vulnerability of water systems to global warming impacts. This involves con-ducting agency assessments of climate change impacts on water supply and working with water managers to evaluate regional vulnerability.

Action 2. Develop response strategies to reduce future impacts of global warming.

Action 3. Prevent future impacts by reducing greenhouse gas emissions by supporting policies such as mandatory caps on emissions.

Action 4. Increase awareness of global warming and water impacts, including educating customers and decision makers and raising public awareness (NRDC, www.nrdc.org).

But even if regulations to reduce global climate change are implemented, they will have no significant impact on short-term changes to water resources. Dealing with climate change will require a long-term commitment on the part of governments, organizations and agencies, and individuals. (See Figure 2.3.)

2.1.3 Sources of Information

The Climate Data Online site (www.ncdc.noaa.gov/oa/ climate/climatedata.html) provides access to an annual summary of monthly temperature means, departures from normal and extremes, heating and cooling degree data, and precipitation totals, departures from normal and extremes. A monthly tally of rain days, snow days, and days within selected temperature thresholds is also included.

The National Climatic Data Center (NCDC, www.ncdc.com) is the world's largest active archive of climate and weather-related data and information. NCDC operates the World Data Center for Meteorology in Asheville, North Carolina, and the World Data Center for Paleoclimatology, located in Boulder, Colorado. NCDC products are based in large part on land-based observations that contain meteorological elements, such as temperature, dew point, relative humidity, precipitation, snowfall, snow depth, wind speed, wind direction, cloudiness, visibility, atmospheric pressure, evaporation, soil temperatures, and weather occurrences such as hail, fog, and thunder. A number of products available from NCDC may be of interest to landscape architects.

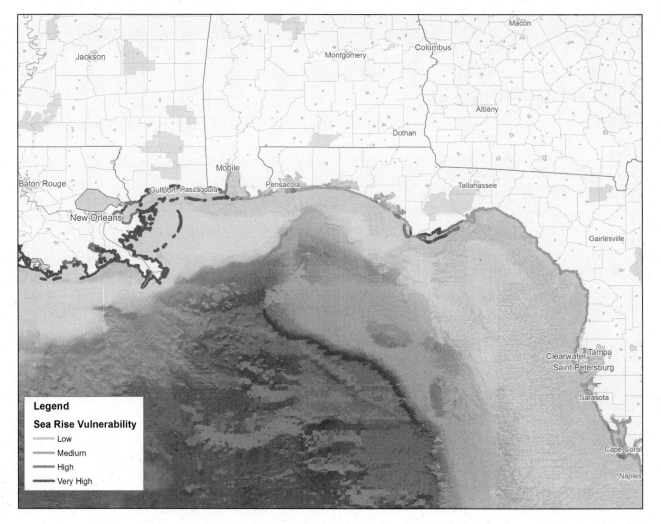

Figure 2.3 *This map shows areas along the Gulf Coast that are vulnerable to sea rise. If sea level rises up to 23 inches, as is predicted, the dark areas along the coastline will be flooded. Image courtesy EDAW.*

2.2 DROUGHT AND WATER WARS

It is difficult to list all of the droughts that have occurred worldwide over the years, much less in the United States—there just have been too many. On average, over the last decade Australia has experienced a 15% to 20% decrease in precipitation, and the drought that has hit the country is often referred to as "the Big Dry." Morocco has had a 50% loss in rainfall over the same time period.

In virtually every decade during which records have been kept, drought occurred in some part of the United States. (See Figure 2.4.)

Figure 2.4 *This image of a dry creek bed in Kentucky helps illustrate how serious recent droughts have been in the South. Image courtesy FEMA.*

When you ask most people about severe droughts, they think of the Dust Bowl days of the 1930s Great Depression era. The Dust Bowl gave us a glimpse of what can happen during periods of extreme drought. The droughts of that time had a devastating impact on the country. Agricultural areas of Colorado, Kansas, Oklahoma, Texas, and New Mexico were hit hard, and crops literally dried up from the lack of water (Tavares, 2009). In July 1934, more than 63% of the United States was considered to be severely to extremely dry, and the droughts led to a mass migration from Midwestern states to California.

Other famous drought years in the United States happened through the 1950s. In the 1960s, a drought hit the Northeast and Midwest that lasted for almost five years in places. A number of significant droughts occurred in the early 1980s in the Northeast and Midwest. The drought of 1988 and 1989 was devastating, killing as many as 17,000 people across the mid-Atlantic, Southeast, Midwest, northern Great Plains, and western states. Crops withered and died, and livestock and farm animals died in droves. The total amount of damages was estimated to be as much

as $120 billion, making it the worst natural disaster ever recorded in the United States. One long-term impact of the 1988 drought is that many aquifers were overpumped by farmers seeking to save their crops and their way of life (Folger, Cody, and Carter, March 2009).

In 1993, much of the southeastern states experienced extended periods of drought and very high temperatures. The 2000 droughts impacted the entire Southeast, extending westward as far as Texas. The Midwest and Rockies were hit hard by the droughts of 2002. Denver, Colorado, imposed mandatory limits regarding water for the first time in 21 years.

Missouri, Arkansas, portions of Louisiana, Tennessee, southeast Iowa, and northern Illinois were hit with severe droughts and heat during 2005, causing more than $1 billion in damages.

What might surprise you, though, is that recent droughts are similar to those in the 1930s. At the height of the 2006 drought season, 49.95% of the contiguous United States was experiencing drought conditions, and

61.5% was experiencing abnormally dry or drought conditions (http://drought.unl.edu/droughtscape/2007Winter/droughtscapewinter2007.htm). In 2007, the Southeast had its driest spring since 1895, and California and Nevada had their driest spring since 1924. According to the California Department of Water Resources, the average flow in the Colorado River is about half of what it was eight years ago. During the drought of 2007, every river in the southern Sierra Nevada received less than half its normal runoff (Noble, 2007).

Toward the end of 2007, the U.S. Government Accountability Office (GAO) projected that at least 36 states will face water shortages within five years because of a combination of rising temperatures, drought, population growth, urban sprawl, waste, and excess. The GAO went on to say that if drought conditions continued, more than 46 states would experience water shortages (http://watercrunch.blogspot.com/2008/02/psst-south-carolina-has-secret.html).

The western and southwestern United States are the most likely to have severe droughts, but the Southeast and upper Midwestern states have had similar problems in recent years.

2.2.1 Worldwide Water Wars

One concern that has been expressed by the U.S. Central Intelligence Agency, Britain's Ministry of Defense, and others is that we may be on the verge of water wars. Some predict that future wars will not be about oil or political boundaries but about water. Klaus Toepfer, director-general of the United Nations Environment Program, says that a future war over water is a distinct possibility (ScienceDaily 1999).

For example, in the Middle East, long a hotbed of conflict, the region has a severe shortage water. To make things worse, 90% of the usable water crosses international borders, so water is part of the political battles as well.

In the city of Bhopal, India, which has a population of 1.8 million, water was rationed to 30 minutes of water supply every other day during the droughts of 2009. More than 100,000 people rely solely on water brought in by trucks, and fights frequently take place as people try to get enough drinking water for a given day. The violence is expected to escalate as water shortages increase.

Some experts agree that we are currently having conflicts over water worldwide but believe that we will stop short of full out war. Fortunately, cooperation over water is far more widespread than conflict, at least for now.

2.2.2 Southwest Water Wars

Mark Twain was quoted as saying "Whiskey is for drinking. Water is for fighting." The Los Angeles Aqueduct was completed in 1913, and it diverted water from the Owens River more than 200 miles to Los Angeles and the San Fernando Valley. In the 1920s, there was literally war over the water, as city employees destroyed the dams and locks of Owens Valley's irrigation system, and, in retaliation, Owens Valley residents sabotaged the aqueduct.

Fortunately, today's water wars in the West typically are settled with lawsuits, not firearms, and the lawyers are staying busy. As of 2009, there were more than a dozen bill draft requests in the Nevada Legislature alone proposing changes to water law (Tavares, 2009). (See Figure 2.5.)

In Nevada, there have been numerous disputes over who owns and who should own the water in more than 230 hydrologic basins. Negotiations on some water allotments have been going on for decades, with no solution in sight. Ranchers need water for their livestock, farmers need water for their crops, environmentalists want water to maintain flora and fauna and natural processes, businesses want water to help manufacture and produce goods, and urban areas want drinking water for their citizens.

Ranchers and environmentalists are fighting the Southern Nevada Water Authority's plan to pump hundreds of thousands of acre-feet of water from rural eastern Nevada and pipe it hundreds of miles to Las Vegas. Much of the West's agriculture depends on irrigation. The federal government, through agencies such as the Bureau of Reclamation, subsidizes most agricultural production. The construction of dams across the rivers of the West has produced tremendous agricultural benefits, but the environmental impacts also have been dramatic.

Southern Nevada depends on Lake Mead, which is created by Hoover Dam, for 90% of its water needs. The region already uses more than its allocated amount of water, so obviously this approach cannot continue. The

Figure 2.5 *Hoover Dam is one of the Bureau of Reclamation's major dams constructed on the Colorado River. Construction on the dam began in 1930 and was completed in less than five years. Las Vegas receives most of its drinking water from Lake Mead through the Southern Nevada Water Project. Lake Mead is located southeast of Las Vegas and it is located in Nevada and Arizona. Image courtesy NRCS.*

only reason that this much water has been allowed to be pulled from Lake Mead is that wastewater is treated and returned back to the lake in order to keep an acceptable level of water.

Many experts believe that the drought and dry conditions that have hit the western United States in recent years are likely to persist and intensify. Scientists from the Department of Energy predict that even in a best-case scenario, the West could experience up to a 70% loss of water as a result of climate change (www.jyi.org/features/ft.php?id=284).

If this happens, it would jeopardize the region's water supply and water quality, compromise the health of rivers and lakes, and increase the risk of flooding for western communities (www.nrdc.org/globalWarming/hotwater/contents.asp).

The drought of 2002 was a real wake-up call for many in the Southwest. The Colorado River basin is the major source of water for people in the driest part of the United States. More than 30 million people in seven states depend on this river for water. The Colorado River drought began in October 1999, and for the next five years, inflow into Lake Powell, which is fed by the Colorado River, was about half of what is considered average. In 2002, inflow was the lowest ever recorded, and the total water available was only 25% of normal. There were real concerns that cities in southern California could lose more than half the water they normally receive from the Colorado River. If climate change results in less water in the Colorado River, as expected, the entire western United States will have to make some dramatic changes in how it manages water.

One of the biggest problems in the West is that water use is based on a misguided premise about the amount of water available. For example, as mentioned, much of the West depends on water from the Colorado River. The problem is that the 1922 Colorado Compact, which determines water allocation to seven western states, was calculated at a time when river flow was at its highest. The compact estimated the river flow as 22 million acre-feet per year, when in reality the average annual flow is closer to 14 million acre-feet. That is problematic because in 2009 water users had legal claims to more than 17.5 million acre-feet of river flow. In other words, more water is allocated than actually exists.

For the past century or so, dams, diversions, and groundwater pumping have been used to distribute water in the West. But water experts warn that these approaches will not work well in the future as demand for water increases, water availability declines, and climate change results in a warmer, drier climate.

Snowpacks in the Rocky, Cascade, and Sierra Nevada mountains are an important part of the hydrologic cycle in the West. The snowmelt in the spring provides much-needed water to maintain the flow in rivers and creeks. Snowpack supplies 70% to 90% of water resources in many parts of the West, so if the snowpack is reduced, we can expect some severe water shortages (NRDC, 2007).

2.2.3 Southeast Water Wars

Water wars in the United States are not limited to the western states. In the last few years, people living in the Southeast have started to appreciate that water is a finite and increasingly threatened resource. Beginning in 1997, there were five consecutive years of drought in many areas of the Southeast, and subsequent water shortages have raised serious questions about who owns the water in rivers, lakes, and aquifers. (See Figures 2.6 and 2.7.)

Figure 2.6 *Hartwell Lake, a man-made lake bordering Georgia and South Carolina, was completed by the U.S. Army Corps of Engineers in 1963. The primary purpose of the lake was to provide flood control, hydropower, and navigation. In 2007, the lake dropped to historic levels because of the drought that year. Image courtesy Steve Kiemele.*

These days, it seems every southern state is suing another. Florida, Alabama, and Georgia have been battling over water resources for decades, and discussions are becoming even more heated. In the early 1990s, North Carolina and Virginia battled over a proposed project by the city of Virginia Beach to divert water from Lake Gaston, a reservoir on the Roanoke River. The project was eventually completed, but not without hard feelings between the two states (http://drought.unl.edu/mitigate/status.htm).

South Carolina is embroiled in lawsuits with the state of North Carolina over water from the Catawba River. South Carolina is trying to prevent the North Carolina cities of Concord and Kannapolis from pumping millions of gallons a day from the river. South Carolina's argument was that a river flowing through one state into another state does not belong to the upstream state only (Associated Press, February 27, 2008).

In 2008, Kentucky, Virginia, and West Virginia all were hit hard by droughts. All three states had extreme drought conditions, the second-worst type of drought, and there were significant concerns about the risks of forest fires from falling leaves and tinder-dry conditions (Associated Press, February 27, 2008).

The state of Alabama also filed suit against Georgia, particularly Cobb County and the city of Marietta, arguing that they were taking more water from Lake Allatoona than allowed via a contract with the U.S. Army Corps of Engineers (Markeshia, 2008).

2.2.4 Peachtree Water Wars

In the southeastern United States, the city of Atlanta seems to be at the center of most recent water wars. Alabama, Georgia, and Florida have disagreed for decades on how to manage the water in the Apalachicola-Chattahoochee-Flint basin, which flows from northwest Georgia south along the border of Alabama and empties into Florida's Apalachicola Bay. One of the biggest issues is the amount of water impounded by Bufford Dam to create Lake Sidney Lanier, a

Figure 2.7 *Lake Oroville is located along the foothills of the Sierra Nevada's in northern California. In 2009, the South Fork of the Feather River was nearly dry because of droughts in the area. Image courtesy California Department of Water Resources.*

Figure 2.8 *Lake Lanier provides water for the Atlanta metro area. In 2007, the lake was more than 19 feet below normal water levels, and Atlanta was within days of running out of water. Image courtesy J. Sipes.*

38,000-acre lake that is metropolitan Atlanta's main source of drinking water. Lake Lanier supplies water for more than 3 million residents in the Atlanta region. More than 1 billion gallons of water are released from the lake every day. The Corps of Engineers bases its water releases on two requirements: The minimum flow needed for a coal-fired power plant in Florida and mandates to protect two mussel species in a Florida river (Nelson, 2007). (See Figure 2.8.)

The majority of Atlanta's water comes from surface water sources, with the Chattahoochee River and Lake Lanier being the biggest suppliers. Unlike other metropolitan areas, Atlanta is not located on a major body of water, and it is located at the headwaters of its rivers and streams, so flow is limited. In addition, the city sits on bedrock, so groundwater sources are limited. For these reasons, Atlanta is dependent on water from its reservoirs much more than most major cities are.

Alabama and Florida have contested metro Atlanta's right to additional drinking water from Lake Lanier since 1990, when the first of many lawsuits was filed. Georgia wants to keep more water in the lake, which is located just

north of Atlanta, to meet the city's water needs. Alabama wants enough water flowing down the Chattahoochee River to float barges, provide coolant for Southern Nuclear Plant Farley near Dothan, and provide water for its own growing communities. Florida wants more water flowing into the Apalachicola River to preserve two federally protected species of mussels in the Apalachicola Bay and to provide water for the Florida Panhandle. Prior rulings have established that the Army Corps of Engineers send more than 3 billion gallons of water a day to Florida during the worst droughts (Shelton, 2008).

In 2007, much of the Southeast experienced the most severe drought in more than 100 years. The drought extended over most of Tennessee, Alabama, and the northern half of Georgia as well as parts of North and South Carolina, Kentucky, and Virginia (Bazemore, 2007). In Atlanta, the drought hit especially hard.

By late October, Lake Lanier was more than 19 feet below normal level, a record low for the lake, and had less than 80 days of stored water left. There was concern that if Lake

Lanier was drained much lower it would be virtually impossible to refill (Bazemore, 2007). The watershed for Lake Lanier is only 1,040 square miles, which is extremely small for such a large lake. As a result, when the lake drops very low, it is very difficult to refill.

Weather forecasters warned that although the region might get some rain, it would not reverse the severe drought (Bluestein, 2007). Atlanta was on the verge of completely shutting down because of lack of water. The city was placed under statewide water restrictions in April that limited outdoor watering to three days a week. By May, Atlanta allowed watering only on weekends, and in September, environmental officials banned virtually all outdoor watering through the northern half of the state (Nelson, 2007). Water fountains were shut off, restaurants provided water only to customers who requested it, and there were even discussions about closing swimming pools and other water-oriented recreation areas.

Many Atlanta residents were amazed that the state had no contingency plans for providing water. According to Governor Sonny Perdue, the state's contingency plan was to "conserve and use our water wisely" (Nelson, 2007).

The state of Georgia sued the Corps, demanding that it send less water downstream to Alabama and Florida.

Both Alabama and Florida argue that Congress did not authorize Lake Lanier to serve as metro Atlanta's water supply when it approved Buford Dam in the 1940s. The dam was built in the 1950s, forming Lake Lanier. According to Alabama and Florida, the dam was approved to control floods, float barges downstream, and generate hydropower. Water released from Lanier runs downstream from Atlanta through a series of lakes and dams; it supplies hundreds of towns, factories, farms, power plants, and recreational facilities in all Georgia, Alabama, and Florida (Vetter, 2008).

If Georgia had spent the money to build the reservoir, it would belong to Georgia, Alabama and Florida say, but since it was funded by federal taxpayers, the reservoir is not just for use in the Atlanta metro area. Former Georgia governor Roy Barnes disagrees, saying his plan was to guarantee metro Atlanta's water supply from Lanier for 20 years while the state built a series of reservoirs to take pressure off the lake (Shelton, 2008). Georgia wanted the Corps of Engineers to hold enough water in Lake Lanier to guarantee metro Atlanta enough water, even during droughts.

In late 2007, Atlanta Mayor Shirley Franklin proposed exploring the option of piping in additional sources of water from Tennessee rivers or even pumping in seawater from the Atlantic coast.

The Georgia governor asked for President Bush's help in 2007 in easing regulations that require the state to send water downstream to Alabama and Florida, calling them "silly rules." Perdue asked the president to exempt Georgia from complying with federal regulations that dictate the amount of water released from Georgia's reservoirs to protect two mussel species downstream (Nelson, 2007). Perdue called the federal regulations a "tangle of unnecessary bureaucracy" that got in the way of the state's ability to manage valuable water resources.

Alabama Governor Bob Riley was not pleased with Governor Perdue's comments. He replied: "The suggestion by Gov. Perdue that the water supply problems of Atlanta are more critical than the needs of the people of Alabama and Florida is . . . disappointing. . . . Until Georgia accepts that its needs are no more critical than those of its downstream neighbors, the prospects for a negotiated solution are indeed dim" (Zeccola, 2008).

Drought

The definition of what drought is and what drought is not has profound implications for the environment and all segments of society, yet it may be different for each. Many attempts have been made to develop a comprehensive and meaningful definition. A generic definition provides a starting point:

> Drought is a persistent and abnormal moisture deficiency having adverse impacts on vegetation, animals, or people.

Source: National Drought Policy Commission Report (http://govinfo.library.unt.edu/drought/finalreport/fullreport/ndpcfullreportcovers/ndpcreportcontents.htm).

When a U.S. circuit court ruled that Georgia does not have authority to use Buford Dam for water storage and that the water being sent downstream would continue, Perdue went to a higher court: He asked hundreds of Georgians to pray to God for rain. Perdue later said, "We have come together, very simply, for one reason and one reason only: To very reverently and respectfully pray up a storm" (Jarvie, 2007) The next day, up to an inch of rain fell in and around Atlanta, and it rained for 9 of the last 12 days of the year (Vetter, 2008).

While waiting for their prayers to be answered, Georgia legislators suggested changing the state's northern border so that the Tennessee River would become part of Georgia. Not surprisingly, Tennesseans did not take kindly to that idea. In early 2008, the city of Chattanooga, Tennessee, had 2,000 bottles of water delivered to the Georgia State Capitol with a note that basically said "This is all the Tennessee water you are going to get" (Zeccola, 2008).

Drought Monitor

The U.S. Department of Commerce, U.S. Department of Agriculture, and National Drought Mitigation Center publish a weekly Drought Monitor on the Internet, posted at http://drought.unl.edu/dm/index.html.

Unfortunately, the bottles of water from Chattanooga were not enough to offset the ongoing drought. In late September 2008, Lake Lanier's water level was at or near a new record low every week, and Lake Hartwell, a federal reservoir between Georgia and South Carolina on the Savannah River, was 14 feet below full level.

By the spring of 2009, water levels in Lake Lanier were much closer to normal, and 60 miles to the west, Lake Allatoona was full or nearly full all year. Many of Georgia's other lakes, including Lakes Burton, Oconee, Rabun, and Seed, were at or near full capacity (Shelton, 2008).

Five Basic Levels of Drought

D0 Abnormally Dry

D1 Drought—First Stage

D2 Drought—Severe

D3 Drought—Extreme

D4 Drought—Exceptional

2.3 WATER DEMANDS

As of July 2009, there were some 6.78 billion people in the world, a number that is increasing daily. China has the largest population with 1.33 billion, or 19.65% of the people on this planet. India is second with 1.17 billion, or 17.23%. Third on the list of most populated countries is the United States.

In 2009, the United States had a population of 307 million people. The United States is the fastest-growing industrialized country in the world, having added 100 million people in the past 39 years. We are expected to add the next 100 million even faster. According to estimates by the U.S. Census Bureau, sometime around 2040, the population in the United States will pass the 400 million mark (El Nasser, 2006).

The one given is that all of these people will need water to survive. One problem in the United States is that on a person-by-person basis, we use more water than any other country. In 2002, it was estimated that Americans were using 60,000 cubic feet of water per person (Organization for Economic Cooperation and Development). Each person currently uses about 80 to 200 gallons of water per day, and estimates of water use in the year 2000 indicated that over 408 billion gallons per day were withdrawn to meet water demands. (See Figures 2.9 and 2.10.)

2.3.1 Meeting Needs

As a general rule, there is plenty of water in the United States on most days. According to the U.S. Army Corps of Engineers, Americans typically use 380 billion gallons of water on a daily basis in this country, and there is usually around 1,400 billion gallons of usable water available every day (USGS. The Water Cycle: Freshwater Storage. http://ga.water.usgs.gov/edu/watercyclefreshstorage.html). (See Figure 2.11.)

Between 1950 and 1980, there was a steady increase in water use in the United States. The expectation seemed to be that even though population was increasing, there would always be available water to meet our needs. We have discovered, though, that the amount of usable water is a finite resource, and we have to take better care of this

---

Figure 2.9 *Lake Powell is the nation's second largest man-made lake, second only to Lake Mead in Nevada. Image courtesy USGS.*

Figure 2.10 *In 2004, Lake Powell was at its lowest water level in over 30 years due to the ongoing drought in the western United States. Image courtesy USGS.*

Figure 2.11 *Yard irrigation is one of the major uses of water by most households. Much of the water used in the traditional spray irrigation system in Clark County, Nevada, will evaporate because of the hot temperatures. Image courtesy NRCS.*

resource in order to ensure that we have sufficient water for the future.

Fortunately, reported water withdrawals declined in 1985 and have remained relatively stable since then in spite of the continuing increase in the nation's population. That is certainly a step in the right direction. Among the reasons for this reduction in withdrawals is improved water technology, greater public awareness of water resource issues, economic issues, and the many state and federal laws and regulations that "encourage" people to do the right thing. Water conservation and technological fixes such as new dams, cloud seeding, desalination plants, and underground water storage have greatly improved the availability of water in most parts of the country.

In general, the country is using water more efficiently today than ever before, particularly in the agricultural industry. But the population of many U.S. cities is growing so fast that it is outstripping these efficiency gains, requiring communities to develop new water supply sources. According to the National Research Council (2007) any gains in water supply will be eventually absorbed by the growing population.

Water demands also vary considerably from one region to the next. Historically, the southeastern United States has had an abundance of water resources. In 2000, average per-capita water use in the South was 1,553 gallons per day, a 2.5% increase from 1990. In comparison, per-capita water use in the rest of the United States was 1,168 gallons per day, an 11.3% *decrease.*

As the population boom continues, western water wars will become even more serious. Many water experts predict that global warming and droughts will turn the region into a dustbowl within the next 50 years.

2.3.2 Demands in Las Vegas

No place exemplifies the problems associated with increased water demands than Las Vegas, Nevada. Las Vegas is the fastest-growing city in the nation and is projected to have a population of over 800,000 by 2020. The city is growing at the rate of 5,000 new residents a month, and there is an ever-increasing demand for more water. It takes a lot of

2.3.3 Uses of Water

It may come as a surprise to some, but the two largest uses of water are thermoelectric power and irrigation. Thermoelectric power accounts for about half of the total water withdrawals in the United States. Irrigation accounts for about a third of water use and is the largest use of freshwater in the nation.

Historically, more surface water than groundwater has been used for irrigation, but that is starting to change. The amount of groundwater being used for agricultural irrigation has increased dramatically over the last few decades. In 1950, for example, 23% of irrigation water was pulled from underground aquifers; in 2000, that figure had increased to 42%. That is a concern because since we cannot see the impact we are having on this water source, we do not seem to be as concerned about what happens.

Primary Water Uses

In the typical household, water is primarily used for:

- Flushing the toilet 40%
- Baths and showers 32%
- Laundry 14%
- Dishwashing 6%
- Cooking and drinking 5%
- Bathroom sink 3%

Source: U.S. Army Corps of Engineers, *Water Supply to the Nation*, 2007.

Figure 2.12 *Urban sprawl in Las Vegas, Nevada, has led to increased demand for water. Image courtesy NRCS.*

water to quench the thirst of that many people. (See Figure 2.12.) The Colorado River is the major water supplier for Las Vegas, providing more than 90% of the city's water. But in recent years, the river has had lower-than-normal flows as a result of increased water demands as well as climate change.

To meet future demands, the city of Las Vegas has proposed a plan to build a $2 billion pipeline that would pump water out of White Pine County, located northeast of the city, and send it to southern Nevada. A concern by residents of White Pine, though, is that there simply is not enough water to send to Las Vegas without having a detrimental impact on the area (Moran and Hinman, 2007).

2.3.4 Options for Meeting Demands

There are a number of different ways to meet water demands. Traditionally, we pulled water from rivers or underground aquifers and built reservoirs to make water available near our cities.

In recent years, water recycling projects have helped reduce the demand for freshwater and will be a major part of the long-term water resource management for many states. Water recycling is especially important in states such as California, which have limited freshwater supplies and are subject to periodic droughts.

Water reuse is becoming an intrical part of water management strategies to meet projected shortages. Water recycling is a low-energy source of water supply and is especially important in areas that have severe water shortages, such as southern California. Southern California imports most of its water via the State Water Project, Colorado River Aqueduct, and Los Angeles Aqueduct, so the energy cost to get usable water is very high. Reusing wastewater also helps improve the overall security and reliability of water supplies, especially in urban areas.

Another possible way to meet water demands is through desalination. Desalination is the process of removing dissolved salts from water. If we can find a cost-effective way to turn seawater into freshwater, and do so in an environmentally friendly way, we can address many of our water resource limitations, especially in coastal areas.

Some water experts believe that desalination plants along the Pacific Ocean in California or Mexico ultimately could provide water for coastal and interior cities, such as Denver, Salt Lake City, and Las Vegas (Woodhouse, 2008).

Desalination water treatment is an option that many are considering because:

- It is reliable.
- There is plenty of saltwater and brackish water available for treatment.
- Costs are becoming more competitive.

Compared to other water treatment options, desalination also can be implemented in a fairly short period of time. The downside of desalination is that the process is more expensive than other techniques, start-up costs are high, and it requires relatively high energy use.

The cost of a desalination plant varies considerably depending on capacity and the type of water being treated since the amount of pretreatment and posttreatment needed is different. A brackish water desalination plant may cost $40 to $50 million to construct; a seawater desalination plant can cost more than double that amount.

The two most common desalination technologies are thermal and membrane technologies. The thermal process heats saline water and produces a water vapor. This vapor is then condensed and collected as freshwater. Membrane processes rely on permeable membranes to separate salts from water.

Researchers have been exploring all potential sources of water to meet growing demands, and those with access to the coasts have been looking seriously at desalination water treatment. In 2006, there were about 12,500 desalination facilities in 120 countries worldwide. Collectively, these facilities have a total capacity of about 4 billion gallons per day. Almost 60% of these plants are located in the Middle East, where desalinated water accounts for more than 70% of the region's water supply. In the United States, there are approximately 250 desalination plants in this country. Florida (114), Texas (38), and California (33) are making the most extensive use of this process, and Texas and California have plans for several more facilities in the near future (Texas Water Development Board, 2005).

In April 2002, Governor Rick Perry directed the Texas Water Development Board to develop a recommendation for a large-scale seawater desalination demonstration project as part of an ongoing effort to address the state's water concerns. Texas has 370 miles of coastline, so access to seawater for desalination is very good. The state also has more than 2.7 billion acre-feet of brackish groundwater that needs to be treated before it can be used. According to a study done by the state, desalinated brackish water can cost about $1.50 per 1,000 gallons, while desalinated seawater may cost anywhere from $2.50 to $3.00 per 1,000 gallons or more (Texas Water Development Board, 2005).

2.3.5 Water Sources

There has also been a significant change in how people access water. In 1950, only 62% of the U.S. population obtained drinking water from public suppliers. Many got their water from surface water, private wells, and other sources. By 2000, more than 85% of the country obtained water from public suppliers. Approximately 34 billion gallons of water are produced by public water systems in the nation on a daily basis. More than 80% of water used for residential activities is for sanitary service and landscape irrigation. Public water distribution systems range in size from small facilities that serve a couple of dozen people to those that serve several million. The fundamental question is how to ensure there is an adequate water supply system to meet future needs. Will it be through public water systems, private systems, or a combination of both?

In 1978, federal funding covered 78% of the cost for new water infrastructure. By 2007, it covered just 3%. Studies from across the country reveal that private water systems charge more—often much more—than public systems (Snitow and Kaufman, 2008).

Many people will argue that the privatization of water will not affect U.S. consumers, but the facts say otherwise. When the French privatized their water services, customer rates went up 150% within a few years. In Britain, in an eight-year period, from 1989 to 1997, four large corporations were prosecuted 128 times for various infractions (Ortega, 2005).

One of the main problems with water privatization is that the public no longer has the right to access information or data about water quality and standards.

2.4 DEVELOPMENT PRESSURES

Water resources have had a tremendous impact on how the United States has developed over the centuries. During the settlement of this country, most communities were established around sources of water. Most major cities east of the Mississippi River are river towns. Major settlement of the western territories took place in the 1840s. Settlers quickly found out the value of water.

Much of the sprawling development patterns across the country have basically ignored the natural constraints of water resources.

The National Resources Conservation Service estimates that between 1992 and 1997, developed land in the contiguous United States increased by more than 11 million acres (NRCS, 2000), with much of this growth occurring around cities. In 2004, NOAA conducted a study to quantify the amount of impervious cover on a national basis. The study estimated impervious surface area for the contiguous United States to be 43,480 square miles, almost the size of Ohio. It also predicts an average of 1 million new single-family homes and over 10,000 miles of new roads per year (Elvidge et al., 2004).

Further complicating the problem is the fact that some of the greatest areas of growth over the past 10 years have been in the driest parts of the western United States. These include:

Nevada	66%
Arizona	40%
Colorado	31%
Utah	30%
Idaho	29%

An evaluation of development pressures can be an effective way to determine potential impacts on water resources. Each state establishes how distribution systems are designed, constructed, operated, and maintained. Environmental regulations and water quality regulations are also the responsibility of the state. (See Figures 2.13 and 2.14.)

2.4.1 Traditional Approaches to Meet Demands

In the past, the United States implemented major water resource, agriculture, and power projects to meet growing demands for water. In the early 1900s, there was a major federal effort to develop water resource projects to encourage settlement of the arid West. Projects such as the Yuma Project on the Colorado River (authorized in 1904) and the Klamath Project on the California–Oregon border (1905) focused on agriculture but eventually became primary providers of urban water and power services (Jones, 2008).

Other federal projects developed to meet demands for water, food, and electricity include the Hoover Dam on the Colorado River (1935), the Grand Coulee Dam on the Columbia River (1942), and the Shasta Dam of California's Central Valley Project (1945). The last of the traditional

Figure 2.13 *This 1984 satellite image shows the development pattern for Las Vegas, Nevada. Image courtesy NASA.*

large-scale reclamation projects to receive congressional authorization was the Central Arizona Project, which was constructed in the mid-1970s. In California, some of the nonfederal large-scale water projects constructed during this time were the Los Angeles Aqueduct (1913), East Bay Municipal Utility District's Mokelumne River Aqueduct (1929), and San Francisco's Hetch Hetchy Aqueduct (1934).

Most of the big water projects in the West were built before passage of the National Environmental Policy Act (1969), the Endangered Species Act (1973), and the Clean Water Act (1972) (Woodhouse, 2008). It is not likely we will ever see projects at that scale anytime soon because it is too difficult for large water projects to meet all of the existing environmental regulations.

2.4.2 Growth in the South

In the South, population growth has exploded in recent decades. As the region continues to grow, so does the

Figure 2.14 *This 2009 satellite image shows how Las Vegas, Nevada, has spread over the years. The increase in development has resulted in a greater demand for water resources. Image courtesy USGS.*

demand for freshwater. Much of the South's growth in recent years has occurred in the Piedmont Region in northern Georgia which has relatively little available groundwater and where the streams hold relatively low volumes of water (www.newscientist.com/article/dn15030).

During the drought of 2007, residential construction slowed down dramatically in the South, and many municipalities even talked about setting restrictions on future growth. Some discussed a moratorium on new residential construction until the water shortage is addressed. Atlanta, Georgia, seriously considered a moratorium because it would allow the city to improve its water infrastructure.

The South has more miles of rivers than any other region of the nation. It has always been considered a water-rich part of the country, but that perception is quickly changing (www.newscientist.com/article/dn15030).

From 1990 to 2000, water use in the Southeast increased 21.5% (from 40,614 million gallons per day [mgd] to

Figure 2.15 *In areas such as Miami, where land is scarce, one approach has been to develop man-made islands that are used for housing. Image courtesy EDAW.*

49,342 mgd) while population grew 18.5% (from 26.8 million to 31.8 million). In comparison, water use in the rest of the United States decreased by 0.4%, while population increased by 12.3% (www.newscientist.com/article/dn15030).

2.4.3 The Corps Meeting Demands

The U.S. Army Corps of Engineers is also working to meet development demands. The Corps is partnering with state and federal water supply agencies and private companies to upgrade the nation's aging water infrastructure (including reservoirs, diversion structures, pipelines, etc.). In many sections of the United States, significant parts of the infrastructure are 50 to 100 years old.

Updating these facilities is expensive and requires careful study to minimize adverse environmental impacts. These updates, though, will have a number of positive benefits for both the environment and the economy including:

- Increasing the efficiency of water supply systems
- Enhancing the quality and quantity of available water supplies
- Improving water conservation

- Achieving economies of scale by combining small systems into regional ones

- Providing increased security against chemical and biological threats

---

Atlanta Regional Council's 2003 Regional Development Plan

Atlanta Regional Council's 2003 Regional Development Plan (RDP) outlines 14 policies to guide regional growth through land use and its relation to transportation, environment, and the economy. These policies are intended to sustain a high quality of life. They include:

1. Provide development strategies and infrastructure to accommodate forecast population and employment growth more efficiently.

2. Guide new development to the Central Business District, transportation corridors, and activity centers.

3. Increase opportunities for mixed-use development, infill, and redevelopment.

4. Increase transportation choices and transit-orientated developments.

5. Provide variety of housing for individuals and families of diverse income and age groups.

6. Preserve existing residential neighborhoods.

7. Advance sustainable development.

8. Protect environmentally sensitive areas.

9. Create a regional network of connected green space.

10. Preserve existing rural character.

11. Preserve historical resources.

12. Inform and involve the public at regional, local, and community levels.

13. Coordinate local policies to support the RDP.

14. Support growth management at the state level.

Source: www.atlantaregional.com/qualitygrowth/qualitygrowth .html.

2.5 ENVIRONMENTAL CONCERNS

According to the U.S. Environmental Protection Agency (EPA), one of the most important areas of environmental concern is our water. Water quality is an issue of concern for human health in both developing and developed countries worldwide. This concern includes both quality and quantity. According to EPA, water is essential for life and plays a vital role in the proper functioning of the Earth's ecosystems. The pollution of water has a serious impact on all living creatures and can negatively affect the use of water for drinking, household needs, recreation, fishing, transportation and commerce (www.epa.gov/indicate/roe/ pdf/tdWater2-2.pdf). (See Figure 2.16.)

The public seems to recognize the environmental concerns associated with water resources. In the 1980s, the oil spill of the *Exxon Valdez* was a wake-up call for many, and it showed the devastating impacts of water pollution.

In a March 2008 survey conducted by Gallup, when Americans were asked to rate their top environmental concerns, their top four concerns were related to water quality. The top concern was pollution of drinking water (53%), followed by: contamination of soil and water by toxic waste (50%); pollution of rivers, lakes, and reservoirs (50%); and maintenance of freshwater for household needs (48%). According the survey, water quality is a more immediate concern, while global warming may seem like a somewhat more remote issue. The survey also indicates that Americans have shown greater concern about environmental problems that touch on water than on any other environmental issue (www.gallup.com/poll/104932/ Polluted-Drinking-Water-No-Concern-Before-Report.aspx).

The concern about water quality is well founded. Ecosystems are being severely changed or destroyed by water pollution. As the world has become more industrialized and the population has grown, problems associated with water pollution have become more of a concern. Growth in urban water use is lowering water tables, and this is having a significant impact on the environment.

If water is polluted enough, it will kill both flora and fauna in a water-based ecosystem. Pollution also disrupts the

Figure 2.16 *Water quality is a major issue in regard to being able to efficiently utilize our water resources. Algae is overtaking this lake in Iowa, greatly reducing water quality and impacting potential uses of the lake. Image courtesy NRCS.*

natural food chain. Discharging untreated wastewater into an ecosystem can affect species downstream.

A fundamental problem with traditional approaches to addressing stormwater is that it has been treated as waste, and the idea was to collect the water and get rid of it as quickly as possible. Yet the answer to stormwater management is not to construct bigger and more expensive stormwater management systems. Cities have tried that for years to no avail.

2.5.1 Wadeable Streams Assessment

One study that seeks to gain a better understanding of our streams is the Wadeable Streams Assessment (WSA). WSA is the first statistically valid survey of the biological condition of wadeable streams in the United States. Wadeable streams are those that are shallow enough to sample without boats. This project is a collaborative effort involving

states, EPA and other federal agencies, tribes, universities, and other organizations.

Beginning with pilot work in the West in 2000 and ending nationwide in 2004, 1,392 random sites were sampled to determine the condition of all streams in regions that share similar ecological characteristics.

The WSA found that 28% of U.S. stream miles are in good condition, 25% are in fair condition, and 42% are in poor condition. Streams in the western states were in the best condition, with 45% of wadeable streams and rivers being in good condition. The most widespread stressors observed in the streams were nitrogen, phosphorus, streambed sediments, and riparian disturbance.

2.5.2 National Rivers and Streams Assessment

The National Rivers and Streams Assessment (NRSA) is a statistical survey of flowing waters of the United States. The

Figure 2.17 *Channel erosion occurs when a riverbed is unstable or when increased runoff upsets the delicate balance that exists within a stream. Image courtesy NRCS.*

NRSA is one of a series of water surveys being conducted by the U.S. Environmental Protection Agency, states, tribes, and other partners. (See Figure 2.17.) In addition to rivers and streams, partners will also study coastal waters, wetlands, and lakes in a revolving sequence. The purpose of these surveys is to generate statistically valid and environmentally relevant reports on the condition of the nation's water resources. The NRSA survey is designed to:

- Assess the condition of the nation's rivers and streams

- Help build state and tribal capacity for monitoring and assessment

- Promote collaboration across jurisdictional boundaries

- Establish a baseline to evaluate progress

- Evaluate changes in condition since the 2004 Wadeable Streams Assessment

2.5.3 Large River Bioassessment Protocols

To address the environmental concerns of nonwadeable water, EPA developed the Large River Bioassessment Protocols. The purpose of the protocols is to assist in the bioassessment of large rivers by states and tribes. These protocols include specific methods for field sampling; laboratory sample processing; taxonomy; data entry, management, and analysis; and final assessment and reporting.

The protocols also review and provide information on development of monitoring designs to address certain types of environmental questions and approaches for documenting and reporting data quality and performance characteristics for large-river biological monitoring.

Our knowledge of river ecosystems has expanded greatly over the last several decades. The flora and fauna of large rivers varies considerably based on the physical, chemical, and hydrologic conditions in a given watershed. Major rivers can be hundreds of miles long, so the characteristics along the river can change. The sheer size and complexity of large rivers makes it difficult to assess their environmental quality. For an adequate assessment of large rivers, the length of the channel that must be sampled to capture the diversity of organisms and habitats is greater than that for smaller, wadeable streams.

2.6 ECONOMIC CONCERNS

Water and economic concerns are inextricably linked. How we deal with water resources has a significant impact on our economy. The Water Integrity Network writes that without water, there can be no economic growth, no industry, no hydropower, no agriculture, and no cities (Water Integrity Network, 2009). The world's gross domestic product (GDP)—the output of goods and services produced by labor and property—was estimated in 2008 to be a little over $60 trillion. The real GDP of the United States was estimated to be $14,075.5 (U.S. Department of Commerce: Bureau of Economic Analysis, 2008) billion in the first quarter of 2009, and this economy is dependent on clean, abundant water resources.

How much is water worth? Perhaps one simple perspective is that in 2007, Americans spent an estimated $16 billion on bottled water. Since 2002, the U.S. market has seen an increase in bottled water production of more than 9% per year, and that trend is expected to continue even with the recent economic downturn. This is ironic, because bottled water costs several *thousand* times as much as tap water, and tests have indicated that in most cases bottled water is not any better in terms of taste or water quality (National Research Council, 2004).

2.6.1 Cost of Water

Water is generally considered to be a public trust resource, not a commodity. It is ironic that water is so valuable and

important to life, yet it has no real market value. Conversely, diamonds and other precious jewels have no practical use yet have a very high price tag.

In the United States, water itself is free; it is the cost of pipes, treatment plants, and infrastructure that is paid by taxpayers. There are several reasons why water prices are kept artificially low. One of the major arguments is that water is a necessity for everyone, and it should not be denied to anyone regardless of their economic status. It would be a little like trying to charge for air. (No offense to Woody Harrelson and his failed Oxygen Bar in Los Angeles.)

Water is heavily subsidized, and prices often do not reflect the full cost of extraction, treatment, and distribution. For example, in the western United States, water for farming from the federal Bureau of Reclamation sells for $10 to $15 per acre-foot, and the cheapest subsidized water sells for as little as $3.50 per acre-foot, even though it may cost $100 to pump the water to farmers. In contrast, residents in urban areas may pay as much as $230 (Milgrom and Roberts, 1992).

2.6.2 Infrastructure Cost

Conventional approaches that use curbs and gutters to handle drainage are extremely expensive to construct and maintain. Also, with traditional curbs and gutters, there is no chance to mitigate the quality or quantity of the water.

One major economic concern is that much of our city's stormwater infrastructure is seriously outdated and will cost billions of dollars to replace or repair (see Figure 2.18). Many municipalities have put off upgrading and replacing their water infrastructure for so long that the situation has reached a crisis point. The EPA estimates that the various water systems in this country will need to invest $276.8 billion between 2003 and 2023 to upgrade or replace aging infrastructure and equipment in order to ensure adequate access to water resources (www.epa.gov/safewater/dwinfo).

The events of September 11, 2001 raised concerns about the security of public water systems. EPA has developed the Water Security Research and Technical Support Action Plan in an effort to protect water systems from terrorist attacks. This added protection will increase the cost of water infrastructure.

Figure 2.18 *In Escondido, California, bioswales are being used to capture stormwater runoff. Bioswales keep the stormwater from running into storm pipes, and this helps reduce the demand on stormwater infrastructure. Image courtesy EDAW.*

In many parts of the country, people have to pay a very high price to get water when and where they need it. In southern California, for example, water distribution systems cost billions of dollars because of the many miles of pipes. EPA estimates that more than 1 million miles of piping are used in the United States to distribute water. Wells must be dug deeper than ever before to tap into aquifers, and that costs money. More extensive treatment plants are needed to make polluted water usable.

Water allocation is the economic problem of deciding how the total supply of water will be allocated among potential users. Among the competing users of water are: residential, industrial, agricultural, forestry, fisheries, recreational, hydroelectric, and transportation. The first four are mostly consumptive users, meaning that they treat water as a nonrenewable resource (http://are.berkeley.edu/~zilber/EEP101/spring02/detailed_text/16.pdf).

2.6.3 Costs of Polluted Water

No one should overlook the impact that poor water management has had on both people and the environment. Polluted water has led to some serious health issues, and in some places Americans are spending a great deal to produce safe, drinkable water. The United States has spent billions on striving to achieve the goals laid out in the Clean Water Act (CWA) of 1972. For example, according to EPA, the total actual cost of water protection in 1994 was almost $45 billion. Recent costs are much higher.

The cost to clean up the environment is also substantial. Every state in the United States has some kind of major water restoration projection in process, and the nation is not anywhere close to addressing all of the problems. For example, the Comprehensive Everglades Restoration Plan, which is intended to help clean up environmental problems in the Everglades in Florida, was originally estimated in 2002 to cost $7.8 billion, but the price tag has already been increased to $10.5 billion. Experts say the project could take more than 50 years to complete, so the total cost will undoubtedly increase significantly. No major water project in the country has ever come in under budget.

There are also costs associated with the lack of water. Because of the drought, real estate agents were having a difficult time selling homes on Lake Lanier and other lakes with low water levels. A house that would have been priced at $1.2 million in 2006 might be 25% to 30% less in 2008. In 2008, there were more than 400 lakeside homes for sale along Lake Lanier, a much higher number than normal (Duffy, 2008). Part of this downturn is undoubtedly the poor economy, but concerns about water level have certainly not helped.

2.6.4 Privatization

In recent years, there has been an increased interest in the privatization of water utilities because of the tremendous costs involved for municipalities. As a result many are turning to private sources to cover the cost. Many of the early water utilities in the United States were developed by private companies, but that changed as cities developed their own water systems to meet public demands. Today, publicly owned systems account for more than 90% of all U.S. water production (www.epa.gov/safewater/dwinfo).

Some municipalities have sold their water utilities outright to private companies, while others maintain ownership but hire private companies to operate and maintain water treatment plants. One benefit of privately owned and operated water utilities is that they often are more efficient and are not as influenced by local politics.

2.7 AGRICULTURAL USES

Agricultural uses are one of the greatest demands for water. About 70% of the water withdrawn from fresh-water sources globally supports agriculture. Of the other

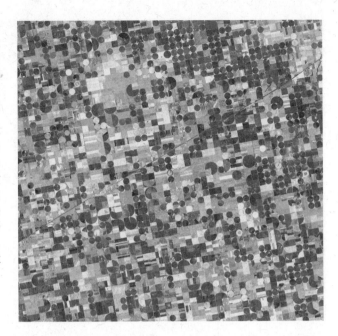

Figure 2.19 *In Kansas, irrigation is required to produce many of the state's agricultural crops. Each dark circle on this satellite image is an irrigated field. Image courtesy USGS.*

30%, two-thirds supports industrial activities and the other one-third is used for municipal supplies. Worldwide, about 93% of the water consumed by humans goes to irrigated agriculture.

In the United States, we have made the decision that agricultural uses are a priority use of available water resources. Farmers rely on rivers to help irrigate their lands and maintain America's reputation as the "bread basket" of the world.

Agriculture accounts for about 85% of the consumptive water use in the United States (see Figure 2.19). The amount of water used varies by region, with aagricultural uses in the West being much more water intensive than elsewhere in the nation. Agriculture uses account for more than 90% of the water usage in California; it is becoming more difficult to use this much water and still meet environmental and development needs (www.jyi.org/features/ft.php?id=284).

Why is agriculture such a priority when it comes to water use? Well, for a starter, U.S. society is based on food that is grown commercially. If we do not irrigate agricultural

Figure 2.20 *The United States seems to have agreed that agricultural uses are a priority for water resources. Image courtesy UDSA.*

fields, then crops do not crow, there is no grain to eat, and we cannot lose sight of the fact that agriculture is a big business in this country. For example, agriculture currently generates an estimated $97 billion for Florida's economy. In 2007, Georgia officials were saying the drought caused more than $787 million in lost agriculture production, and 60% of Georgian farmers lost all of their crops (NOAA, 2008). In Tennessee in 2008, Governor Phil Bredesen requested a federal designation of agricultural disaster for 39 counties because of crop and livestock losses that were primarily a result of drought conditions (Bredesen, 2008).

2.7.1 Impacts

In many parts of the world, agricultural production is constrained by a lack of irrigation water or systems, and the amount of land per capita that is under irrigation is falling for the first time. Agriculture is the main source of sediment erosion in many parts of the United States. (See Figure 2.21.) Thousands of acres of wetlands across the country

have been drained and put into agricultural production over the years. Excessive runoff from agricultural areas also may compound flooding problems.

Another big issue with agricultural uses of water is the impact they have on water quality. Pastured livestock are a source of phosphorous loading to surface waters through defecation in the water or on banks of rivers and lakes. Livestock often destabilize banks, causing significant erosion problems. Surprisingly, in some states, no rules prohibit cattle from watering or grazing in or along riparian areas. More must be done to encourage livestock farmers to establish stream buffers and other effective riparian protections. A minimum base buffer width of 50 to 100 feet is recommended to provide adequate stream protection, with buffers of 100 to 300 feet used for more sensitive wetlands and water resources. At a bare minimum, fencing should be used to keep livestock from contaminating water. (See Figure 2.22.)

Excessive phosphorous contributes to declining water quality because it leads to abundant algae growth and it can upset a lake's ecosystem. According to the Virginia

Figure 2.21 *The 2008 Farm Bill made water conservation funding available nationally. One of the objectives of this funding was to improve the efficiency of agricultural irrigation systems. Image courtesy USDA.*

Figure 2.22 *Contour stripcropping helps reduce erosion and surface runoff. It is one of many measures that are being used to reduce the environmental impact of agricultural uses. Image courtesy NRCS.*

Figure 2.23 *Allowing livestock in a stream can have a negative impact on water quality and riparian habitation. The use of a concrete water crossing allows livestock to cross the creek with minimal impact. Image courtesy NRCS.*

Department of Environmental Quality, pasturelands are by far the predominant source of bacteria in several impaired river and stream segments in Albemarle County. Most other states around the country echo this sentiment (Virginia Department of Conservation and Recreation, 2006).

Most of the phosphorus loads in our lakes and rivers come from agricultural uses. One problem in the Lake Okeechobee, Florida, watershed, for example, is that although dairies and row crops occupy only about 4% of the watershed, they are the cause of more than 50% of the phosphorus that goes into the lake annually. Decades of phosphorus loading have resulted in the accumulation of a thick layer of organic muck over 300 square miles of Lake Okeechobee's bottom. It has been estimated that there are more than 51,000 tons of phosphorus in the lake (Environment News Service, 2008).

2.7.2 Reducing Impacts

There have been efforts to be more efficient in using water for agricultural uses. (See Figure 2.23.) Agricultural permits limit when and how much water can be used for irrigation. Water use allocations are determined by irrigation best management practices for specific crop production.

The Conservation Reserve Program of the U.S. Department of Agriculture Natural Resources Conservation Service (NRCS) pays farmers to convert environmentally sensitive land to vegetative cover, such as native grasses or riparian buffers. County soil and water conservation districts often have cost-share programs to help riparian landowners with fencing projects to keep livestock away from lake edges.

Water use measures such as modest crop shifting, smart irrigation scheduling, advanced irrigation management, and efficient irrigation can dramatically improve water efficiency. For example, switching from flood irrigation, which is commonly used for a number of agricultural uses, to drip irrigation can decrease water use by as much as 40%.

In 2004, the state of Georgia installed 177 meters on farm irrigation systems in southwest Georgia in order to measure how much water is being used. The state has talked about the need to install as many as 21,000 water meters (Hollis, 2002). The idea behind water meter use is that a better understanding of how water is used for agricultural purposes will lead to better policies and plans.

2.8 WATER QUALITY

For many, the impact that humans have had on water quality was epitomized when the Cuyahoga River in Cleveland, Ohio, caught fire in June 1969. That is not a typo . . . the river actually had so much oil and debris in it that it caught fire. Randy Newman wrote about the event in his song "Burn On," and Cleveland was the laughingstock of the nation.

The quality of U.S. rivers, streams, lakes, bays, and groundwater must be maintained in order to meet goals for sustainability. Water quality standards are the foundation of EPA's water quality protection efforts. States assess the quality of their waters based on water quality standards they develop in accordance with the Clean Water Act.

Water quality standards may differ from state to state but must meet minimum requirements. EPA must approve these standards before they become effective under the Clean Water Act. (See Figure 2.24.)

After setting water quality standards, states assess their waters to determine the degree to which the standards are being met. State water quality assessments normally are based on five broad types of monitoring data: biological integrity, chemical, physical, habitat, and toxicity.

Monitoring enables water quality managers to identify existing or emerging problems. It also facilitates responses to emergencies, such as spills and floods, and helps water quality managers target specific pollution prevention or remediation programs to address these problems. State pollution control agencies, Indian tribes, local governments, and federal agencies typically are responsible for watershed assessment and monitoring activities (National Management Measures to Control Nonpoint Source Pollution from Urban Areas, 2005).

Figure 2.24 *The water clarity of Lake Tahoe has declined from about 100 feet in the 1960s to about 70 feet today. Scientists believe lake clarity can be restored in 20 years if one-third of the nitrogen, phosphorous, and fine sediment now entering the lake is eliminated. Image courtesy J. Sipes.*

A body of water is considered impaired if it does not attain the water quality criteria associated with its designated use. Threatened waters are those that meet standards but exhibit a declining trend in water quality such that they will likely exceed standards in the near future (EPA, 2008).

2.8.1 Water Quality Regulations

A number of acts, legislation, and studies in the United States are intended to help protect the quality of the nation's water. Some of these are listed next.

Section 303(d) and TMDL

Under Section 303(d) of the Clean Water Act, states are required to compile a list of impaired waters that fail to meet any of their applicable water quality standards. This list, called a 303(d) list, is submitted to Congress every two years, and states are required to develop a total maximum daily load (TMDL) for each pollutant causing impairment for water bodies on the list.

Based on recent state 303(d) lists, more than 38,000 bodies of water in the United States are impaired, and 63,000 have associated impairments. Pollutants are the most common problem (EPA, Handbook for Developing Watershed Plans to Restore and Protect Our Waters, 2008).

A TMDL is the maximum amount of a pollutant that can be released into a water body without causing the water body to become unable to serve its beneficial use. Each state is required to develop TMDLs for all water bodies on its 303(d) list.

Section 303(d) and subsequent regulation prescribe a five-step process for TMDL development:

1. Identify stream segments that are water quality limited (i.e., unable to support additional development).

2. Prioritize water quality.

3. Develop TMDL plans for these waters.

4. Implement water quality improvement actions.

5. Assess improvement actions.

The National TMDL Tracking System (NTTS) houses the 303(d) lists and tracks TMDL approvals. The NTTS includes the information necessary to ensure that TMDLs are being addressed appropriately.

Section 401, typically referred to as the Water Quality Certification, is also a part of the Clean Water Act. Section 401 requires that any applicant for a federal license or permit involving actions that may impact navigable waters must obtain a certification from the state or tribe in which the discharge originates.

Section 305(b)

As required by Section 305(b) of the Clean Water Act, EPA transmits to Congress the National Water Quality Inventory Report (305(b) Report). Based on water quality information submitted by states, tribes, and territories, including information on lakes, this document characterizes water quality, identifies widespread water quality problems, and describes various programs implemented to restore and protect U.S. waters.

Forty-six states, Puerto Rico, and the District of Columbia rated lake water quality in their 2000 Section 305(b) reports. These states assessed 17.3 million acres of lakes, reservoirs, and ponds, which equals 43% of the 40.6 million acres of lakes in the nation. The states based 68% of their assessments on monitored data and evaluated 28% of the assessed lake acres with qualitative information (EPA, 2007).

Good water quality was found in 55% of the assessed 17.3 million lake-acres. Fifty-four percent fully support their designated uses, and 44% are impaired for one or more uses. Nutrients affect more lake-acres than any other pollutant or stressor. States reported that excess nutrients pollute 3.8 million lake acres (EPA, 2007).

Healthy lake ecosystems contain nutrients in small quantities from natural sources. The addition of extra nutrients, such as nitrogen and phosphorus, disrupt the balance of lake ecosystems by stimulating population explosions of undesirable algae and aquatic weeds. Bacteria flourishes because of the added food source of the algae, and the bacteria consume dissolved oxygen. Fish kills and foul odors may result if dissolved oxygen is depleted (EPA, 2007).

In 2001, the National Research Council recommended EPA, states, and tribes promote a uniform, consistent approach to monitoring and data collection. The aim is to support core water quality programs to help address the problem of inadequate data for national reporting on freshwater, coastal, and ocean water quality indicators (USEPA, 2006).

National Pollutant Discharge Elimination System

The National Pollutant Discharge Elimination System (NPDES) permit program, established by Section 402 of the Clean Water Act, functions as the primary regulatory tool for assuring that state water quality standards are met. NPDES permits, issued by EPA or an authorized state agency, contain discharge limits intended to meet water quality standards and national technology-based effluent regulations.

Phase I of NPDES was initiated in 1990, and it covers municipalities with populations over 100,000, construction sites over five acres in size, and several industrial activities. Phase II of the program, adopted in 1999, includes smaller municipalities, urban areas adjacent to municipalities, and construction sites between one and five acres in size.

To meet NPDES requirements, each local stormwater program is responsible for establishing a Stormwater Management Plan (SWMP). These SWMPs give specific local requirements targeted to meet the environmental needs of each watershed and reflect the political consensus of each community.

Regulations under the NPDES stormwater program offer a structure for considering the water quality benefits associated with smart growth techniques. NPDES permits regulate the discharge of pollutants from point sources, such as pipes, outfalls, and conveyance channels. In general, facilities that discharge wastewater into water bodies are required to have a permit under the NPDES program.

The *Water Quality Trading Toolkit for Permit Writers* (*Toolkit*) (EPA, 2007) provides NPDES permitting authorities with the tools they need to facilitate trading and to authorize and incorporate trading in NPDES permits.

EPA Lakes Survey

EPA's Survey of the Nation's Lakes is intended to provide important information to states and the public about the condition of the nation's lake resources and key stressors on a national and regional scale (USEPA, 2006). The lakes survey has two main objectives:

1. Estimate the current status, trends, and changes in selected trophic, ecological, and recreational indicators of the condition of the nation's lakes with known statistical confidence.

2. Seek associations between selected indicators of natural and anthropogenic stresses and indicators of ecological condition.

The survey consists of 909 lakes, including natural and man-made freshwater lakes, ponds, and reservoirs greater than 10 acres, at least 3 feet in depth, and located in the coterminous United States. For each lake, a folder was prepared that contains applicable information, such as: road maps, written access permissions, scientific collection permits, lake site coordinates, information brochures, bathymetric map, and local area emergency numbers (USEPA, 2006).

A water body stays on the 303(d) list until it meets water quality standards. To develop the 303(d) list, most states started with the information in their 305(b) report and then augmented it with information from sources such as the EPA report of waters affected by nonpoint sources.

The states included in the survey reported metals as the second most common pollutant in assessed lake acres, impairing 3.2 million lake acres. This is mainly due to the widespread detection of mercury in fish tissue samples. In addition to nutrients and metals, the states report that siltation (sedimentation) pollutes nearly 1.6 million lake acres; total dissolved solids affect nearly 1.5 million acres; and enrichment by organic wastes that deplete dissolved oxygen in lake waters affects over 1.1 million lake acres (EPA, 2007).

The most commonly reported sources of impairment in lakes include agriculture, hydrologic modifications, and urban runoff/storm sewers. Agriculture is the most widespread source of impairment in the nation's assessed lake acres, generating pollutants that degrade aquatic life or interfere with public use of over 3 million lake acres. Riparian pasture grazing and irrigated and nonirrigated crop production were the most frequently cited types of agriculture impairments. Hydrologic modifications, the second most commonly reported source of impairment, include flow regulation and modification, dredging, and construction of dams (EPA, 2007).

Pollution from urban runoff and storm sewers degrades nearly 1.4 million lake acres; generalized nonpoint sources of pollution impair about 1 million lake acres; atmospheric deposition of pollutants impairs 1 million lake acres; and municipal sewage treatment plants pollute 943,715 lake acres (EPA, 2007).

EPA's *Field Operations Manual* describes field protocols and daily operations for crews to use in the Survey of the Nation's Lakes. The survey is a statistical assessment of the condition of U.S. lakes, ponds, and reservoirs and is designed to:

1. Assess the condition of the nation's lakes

2. Establish a baseline to compare future surveys for trends assessment and to evaluate trends

3. Help build state and tribal capacity for monitoring and assessment and promote collaboration across jurisdictional boundaries (USEPA, 2007)

Clean Lakes Program

EPA's Clean Lakes Program was established in 1972 as Section 314 of the Federal Water Pollution Control Act. Its objective was to provide financial and technical assistance to states in restoring publicly owned lakes. The Section 314 Clean Lakes Program was reauthorized in September 2000 as part of the Estuaries and Clean Water Act of 2000. EPA has not requested funds for the Clean Lakes Program in recent years; rather, it has encouraged states to use funds from the December 1999 Supplemental Guidance for the Award of Section 319 Nonpoint Source Grants in FY 2000 (and previous guidance) for eligible activities that might have been funded in previous years under Section 314.

Drinking Water

Safe drinking water is a top priority for water managers around the country. Water quality regulations are intended

Figure 2.25 *Over 1 billion people lack access to safe drinking water worldwide. Image courtesy EDAW.*

to ensure that drinking water is adequately treated and monitored to protect public health. Under the 1996 amendments to the federal Safe Drinking Water Act, states must conduct studies that provide basic information about public drinking water. Each program is intended to be developed for a state's specific water resources and drinking water priorities.

Drinking water contaminated with chemicals or bacteria can make people sick, especially children and the elderly. (See Figure 2.25.) Water can be contaminated with bacteria when it comes into contact with untreated human waste.

Polluted water can carry harmful microbial or chemical contaminants. Waterborne diseases, such as dysentery, typhoid, and cholera, have been eliminated, but other bacteria, such as *Legionella* and *Salmonella,* are still a concern. For example, *Legionella*, which causes Legionnaire's disease, causes 8,000 to 18,000 illnesses each year in the United States (National Research Council, 2004).

Chlorine has been used to kill bacteria in public water systems for more than 100 years. One concern is that high levels of chlorine can cause health problems. Some communities use ozone and ultraviolet radiation instead, but even if they do, they typically add small amounts of chlorine to provide protection throughout the distribution system.

Herbicides, pesticides, pharmaceuticals, antibiotics, industrial pollutants, and radioactive materials all present potential health threats in drinking water, but they usually are present in such low levels that they do not cause serious problems. One concern is that increased levels of chlorine can cause a chemical reaction that produces lead in the water. The EPA estimates that 10% to 20% of lead exposure comes from contaminated drinking water.

Source Water Assessments

Source Water Assessment Programs (SWAPs) are intended to analyze existing and potential threats to the quality of the public drinking water. Every state was required to implement assessments of its public water systems by 2003. The SWAPs vary from state to state, but all must include four major elements:

1. Map of the source water assessment area

2. Inventory of potential sources of contamination

3. Determination of the susceptibility of the water supply to contamination sources

4. Availability of the results to the public

Pollutants

Water plays an essential role in sanitation and public health. According to the second United Nations World Water Development Report (UNESCO, 2006), more than 1 billion people—almost one-fifth of the world's population—lack access to safe drinking water, and 40% lack access to basic sanitation. The global water crisis is the leading cause of death and disease in the world, with more than 14,000 people dying each day. The leading cause of child death in the world is diarrhea. This often results from a lack of clean drinking water. Each year, children under age 5 suffer 1.5 billion episodes of diarrhea, and 4 million of these cases are fatal.

Some materials typically removed during the water treatment process include bacteria, algae, viruses, fungi, chemicals, and minerals such as iron, manganese, and sulfur. Water is a solvent, and the most common dissolved mineral substances found in water are sodium, calcium, magnesium, potassium, chloride, bicarbonate, and sulfate. Water is considered unsuitable for drinking if the quantity of dissolved minerals exceeds 1,000 milligrams per liter (http://pubs.usgs.gov/gip/gw/gw_a.html).

Pollutants typically are classified as being point or nonpoint pollution. Traditionally under the Clean Water Act, controls were focused on reducing pollutant impacts on local water quality from point sources, such as wastewater treatment plants. The CWA Act requires that all point-source dischargers obtain permits, which establish the levels of contaminants allowed.

Practices for Controlling Chemicals and Pollutants

- Equipment runoff control

- Fuel and maintenance staging areas

- Locate potential land-disturbing activities away from critical areas

- Pesticide and fertilizer management

- Pollutant runoff control

- Spill prevention and control program

Source: EPA 841-B-07-002 4-1

Nonpoint sources are all of the man-made sources of water contamination that are not point sources. They are often difficult to identify because they are so diverse. Nonpoint source pollution comes from diffuse sources, with surface water runoff being a major nonpoint source in both urban and rural areas. Nonpoint source pollutants carried by urban runoff include sediment, heavy metals, sewage discharges, detergents, solvents, oxygen-demanding organic matter, bacteria, excess nutrients, pesticides, oils, and lubricants.

Watershed plans typically focus on nonpoint pollution sources. Watershed models can be used to forecast or estimate future conditions that might occur under various conditions. These models provide an opportunity to explore a wide range of scenarios to determine which approach would be best.

Controlling pollutants at the site (source control) is usually the simplest and most cost-effective way to reduce stormwater pollution at many commercial sites. Source control measures include proper handling and storage of pollutants and site design practices. Handling and storage practices focus on the storage of materials and vehicles in outdoor areas, while site design practices include designing better loading docks, covering materials stored outdoors, and containing dumpsters and fueling areas. Other source-control opportunities exist at fleet parking areas, outdoor maintenance areas, landscaping areas, and above-ground storage tanks (Rowe and Schueler, 2006).

Among the most common water quality problems are:

- Eutrophication
- Trash and debris
- Bacteria levels
- Aquatic life toxicity
- Sediment and fish tissue contamination

EPA has identified sediment as the most widespread pollutant in the nation's rivers and streams. Contamination of surface waters by sediment is currently regulated primarily by the Sedimentation Pollution Control Act. This act requires approved erosion control plans for any land-disturbing activities that will uncover more than one acre. Agricultural production is exempt from this law.

Nine Critical Elements

EPA has identified nine elements that are critical for achieving improvements in water quality. EPA requires that these nine elements be addressed for Section 319-funded watershed.

a. Identification of causes of impairment and pollutant sources or groups of similar sources that need to be controlled to achieve needed load reductions, and any other goals identified in the watershed plan.

b. An estimate of the load reductions expected from management measures.

c. A description of the nonpoint source management measures that will need to be implemented to achieve load reductions and a description of the critical areas in which those measures will be needed to implement this plan.

d. Estimate of the amounts of technical and financial assistance needed, associated costs, and/or the sources and authorities that will be relied on to implement this plan.

e. An information and education component used to enhance public understanding of the project and encourage early and continued participation in selecting, designing, and implementing the nonpoint source management measures that will be implemented.

f. Schedule for implementing the nonpoint source management measures identified in this plan that is reasonably expeditious.

g. A description of interim measurable milestones for determining whether nonpoint source management measures or other control actions are being implemented.

h. A set of criteria that can be used to determine whether loading reductions are being achieved over time and substantial progress is being made toward attaining water quality standards.

i. A monitoring component to evaluate the effectiveness of the implementation efforts over time, measured against the criteria established under item h immediately above.

Source: www.epa.gov/owow/nps/cwact.html.

2.9 LEGAL ISSUES

There have been legal battles over water in the United States for centuries, and they are not likely to be cleared up anytime soon. All surface and groundwaters are legally considered "waters of the state" and cannot be privately owned. The legal structure in the United States varies depending on where you live.

2.9.1 Riparian Rights

Most states east of the Mississippi River are known as riparian rights states, meaning that if you own land along a natural body of water, you have a legal right to access and use the water that touches or runs through your property. Riparian rights are tied to the land, so they cannot be sold or transferred to other users.

In most riparian rights states, the courts have generally ruled that a riparian owner's use of water has to be "reasonable." The problem, though, is that not everyone agrees on what "reasonable" actually means. This "reasonable use" standard gives courts a lot of flexibility to resolve disputes, but it can be confusing for landowners because there are no hard and fast rules. The definition of "beneficial use of water" has expanded in recent years. One basic idea is that reasonable use must be accomplished in a way that does not impose undue restrictions on other users and uses of the water resource. The reasonable use doctrine also applies to groundwater, and landowners are allowed to withdraw water for reasonable use on their property. Agricultural and industrial uses are generally considered to be "reasonable" as long as they do not cause unreasonable adverse effects to adjacent landowners.

It is no coincidence that the riparian rights concept was embraced in the states where water was considered to be abundant. All eastern states, with the exception of Mississippi, follow the riparian doctrine. These states were the first settled by Europeans and therefore most influenced by English law. With the perception of having plenty of water, the focus was primarily on how to share this resource.

One problem with riparian rights is that it is not a good system for resolving disputes when water is scarce. If anything, riparian rights for water allocation actually encourage the use of water. In times of drought or water shortages, most states use regulatory mechanisms for allocating water.

Many eastern states are transitioning to a system called a regulated riparian system, which replaces traditional riparian rights with a water permit system. Georgia and North Carolina have already established a permitting process for tapping surface water supplies.

South Carolina is a riparian rights state, so if you live next to a river, you have a right to use it. Surprisingly enough, you do not need any permit to withdraw water from a stream in South Carolina as long as no interbasin water transfer is involved. If you withdraw water over a certain threshold, you will only need to notify South Carolina of the amount.

The state of Florida takes the position that natural flow regimes must be maintained to protect environmental resources.

Many of the states in the western United States are governed by the doctrine of prior appropriation, which is also called "first in time," or the "Colorado Doctrine" of water law (Castle, 1999).

2.9.2 First in Time

Western states utilize a prior appropriation system for water allocation. Basically, "prior appropriation" means that no one actually owns the water in a stream, but all persons, corporations, and municipalities have the right to use the water for beneficial purposes. Water is allocated based on the concept of "first in time, first in right," meaning that those who used the water first have a priority. Legal issues involving water resources have long been a point of contention in the West, and this first-in-time allocation is at the heart of many battles. Colorado water law is generally considered to be the authority and is used by other western states that follow the prior appropriation doctrine (http://www.blm.gov/nstc/WaterLaws/appsystems .html).

Some western states recognize both absolute and conditional water rights. Absolute water rights assume that water is appropriated when it is permitted. With conditional rights, the water is allocated before it is actually available. This approach is used for large water projects, which can take a long time to complete.

Several western states allow for the use of replacement plans that seek to balance new water uses with existing water rights. For example, a replacement plan would allow water to be diverted from a stream if it can be replaced from another source.

In Arizona, a dual system uses a prior appropriation for surface water and a "beneficial and reasonable" use approach for groundwater. Arizona also follows the legal concept of adequacy, which is based on availability of sufficient water to support a proposed use for 100 years. Some argue that the 100-year time frame is inadequate to ensure that the source of water is sustained for future generations.

California's water management practices are based on two laws: (1) public trust doctrine, which says that resources such as surface water are accessible by everyone, and (2) landowners own all groundwater beneath their land. The public trust doctrine is part of the constitutions of most U.S. states. Some have argued that public trust applies only to navigable waters and tidelands, and the scope of public trust is restricted to surface water resources. This is an issue that will surely be battled in the courts for years to come. The Colorado River management between the states of Arizona and California is a good example of the benefits of federal arbitration.

In the West, because the water right system is founded on beneficial use of the resource, a lack of use can result in an "abandonment' or "forfeiture" of the right. Most western state laws determine you have forfeited your legal rights if you have not diverted and used water for a specific period of time. That period varies from state to state but can be as few as five years. Some states do not just make such an assumption and instead require submittal of an "intent to abandon" the water right.

A century ago in western states, it was acceptable for an approved user to remove all the water from a stream, but today federal statutes typically require a minimum instream flow to protect endangered species or to maintain downstream uses.

2.9.3 Groundwater, Soil Moisture, and Precipitation

Surface water is not the only resource that has to be addressed in order to ensure we have enough water for future uses. Groundwater initially was considered part of the land, and there were no separate water rights. Today, a right to water from underground sources varies from state to state. Some states treat tributary groundwater the same way they do surface water. For example, New Mexico has managed surface and groundwater together since the 1950s.

Soil moisture typically is considered to be part of the land, so water rights are not applied.

In the states of Utah, Colorado, and Washington, rainfall is considered essential for replenishing groundwater, so it is illegal to collect rainfall. Although it is not likely you will get arrested for installing a rain cistern, it is against the law. Colorado law explicitly states that every drop of moisture suspended in the atmosphere must be divvied up according to previous water claims (Simon, 2009). Taken literally, that means that the state owns every drop of rain. In the state of Washington, rainwater harvesting is allowed in only a few areas, including Seattle and the San Juan Islands.

Despite these prohibitions, many cities, especially in the West, are encouraging rain harvesting through tax credits, rain barrel subsidies, and changes in building codes (Simon, 2009).

In the past, water rights did not apply until the water reached the land surface. At that point, the water was absorbed by the soil, run off into rivers and streams, or percolated through the soil into underground aquifers. The difficulty with this approach is that it is difficult to measure the amount of rainfall that falls in a given area of a watershed.

Water rights applying to man-made bodies of waters are different, because whoever constructs the water body typically determines how rights are defined. In most states, land under freshwater or saltwater, and land that is subject to the ebb and flow of the tide are considered to be public land. Smaller creeks, lakes, and ponds are not considered to be public lands and can be privately owned. There is no public right to travel over private property to obtain access to streams, lakes, tidal areas, or other waters that the public has a right to use.

Many property boundaries, including those of states, run to the center of a river. That is problematic because rivers are constantly shifting and cutting new channels.

2.9.4 Direct Flow and Storage

Water rights are of two general types: direct flow and storage. A direct flow right generally is measured in terms of a rate of flow and is used when discussing rivers, streams, and other moving water. A storage water right is measured in terms of volume. Storage rights are usually only for one filling of the storage vessel per year.

2.9.5 Water Law

Water law is used to resolve conflicts over water resources by determining the rights and obligations of the parties involved in a dispute. U.S. water law is very complicated because so many different uses compete for the water and because of the mix of federal and state regulations that seek to make sense of all the regulations. A major problem is that uses are consumptive and alter the hydrologic cycle. This may result in significant environmental impacts.

Water law is a system of enforceable rules that control the use of water resources. In the United States, these rules are created by statutes, court decisions, and administrative regulations. Either state or federal laws can create public and private water rights. If there is water conflict between users in different states, the federal courts take over.

Water law in the western United States is defined by state constitutions (i.e., Colorado, New Mexico) statutes, and case law. Each state uses variations on the basic principles of the prior appropriation doctrine. Texas and the states directly north of it, the West Coast states, and Mississippi have a mixture of systems (http://www.blm.gov/nstc/WaterLaws/appsystems.html).

State Laws Regarding Water

Alabama: Title 33

Alaska: Title 46

Arizona: Title 45

Arkansas: Title 15

California: Title 23

Colorado: Title 37

Connecticut: Title 25

Florida: Title XVIII

Georgia: Title 52

Idaho: Title 70

Illinois: Chapter 615

Indiana: Title 14, Articles 25–33

Iowa: Title XI, Subtitles 1–3

Kansas: Chapters 24, 42, 82a

Kentucky: Title IX, Chapters 74, 104

Louisiana: Title 19

Maine: Titles 12, 38

Maryland: Title 16

Massachusetts: Chapter 91

Michigan: Chapters 121, 323, 486

(continues)

(continued)

Minnesota: Chapters 103A–114B

Mississippi: Title 51

Missouri: Title 15

Montana: Title 85

Nebraska: Chapters 31, 46, 56

Nevada: Title 48

New Hampshire: Title 50

New Jersey: Title 58

New Mexico: Chapter 72

New York: Chapter 43B

North Carolina: Chapter 77

North Dakota: Title 61

Ohio: Title LXI

Oklahoma: Title 82

Oregon: Chapters 536–558

Pennsylvania: Title 32, Chapters 21–50

Rhode Island: Title 46

South Carolina: Title 49

South Dakota: Titles 46, 46A

Tennessee: Title 69

Texas Title 30

Utah: Title 73

Vermont: Title 25

Virginia: Titles 28.2, 62.1

Washington: Titles 90, 91

West Virginia: Chapters 20, 22

Wisconsin: Chapters 280, 281

Wyoming: Title 41

Source: www.megalaw.com/top/water.php.

3.0 SUSTAINABLE PLANNING APPROACHES FOR WATER RESOURCES

3.1 AN INTERNATIONAL AND U.S. NATIONAL PERSPECTIVE ON WATER RESOURCES LAWS, POLICIES, REGULATIONS, AND PERMITS

International waters, or transboundary waters, are those that transcend international boundaries. Rivers, groundwater, oceans, seas, and estuaries do not seem to care about political boundaries. They follow a natural pattern regardless of where they go or what country they cross into.

A number of global and regional water resource agreements have been implemented over the years. These include the Helsinki Rules on the Uses of the Waters of International Rivers (1966); the Seoul Rules on International Groundwaters (1986), Transboundary Groundwaters: The Bellagio Draft Treaty (1989); and the United Nations Convention on the Law of the Non-navigational Uses of International Watercourses (1994), just to name a few.

It is important to note, however, that most water policies are made at a more local level. Most of the world's transboundary river basins, for example, lack adequate legal protection. In the last decade or so, there has been a call for global policies that help protect and manage water

resources, but establishing such policies is an arduous task and is not likely to happen quickly. (See Figure 3.1.).

It may come as a surprise to some, but the United States does not have a comprehensive national program for all water resources. Instead, we have a fragmented approach

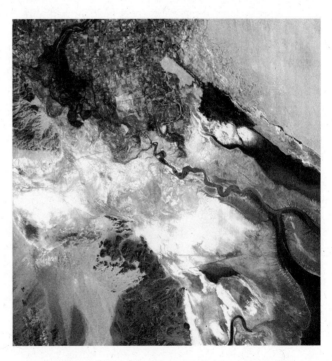

Figure 3.1 *The Colorado River flows from northern Colorado through Utah, the Grand Canyon, Arizona, and Mexico before pouring out into the Gulf of California. This satellite image, which was taken on September 8, 2000, shows the impact that irrigation and urban sprawl have had on the river. Image courtesy NASA/GSFC/METI/ERSDAC/JAROS.*

to laws and regulations when it comes to water resources and watershed issues. Federal laws and regulations about water relate mainly to environmental protection, water pollution, dam regulation for hydropower, endangered species, and wetland conservation. Laws regulating water quantity, resource management, and non point source pollution are implemented at the state level. Land use management, however, is generally a question for local government.

3.1.1 Federal Reserved Water Rights

The United States has a federal reserved water rights doctrine, which ensures that the government is able to reserve sufficient water resources for public land uses, such as Indian reservations, military reservations, and national parks. The doctrine was established in 1908 by the U.S. Supreme Court when it ruled in *Winters v. United States* that the federal government could reserve water for future use in order to meet the needs of federal properties. An amendment was approved in 1952 that required federal agencies claiming a federal reserved water right to go through a state's legal process. Today, federal reserved water rights can be asserted on most lands managed by the federal government.

3.1.2 National Laws, Acts, and Policies

In the United States, a handful of acts implemented at the federal level have laid the foundation of how we deal with water resources in this country.

Rivers and Harbors Act

The Rivers and Harbors Act (Refuse Act), which was enacted in 1899, was the first statute to address water quality in the United States. It prohibited the dumping of solid waste into navigable waterways, prohibited the obstruction of waterways, and specifically excluded wastes "flowing from the streets and sewers." The construction of any bridge, dam, dike, or causeway over or in navigable waterways of the United States was prohibited without congressional approval.

Public Health Service Act of 1912

This Public Health Service Act of 1912 expanded the mission of the United States Public Health Service to study problems of sanitation, sewage, and pollution. At the time there were major concerns about water supply, pollution, sanitation, and hygiene in cities because of the rapid growth that was occurring. The act granted the Public Health Service the authority to pursue studies of the "diseases of man and conditions affecting the propagation and spread thereof, including sanitation and sewage and the pollution either directly or indirectly of navigable streams and lakes" (http://findarticles.com/p/articles/mi_qa3912/is_200012/ai_n8921941/).

Federal Power Act of 1935

The Federal Power Act of 1935 authorized the Federal Energy Regulatory Commission (FERC) to regulate nonfederal hydroelectric projects. Included in FERC's regulatory mandate are specific requirements for protecting nonpower resources, including fish and wildlife habitat, irrigation, water supply, recreation, flood control, and water quality. In addition, Section 4(e) of the Federal Power Act, as amended by the Electric Consumers Protection Act of 1986, requires that the commission, when issuing a license, give "equal consideration to the purposes of energy conservation, the protection, mitigation of, damage to, and enhancement of, fish and wildlife (including related spawning grounds and habitat), the protection of recreational opportunities, and the preservation of other aspects of environmental quality."

Federal Water Pollution Control Act of 1948

The Federal Water Pollution Control Act of 1948 was the first statute to deal directly with pollution from sewage outfalls. It created a comprehensive set of water quality programs that also provided some financing for state and local governments. It also broadened the federal government's authority in water pollution control and mandated the Public Health Service, in cooperation with other federal, state, and local entities, to prepare comprehensive programs for eliminating or reducing the pollution of interstate waters and tributaries and improving the sanitary condition of surface and underground waters. Water Pollution Control Act Amendments of 1956 strengthened enforcement provisions and addressed cost-sharing programs with municipalities.

Water Resources Planning Act of 1965

In 1965, Congress passed the Water Resources Planning Act, which created the Water Resources Council. The council included representatives of each of the major federal agencies involved with water policy. Funding was cut off in the early 1980s because of the general feeling that the council was not cost effective.

The Wild and Scenic Rivers Act of 1968

The Wild and Scenic Rivers Act of 1968 states:

> [C]ertain selected rivers of the nation which, with their immediate environments, possess outstandingly remarkable scenic, recreational, geologic, fish and wildlife, historic, cultural, or similar values, shall be preserved in free-flowing condition, and that they and their immediate environments shall be protected for the benefit and enjoyment of present and future generations.

If a stream or river segment is designated as "wild and scenic," restrictions are placed on modifications that can be made. One of those restrictions is that water flow must be preserved and protected.

National Environmental Policy Act of 1970

National Environmental Policy Act of 1970 (NEPA) is one of the first environmental laws ever written. The act establishes national environmental policy and goals for the protection, maintenance, and enhancement of the environment and provides a process for implementing these goals within the federal agencies. Federal agencies have to consider the environmental impacts of proposed federal projects that could significantly affect the environment and set up procedural requirements for preparing environmental assessments and environmental impact statements. The NEPA review process often covers a wide range of natural resource issues and socioeconomic impacts, including water resources. The act also establishes the President's Council on Environmental Quality.

Clean Water Act of 1972

The Clean Water Act of 1972 is the most comprehensive legislation relating to water quality in the United States. It provided national programs to clean up the nation's waters, and gave the Environmental Protection Agency (EPA) authority to establish objectives, goals, and policies to enable this legislation. The principal body of law currently in effect is based on the Federal Water Pollution Control Amendments of 1972, which significantly expanded and strengthened earlier legislation. In 1987, amendments to the act established a national policy for nonpoint source (NPS) pollution and reaffirmed the states in implementing water quality goals, among other changes.

Endangered Species Act of 1973

The Endangered Species Act of 1973, as amended, states in part: "All Federal departments and agencies shall seek to conserve endangered and threatened species and shall utilize their authorities in furtherance of the purposes of this Act." No permits will be issued that conflict with the enhancement or preservation of the habitat of endangered and/or threatened plant and animal species. Although not specifically intended to address water resources, the Endangered Species Act has had a tremendous impact on water management issues.

Safe Drinking Water Act of 1974

The Safe Drinking Water Act of 1974 requires that public water systems monitor and comply with established contaminant limits. These limits, which are set by EPA, are commonly referred to as maximum contaminant limits. A 1996 Amendment to the Safe Drinking Water Act required stricter monitoring and also required states to develop programs to protect water supply areas.

Clean Water Act of 1977

The Clean Water Act of 1977 (CWA), an amendment to the Federal Water Pollution Control Act of 1972, sets the basic structure for regulating discharges of pollutants into waters of the United States. The law gives EPA the authority to set effluent standards and continues the requirements to set water quality standards for all contaminants in surface waters. In particular, the CWA focuses on point source pollution and toxic pollutants. In 1987, the CWA was reauthorized and again focused on toxic substances.

Water Quality Act of 1987

Congress revised Section 101 of the 1987 Act, "Declaration of Goals and Policy," to add this fundamental principle: It is the national policy that programs for the control of nonpoint sources of pollution be developed and implemented in an expeditious manner so as to enable the goals of this act to be met through the control of both point and nonpoint sources of pollution.

National Estuary Program

The National Estuary Program (NEP) was established in 1987 by amendments to the Clean Water Act. The purpose of the program is to identify, restore, and protect nationally significant estuaries of the United States. There are currently 28 active NEPs along the nation's coasts.

National Drought Policy Act of 1998

Congress passed the National Drought Policy Act, which created the National Drought Policy Commission. The commission makes recommendations concerning the creation and development of an integrated, coordinated federal drought policy. The policy is a marked shift from emphasis on drought relief. The commission summarized its findings by stating that:

- Preparedness is the key to successful drought management.

- Information and research are needed to support and achieve preparedness.

- Insurance against drought impacts needs to be reevaluated and revamped.

- A safety net is needed for the period of transition from relief-oriented drought programs to drought preparedness.

Water for the Poor Act

In 2005, Congress passed the Water for the Poor Act, which made the provision of safe water and sanitation a cornerstone of U.S. foreign aid by integrating water sanitation into all U.S. development programs.

3.1.3 Other Acts

Other acts also have had a significant impact on how water resources are utilized in the United States. For example, the Homestead Act of 1862 and the Desert Lands Act of 1877 encouraged settlement in the West. These acts supported the spread of small farms in the sparsely inhabited states and territories.

President Theodore Roosevelt signed the National Reclamation Act in 1902, paving the way for water reclamation projects to enhance settlement of western states (Woodhouse, 2008). This act provided the funding for the construction and maintenance of western irrigation projects.

Congress enacted the National Historic Preservation Act of 1966, the Archaeological and Historic Preservation Act of 1974, and the Archaeological Resources Protection Act of 1979, mandating that federal agencies protect cultural, historical, and archaeological sites. These acts all have an impact on water resource projects.

In 1998, EPA and the U.S. Department of Agriculture (USDA) released the Clean Water Action Plan as a means to fulfill the original goal of the Clean Water Act. A key component of the plan was the development of watershed restoration action strategies (WRASs). The WRASs addressed watershed restoration, including a balance between discharge control for specific chemicals and prevention of broader water-related problems, such as wetland loss and habitat degradation.

The Water Quality Financing Act of 2007, which was passed by the House of Representatives, authorized $14 billion for fiscal years 2008 to 2011 for wastewater state revolving loan fund programs.

3.1.4 Water for America Initiative

In fiscal year 2009, the Bureau of Reclamation partnered with the U.S. Geological Survey (USGS) to implement the Water for America Initiative. This initiative is intended to secure water resources for future generations and address decreasing water supplies caused by potential climate change and population growth. The initiative includes three strategies:

1. Plan for our nation's water future.

2. Expand, protect, and conserve our nation's water resources.

3. Enhance our nation's water knowledge (www.usbr .gov/wfa/).

The plan incorporates elements of Water 2025 and the Water Conservation Field Services Program. Through these two programs, the Bureau of Reclamation seeks to increase water conservation, improve efficiency, and help secure future water supplies through competitive grants and technical assistance.

As part of the Water for America Initiative, USGS plans to conduct seven regional studies and three focused area studies every three years between fiscal years 2009 and

2019. The studies will develop water budgets and analyze hydrologic trends in each of the 21 major river basins in the nation over the next 10 years.

3.1.5 Federal Agencies Involved with Water Resources

A number of U.S. federal agencies are involved in water resource management and watershed protection. Each agency has a different focus, but all are involved to some degree in activities such as data collection, regulation development, technical oversight, environmental education, and planning processes.

Most federal agencies have regional or state liaisons to help administer their programs. For example, the Environmental Protection Agency divides the country into 10 regions, with each region being responsible for the programs within its respective states.

Environmental Protection Agency

The EPA was established in July of 1970 by the White House and Congress in response to the growing public demand for cleaner water, air, and land. EPA is responsible for environmental protection and pollution control in the United States. It also is responsible for administering the Clean Water Act and other acts that involve pollution control. The agency is involved with writing regulations, which are mandatory requirements that can apply to individuals, businesses, state or local governments, or nonprofit institutions. EPA's Office of Water is responsible for the agency's water quality activities, including development of national programs, technical policies, and regulations relating to drinking water, water quality, groundwater, pollution source standards, and the protection of wetlands.

U.S. Army Corps of Engineers

The U.S. Army Corps of Engineers is the federal agency with primary responsibility for regulating wetlands, although

EPA, the Soil Conservation Service, and the U.S. Fish and Wildlife Service all have various levels of responsibility. EPA, for example, has veto power over the Corps' decisions to grant permits.

The Corps works with a wide variety of federal agencies, including the Federal Emergency Management Agency (FEMA), EPA, the USDA, and the U.S. Fish and Wildlife (www.CorpsResults.us).

The Corps manages for long-term public access to, and use of, the natural resources in cooperation with other federal, state, and local agencies as well as the private sector. The two basic goals of Corps stewardship are to manage lands and waters to ensure their availability for future generations, and to help maintain healthy ecosystems and biodiversity. The Corps' Natural Resources Management mission is to manage and conserve those natural resources, consistent with ecosystem management principles, while providing quality public outdoor recreation experiences to serve the needs of present and future generations.

The Corps is responsible for approximately 12 million acres of lands and waters in 43 different states. These lands and waters include streams, rivers, lakes, and their adjacent lands. Most Corps land is east of the Mississippi, and 80% is near a major city. The Corps manages hundreds of reservoirs filled with 330 million acre-feet of water and having more than 56,000 miles of lake shore. It oversees 5,700 recreation areas at 419 lakes, and about 386 million people visit Corps lakes each year, including: 130 million for sightseeing; 100 million for fishing; 84 million for boating; 49 million for swimming; 46 million for picnicking; 10 million for hunting; and 5 million for camping. Visitors to Corps lakes spend nearly $15 billion a year.

Of the Corps' 600 reservoir projects, 117 are used for water supply storage. Collectively they provide more than 3 trillion gallons of water for use by local communities and businesses. That is enough water to supply the average household needs of about 85 million Americans for a year.

Environmental considerations are a top priority in all of the Corps' water supply projects. An example of the watershed approach in action is the Corps' Savannah (GA) River Basin Comprehensive Study. The goal of this study is to develop, with the help of key stakeholders, a comprehensive plan for this watershed that will conserve, restore, and protect this valuable ecosystem while allowing for the appropriate balancing of multiple uses.

The Corps is also the largest operator of hydroelectric power plants in the United States and one of the largest in the world. Corps hydropower plants provide 100 billion kilowatt-hours annually, enough power to serve more than 10 million households. Hydropower plants contribute to cleaner air, because they do not burn fossil fuels, such as coal and oil, and they are good for the economy because they provide an inexpensive source of power, which helps keep energy prices down.

Bureau of Reclamation

The Bureau of Reclamation (BOR) is a water management agency within the Department of Interior. The BOR's mission is to manage, develop, and protect water and related resources in an environmentally and economically sound manner in the interest of the American public. The National Reclamation Act was enacted in 1902, and its purpose was to provide funding for the construction and maintenance of western irrigation projects. The Bureau of Reclamation was created to administer this program. Most large water resource projects in the West have involved BOR.

Natural Resources Conservation Service

USDA's Natural Resources Conservation Service (NRCS) provides support for funding watershed-oriented projects, such as agricultural management practices, wetland restoration, and land retirement. The NRCS administers the USDA Watershed Program, which assists federal, state, and local agencies; local government sponsors; tribal governments; and other program participants in protecting watersheds.

Federal Energy Regulatory Commission

The Federal Energy Regulatory Commission is an independent agency that regulates the interstate transmission of electricity, natural gas, and oil. Among other responsibilities, the FERC oversees environmental matters related to hydroelectricity projects. It also regulates the activities of municipal power systems; federal power marketing agencies, such as the Tennessee Valley Authority; and most rural electric cooperatives. Most nonfederal hydroelectric projects in the United States operate under licenses issued by the FERC. In order to continue operating and maintaining an existing hydroelectric project, licenses must be renewed periodically. The relicensing process addresses power generation, natural resources, recreation, and aesthetics at hydroelectric projects. (See Figure 3.2.)

FERC is also mandated to protect fish and wildlife habitat, irrigation, water supply, recreation, flood control, and water quality. A licensee for a FERC project is responsible for operating and maintaining these projects in accordance with license requirements and project purposes.

U.S. Geological Survey

The U.S. Geological Survey is a science organization that focuses on biology, geography, geology, geospatial

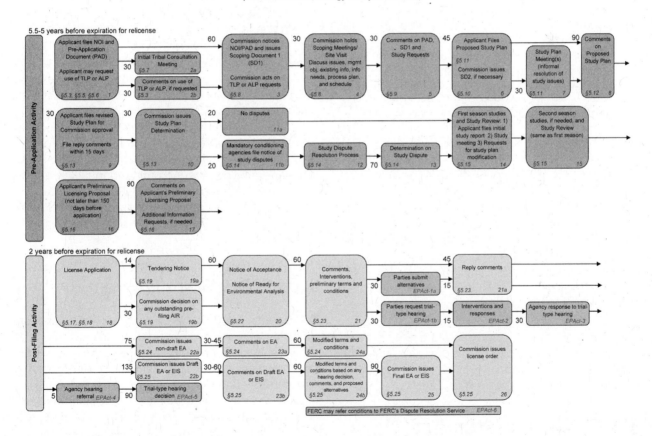

Figure 3.2 *The Federal Energy Regulatory Commission has developed a process that defines the steps for getting approval for hydroelectric projects in the United States. Image courtesy FERC.*

FERC Applications

General information that should be included in FERC applications for proposed nonproject uses or facilities includes:

1. Description of proposed nonproject use or facility.

2. Description of affected environment (the immediate area surrounding the site of the proposed facility or use).

3. Evaluation of how the proposed use is compatible with existing uses.

4. Documentation of consultation (copies of correspondence) with appropriate federal, state, and local government agencies and interested nongovernmental organizations (NGOs).

5. A description of the proposed use's potential impact on each resource area identified under item (2).

6. A description of any proposed construction, design, and/ or operation practices or measures to minimize or mitigate for any specific impacts identified under item (5).

---

information, and water. USGS's stated mission is to provide "reliable scientific information to describe and understand the Earth; minimize loss of life and property from natural disasters; manage water, biological, energy, and mineral resources; and enhance and protect our quality of life" (www .usgs.gov/aboutusgs). Founded in 1879, UGSG is one of the nation's oldest and most respected agencies because of the data they have produced and made available to the public for free, and is also the largest water, earth, and biological science and civilian mapping agency.

3.1.6 Clean Water Act

The Clean Water Act has had a significant impact on how water resources are managed in the United States. The major sections of the act are discussed next.

Section 303(d) of the Clean Water Act

Under Section 303(d), states are required to compile a list of impaired waters that fail to meet any of their applicable water quality standards or cannot support their designated or existing uses. This list, called a 303(d) list, is submitted to Congress every two years. States are required to develop a total maximum daily load (TMDL) for each pollutant causing impairment for water bodies on the 303(d) list.

Section 305(b) and the National Water Quality Inventory: Report to Congress

Every two years, states are required to submit a report to Congress detailing the health of their waters. The 305(b) reports evaluate whether U.S. waters meet water quality standards, what progress has been made in maintaining and restoring water quality, and the extent of remaining problems. EPA compiles the data from the state reports, summarizes them, and transmits the summaries to Congress. According to the EPA's *National Water Quality Inventory: 2000 Report to Congress* (required under Section 305(b)), approximately 39% of surveyed rivers and streams were significantly impacted by pollution.

Section 319 Grant Program

Under Section 319 of the Clean Water Act, EPA awards funds to states and eligible tribes to implement nonpoint source management programs. States may use funding under Section 319 of the Clean Water Act to develop and implement watershed plans. State and tribal NPS include a variety of components, including technical assistance, financial assistance, education, training, technology transfer, demonstration projects, and regulatory programs. Each year, EPA awards Section 319(h) funds to states in accordance with a state-by-state allocation formula that EPA has developed in consultation with the states.

66   Sustainable Planning Approaches for Water Resources
result

Nine Important Elements

EPA requires that nine elements be addressed in watershed plans funded with incremental Clean Water Act Section 319 funds. EPA also recommends that they be included in all other watershed plans intended to address water quality impairments.

1. Identification of causes of impairment and pollutant sources or groups of similar sources that need to be controlled to achieve needed load reductions and any other goals identified in the watershed plan.

2. An estimate of the load reductions expected from management measures.

3. A description of the nonpoint source management measures that will need to be implemented to achieve load reductions and a description of the critical areas in which those measures will be needed to implement this plan.

4. Estimate of the amounts of technical and financial assistance needed, associated costs, and/or the sources and authorities that will be relied on to implement this plan.

5. An information and education component used to enhance public understanding of the project and encourage early and continued participation in selecting, designing, and implementing the nonpoint source management measures that will be implemented.

6. Schedule for implementing the nonpoint source management measures identified in the plan that is reasonably expeditious.

7. A description of interim measurable milestones for determining whether nonpoint source management measures or other control actions are being implemented.

8. A set of criteria that can be used to determine whether loading reductions are being achieved over time and whether substantial progress is being made toward attaining water quality standards.

9. A monitoring component to evaluate the effectiveness of the implementation efforts over time.

Source: Handbook for Developing Watershed Plans to Restore and Protect Our Waters, http://epa.gov/nps/watershed_handbook/pdf/handbook.pdf.

Section 401 of the Clean Water Act

Section 401 requires federal agencies to obtain certification from states, territories, or Indian tribes before issuing permits that would result in increased pollutant loads to a water body.

Section 404 Discharge of Dredged and Fill Material

Any project involving discharge of dredged or fill material to wetlands or other waters of the United States must obtain authorization from the U.S. Army Corps of Engineers. Implementation of Section 404 is shared between the Corps and EPA, with the Corps being responsible for permitting. The Section 404(b) guidelines are the environmental criteria that the Corps applies when deciding whether to issue permits.

404 Permits for Wetlands

Activities in wetlands for which 404 permits may be required include but are not limited to:

- Placement of fill material
- Ditching activities when the excavated material is cast to the side instead of being removed
- Levee and dike construction
- Mechanized land clearing
- Land leveling
- Most road construction
- Dam construction

Source: U.S. Army Corps of Engineers (http://www.spl.usace.army.mil/regulatory/)

Section 404 of the Clean Water Act requires approval prior to discharging dredged or fill material into the waters of the United States, including special aquatic sites, such as wetlands. A Section 404 permit can be authorized by the Corps. There are four different types of permits: a standard individual permit, letter of permission, nationwide permit, or regional permit. The Corps determines what type of permit is needed.

A *standard individual permit* is used for most site-specific projects. *A letter of permission* is normally used for activities in navigable waters where objections are unlikely.

Limitations of the Section 404 Program

- It does not protect wetlands from indirect impacts that occur within wetland-contributing drainage areas.

- Some isolated wetlands may be outside the geographic jurisdiction of the program.

- Some activities are not subject to regulation.

- Most activities that are subject to regulations are authorized by general permits, which do not have as extensive a review process and may not require any mitigation.

- It does not address cumulative impacts to wetlands due to the permit-by-permit approach as opposed to a watershed approach.

- It does not successfully replace wetland types or functions because mitigation wetlands often are not of the same type as the wetland they are replacing, and insufficient guidance exists on how to mitigate for functions and measure success.

- It does not always replace lost wetland acreage due to high failure rates of mitigation wetlands or lack of implementation and enforcement.

Source: Tiffany Wright et al., Center for Watershed Protection, "Direct and Indirect Impacts of Urbanization on Wetland Quality Wetlands & Watersheds," prepared for Office of Wetlands, Oceans and Watersheds, U.S. Environmental Protection Agency (December 2006).

A *nationwide permit* is a form of general permit that authorizes a category of activities throughout the nation. *Regional permits* are issued by the district engineer for a general category of activities when: (1) the activities are similar in nature and cause minimal environmental impact (both individually and cumulatively); and (2) the regional permit reduces duplication of regulatory control by state and federal agencies (U.S. Army Corps of Engineers, www.spl.usace.army.mil/regulatory).

Processing time for individual permits can range from 6 to 24 months. Nationwide permits usually are processed within 3 to 6 months, although it can take up to 12 months. The time frame is dependent on the complexity of the impacts on aquatic resources, endangered species, archaeological or tribal concerns, and workload. A nationwide permit applicant will get a response within 45 days from the Corps, although processing time may be extended due to endangered species. If a project might affect threatened or endangered species, a biological evaluation will be required. Applicants requiring an environmental impact statement average about three years to process.

Typical activities requiring Section 404 permits are:

- Depositing fill, dredged, or excavated material in waters of the United States and/or adjacent wetlands.

- Grading or mechanized land clearing of wetlands.

- Placement of spoils from ditch excavation activities in wetlands.

Processing Steps for Individual Permits (U.S. Army Corps)

1. Preapplication consultation (optional).

2. Applicant submits Joint Aquatic Resource Permits Application form.

3. Application received and assigned identification number.

4. Public notice issued (within 15 days of receiving all information).

5. Comment period of 15 to 30 days depending on the nature of the activity.

(continues)

(continued)

6. Proposal is reviewed by Corps and the public; special interest groups; and local, state, and federal agencies.

7. Corps considers all comments.

8. Other federal agencies are consulted, if appropriate.

9. District engineer may ask the applicant to provide additional information.

10. Public hearing is held, if needed.

11. District engineer makes a decision.

12. Permit is issued, or permit is denied and applicant is advised of the reason(s).

- Soil movement during vegetation clearing in wetlands.
- Site development fills for residential, commercial, or recreational developments.
- Construction of revetments, groins, breakwaters, beach enhancement, jetties, levees, dams, dikes, and weirs.
- Placement of riprap and road fills.

Nationwide, only 3% of all 404 requests for permits are denied.

Security

September 11, 2001 raised concerns about the security of the nation's water supply. In the wake of those events, the Corps heightened its levels of security to ensure the safety of the water supply. Steps taken include:

- Providing specialized training for all personnel at Corps water supply facilities

- Reevaluating security requirements at each site and making any necessary changes

- Upgrading physical security precautions such as fences, gates, and electronic monitoring systems

- Coordinating security plans with local and national law enforcement agencies

3.1.7 Water for America Initiative

In the fiscal year 2009 budget, President Bush provided $21.3 million for the Water for America initiative. This initiative contains three basic strategies: (1) plan for our nation's water future; (2), expand, protect, and conserve our nation's water resources; and (3) enhance our nation's water knowledge. The Department of Reclamation would focus on the first two, and USGS will handle the third. The goal is to stretch water supplies while managing and protecting endangered species. Reclamation will also address using climate change information in operations and planning through project-specific studies. USGS will conduct a national water census and groundwater research project and enhance stream-gauging networks. The national water census will be the first in more than 30 years and is expected to be completed in 2012.

In 2009, the Bureau of Reclamation started working with state and local partners to implement several comprehensive water supply and demand studies in the West. These basin studies are critical to understanding how best to deal with water resources there. The studies focused on major river basins and subbasins in selected parts of the 17 western states.

3.1.8 Flood Management at a National Level

Floods inflict more damage and economic losses on the United States than any other natural disaster. Perhaps one reason is that more than 30 million Americans live in areas that have a high risk of flooding. In response to the rising cost of taxpayer-funded disaster relief for flood victims and the increasing amount of damage caused by floods, Congress created the National Flood Insurance Program (NFIP) in 1968. To date, NFIP has paid about $12 billion in insurance claims, primarily from policyholder premiums, that otherwise would have been paid, at least in part, from taxpayer-funded disaster relief.

During the 10 years from fiscal year 1992 through fiscal year 2001 (October to October), according to the U.S. Army Corps of Engineers (GAO, 2001), flooding caused over 900 deaths and resulted in approximately $55 billion in damages. In recent years, the cost of flooding has increased significantly. The greatest loss was in 2005, when loss payments totaled $17.4 billion, in large part because of flooding caused by hurricanes Katrina, Rita, and Wilma. If recent years have shown us anything, it is that problems with flooding and other natural disasters are escalating, as are costs.

Why is flooding such a big problem? One reason is that FEMA flood maps, which are intended to define areas that are "safe" from flooding, are outdated and inaccurate. Flood maps have been produced and used for 35 years, and many have not been updated in years. According to FEMA, nearly 70% of the nation's approximately 92,222 flood maps are more than 10 years old, and many no longer accurately reflect current flood hazard risks. As a result, development is occurring in areas that should be restricted because of flooding hazards, and about 25% of all flood insurance claims occur in areas mapped as being moderate or minimal flood risk.

As part of the nation's effort to reduce the damages and costs of flooding, Congress appropriated funding to update flood maps across the entire country. FEMA's Flood Map Modernization (Map Mod) program is a five-year initiative to update the nation's flood hazard maps, expected to cost more than $1 billion. FEMA intends to use advanced technologies to produce more accurate and accessible digital flood maps available on the Internet. The basic idea is to reduce the damages and costs of flooding across the nation. FEMA Map Modernization is part of a larger effort to develop a National Spatial Data Infrastructure, which is a physical, organizational, and virtual network that enables the development and sharing of digital geographic information resources across the country.

One objective of FEMA's Map Modernization program is making digital floodplain data available in Geographic Information Systems (GIS) formats. GIS experts are expecting this attempt to be much more successful than their first attempt in the 1990s, when FEMA made an effort to transfer paper maps to digital format. This process produced the Q3 Flood Data, which has been the foundation for many design and planning decisions over the years.

To be blunt, many problems are associated with Q3 Flood Data. The horizontal control of Q3 flood data is consistent with that used for 1:24000 scale maps, which is acceptable for community- and regional-scale planning projects but is not useful for site-scale projects.

The Q3 data displayed on FEMA's Web site (www.fema.gov/hazard/flood/index.shtm) was developed by scanning existing original paper maps, called Flood Insurance Rate Maps (FIRMs). A major limitation is that during the digitizing and postprocessing steps, edge-matching errors, overlaps, deficiencies in coverage, and other types of problems were not corrected. As a result, maps developed with Q3 data are not nearly as accurate or have the same level of detail as FIRM maps. Base flood elevations, river cross sections, study data, river depths, and other features were missing from Q3 data, and quality control was not very good.

FEMA's Q3 data are being replaced through Map Mod by Digital Flood Insurance Rate Maps (DFIRMs). These new maps greatly improve the quality and put information in the hands of people who need it. The mapping technologies used in Mod Map have improved significantly in recent years, and the newer DFIRM maps created through Map Mod are much more detailed and accurate than Q3 or the earlier paper maps. The DFIRM Database is derived from FEMA's Flood Insurance Studies and previously published Flood Insurance Rate Maps (FIRMs) as well as flood hazard analyses and additional mapping data accumulated in many locations. This approach helps increase the quality, reliability, and availability of flood hazard maps and data. (See Figure 3.3.)

To ensure that the new DFIRMs provide the required level of accuracy, FEMA is incorporating data from a variety of sources. These include: the National Digital Orthophoto Program (NDOP); National Elevation Dataset (NED) and Similar USGS Holdings; National Agriculture Imagery Program (NAIP); NRCS/USDA Geospatial Data Gateway; Seamless Data Distribution System, U.S. Census/TIGER (Topologically Integrated Geographic Encoding and Referencing system) Accuracy Improvement Project; National

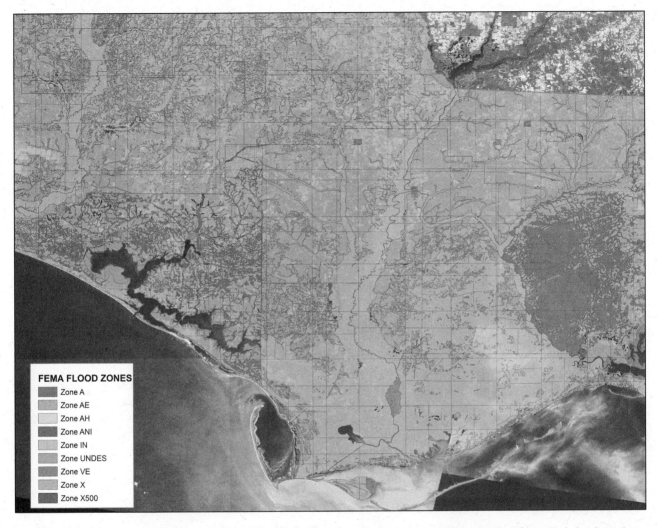

FEMA FLOOD ZONES
- Zone A
- Zone AE
- Zone AH
- Zone ANI
- Zone IN
- Zone UNDES
- Zone VE
- Zone X
- Zone X500

Figure 3.3 *FEMA produces maps that identify flood zones. Each zone has a different potential of flooding. This information helps determine where to build, where not to build, and where special consideration needs to be taken when considering potential building options. Image courtesy FEMA.*

Geospatial-Intelligence Agency; and the National Oceanic and Atmospheric Administration Coastal Services Center.

The NDOP was introduced in 1993 by a consortium of federal agencies to develop, distribute, and maintain orthoimages as part of the public domain. In 2002, USDA started the NAIP to support the continued development of its own GIS program through the acquisition of digital orthophotography.

The USGS NED has been developed by merging the highest-resolution, best quality elevation data available across the United States into a seamless raster format.

Maps through the Map Mod program can be accessed from a number of sources. Flood maps and data may be obtained online via the FEMA Mapping Information Platform. Many municipalities and organizations have incorporated FEMA's

Map Modernization program into Web-based services that make the data available to constituents. Flood maps for any community participating in the NFIP are available through the Community Map Repository, which typically is maintained by a local floodplain administrator or a local planning and zoning department. Landscape architects working on projects for one of these communities may find this to be the easiest way to get access to the most up-to-date flood maps.

The Geospatial Data Gateway provides access to DFIRM maps as well as many other data layers. Some of these data are updated weekly, while other data may be slightly older. FEMA's Web Map Service (WMS) provides public access to Nationwide DFIRM and Q3 Flood Maps. Maps generated by WMS can also be viewed in Google Earth. Many landscape architects have already discovered that Google Earth is a great tool for presenting information, and being able to add flood hazard data just provides one more layer of valuable geospatial information.

Information about the best resolution available and methods of production are available through the USGS GISDATA (http://gisdata.usgs.net/website/USGS_GN_NED_DSI/viewer .htm) Map Studio Interactive Viewer. This is one site that landscape architects need to save as a "Favorite" Internet site.

At the end of 2007, FEMA performed a midprogram evaluation to determine whether the Map Mod program was meeting expectations. FEMA is continuing to make changes in how it is implementing Map Mod in order to produce more accurate flood maps. At the time of the evaluation, more than 50% of flood maps across the nation had been updated. FEMA estimates that access to better flood data from the Map Modernization program will save more than $160 billion over the next 40 years.

U.S. Army Corps Environmental Operating Principles

- Strive to achieve environmental sustainability. An environment maintained in a healthy, diverse, and sustainable condition is necessary to support life.

- Recognize the interdependence of life and the physical environment. Proactively consider environmental consequences of Corps

programs and act accordingly in all appropriate circumstances.

- Seek balance and synergy among human development activities and natural systems by designing economic and environmental solutions that support and reinforce one another.

- Continue to accept corporate responsibility and accountability under the law for activities and decisions under our control that impact human health and welfare and the continued viability of natural systems.

- Seek ways and means to assess and mitigate cumulative impacts to the environment; bring systems approaches to the full life cycle of our processes and work.

- Build and share an integrated scientific, economic, and social knowledge base that supports a greater understanding of the environment and impacts of our work.

- Respect the views of individuals and groups interested in Corps activities, listen to them actively, and learn from their perspective in the search to find innovative win-win solutions to the nation's problems that also protect and enhance the environment.

Source: www.usace.army.mil/Environment/Pages/eop.aspx.

3.1.9 National Drought Policy

Efforts to deal with drought in the United States have been somewhat haphazard. A couple of years ago, EPA determined that there were 47 federal programs with elements of drought-related relief, focusing primarily on agricultural droughts. UDSA had relief programs for drought assistance, but the application process was too cumbersome; it took too long to make decisions, and placing federal decision making outside the local level often results in disconnection among the applicants and the programs (National Drought Policy Commission Report 2002, http://govinfo.library.unt .edu/drought/finalreport/fullreport/ndpcfullreportcovers/ ndpcreportcontents.htm).

Five Major Goals of the National Drought Policy Commission Report

Goal 1. Incorporate planning, implementation of plans and proactive mitigation measures, risk management, resource stewardship, environmental considerations, and public education as the key elements of effective national drought policy. In accordance with the law that established the National Drought Policy Commission, we strongly endorse preparedness as a key element to reduce the impacts of drought on individuals, communities, and the environment. We believe that sound drought preparedness programs will lessen the need for future emergency financial and other assistance.

Goal 2. Improve collaboration among scientists and managers to enhance the effectiveness of observation networks, monitoring, prediction, information delivery, and applied research and to foster public understanding of and preparedness for drought. Our findings and conclusions point out the value of observation networks, monitoring, prediction, information gateways and delivery, and research to drought preparedness.

Goal 3. Develop and incorporate comprehensive insurance and financial strategies into drought preparedness plans. We firmly believe that preparedness measures will go far to reduce this country's vulnerability to drought. But we also recognize that prolonged drought causes risks that the best preparedness measures may not adequately address. The most significant approach to such risks in recent years is the federal government's crop insurance program for farmers. We had neither the expertise nor the resources to investigate thoroughly the various options to improve the crop insurance program or the other proposals that were presented during our deliberations and that Congress has grappled with for many years. (Our full report briefly describes several alternative plans.) Still, we are convinced that sound insurance and financial strategies are essential if the country is to move away from emergency relief in response to widespread drought.

Goal 4. Maintain a safety net of emergency relief that emphasizes sound stewardship of natural resources and self-help. The Commission recognizes that over time, efforts at drought preparedness, including risk management, can greatly reduce, but not eliminate, drought-related emergencies. Response measures for drought emergencies can also be useful to respond to water shortages not caused by drought. In all cases where emergency response is required, it should be effective and timely.

Goal 5. Coordinate drought programs and response effectively, efficiently, and in a customer-oriented manner. Federal drought programs are a collection of initiatives run by different departments and agencies. Every analysis of past responses to major droughts notes that these programs need to be better coordinated and integrated. We strongly agree. In accordance with our policy statement, we emphasize that coordination of federal drought programs should ensure effective service delivery.

Source: http://govinfo.library.unt.edu/drought/finalreport/full report/ndpcfullreportcovers/ndpcreportcontents.htm.

On July 16, 1998, Congress passed the National Drought Policy Act of 1998, Public Law 105-199, which established the National Drought Policy Commission. The commission was charged by Congress to provide advice and recommendations on the creation of an integrated, coordinated federal policy that would provide a plan for preparing and responding to serious drought emergencies. The National Drought Policy Commission's report to Congress and the president, "Preparing for Drought in the 21st Century," emphasizes the need for drought planning at the state, local, federal, and tribal levels of government (http://drought.unl.edu/pubs/pfd21main.html).

Among other tasks, the commission was to help the federal government coordinate its more than 80 drought-related programs and to integrate them with ongoing nonfederal drought programs.

The National Drought Policy Commission recommended that Congress pass a National Drought Preparedness Act, which would establish a nonfederal/federal partnership through a National Drought Council. The primary function of the council would be to ensure that the goals of national drought policy are achieved. The commission's drought preparedness plans contain three critical components (http://drought.unl.edu/mitigate/status.htm):

1. A comprehensive early-warning system
2. Risk and impact assessment procedures
3. Mitigation and response strategies

The National Drought Policy Commission (http://govinfo.library.unt.edu/drought/finalreport/fullreport/ndpcfullreportcovers/ndpcreportcontents.htm) recommended three guiding principles for a national drought policy. They are:

1. Favor preparedness over insurance, insurance over relief, and incentives over regulation.

2. Set research priorities based on the potential of the research results to reduce drought impacts.

3. Coordinate the delivery of federal services through cooperation and collaboration with nonfederal entities.

The emphasis of these principles is on preparedness and shifting away from a policy that emphasized drought relief. This forward-looking approach will greatly reduce this nation's vulnerability to the impacts of drought. Preparedness includes drought planning, plan implementation, proactive mitigation, risk management, resource stewardship, consideration of environmental concerns, and public education.

Consultative Group on International

The Consultative Group on International Agricultural Research (CGIAR), a network of 60 governments, private foundations, and international and regional organizations, was established to apply science to the challenge of feeding the world's poor and enabling them to escape poverty. CGIAR has identified three strategic objectives that define the need for action:

1. **Food for People.** Create and accelerate sustainable increases in productivity and production of healthy food by and for the poor.

2. **Environment for People.** Conserve, enhance, and sustainably use natural resources and biodiversity to improve the livelihoods of the poor in response to climate change and other factors.

3. **Policies for People.** Promote policy and institutional change that will stimulate agricultural growth and equity to benefit the poor, especially rural women and other disadvantaged groups

Source: www.cgiar.org.

National Drought Policy

Studies show that the federal government spent $3.3 billion responding to the drought of 1953 to 1956, at least $6.5 billion during the 1976–1977 drought, and about $6 billion during the 1988–1989 drought. The National Drought Policy Commission contends that the nation's vulnerability to the impacts of drought can be reduced by making preparedness the cornerstone of national drought policy.

Source: National Drought Policy Commission Report
http://govinfo.library.unt.edu/drought/finalreport/fullreport/ndpcfullreportcovers/ndpcreportcontents.htm.

3.2 PLANNING AT THE STATE LEVEL

In addition to federal regulations, most states have enacted laws to protect the natural resources within their jurisdiction.

Water Planning Regions

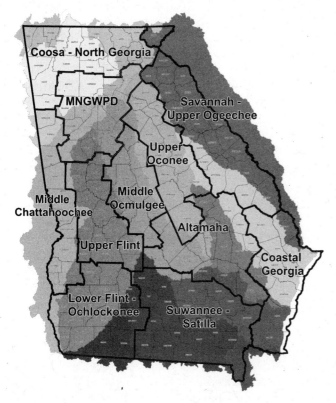

Figure 3.4 *The state of Georgia is broken down into 11 water planning regions. Each region is able to establish its own goals and objectives. Image courtesy Georgia Department of Water Resources.*

As a general rule, water resource planning and policies are implemented at the state level rather than at the federal level. Each state in the United States has the right to establish its own water resource approach. The federal acts have laid the foundation of how water resources are dealt with in the United States; it is up to the states to implement the actions. State regulations can be more restrictive than federal regulations.

States have the authority and responsibility to enforce state water quality laws. They also are authorized by the Environmental Protection Agency to enforce the Federal Clean Water Act. States are encouraged to develop statewide watershed planning frameworks that integrate and coordinate plans for large drainage areas. (See Figure 3.4.)

This watershed protection approach is used to develop statewide instream flow policies to protect water quantity and quality. Plans for larger basins should contain general or summarized quantitative analyses of current water quality problems and the load reductions or other benefits expected from the implementation of best management practices (BMPs) (EPA, 2008).

Under the 1996 amendments to the federal Safe Drinking Water Act, states must conduct source water assessments and produce studies or reports that provide basic information about public drinking water. States establish nonpoint source programs that are intended to reduce (NPS) pollution statewide. State NPS programs provide technical assistance as well as funding sources for developing and implementing specific plans.

10-Step Planning Process for Developing a Drought Policy

1. Appoint a drought task force.

2. State the purpose and objectives of the drought preparedness plan.

3. Seek stakeholder participation and resolve conflict.

4. Inventory resources and identify groups at risk.

5. Prepare/write the drought preparedness plan.

6. Identify research needs and fill institutional gaps.

7. Integrate science and policy.

8. Publicize the drought preparedness plan and build public awareness.

9. Develop education programs.

10. Evaluate and revise drought preparedness plan.

Source: National Drought Mitigation Center, University of Nebraska, Lincoln, Nebraska (http://drought.unl.edu).

Many states have statewide watershed management programs that provide an evaluation of cumulative effects on water resources. Many utilize unified watershed assessments, which were initiated in 1999 to assess the health of watersheds and identify watersheds in need of restoration or repair. These assessments also identified watersheds that need preventive action to sustain water quality using ongoing state, tribal, and federal programs as well as pristine or sensitive watersheds on federal lands that need an extra measure of protection. The results of these assessments can be obtained from state environmental protection departments. A detailed description of water quality models of all types can be found in the *Compendium of Tools for Watershed Assessment and TMDL Development* (EPA, 1997).

Evaluation Factors for USACE Permitting

The decision whether to grant or deny a permit is based on a public interest review of the probable impact of the proposed activity and its intended use. Benefits and detriments are balanced by considering the effects on items such as:

- Conservation
- Economics
- Aesthetics
- General environmental concerns
- Wetlands
- Cultural values
- Flood hazards
- Floodplain values
- Food and fiber production
- Navigation
- Shore erosion and accretion
- Recreation
- Water supply and conservation
- Water quality
- Energy needs
- Safety
- Needs and welfare of the people
- Considerations of private ownership

Source: U.S. Army Corps of Engineers (http://www.spl.usace .army.mil/regulatory/).

Many states and counties have developed wetland protection programs, which vary considerably from state to state. State water quality reports are produced to meet federal requirements.

3.2.1 State Actions

Each state makes its own decision about how to address water resource issues. Florida delegates drought planning to local authorities. South Carolina, North Carolina, Virginia, West Virginia, and Kentucky all have drought plans that emphasize response. Georgia's drought plan emphasizes mitigation. As of October 2006, Alabama, Arkansas, Louisiana, Mississippi, and Tennessee were all states without a comprehensive drought plan (http://drought.unl.edu/mitigate/status.htm).

Examples of what some states are doing to protect their water resources are presented next.

Alabama

In the past, Alabama lacked any significant laws to manage water resources within the state. The Southern Environmental Law Center and the Alabama Rivers Alliance produced the first Alabama Water Agenda in January 2007. The agenda identified the six most urgent threats to the state's waters and outlined a series of actions. The threats include a lack of coordination among the many agencies responsible for water protection, a lack of funding for these agencies, and lax enforcement of rules and regulations. Other threats identified in the report include suburban sprawl, stormwater pollution, and growing water consumption (Alabama Rivers Alliance, 2007).

The Alabama Water Agenda is designed to create permanent change in water policy through proactive solutions. Water threats were reduced to the 16 primary threats most frequently submitted. A peer review group narrowed the focus to the 6 priority threats that represent the greatest detrimental impacts to the state's waters and have the most potential for success through policy change. The priority threats identified are: agency coordination and enhancement, enforcement, state agency funding, instream flow, stormwater, and suburban sprawl (www .AlabamaWaterAgenda.com).

Alabama has more than 77,000 miles of rivers and streams, making in seventh in the nation in total miles of perennial streams. The Alabama Department of Environmental Management has only fully assessed about 7%

of Alabama's rivers. Forty percent of the assessed streams are considered to have poor water quality. Groundwater from underground aquifers also supplies many Alabamians with drinking water and often provides a base flow to surface waters. Alabama also ranks fifth in the nation in plant and animal diversity and first in freshwater species diversity, but it also ranks fourth in the number of species at risk for extinction (Alabama Rivers Alliance, 2007).

The Alabama Office of Water Resources is responsible for tracking water withdrawals, developing a drought management plan, and water negotiations with other states. The Alabama Department of Environmental Management ensures water quality standards are met and issues permits to the facilities discharging pollutants into the state's rivers.

In February 2008, when a federal appellate court panel ruled the state of Georgia could not withdraw as much water as it had planned from Lake Lanier, Governor Bob Riley of Alabama hailed the decision as "one of the most important in the history of the State of Alabama" ("Southeast Drought Update," 2008).

Arkansas

Arkansas residents utilize groundwater to meet approximately 93% of their water needs. That is problematic because there is no balance, and if the alluvial aquifers are no longer recharged at the same rate as in the past, the state could face some significant water shortages. It is already being predicted that the eastern part of the state will experience severe shortages in the next few years. When it comes to surface water use, Arkansas relies on a "reasonable use riparian doctrine."

California

The state of California has some of the most stringent water regulations in the nation. The Water Plan is a strategic planning document that describes the role of state government and the growing role of California's regions in managing the state's water resources. The 2009 update of the plan integrates information and recommendations from companion planning documents of other state agencies. The California Department of Transportation has one of the most comprehensive stormwater drainage systems in the country. It has

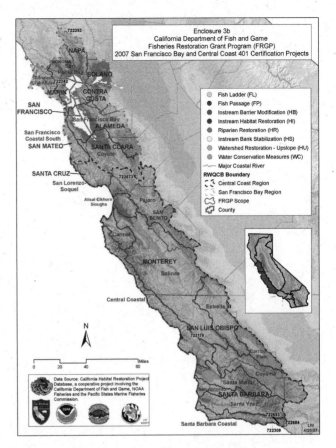

Figure 3.5 *The California Department of Fish and Game provides grants for improving fish habitat and access in the state. This map shows the San Francisco Bay and Central Coast projects. Image courtesy California Department of Fish and Game.*

implemented a Storm Water Task Force to monitor, train, and educate its employees and hired contractors about pollution prevention measures. The California Watershed Assessment Manual was developed to help watershed groups, local agencies, and private landowners evaluate the condition of their watershed. (See Figure 3.5.)

The California Water Plan provides a framework to help decision makers determine what is best for the state's water future. The goal of the plan is "to meet Water Code requirements, receive broad support among those participating in California's water planning, and be a useful document for the public, water planners throughout the state,

legislators, and other decision makers" (www.waterplan
.water.ca.gov). The Water Plan is updated every five years,
but because water resources are such a major issue in
the state, Department of Water Resources (DWR) and the
California Water Plan publish a weekly electronic newsletter with updated information about the plan.

Colorado

In April 2008, Governor Bill Ritter signed House Bill 1280,
which is referred to as the Healthy Rivers Act. This program allows the Colorado Water Conservation Board to
acquire consumptive use water rights and to leave that
water in the rivers. This approach can help protect the
natural environment of streams and rivers in the state. In
the West, a use-it-or-lose-it constraint has been the norm,
but this approach made it risky for water rights owners to
lease water to the state because of their concern that they
would lose rights to the water. The Healthy Rivers Act gives
assurance to water rights owners that their rights will not
be diminished for the time it is leased to the instream flow
program ("Water Projects Writ Large," 2008).

Florida

The challenge for Florida is how to ensure an adequate
water supply for its growing population while also protecting the state's natural resources. The Florida Water
Resources Act of 1972 is considered to be one of the
most comprehensive and progressive water regulatory
systems in the nation. The Florida Legislature mandates
that water management districts must identify sustainable
water source options and evaluate alternative water supply
options that can be developed and used while still protecting environmental resources.

In 1993, Florida and the U.S. government initiated a 20-
year project that would appropriate up to $7.8 billion for
the U.S. Army Corps of Engineers to review, revise, and
carry out changes to restore the Everglades (Totty, 2003).
This is just one of the major efforts within the state.

Preservation 2000 and Florida Forever are two programs
that are intended to acquire and preserve natural lands.
The state has led the country in establishing these types

of programs. The Century Commission for a Sustainable
Florida's Critical Lands and Waters Identification Project is
intended to identify Florida's critical natural resources and
make this information available for strategic conservation
planning at a statewide and regional scale (Totty, 2003).

The Century Commission for a Sustainable Florida is a
strategic planning commission appointed by the governor
to help outline Florida's future growth and development.
The commission identified 12 critical issues that will challenge Florida during the next two generations. These
essential state interests are organized under three general
categories: (1) Providing for Floridians' Needs; (2) Preparing
Floridians for Careers; and (3) Protecting Florida's Lands
and Waters. This last category recognizes that Florida is an
exceptional state, endowed with natural beauty, and that
the vitality of the state depends on preserving and conserving this natural landscape.

The Water Resources Management for 2050 Plan, developed by the Hesperides Group, LLC, (2007) recommends
a series of actions for water supply planning, integrated
water resource management, and land use development.
The idea is to create a long-range vision for water resources
in Florida.

Georgia

In Georgia, House Bill 237 was passed in 2004, enacting
the state's "Comprehensive State-wide Water Management
Planning Act." The plan was approved by the Water
Council on January 8, 2008.

The Georgia management plan is designed to help guide
the stewardship of the state's precious water resources
to ensure that those resources continue to support
growth and prosperity statewide while maintaining healthy
natural systems. The plan is based on three fundamental
concepts:

1. Completion of a thorough evaluation of resources,
   called Water Resource Assessments

2. Development of regional forecasts of water supply
   and assimilative capacity demands

3. Development of regional water development and
   conservation plans

Georgia's current approach to water management has evolved in a piecemeal fashion over several decades. Many states have taken the same approach, and their policies have mainly been reactionary, responding to federal legislative mandates and immediate water issues, such as droughts and water wars.

The purpose of the Georgia Comprehensive State-wide Water Management Plan, as stated by the Official Code of Georgia (O.C.G.A.) Section 12-5-522(a), is to guide Georgia in managing water resources in a sustainable manner to support the state's economy, to protect public health and natural systems, and to enhance the quality of life for all citizens. The plan lays out statewide policies, management practices, and guidance for regional planning. The provisions of this plan are intended to guide river basin and aquifer management plans and regional water planning efforts statewide in a manner consistent with O.C.G.A. Sections 12-5-522 and 12-5-570 et seq. (Georgia Comprehensive State-wide Water Management Plan, 2008).

Georgia's water management plan depends on the development of regional water plans. Regional forecasts of future needs for water and wastewater will be completed, then management practices will be identified to ensure that these anticipated demands can be met. Once the regional plans have been developed and approved, they will be implemented primarily by various water users in the region.

Some of these statewide policies and practices will require rulemaking, and this will involve a public involvement process before being brought to the Board of Natural Resources for consideration.

In Georgia, Act 599 of the O.C.G.A. requires that governing authorities of Georgia's 159 counties and 537 incorporated municipalities adopt comprehensive ordinances governing land-disturbing activities within their boundaries (Georgia Soil and Water Conservation Commission, 2000).

Iowa

The state of Iowa updated its State Water Plan in 2007. Prior to this plan, the last comprehensive state water plan in Iowa was completed in 1978. A number of different reports that included water resources had been developed over the years, but they are not integrated, and the general consensus was that Iowa was not taking adequate care of its water resources. The new State Water Plan states: "Further deterioration of Iowa's water quality is no longer acceptable to the citizens of Iowa." The stated goal of implementing a state water plan is "to establish a framework in which to restore, preserve, and enhance Iowa's ground and surface water resources" (2007 Iowa State Water Plan Proposal).

Kansas

The Kansas Water Plan is used to coordinate the management, conservation, and development of the water resources of the state. The Kansas Water Office is responsible for developing the water plan, which is produced in three volumes, plus a state atlas. The most recent version of the plan was approved on January 29, 2009.

Louisiana

The Louisiana Department of Environmental Quality is responsible for administering the state's stormwater program. Louisiana requires that stormwater be treated to the maximum extent practicable. Many of the state's large municipalities have stormwater programs in place, and additional treatment requirements are possible at the local level.

Maryland

The state of Maryland is very environmentally conscious, in large part because of its location around the Chesapeake Bay. The state's Bay Watershed Restoration Strategy is the largest interstate effort in the nation to control nutrient pollution to a major water body. The strategy includes new water quality standards that require specific nutrient-loading limits in all new or renewed permits for Maryland's major wastewater treatment plants in the Chesapeake Bay watershed. The Maryland Department of the Environment (MDE) completed and released to the public the TMDL Guidance for Local Government. The document is a planning aid to counties and municipalities throughout the state.

Maryland's Department of the Environment developed the Environmental Benefits District (EBD) initiative to identify locations where state government and stakeholders could focus their resources to benefit targeted communities. In 2004, MDE designated its first EBDs in portions of central Prince George's County and eastern Baltimore City. Since then MDE has infused a variety of program resources into those districts, including grant funding of nearly $1 million to improve conditions in those areas. These areas have sensitive populations (e.g., children, elderly) and are at increased health risk from high levels of toxic air pollution as well as concerns about water resources.

In 2006, MDE established two additional EBDs: Easton and 10 neighborhoods in the Monroe-Fulton corridor of southwest Baltimore City, including Washington Village. To date, MDE has contributed funding as part of a matching grant for stormwater management projects in Watershed 263 and allocated additional funding to rehabilitate an environmentally friendly community playground. Funds for these projects came from the Maryland Used Tire Cleanup and Recycling Fund, which collects 80 cents per tire at purchase (MDE Accomplishments Report, 2002–2006).

Nevada

The Nevada State Water Plan is published in five volumes, which include (1) a summary; (2) background and resource assessment; (3) water use and forecasts; (4) water planning and management issues; and (5) appendices that include supporting materials. All data in the appendices are accessible digitally by a Web-based state map, allowing direct access to individual state and county water and socioeconomic data and forecasts (http://water.nv.gov).

New Mexico

New Mexico's water law is based on the doctrine of prior appropriation. All waters in the state are considered to be public and therefore have to meet the "beneficial use" requirement for appropriation. There are five basic components of a water right in New Mexico: point of diversion, place of use, purpose of use, owner, and quantity. Although these factors are statutorily required, the state engineer makes decisions about the appropriation and distribution of the state's surface and groundwater resources. Since the state does not have an official list of approved beneficial uses, the state engineer has broad authority on making that determination.

The groundwater procedures closely parallel those for surface water, with underground water basins being regulated by the state. There are currently 33 declared underground water basins throughout New Mexico. In the state, water rights are considered real property and can be bought or sold separately. New Mexico's instream flow program is complex, unclear, and continually evolving. The state does not have a legislated instream flow program, and instream flow is not a recognized beneficial use; however, in a 1998 court case, the New Mexico Attorney General determined that the transfer of a consumptive water right to an instream flow right is allowable under state law (www.ose.state.nm.us/water-info/NMWaterPlanning/2003StateWaterPlan.pdf).

Pennsylvania

Pennsylvania's Act 167 requires that watershed assessments consider these objectives:

- Implement nonpoint source pollutant removal methodologies
- Maintain groundwater recharge
- Reduce channel erosion
- Manage overbank flood events
- Manage extreme flood events

The state established four subtasks to achieve these objectives:

1. Determine the water quality design storm.
2. Determine the runoff capture for a selected design storm (recharge/retention).
3. Establish streambank erosion requirements.
4. Establish overbank/extreme event requirements (release rates).

(Pennsylvania DEP, 1999. www.depweb.state.pa.us/dep/cwp/view.asp?a=3&q=503359.)

Texas

In the 1950s, the Texas Legislature created the Texas Water Development Board (TWDB) to develop water supplies and prepare plans to meet the state's future water needs. The

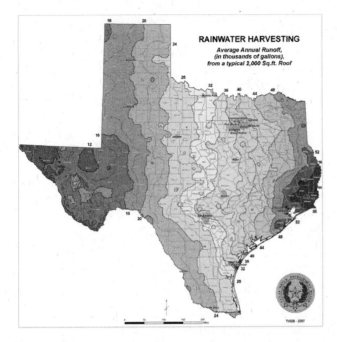

Figure 3.6 *This map of Texas shows the average annual runoff from a typical 2,000-square-foot roof. The eastern part of the state receives considerably more rainfall, so the potential for rainwater harvesting is greater in these areas. Image courtesy Texas Department of Water Resources.*

state's water plan is coordinated by 16 Regional Water Planning Groups that each is in charge of one of the regional water planning areas. TWDB is required to review and update the planning area boundaries at least once every five years (www.twdb.state.tx.us). (See Figure 3.6.)

Virginia

In 2003, following a major drought, the state of Virginia passed its Water Supply Planning Act. This act required development of a comprehensive statewide water-supply planning process to address potential issues associated with water resources. The act was to ensure adequate and safe drinking water, protect other beneficial uses of the state's waters, and promote alternative water sources. The state requires communities to develop a water resource map, and these plans will be assembled to develop a statewide plan outlining needs and potential alternatives for the next 30 years.

One of the primary regulatory mechanisms in Virginia is the Erosion and Sediment Control program, which requires developers to submit and implement a plan that identifies how they are reducing sedimentation. The program includes 19 guidelines that function as the minimum standards for all submitted plans (http://dls.virginia.gov/pubs/legisrec/2009/water1.htm).

Wyoming

In 1997, the Wyoming Legislature directed the state's Water Development Office to conduct a water planning feasibility study with the assistance of the University of Wyoming. Two years later, a planning framework was recommended and authorized the Bear and Green Basin Plans, and five other river basin plans were developed in subsequent years. The water plan for the seven basins has two objectives: (1) conduct an inventory and project future water needs, and (2) provide future water resource planning direction to the state of Wyoming (http://wwdc.state.wy.us).

Wetland Resource Vulnerability

The Association of State Wetland Managers recommends that states take these actions to evaluate and reduce the extent of potential vulnerability to their wetland resources:

- Monitor Corps' determinations to evaluate the extent of reductions in Clean Water Act jurisdiction.

- Document any associated loss of wetland benefits and services.

- Work with the Corps and EPA to determine "significant nexus" guidance.

- Provide clarifying information to the public regarding regulated waters.

- Expand state permitting programs or water quality statutes to provide protection for vulnerable streams and wetlands.

Source: Adapted from Christie and Kusler, 2006.

3.3 REGIONAL APPROACHES TO WATER MANAGEMENT

Because water issues do not respect political boundaries, water resources often have to be addressed at a regional scale. Even when a river defines the boundary between two states, for example, the states have to work together to manage the water—or they spend a lot of time in court. Taking legal actions certainly has been a common approach in recent years.

There are a number of regional approaches to addressing water resources. Some involve states working together, some involve counties and cities within a state combining forces, and some involve nonprofit organizations that take a broad, watershed approach to water management.

3.3.1 Interstate Water Commissions

There is often a need for different states to work together to address water quality and water quantity issues. Interstate water commissions seek to do just that. Some examples of interstate commissions include: New England Interstate Water Pollution Control; Interstate Commission on the Potomac River Basin; Ohio River Valley Water Sanitation Commission; Susquehanna River Basin Commission; Delaware River Basin Commission; Great Lakes Commission; and Interstate Environmental Commission. A good source of information about these commissions is the Association of State and Interstate Water Pollution Control Administrators, which is a national organization representing the officials responsible for implementing surface water protection programs throughout the United States (www.asiwpca.org).

New England Interstate Water Pollution Control Commission

The New England Interstate Water Pollution Control Commission (NEIWPCC) is a not-for-profit interstate agency that serves the states of Connecticut, Maine, Massachusetts,

New Hampshire, New York, Rhode Island, and Vermont. Founded in 1947, emphasis was originally on surface water protection, but the commission's programs have grown to include watershed planning, wetlands, nonpoint source pollution, drinking water, source water protection, wastewater treatment plant security, underground storage tanks, and policy development. The NEIWPCC has three main divisions: Water Quality, Wastewater and Onsite Systems, and Drinking Water.

Interstate Commission on the Potomac River Basin

The Interstate Commission on the Potomac River Basin (ICPRB) was established by Congress in 1940 to help the Potomac basin states and the federal government enhance, protect, and conserve the resources of the Potomac River basin. The Potomac Basin stretches across parts of four states (Maryland, Pennsylvania, Virginia, and West Virginia) as well as the District of Columbia, includes 14,670 square miles, and is home to more than 5 million people. The ICPRB does not have the authority to establish water quality standards or regulations; instead it works within existing state and federal laws and regulations.

Ohio River Valley Water Sanitation Commission

The Ohio River Valley Water Sanitation Commission (ORSANCO) is an interstate commission representing eight states and the federal government. Its mandate is to control and abate pollution in the Ohio River Basin. ORSANCO was established in 1948, and member states include Illinois, Indiana, Kentucky, New York, Ohio, Pennsylvania, Virginia, and West Virginia. Emphasis is on improving water quality, and ORSANCO is involved with setting wastewater discharge standards, performing biological assessments, monitoring for the chemical and physical properties of the waterways, and conducting special surveys and studies.

Susquehanna River Basin Commission

The Susquehanna River Basin Commission is an interstate watershed agency that manages the 27,510-square-mile Susquehanna River watershed. The commission was founded in 1970, and its members include New York, Pennsylvania, Maryland, and the federal government. The Susquehanna River is the nation's sixteenth largest river and is the largest U.S. river flowing into the Atlantic Ocean. The commission has the authority to address water resource problems anywhere in the drainage area, and it serves as a forum to provide coordinated management, promote communication among the members, and resolve water resource issues. The master plan for the Susquehanna Basin identifies six major areas of interest:

1. Flood plain management and protection
2. Water supply
3. Water quality
4. Watershed protection and management
5. Recreation, fish, and wildlife
6. Cultural, visual, and other amenities

Delaware River Basin Commission

The Delaware River Basin Commission (DRBC) was created in 1961 to help protect the resources in the Delaware River watershed, which stretches 330 miles from the Delaware River's headwaters near Hancock, New York, to the mouth of the Delaware Bay. The commission includes representatives from Delaware, New Jersey, Pennsylvania, and New York as well as the federal government. One of the major tasks of the DRBC is to help coordinate activities of the 43 state agencies, 14 interstate agencies, and 19 federal agencies that are involved in the basin. Commission programs include water quality protection, water supply allocation, regulatory review, water conservation initiatives, watershed planning, drought management, flood loss reduction, and recreation. The DRBC is funded by the signatory parties, project review fees, water use charges, and fines as well as federal, state, and private grants.

Great Lakes Commission

The Great Lakes Commission is an interstate compact agency established in 1955. Its mission is to promote the orderly, integrated, and comprehensive development, use, and conservation of the water resources of the Great Lakes Basin and the St. Lawrence River. Its members include the eight Great Lakes states with associate member status for the Canadian provinces of Ontario and Québec, making

it the only state/provincial organization of its kind in the world. The commission provides leadership in the areas of communication and education, information integration and reporting, facilitation and consensus building, and policy coordination and advocacy.

Interstate Environmental Commission

The Interstate Environmental Commission (IEC) is a joint agency of the states of New York, New Jersey, and Connecticut. The IEC was established as a partnership between New York and New Jersey in 1936, with Connecticut joining five years later. The IEC's area of jurisdiction runs west from Port Jefferson and New Haven on the Long Island Sound, from Bear Mountain on the Hudson River down to Sandy Hook, New Jersey, the Atlantic Ocean out to Fire Island Inlet on Long Island, and the waters abutting the five boroughs of New York City. The primary focus of the IEC is on water quality, but the commission also addresses air pollution, resource recovery facilities, and toxins.

Chesapeake Bay Program

The Chesapeake Bay Program is a regional partnership involved with the restoration of the Chesapeake Bay. Partners of the program include the states of Maryland,

---

Chesapeake Bay Restoration Fund

The Chesapeake Bay Restoration Fund, which is administered by Maryland Department of the Environment, is one of the most important pieces of environmental legislation enacted in Maryland in the past quarter century. A $2.50 monthly fee collected from homes on public sewerage pays for upgrading the 66 largest wastewater treatment plants to state-of-the-art enhanced nutrient removal levels. A $30 annual fee is collected from onsite septic system homes; 60% of the funds are allocated for septic system upgrades and 40% for farmland cover crops to absorb nitrogen.

Source: MDE Accomplishments Report 2002-2006, www .mde.state.md.us/assets/document/MDE_Accomplishments_ Report02_06.pdf.

Pennsylvania, and Virginia; the District of Columbia; the Chesapeake Bay Commission; and EPA.

3.3.2 Regional Approaches within States

A number of regional water initiatives are conducted within the boundaries of a particular state. These initiatives involve multiple political entities, but instead of states they are counties, cities, towns, and other local entities.

Central and South Florida Project for Flood Control and Other Purposes

The Central and South Florida Project for Flood Control and Other Purposes, which began in 1947, has made significant changes in South Florida. This project provided the U.S. Army Corps of Engineers funding to build levees, pump stations, and flood control structures. When combined with the projects to channelize the Kissimmee River and construct a dike around Lake Okeechobee, the engineering efforts in South Florida were designed to disconnect the natural flow patterns in an effort to enhance both flood control and agricultural production (Steinman, Luttenton, and Havens, 2004).

Comprehensive Everglades Restoration Plan

Another water resource initiative in Florida is the Comprehensive Everglades Restoration Plan (CERP). The CERP is a large-scale, comprehensive restoration program for the South Florida hydroscape, and its major goal is to improve the timing and distribution of water throughout the region. One reason for the estimated $8 billion project is the need to store some of the more than 1.7 billion gallons of water that is being discharged into the oceans each day. CERP focuses on the use of aquifer storage and recovery, which involves injecting up to 1.6 billion gallons per day of treated surface water into the Upper Floridian

aquifer and storing the water for later use. The project calls for up to 333 wells, approximately 200 of which will be located around Lake Okeechobee. The wells will range in depth from 600 to 1,000 feet (Steinman et al., 2004).

The CERP and the Lake Okeechobee Protection Plan are designed to reduce phosphorus inflows to Lake Okeechobee by about 400 tons per year. This plan is expected to cost nearly $1 billion a year (ENS, www.ens-newswire.com/ens/nov2007/2007-11-26-093.asp).

In the West

Watersheds throughout the West continue to be challenged by chronic water supply shortages, dramatic population growth, climate variability, and heightened competition for finite water supplies by cities, farms, and the environment (www.usbr.gov/wfa/).

The water transfer projects of the 20th century have had a major impact at a regional level by expanding agriculture use, growing industry, and allowing municipalities to grow. Half of the nation's produce is grown in California, a result of water transfer projects. Laws and policies allowed water in the West to be distributed for beneficial use, encouraged interstate compromise when it came to competition for resources and development, and allowed the interbasin transfer of water (Ellison, 2008).

In the next few years, there will have to be some major decisions on how existing large water projects are managed. These projects typically are not operating as they were intended, largely because much of the water is being used to meet the needs of urban areas instead of agricultural uses as was originally planned.

In the late 1970s and early 1980s, then-Governor Jerry Brown and Los Angeles Mayor Tom Bradley developed a proposal to construct a canal to transport Sacramento River water around the Sacramento–San Joaquin Delta to the head of the California Aqueduct. The proposal received a lot of opposition from both environmentalists and agribusinesses in the San Joaquin Valley. After a heated battle, the bill was finally moved through the legislature, but the opposition coalition immediately challenged it via referendum and in 1982 persuaded voters to reject the canal (Walters, 2008).

Thirty years later, Governor Arnold Schwarzenegger revisited the idea of the canal because of increased battles over water. The courts have ordered reductions in pumping water out of the delta in order to protect endangered fish species, and this has caused severe problems for other uses that depend on the water. In the very near future, something will have to be done to address the battles over water in the delta (Walters, 2008).

In California's Sacramento–San Joaquin Bay Delta, a 2007 federal district court imposed limits on the amount of water that can be pumped by the projects in order to protect endangered fish (Woodhouse, 2008).

The Bureau of Reclamation has initiated an 8,000-acre-foot storage reservoir near Drop 2 on the All-American Canal in southern California. The reservoir is intended to store water from the Colorado River for use downstream. Currently the water flows into Mexico. The reservoir is being funded entirely by the Southern Nevada Water Authority, Metropolitan Water District of Southern California, and the Central Arizona Water Conservation District and is being constructed by the Bureau of Reclamation (www.usbr.gov/lc/region/programs/drop2reservoir.html).

States are responding to increased demands for water by taking a more comprehensive approach to water management. Although some court decisions have resolved issues between states, no interstate compacts have been created in the eastern United States since the 1960s, prior to the passage of much of the federal and state environmental legislation (Kundell, 2008).

The West has become drier in recent years, and many believe this is in part a result of climate change. Farmers in California and other states are irrigating fewer acres or abandoning fields altogether because of the lack of available water (Ellison, 2008).

More than 80% of the people living in the Colorado River Basin are in urban areas. When the Colorado River Compact and other water management policies were put in place, the idea was to ensure that decisions about water resources were made by experts, not politicians. But as demands for water increase, the process has become increasingly political. The Colorado River Compact allows water that is allocated but unused in one state to be used by another.

In the late 1990s, the Southern Nevada Water Authority (SNWA) worked with the U.S. Bureau of Reclamation and the Colorado River Basin states to develop agreements that would ensure the Las Vegas Valley had sufficient water. Facilities to transport the water include 327 miles of underground pipeline, pumping stations, regulating tanks, power facilities, and a water treatment facility, located largely on federal land. The SNWA agreement is important because Las Vegas, Reno, Carson City, Wendover, Tonopah, and other municipalities all draw water from outside their own valleys. The cost of the project is projected to be $3.5 billion in 2007 dollars (Johnson, 2008).

In Georgia

The characteristics of water resources and water users vary significantly in different regions across Georgia. Georgia has several regional programs that focus on water resources. The state is one of the fastest growing in the nation, and population growth and economic development are dependent on the availability of water resources. The state has 14 major river systems and multiple groundwater aquifer systems.

Each of Georgia's regional water planning councils identified in the Comprehensive Statewide Water Management Plan consists of 25 members and three alternates. Each council will be represented to include agriculture, forestry, industry, commerce, local governments, water utilities, regional development centers, tourism, recreation, and the environment.

The Metropolitan North Georgia Water Planning District was created by the Georgia General Assembly in 2001 to establish policy, create plans, and promote intergovernmental coordination of all water issues in the district from a regional perspective.

The Environmental Protection Division (EPD) is a section of the Georgia Department of Natural Resources (DNR). Regional water development and conservation plans will be prepared by a water planning council or by EPD. Long-term regional water development and conservation plans are developed for each of the state's major surface water and groundwater resources. Water planning councils throughout the state are responsible for overseeing the preparation of a recommended plan based on EPD guidelines.

EPD has developed water quantity and water quality assessments for each major water resource in the planning region. According to data collected by EPD in the 55 north Georgia counties where a level 4 drought response was in effect, water use in June 2008 decreased by 20% compared to water use in June 2007. That is a savings of nearly 180 million gallons of water per day (Georgia DNR, 2008).

The Atlanta Regional Commission (ARC) is the regional planning and intergovernmental coordination agency for the 10-county area including Cherokee, Clayton, Cobb, DeKalb, Douglas, Fayette, Fulton, Gwinnett, Henry, and Rockdale counties, as well as the city of Atlanta. ARC is a comprehensive land use planning agency that advises communities on decisions and actions that have impacts beyond any one jurisdiction. ARC's Land Use Division develops regional plans and policies that address key land use issues and needs of the Atlanta region. ARC's Regional Development Plan serves as the comprehensive plan for the Atlanta region. In addition, each local government in the region prepares a local comprehensive plan for its respective county or city.

The Northwest Georgia Regional Water Resources Partnership consists of a collaboration of water withdrawal permit holders, local governments, and other advocacy entities across a 15-county region in northwest Georgia. Centralized water service there is provided by about 41 entities, with water being supplied from 35 surface water sources and 21 wells. Some water is also purchased from outside the region. About 200 million gallons per day are permitted to be drawn from the existing water sources.

3.3.3 Power Companies

Duke Energy

Duke Energy is one of the largest electric power companies in the United States, supplying energy to approximately 4 million customers. The company provides electricity in the Midwest and the Carolinas and natural gas distribution services in Ohio and Kentucky. Duke Energy creates lakes primarily as a source of electric power production. Before making changes to waterfront property on a Duke Energy lake, landowners are required to contact the company's Lake Management Office, which is responsible for the permitting process that is used to approve such changes.

Southern Company

Based in Atlanta, Southern Company is one of the largest generators of electricity in the nation, serving both regulated and competitive markets across the southeastern United States. The company serves about 75 investor-owned utilities, electric cooperatives, and municipalities in Alabama, Florida, Georgia, Mississippi, North Carolina, and South Carolina. Southern Company's four electric utilities are Alabama Power, Georgia Power, Gulf Power, and Mississippi Power. Collectively they serve more than 4.3 million retail customers. Southern Power, a subsidiary of Southern Company, is the largest wholesale energy provider in the Southeast. The company currently owns and operates more than 6,700 megawatts of generation assets in Alabama, Georgia, Florida, and North Carolina.

Tennessee Valley Authority

The Tennessee Valley Authority (TVA, www.tva.com) is the nation's largest public power provider, generating electricity that serves about 8.6 million people across seven states through local distributors. TVA covers almost all of Tennessee and parts of Alabama, Georgia, Kentucky, Mississippi, North Carolina, and Virginia. (See Figure 3.7.)

In 1933, as part of his New Deal, President Franklin D. Roosevelt asked Congress to create TVA as "a corporation clothed with the power of government but possessed of the flexibility and initiative of a private enterprise." TVA's first hydroelectric project was Norris Dam, located on the Clinch River in eastern Tennessee. The dam was completed in 1936. In the following years, TVA built dams to harness the power of the region's rivers and provided electricity for the region. In the 1950s, TVA became the nation's largest electricity supplier, but demand continued to increase. Congress passed legislation in 1959 to make the TVA power system self-financing, and this enabled it to issue bonds and greatly expand capacity. In the 1960s, TVA began building nuclear plants as a new source of economical power. But in the early 1980s, with energy demand

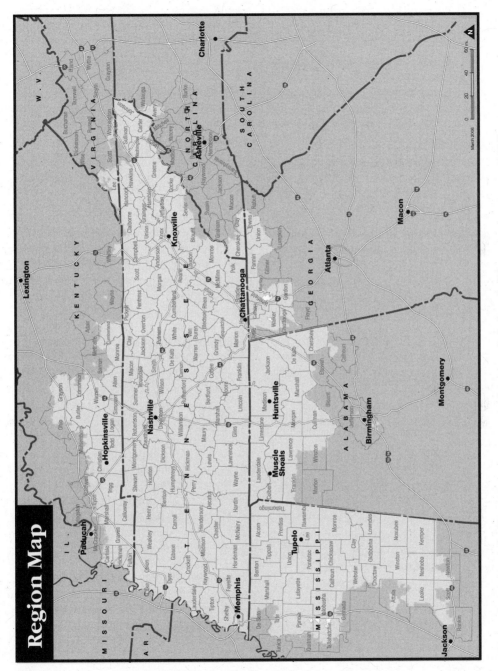

Region Map

Figure 3.7 *The Tennessee Valley Authority covers parts of six states, including all of Tennessee. Image courtesy TVA.*

dropping and construction costs rising, TVA canceled several nuclear plants and focused more on improving efficiency and productivity while cutting costs.

TVA is currently responsible for the management of more than 293,000 acres of public land and 11,000 miles of public shoreline in the Tennessee Valley. Originally it acquired approximately 1.3 million acres of land in the Tennessee Valley. The construction and operation of the reservoir system inundates approximately 470,000 acres with water. TVA operates its 34 flood control dams and generates electricity at 29 hydroelectric dams, 11 coal-fired plants, 6 combustion turbine sites, 3 nuclear plants, a pumped-storage hydropower plant, and 18 green power sites that employ wind turbines, methane gas, and solar panels.

Georgia Power

Georgia Power (www.georgiapower.com) is the largest nongovernment provider of recreation facilities in Georgia, serving 2.25 million customers in 155 of Georgia's 159 counties. The company is responsible for 14 reservoirs throughout the state, including some 60,000 acres of lakes, 1,350 miles of shoreline, and dozens of parks developed for family enjoyment. Georgia Power also leases about 30,000 acres of prime hunting land to the state of Georgia for use as wildlife management areas.

FirstEnergy Corporation

FirstEnergy (www.firstenergycorp.com) serves more than 4.4 million customers over a 36,100-square-mile area of Ohio, Pennsylvania, and New Jersey. It is the fifth-largest investor-owned electric system in the nation. In 2004, FirstEnergy organized three trade missions that took utility customers to Mexico City, Monterrey, and Toronto. The company has facilitated 304 separate corporate projects during 2004.

Xcel Energy

Xcel Energy (www.xcelenergy.com) is a major U.S. electric and natural gas utility, providing energy to more than

3.3 million electric customers and 1.8 million natural gas customers in eight states (Colorado, Michigan, Minnesota, New Mexico, North Dakota, South Dakota, Texas, and Wisconsin). It also operates 27 hydroelectric power plants in Wisconsin, Minnesota, and Colorado.

3.4 PLANNING AT THE DISTRICT LEVEL

Water districts are local governmental agencies that are responsible for building dams and canals to supply water to agriculture and to supply hydropower to local municipalities. The goal of water districts is to supply water for the public good. It is against federal and state law for a water district to profit from the sale of water and electricity (http://are.berkeley.edu/~zilber/EEP101/spring02/detailed_text/16.pdf).

Water districts appear to be about the right size to manage many of the day-to-day decisions regarding water resources. Virtually every state in this country utilizes some type of water district structure. Many districts use some type of local ordinances or regulations to address sediment control, river corridors and wetland buffers, protection measures, and other provisions to help manage water resources. In many counties, the Planning and Zoning Office and the Soil and Water Conservation District are the major local government players. For example, Albemarle County (VA) has established a comprehensive plan that sets a goal of "minimizing the negative impacts of increased stormwater discharges from new land development (www.albemarle.org/upload/images/forms_center/departments/county_attorney/forms/Albemarle).

Recommendations in Albemarle County focus primarily on limiting runoff from new land development, but retrofitting existing developments is considered to be a part of stormwater management (SELC, 2008).

Conservation districts are local units of government responsible for soil and water conservation work within their boundaries. A district's role is to increase voluntary conservation practices among farmers, ranchers, and other

Figure 3.8 *The South Florida Water Management District has developed a master plan to guide future decisions within the district. Image courtesy EPA.*

land users. Depending on the location of the districts, their programs and available information vary.

Many water districts issue some type of permits to allocate water that can be used to meet water demands of residents and businesses. Permits set limits on how much water can be withdrawn at each location in an effort to help protect water resources. Most also use minimum flows and levels (MFLs) that have been determined to be necessary to prevent harm to the water resources or environmental resources. In setting MFLs, water management districts collect water data and evaluate the results to consider the possible impacts of water withdrawal on a water body.

Water management districts are required to update their water plans on a regular basis and define areas that are likely to experience significant water supply problems. Some are using special area management plans (SAMPs), which is a type of watershed planning approach promoted by the U.S. Army Corps of Engineers. SAMPs are designed to be conducted in geographic areas of special sensitivity under intense development pressure. These efforts involve the participation of multiple local, state, and federal agencies and work with EPA. (See Figure 3.8.)

Steps In Developing a Water Management Plan for a Water District

- Establish a basin forum.
- Collect and review information.
- Gather public input on water issues.
- Analyze basin hydrology to determine historical and future water supply.
- Conduct water demand analyses and forecasts.
- Develop a vision and goals.
- Gather public input on vision and goals (Newsletter and Response Form #2).
- Develop actions for water management.
- Develop alternatives for augmenting supply.
- Conduct technical studies (on water conservation and alternative opportunities for water storage, and maintaining river flows).

(continues)

(continued)

- Identify trade-offs among supply alternatives.
- Develop a "preferred supply alternative."
- Gather public input on preferred supply alternative and actions for water management.
- Prepare a draft water management plan (WMP).
- Seek approval and adoption of the draft WMP by the planning partners.

Source: EPA, Developing a Water Management Plan.

3.4.1 St. Johns River Water Management District

The St. Johns River Water Management District is one of five regional agencies in Florida that have authority to tax,

issue water permits, and regulate wetlands. The district includes the northeast part of the state. Its water supply planning program addresses future water demands, traditional and alternative water sources, and water supply infrastructure improvements required to meet future water supply needs without causing harm to water resources or water dependent natural systems. (See Figure 3.9.)

Legislation passed in 1997 requires the Florida's water management districts to complete specific water supply planning activities and initiate water resource development projects. The districts' first Water Supply Assessment (WSA) was completed in 1998. The *WSA 1998* was used to develop the *District Water Supply Plan, 2000* (*DWSP 2000*) (www.sjrwmd.com/dwsp.html). Work is currently in progress on *DWSP 2010,* which will address a planning horizon through 2030. The plans identify water resource development projects, alternative water supply development projects, and strategies that can be implemented to meet the anticipated water supply needs through 2025 without

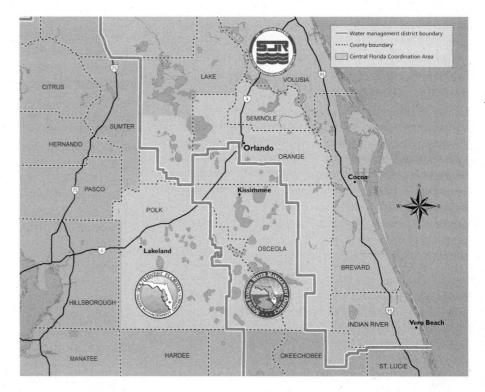

Figure 3.9 *The St. Johns River Water Management District is one of five regional agencies in Florida. It includes the area around Orlando. Image courtesy St. Johns River Water Management District.*

resulting in unacceptable impacts to water resources (http://sjr.state.fl.us/waterprotectsustain/index.html).

Cost-share funding is available for alternative water supply projects identified in the St. Johns River Water Management District. Emphasis in the district is on multijurisdictional, regional projects (*DWSP 2005*). The district will match state funds for construction costs: 20% for reclaimed water projects, 30% for surface water augmentation, and 40% for new source public supply. The district approved 55 projects for fiscal years 2006, 2007 and 2008.

The district issues water use permits for agricultural purposes, and these often require the use of reclaimed water or recycled water on-site to minimize withdrawals from groundwater or surface water supplies. In addition, agricultural water users must demonstrate water conservation techniques by upgrading to more efficient irrigation systems and implementing improvements that result in water savings.

In 2005, total freshwater use in the district averaged approximately 1.19 billion gallons per day. Approximately 200 million gallons per day of alternative water supplies are expected to be needed by 2025 to meet the growing demand for water. In some areas, additional supplies will be needed as early as 2013. Strategies to meet water supply needs include increased water conservation, improved efficiency, increased water reclamation and reuse, and development of alternative water sources.

In the most recent *District Water Supply Plan* (2005), the district identifies options for alternative sources of water supplies. Eighty-four project options are identified, including reclaimed water (highly treated wastewater), brackish (slightly salty) groundwater, brackish and fresh surface water, and seawater.

The city of Cocoa, Florida, utilizes surface water from Taylor Creek Reservoir, a tributary of the St. Johns River, most of the time, but the city treats and stores additional amounts underground for use when surface water is not available. There are other efforts in central Florida to provide an adequate amount of drinking water. Recently, Central Florida utilities proposed to divert more than 200 million gallons per day from the St. Johns and Ocklawaha rivers at an estimated cost of $800 million to $1.2 billion.

3.4.2 Metropolitan North Georgia Water Planning District

The Metropolitan North Georgia Water Planning District was created by an act of the Georgia General Assembly in 2001. Funding for the district is generated from state appropriations and per-capita local government dues. The Atlanta Regional Commission Environmental Planning Division provides staffing for the district, and it is governed by an elected/appointed governing board.

The Metro Water District includes 16 counties and over 90 cities within the metro Atlanta region. The legislation creating the district mandates the preparation of three long-term plans:

1. District-Wide Watershed Management Plan (WMP)
2. Long-Term Wastewater Management Plan
3. Water Supply and Water Conservation Plan

The District-Wide WMP provides strategies and recommendations for effective watershed management and the control of stormwater runoff. Its overall goal is to meet and maintain water quality standards and designated uses of streams and other water bodies within the district (District-Wide Watershed Management Plan, 2003) (www.northgeorgiawater.com).

This plan builds on the existing watershed and stormwater management planning efforts that have taken place in the district. The WMP includes recommendations for six distinct watershed management strategies (District-Wide Watershed Management Plan, 2003):

1. **Local stormwater management program activities.** These are the day-to-day program activities that local governments implement to address watershed protection and stormwater management. They include maintaining water quality as new development occurs, encouraging stormwater pollution prevention, and improving enforcement of existing ordinances and laws.

2. **Total maximum daily load (TMDL) strategies.** These management measures address specific

pollution problems in waterways that appear on the Georgia Environmental Protection Division TMDL list.

3. **Source water protection strategies.** These management measures focus on protecting drinking water supply watersheds.

4. **Watershed improvement strategies.** These strategies address watersheds that already have been impacted substantially by development, identifying needed retrofits and restoration.

5. **Land use strategies.** These strategies include land use and zoning measures that local governments can use to meet watershed management and protection goals. Specific strategies include initiatives such as greenspace preservation, alternative development patterns, and other innovative land use practices.

Basic Concepts for Water Districts

Each water district should incorporate a few basic concepts that focus on preserving and restoring the hydrologic cycle. These include:

- **Every site is in a watershed.** Rain falls on every site, and understanding that each site has a position in the larger context is essential to stormwater management.

- **Start at the source.** Water quality is most easily and economically achieved if stormwater management starts at the point where water hits the earth.

- **Think small.** Small-scale techniques, applied consistently over an entire watershed, can have a big impact in improving stormwater quality and reducing overall runoff volume.

- **Keep it simple.** An array of simple techniques throughout a site can improve stormwater management in an economically viable way.

- **Integrate the solutions.** Integrate solutions into an overall site plan and ensure stormwater facilities provide recreational, aesthetic, habitat, and water quality benefits.

Source: BASMAA. Start at the Source. 1999.

---

6. **Basin-specific strategies.** Specific management issues are delineated for each major river basin in the district.

The WMP identifies model ordinances that can be used in the 16 counties as a key component of the local stormwater management program activities for watershed management.

3.5 WATERSHED PLANNING

A watershed plan is a strategy that provides assessment and management information for a watershed, including the analyses, actions, participants, and resources related to developing and implementing the plan (EPA, 2008). The basic goals of a watershed planning approach are to protect, maintain, and restore water resources. At an international level, there is an increased effort to implement comprehensive watershed planning.

Why Watershed Plans Fail

The Center for Watershed Protection conducted a broad assessment of the value of planning documents in protecting water resources and identified a number of reasons why some plans had failed:

- Planning activities were conducted at too great a scale.

- The plan was a one-time study rather than a long-term management process.

- Stakeholder involvement and local ownership were lacking.

- The plan skirted land use/management issues in the watershed.

- The document was too long or complex.

- The recommendations were too general.

- The plan failed to identify and address conflicts.

Source: EPA, *Handbook for Developing Watershed Plans to Restore and Protect Our Waters March 2008,* (www.epa.gov .nps/watershed_handbook).

Comprehensive water management planning usually is conducted by entities that range from water districts and large multicounty urban areas to state water resources agencies and regional river basin compacts and commissions.

Many watershed management districts have begun to implement a more holistic approach to managing aquatic resources by focusing on watersheds. This approach recognizes that rivers, lakes, wetlands, and coasts are complex systems that interact with one another in numerous ways (www.CorpsResults.us). EPA recommends the use of a watershed approach as the key framework for dealing with problems caused by runoff and other sources that impair surface waters (EPA, *Handbook for Developing Watershed Plans to Restore and Protect Our Waters*, March 2008). A watershed protection approach is a comprehensive planning process that considers all natural resources in the watershed as well as social, cultural, and economic factors. Incentives, rather than regulations, and models that can be adapted to local conditions, rather than one-size-fits-all prescriptions, are used in watershed planning.

3.5.1 Conservation Approach

Conservation is an important part of any watershed planning effort. Water conservation is one of the highest priorities in helping to ensure we are able to balance human needs with environmental requirements. It is the foundation of all sustainable water supply options for the future. The basic idea is to have a water conservation approach that is aggressive while also being reasonable. Although water conservation efforts are important, conservation and reuse alone will not yield enough water to meet future demands in many areas. For example, in northeast Florida, water supply utilities in the 18-county service area of the St. Johns Water Management District are moving forward with decisions to develop supplemental alternative water sources because many utilities are unlikely to receive permits to take additional water supplies from groundwater (http://sjr.state.fl.us/waterprotectsustain/index.html).

Comprehensive water conservation planning has the potential to improve water quality and instream flow levels, decrease the need for new capital investments, reduce vulnerability to drought, and protect valuable cultural and natural resources. Water conservation will continue to play

a vitally important role in sustaining the water supply in the Southeast, as it is one of the most efficient and least expensive ways to protect water resources. Conservation measures do have an impact. In Sarasota County, Florida, for example, the per-capita water use has been reduced from 158 gallons to about 96 gallons per day simply by the community conservation efforts (Angelo, Hamann, and Klein, 2008).

Integrating watershed planning with economic development master planning builds efficiencies and effectiveness in both processes and ensures compatibility among activities that might have competing objectives. The watershed planning process is intended to be iterative, holistic, geographically defined, integrated, and collaborative (EPA, 2008). (See Figure 3.10.)

Watershed protection management practices fall under four categories (EPA, 2008):

1. Focus on drainage protection. Includes descriptions and applications of zoning techniques that can be used to limit development density or redirect density to less environmentally sensitive areas.

2. Establishment and protection of stream buffers. Describes important steps for protecting or establishing riparian buffer zones to enhance water quality and pollutant removal.

3. Emphasis on NPS contributions. Involves identifying potential upstream sources of nonpoint source pollution as well as providing solutions to minimize those impacts.

4. Identify and preserve critical areas. Entails identifying properties that if preserved or enhanced could maintain or improve water quality and reduce the impacts of urban runoff as well as preserving environmentally significant areas (includes land acquisition, easements, and development restrictions of various types).

A watershed-based planning approach can help communities make better decisions on watershed restoration priorities and make the most out of limited funding and staffing resources. Many communities are proving they can extend their existing water supplies simply by encouraging water efficiency. Cary (NC) reduced its water consumption by

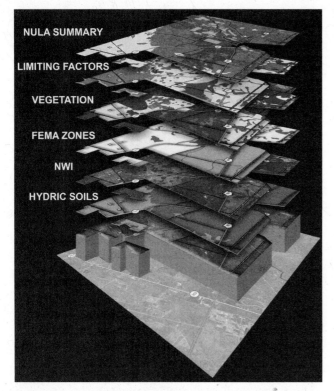

NULA SUMMARY

LIMITING FACTORS

VEGETATION

FEMA ZONES

NWI

HYDRIC SOILS

Figure 3.10 *A watershed planning process requires the combination of different types of geospatial data that help define the characteristics of the watershed. Image courtesy EDAW.*

square miles or less. Watersheds larger than that are simply too complicated and involve too many diverse stakeholders to be able to develop a planning process that will meet sustainability objectives.

The future effects of climate change on water resources in the United States will depend in large part on the policies established and the watershed planning approaches implemented to help protect these resources. Water conservation is one of the highest priorities in helping to ensure we are able to balance human needs with environmental requirements, but conservation alone will not solve the water supply challenges. Large reclamation projects enhanced settlement of western states, but these were developed prior to the implementation of environmental regulations. It is much more difficult to develop these types of large reclamation projects now than in the past. Desalination is not a viable option in most places because it costs 10 times more than traditional surface water treatment. Regardless of what approach is taken to ensure there is adequate water for future generations, landscape architects will play a major part in the process. The better we understand the problems and the opportunities, the better the decisions we will make about water resources.

15% in 11 years, and Tampa Bay (FL), with a population of over 2.5 million, reduced its consumption by 26% over 12 years (Wodder, 2008).

One major benefit of a watershed planning approach is that it creates a unified framework to address many different programs, regulatory mandates, and permit requirements that confront municipalities. These regulatory drivers are often complex, costly, and confusing to implement (Rowe and Schueler, 2006).

The best method for integrating watershed planning programs is the small watershed plan, which analyzes the unique characteristics of each subwatershed, evaluates restoration potential, and ranks priority restoration practices for long-term implementation. As a general rule, watershed planning is most effective at a scale of 100

Watershed Management Planning Process

- Develop district policy goals.
- Characterize existing watershed conditions and identify key issues.
- Develop water quality model to estimate existing and future pollutant loads.
- Evaluate strategies: best management practices, regulatory strategies.
- Develop watershed management alternatives.
- Prepare draft watershed management plans.
- Prepare a final water management plan.

3.5.2 Watershed Assessment

Watershed assessment is a critical component of a watershed-based approach. Watershed planning should include a baseline assessment of existing water resources. This enables users to have a better understanding of the changes that occur within a particular watershed. The better these changes are understood, the better we understand which decisions are effective and which ones are not.

A watershed assessment program characterizes watershed conditions and establishes a set of watershed indicators. Watershed assessment and monitoring are tools used to characterize water quality and to identify trends in water quality over time (EPA, *Handbook for Developing Watershed Plans to Restore and Protect Our Waters*, March 2008). Watershed assessment is needed to develop both protection and restoration strategies, identify priorities, and adjust management prescriptions based on trend analyses.

Santa Fe County, City of Santa Fe Reach Water Agreement

U.S. Water News Online reported in October 2009 that a "historic" agreement had been reached on a water-sharing project between Santa Fe County and the city of Santa Fe, New Mexico, where each would share 50% in the ownership of a Rio Grande water diversion project. Initial costs are $60 million for design and construction, and the total cost of the project will be twice that. The project involves diverting water directly from the Rio Grande. For the city of Santa Fe, this project was important because of recent droughts and water shortages, and it allows the county to more than triple the amount of water it can access. The county will be allowed to take 1,700 acre-feet per year in addition to the 500 acre-feet per year it buys from the city.

Source: www.uswaternews.com.

Regardless of whether it is for a national, state, or local level, developing a better understanding of precipitation and drought will enable landscape architects and planners to make better decisions about how to protect water resources. This knowledge will also help government agencies, private institutions, and stakeholders make more informed decisions about risk-based policies and actions to mitigate the dangers posed by floods and droughts.

3.5.3 Tools for Water Resource Analysis

It is difficult to predict future changes in regional precipitation patterns and identify areas where drought is a priority, but digital tools realistically generate forecasts across the United States with seasons and geographic areas. Advanced Hydrologic Prediction Service (AHPS) is a Web-based suite of forecast tools that are part of the National Weather Service's Climate, Water, and Weather Services. AHPS products are developed using sophisticated computer models and large amounts of data from multiple sources, including automated gauges, geostationary satellites, Doppler radars, weather observation stations, and the Advanced Weather Interactive Processing System. AHPS tools can be used to model floods or droughts and make predictions from hours to months in advance. The tools allow users to view a national composite map or to zoom into regions, states, and county-level areas over multiple time periods, including for the previous day and precipitation totals over the last 7, 14, 30, or 60 days. Archived data are available back to 2005 with monthly estimates of departure from normal and percent of normal precipitation.

The AHPS Web site (www.nws.noaa.gov/oh/ahps) includes maps of individual river basins as well as points along the rivers for which information is available. The maps provide information on impacts of high water or flood, impacts of low stage or level, agricultural impacts, short-term and long-term hydrologic forecasts, water supply forecasts, documented drought conditions, and potential drought areas.

Data from AHPS can also be downloaded in a shapefile format for use with Geographic Information Systems programs or in a KMZ format for use with Google Earth, a popular geospatial browser. Data are updated every 15 minutes.

3.5.4 Watershed Boundaries

Defining the geographic boundaries of a watershed planning effort is one of the first steps in developing a watershed management plan. Watersheds have traditionally been defined based on United States Geological Survey Hydrologic Units. A hydrologic unit is part of a watershed mapping classification system showing various areas of land that can contribute surface water runoff to designated outlet points, such as lakes or stream segments. The USGS system breaks down watershed into six different levels: regions, subregions, basins, subbasins, watersheds, and subwatersheds. Each hydrologic unit is identified by a unique hydrologic unit code consisting of 2 to 12 digits. (See Figure 3.11.)

USGS estimates that there are 2,150 subbasins in the United States, with most of these being more than 700 square miles in size. USGS also estimates there are 22,000 watersheds and 160,000 subwatersheds in the country. GIS coverage of the different watershed levels is available

Figure 3.11 *The United States is categorized as a series of Hydrologic Units that are defined by the USGS. Image courtesy USGS.*

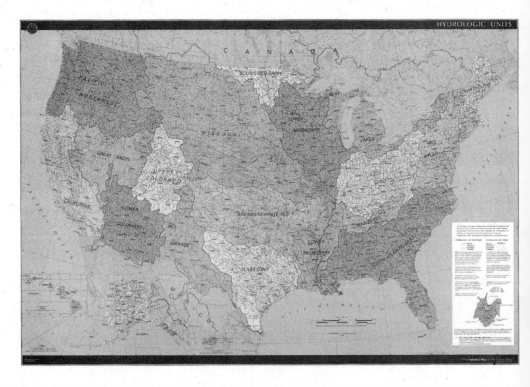

Eight Tools Audit

The Eight Tools Audit is designed to identify regulatory and programmatic tools and gaps in watershed protection arsenals. The self-assessment is organized by the eight categories of protection tools available in most communities.

1. **Land use planning.** Identify which regulatory measures and/or planning techniques are in use in your community to manage growth, redirect development where appropriate, and protect sensitive areas (i.e., zoning, overlay districts, growth boundaries).

2. **Land conservation.** Outline programs or efforts to conserve undeveloped, sensitive areas or areas of particular historical or cultural value (i.e., purchase of development rights, land trusts, agricultural preservation, tax incentives).

3. **Aquatic buffers.** Evaluate criteria for the protection, restoration, creation, or reforestation of stream, wetland, and urban lake buffers (i.e., width, vegetative standards, and incentives).

4. **Better site design.** Assess flexibility of local codes and ordinances to reduce impervious cover, integrate stormwater management, and conserve natural areas in the design of new and redevelopment projects.

5. **Erosion and sediment control.** Examine criteria for the use of erosion prevention, sediment control, and dewatering practices at all new development and redevelopment sites. (See Figure 3.12.)

6. **Stormwater management.** Assess criteria for design of structural practices in new development, redevelopment, or the existing landscape to help mitigate the impacts of stormwater runoff on receiving waters.

7. **Non-stormwater discharges.** Evaluate operations and maintenance programs for locating, quantifying, and controlling non-stormwater pollutant sources in the watershed.

8. **Watershed stewardship program.** Identify extent of existing stormwater and watershed education or outreach programs; restoration efforts, and monitoring activities.

Source: Karen Cappiella, Anne Kitchell, and Tom Schueler, Center for Watershed Protection, "Using Local Watershed Plans to Protect Wetlands," *Wetlands & Watersheds,* Office of Wetlands, Oceans and Watersheds, U.S. Environmental Protection Agency, Washington, DC (June 2006).

Figure 3.12 *In Shelby County, Iowa, this agricultural field is terraced to prevent stormwater runoff, sedimentation, and erosion. Image courtesy NRCS.*

by EPA region in EPA's BASINS modeling system (www.epa.gov/ost/basins).

One goal of the USGS is to develop a comprehensive watershed boundary data set for the United States. A goal of this initiative is to provide a hydrologically correct, seamless, and consistent national GIS database of watersheds at a scale of 1:24,000.

In addition to the USGS and NRCS classification, many states have created their own watershed or planning unit delineations that break the USGS cataloging units into smaller watersheds.

Watershed Planning Process

EPA organizes the watershed planning process into six major steps:

1. Build partnerships.
2. Characterize the watershed to identify problems.
3. Set goals and identify solutions.
4. Design an implementation program.
5. Implement the watershed plan.
6. Measure progress and make adjustments.

Source: EPA, *Handbook for Developing Watershed Plans to Restore and Protect Our Waters*, EPA 841-B-08-002 (March 2008).

3.6 WATER MARKETS AND WATER SUPPLY SYSTEMS

Water quality trading is a market-based approach that can achieve water quality standards more efficiently and at lower cost than traditional approaches. It is based on the fact that the cost to control sources of pollutants varies within a watershed. In certain conditions, water quality trading can be an effective tool for meeting pollutant reduction goals. The programs are tailored to meet the needs of a specific watershed.

Trading programs allow facilities with higher pollution control costs to meet their regulatory obligations by purchasing pollution reductions from another source at lower cost within the same watershed. The idea is similar to a transfer of development rights or purchasing carbon credits. With water quality trading, the concept is to achieve the same water quality improvement but at a much lower and more affordable overall cost.

Models for Watershed Assessments

EPA supports a number of models that can be used for watershed assessments. These include:

- **BASINS.** A multipurpose environmental analysis system that integrates GIS, national watershed data, and environmental assessment and modeling tools.

- **AQUATOX: A Simulation Model for Freshwater Ecosystems.** It predicts the effects of pollutants on the ecosystem.

- **DFLOW: A Tool for Low Flow Analysis.** This tool calculates design flow statistics.

- **QUAL2K Model.** This tool is a river and stream water quality model.

Source: www.epa.gov/waterscience/wqm.

EPA's Trading Policy states that all water quality trading should occur either within a watershed or within a defined area for which a total maximum daily load has been approved. Water quality trading is intended to provide opportunities for efficiently achieving water quality standards within a specific watershed.

The goal of a water supply planning program is to identify sustainable water supply options that are consistent with the protection of minimum flows and levels. When issuing a consumptive use permit, water districts limit the withdrawal of water in order to meet of minimum flows and levels requirements. Permits for consumptive use are issued for a specific duration. When they expire, the permit has to be renewed.

The EPA has promoted the concept of water quality trading to achieve water quality standards for the past decade. EPA issued its Trading Policy to encourage state regulatory agencies to include trading as an option for a point source to meet water quality standards.

Despite the promise of water quality trading and EPA's efforts, water quality trading has met with only limited success. As of a couple of years ago, more than 80% of all water quality trades occurred in the Long Island Sound (NY). Most of the trading programs have been implemented at a relatively small scale and have not had a significant impact on improving water quality or reducing the costs of controlling pollution.

Even with the limited success of water quality trading programs to date, many believe that the programs will gain in popularity in upcoming years. EPA is continuing to promote the programs, and USDA's NRCS works directly to support water quality trading among nonpoint sources through tool development and outreach efforts. The North Carolina Department of Environment and Natural Resources (DENR) works with any watershed group interested in water quality trading under a permit for an overlay district. Other states are following DENR's lead.

EPA Reporting Categories

EPA recommends that states use five reporting categories to report on the water quality status of all waters in their states. They are:

Category 1. All designated uses are supported, no use is threatened.

Category 2. Available data and/or information indicate that some but not all of the designated uses are supported.

Category 3. There are insufficient available data and/or information to make a designated use support determination.

Category 4. Available data and/or information indicate that at least one designated use is not being supported or is threatened but a TMDL is not needed.

Category 5. Available data and/or information indicate that at least one designated use is not being supported or is threatened, and a TMDL is needed.

One major issue with water quality trading is determining which pollutants may be traded. Some pollutants are considered to be too toxic to be included in the program. EPA's Trading Policy does not support trading of persistent bioaccumulative toxics (PBTs) because they are considered to be too dangerous. EPA has a list of PBTs that are not appropriate to be traded (www.epa.gov/pbt/index.htm).

Many water quality experts predict that water quality trading systems will soon be a common way to meet water requirements.

3.7 WETLAND PLANNING AND WETLAND BANKING

Over the years, many of the wetlands in the United States have been destroyed. In recent years, though, people have discovered the value of wetlands and are doing a better job of taking care of them. Wetland loss has slowed considerably in the last two decades due to federal and state wetland permitting and increased wetland restoration. At the federal level, Executive Orders 11988, *Floodplain Management*, and 11990, *Protection of Wetlands,* identify the actions federal agencies must take to:

- Identify and protect wetlands and floodplains.

- Minimize the risk of flood loss and destruction of wetlands.

- Preserve and enhance the natural and beneficial values of both floodplains and wetlands.

Over the past 30 years, the primary authority protecting U.S. water bodies has been the federal Clean Water Act. The CWA gives states the authority to establish their own regulatory programs for wetlands. States can also adopt more stringent criteria than those established under the federal program, and a number have done so.

Many states, tribes, and local governments rely solely on Section 401 of the CWA to protect their local wetland resources. As of 2007, 21 states depended entirely upon the CWA and had no other regulations in place. One major concern is that in 2001, the U.S. Supreme Court ruled that

Figure 3.13 *Boardwalks can be constructed as a way to provide access to wetlands without having a significant negative environmental impact. Image courtesy NRCS.*

isolated, nonnavigable, and intrastate waters wetlands are not protected under the CWA Section 404 based solely on the Migratory Bird Rule. This ruling, known as the SWANCC ruling, means that more than 20 million acres of wetlands are at risk (Cappiella et al., 2006). A few states, such as Ohio, Wisconsin, Indiana, and North Carolina, have recently adopted new regulations to fill the gaps in federal protection (Cappiella and Fraley-McNeal, 2007). (See Figure 3.13.)

Vulnerable streams and wetlands are those that are no longer protected under the CWA due to their periodic dryness, isolation, or nonnavigability. Vulnerable streams and wetlands include the smallest streams and wetlands. Estimates made by EPA, the Natural Resources Defense Council, and the National Wildlife Federation state that approximately 20% to 30% of the wetland acreage in the contiguous United States could be considered "isolated," and are therefore not protected by the Clean Water Act.

A 2005 study (Comeer et al.) found that the South Atlantic and Gulf coastal plain had the greatest diversity of isolated wetland types. The same study also reported that the highest proportions of isolated wetlands when viewed as

a percent of total wetlands were found in the upper Great Lakes, north-central interior, and Great Plains regions.

There are other limitations to current wetland protection strategies. Most states, tribes, and local governments currently do not have the regulatory tools in place to protect wetlands and headwater streams. In addition, the indirect impact of upland development on wetlands is not currently regulated by state or federal agencies. (See Figure 3.14.)

3.7.1 Wetland Recommendations

State wetland conservation plans are strategies developed by states to achieve no net loss and other wetland management goals by integrating both regulatory and nonregulatory approaches to protecting wetlands. In the past, states frequently tried to manage wetlands on a site-by-site basis. Although this is effective for individual wetlands, it does not help achieve a "no net loss" of wetlands. The reason is

Figure 3.14 *Restoration efforts were taken to repair a vital section of the Lake Tahoe Basin watershed after it was damaged by development. The project was funded by the California Tahoe Conservancy. Image courtesy AECOM.*

that a site-by-site approach does not take into consideration cumulative impacts to wetlands. Wetland information needs to be compiled and managed at the watershed level.

Wetland recommendations focus on three types of measures:

1. **Wetland protection.** Involves the application of land development regulations and other measures to prevent or reduce impacts to wetlands as a result of land development and other activities.

2. **Wetland conservation.** Includes the use of land acquisition, easements, and other conservation tools to permanently protect high-quality wetlands from future development.

3. **Wetland restoration.** Involves changing the hydrology, elevation, soils, or plant community of a currently degraded wetland or a former wetland. (See Figure 3.15.)

Wetlands function as natural filters and help maintain water quality in lakes, rivers, streams, and groundwater. Wetlands can remove, retain, or transform a variety of pollutants. Fringe wetlands protect streams and shorelines from erosive winds, waves, and currents. Lakes with a high percentage of wetlands in their watershed tend to have higher-water quality than watersheds where most of the wetlands have been drained or filled. Restoring drained wetlands may be one way to improve water quality. States such as Florida and Louisiana are restoring coastal wetlands to serve as a buffer between development and hurricane storm surges.

3.7.2 Wetlands Data

There has been a concentrated effort in recent years to collect more information about wetlands. A wetland inventory in a watershed consists of six steps (Cappiella et al., 2006):

1. Update existing wetland maps.
2. Estimate historic wetland coverage.
3. Delineate wetland contributing drainage areas.
4. Estimate wetland functions.
5. Estimate wetland conditions.
6. Estimate effects of future land use changes on wetlands.

(See Figure 3.16.)

Figure 3.15 *This restored wetland in Calhoun County, Iowa, is part of the state's Conservation Reserve Enhancement Program, which is a state, federal, local, and private partnership. The goal of this program is to establish wetlands for water quality improvement and reduce nitrogen loads from croplands to streams and rivers. Image courtesy NRCS.*

Figure 3.16 *We have a much better understanding of existing wetlands because of recent efforts to develop a nationwide wetland inventory. Image courtesy NRCS.*

3.7.3 Wetlands of International Importance

In 1971, the Convention of Wetlands of International Importance, especially as Waterfowl Habitat, was held in Iran. The convention, often called the Ramsar Convention, is an intergovernmental treaty that provides a framework encouraging international cooperation to help conserve wetlands and wetland habitat. More than 122 countries are involved; the United States became a member of the organization in 1986.

As a result of the convention, a list of wetlands of international importance was developed. At last count, there were 1,031 designated sites covering more than 193 million acres. This list has had a significant impact on efforts made to conserve these wetlands.

3.7.4 National Wetlands Inventory

The U.S. Fish and Wildlife Service (USFWS) is the principal federal agency that provides information to the public about wetlands. The agency has developed a series of topical maps to show wetlands and deepwater habitats. Two of the primary goals of the National Wetlands Inventory (NWI) mapping efforts are to increase map accuracy for wetlands, and to reduce map production costs. The NWI has been completed for approximately 42% of the continental U.S. and about 13% of Alaska.

NWI digital data files are records of wetlands location and classification as defined by the USFWS. In the NWI, there are more than 6,000 possible combinations of coding nationwide. These include different categories for marine, estuarine, riverine, lacustrine, and palustrine areas.

NWI data are produced from an analysis of high-altitude imagery, collateral data sources, and fieldwork, and maps are produced at a nominal scale of 1:24,000. Delineated wetland boundaries are manually transferred from interpreted photos to USGS 7.5-minute topographic quadrangle maps and then labeled manually. These quad maps contain ground planimetric coordinates of wetlands point, line, and area features and wetlands attributes.

The Wetlands Geodatabase and the Wetlands Mapper are two sources of information available on the Internet (www.fws.gov/wetlands/data/index.html). A congressional mandate also requires the USFWS to produce wetlands status and trends reports for the nation and to report to the Congress at periodic intervals. The latest report is the Wetlands Master Geodatabase Annual Report 2008.

Most jurisdictions rely on USFWS's NWI for mapping information about their wetlands. The National Wetlands Inventory program was established in the mid-1970s to inventory the nation's wetlands and report on their status. By 2001, most of the wetlands in the United States had been mapped. Numerous local and regional status and trends analyses have also been completed, including those of the Texas Coast, the Mid-Atlantic States, and the Chesapeake Bay Watershed.

The NWI has several limitations, though. It has an inherent margin of error and is best used for community- or regional-scale planning projects. The accuracy of wetland data from aerial and satellite imagery is based on the quality of the imagery, how the imagery is processed, and the amount of cross-referenced data as well as ground truth verification. Most NWI data were developed with aerial images taken between 1971 and 1992, and this imagery was processed to delineate wetlands. In areas with minimal vegetative cover, such as open plains and prairies, the minimum size of wetlands being mapped is around one-quarter acre. In forested areas, the minimum size ranges from one to three acres, depending on wetland type and the quality of the aerial imagery. In areas with evergreen forests, wetlands have to be at least three acres or so in size to be mapped. This means that many wetlands smaller than three acres do not show up on NWI maps.

In 1999, a study by the National Aeronautics and Space Administration Office of Space Access and Technology discovered that NWI maps could have a discrepancy of up to 130 yards as compared to wetland maps delimited in a field survey. For regional mapping projects, this level of accuracy is acceptable, but it does not work for site scale design that many landscape architects are involved with.

Problems include the fact that much of the data used in NWI are over 20 years old and NWI does not include wetlands smaller than one acre in size. Data collection methods used by the USFWS have improved in accuracy over the years, allowing the NWI to capture smaller wetlands or wetland types that would not have been included in previous inventories. USFWS methods do not include ephemeral wetlands (wetlands that are dry for some portion of the year), those smaller than one to three acres, Pacific Coast estuarine wetlands, or wetlands that were previously converted for agricultural use (Dahl, 2000). Another limitation is that USFWS reports do not consider the quality of the wetlands in question.

For future efforts, the USFWS states that it:

> [W]ill intensify program efforts to expand and improve the electronic availability of resource information, and more rapidly distribute wetland and aquatic habitat information. This will be accomplished through developing and enhancing public and private partnerships to promote fish and wildlife habitat protection, restoration, and creation activities.

> The Service will draw on remotely-sensed information, enhanced geographic information system capabilities, and the development of new partnerships to ensure a quick turnaround of information analyses. The products will be of substantial benefit to the Service and our partners as tools for directing resource restoration efforts, assessing and quantifying water resource development effects, and in assisting land use planning activities (http://fgc3 .wr.usgs.gov/ppt/fws_nwi_fgc3.ppt).

In addition to analyzing national wetlands trends, the USFWS will continue to target watersheds in the country where impacts may be substantial. The idea is that more intensive and frequent sampling will provide a greater understanding of the changes and the pressures affecting aquatic habitats.

For most of the projects landscape architects work on, wetlands are delineated on a project-by-project basis. On virtually every site design project, we start by sending out surveys to document property boundaries, topography, existing site features, and other critical characteristics of the site, including wetlands. Wetlands are delineated and mapped, and this information is used to make design and planning decisions about the site.

Planning Ahead

Plans that you might want to integrate into your watershed planning activities.

- Source water assessments
- TMDL implementation plans
- Stormwater management plans
- Resource management plans
- Master plans
- Facility plans
- Wetland assessments
- Wildlife action plans
- Aquatic Green Acres Project analyses

Source: EPA, Handbook for Developing Watershed Plans to Restore and Protect Our Waters. http://epa.gov/nps/watershed_handbook/pdf/handbook.pdf.

It is important to review historic information about wetlands in order to understand where they were once located. In an ideal world, we would focus on restoring many of these wetlands.

3.7.5 National Data

There is no shortage of hydrological data in digital format. One popular source is the USGS Seamless Data Distribution site. Among the hydrography data from this site, you can find: Ground Water Climate Response Network; Alluvial and Glacial Aquifers; Hydrologic Unit Regions; Principal Aquifers; National Hydrography Dataset (NHD) Streams; NHD Streams; and Arsenic in Ground Water.

The mission of the USGS Water Resources is to provide water information that benefits the nation's citizens in the form of publications, data, maps, and applications software. USGS Water Resources offices are located in every state. The NWISWeb Water Data site provides access to water resources data collected at approximately 1.5 million sites throughout the nation. It includes real-time, surface water, groundwater, water quality, and site inventory data.

The USGS provides access to near-real-time data about water resources through its Web site. As part of the

National Streamflow Information Program, the USGS operates and maintains approximately 7,300 stream gauges that provide long-term, accurate, and unbiased information and stream flow. Stream gauges are used to monitor the flux of water and associated components in streams and rivers. The purpose of this program is to help manage water resources. USGS's WaterWatch is on online map that tracks short-term stream flow changes in rivers and streams. The map depicts stream flow conditions as computed at USGS gauging stations.

Data for hydrologic units is available from USGS. Most of this information was originally collected for the Geographic Information Retrieval and Analysis System at a scale of 1:250,000, although many major cities in the West were mapped at a scale of 1:100,000. This data was also compiled to create river basin boundaries that are part of the National Water Quality Assessment (NAWQA) study.

Some of the other water resources maps and GIS data sites that USGS identifies include:

- EarthExplorer
- Geospatial One Stop
- Hydrologic Unit Maps
- National Geospatial Data Clearinghouse
- National Hydrography Dataset
- National Map Seamless Data Distribution System
- NAWQA Digital Maps
- Science in Your Watershed
- USGS GeoData
- Historical Water Conditions (1921–2002)

3.7.6 Wetland Mapper

The U.S. Fish and Wildlife Service developed the Wetlands Mapper in an effort to expand and improve the availability of digital wetlands data. Wetlands Mapper identifies areas in this country that have been mapped as part of the National Wetlands Inventory program. Like many other portal sites, Wetlands Mapper also provides links to other data sites. It includes accessing wetlands habitat data from the National Map, which provides public access to high-quality, geospatial data. The site provides geospatially referenced information on the status, extent, characteristics, and functions of wetlands, riparian, deepwater, and related aquatic habitats. These features are displayed at a scale of 1:100,000 or larger.

Metadata for Wetlands Mapper data includes:

- Date of the satellite imagery
- Type of imagery
- Date the map was produced
- Available data formats
- Intent of mapping
- Constraints
- Contributing data sources
- Datum
- Other information directly related to a particular map

Features in Wetlands Mapper are stored as part of the Wetlands Master Geodatabase. This approach provides a seamless digital wetland data layer and map data in a single standard projection. Wetland Mapper also meets standards of the Open GIS Consortium, which means that it is available for use by other software developers.

The Wetlands Data Extraction Tool is used to download data viewed with Wetlands Mapper. It can download a National Wetlands Indicator wetland polygon, metadata that describes the wetland polygon, and historic maps that may be useful for understanding landscape changes. The Wetlands Data Extraction Tool uses the USGS topographic quadrangle names for area selection and extraction.

3.7.7 Wetlands Master Geodatabase

The U.S. Fish and Wildlife Service also produced the Wetlands Master Geodatabase (MGD), a national digital library that provides a seamless layer of digital wetlands and deepwater habitat. It also includes links to hydrographic data in an effort to improve scientific research, strategic planning, resource management, and tactical analysis for habitat conservation. The MGD was developed in response to the demand to be able to better integrate geospatial data together to create one map.

The MGD contains available digital wetland and deepwater map data, including approximately 27,000 wetland coverage maps combined to create a seamless ArcSDE Geodatabase. The MGD also accommodates upland, riparian habitats, and hydrogeomorphic coding of features within the data set.

Geodatabases like MGD are storage mechanisms for spatial and attribute data. They help standardize the updating of spatial data and strengthen the overall quality and integrity of the information. Geodatabases are able to work with a wide range of geospatial formats, and this approach helps integrate data.

3.7.8 Data at the State Level

One limitation that many states have is that the only geospatially referenced data they have about wetlands is the National Wetlands Inventory. Many states are making efforts to develop their own geospatial data for wetlands. In Oregon, for example, a subcommittee of the Oregon Geographic Information Council developed a state-wide prototype wetland mapping framework to help facilitate the integration and sharing of wetland mapping data. The Oregon Wetland Mapping Standard (OWMS) is a collection of georeferenced features depicting wetlands within the state. OWMS defines standards for data quality, including completeness, level of detail, positional accuracy, and attribute accuracy. The format used for OWMS is similar to that developed by USFWS for NWI. This format provides a consistent structure for wetland data. The adoption of this standard will help improve compatibility of data sets and make it easier for different organizations to share information. (See Figure 3.17.)

Within Oregon, data includes wetland and vegetation information from Natural Heritage Information Center; data on "Oregon's Greatest Wetlands" from the Wetlands Conservancy; and local wetland inventories and delineations from the Oregon Department of State Lands.

The North Carolina Division of Coastal Management (DCM) has created a wetlands conservation plan for improving wetlands protection and management in areas along the coast. The plan consists of six components:

1. Wetlands mapping and inventory
2. Functional assessment of wetlands
3. Wetland restoration identification and prioritization

Figure 3.17 *Wetlands along the Texas coast have been damaged by hurricanes in recent years. One reason is that barrier islands, which once provided a level of protection for the wetlands, have been disappearing. Image courtesy USGS.*

4. Coordination with wetland regulatory agencies
5. Coastal area wetland policies
6. Local land use planning

To develop the Wetlands Conservation Plan, the DCM combined data from the NWI maps, Natural Resource Conservation Service County Soil Surveys, and TM LandSat imagery.

One primary focus of the conservation plan is to provide an accurate functional assessment of wetland significance. To help achieve this goal, DCM developed the North Carolina Coastal Region Evaluation of Wetland Significance (NC-CREWS), a GIS-based functional assessment model used to evaluate the ecological significance of wetlands. It is intended to be used as a planning and decision support tool to help planners, developers, and managers to define appropriate development or conservation practices to maintain and protect ecosystems. NC-CREWS evaluates 39 separate functions, such as water quality, wildlife habitat, water storage, and bank stabilization. DCM has also conducted a comprehensive accuracy assessment to determine the accuracy of the wetland type data.

3.8 STORMWATER MANAGEMENT AND EROSION CONTROL

There are two basic approaches to stormwater management: (1) conveyance and (2) infiltration. The conveyance approach focuses on getting rid of the water as quickly as possible. Landscape architects typically use curbs and gutters that capture stormwater that falls onto streets, parking lots, and other paved areas, and then redirect the water into ditches or underground pipes. Virtually every city in the United States was based on a conveyance approach that uses underground pipes, drainage ditches, and curbs and gutters.

The benefit of using a conveyance approach is that it solves immediate flooding problems. The downside is that by diverting all the water, we create problems downstream. The increased volume of water can lead to severe erosion problems and downstream flooding. As a result, we often had to resort to structural solutions to control water movement and prevent flooding.

Coal Bed Methane Dewatering Treatment Wetlands

One innovative multiuse wetland project was developed in conjunction with a southern Colorado coal bed methane (CBM) production operation. The Southern Colorado Treatment Wetlands Project facilitates collection and treatment of coal bed methane discharge water within a series of aesthetic and functional constructed wetlands. The coal seam fractures where CBM is found are effectively aquifers, so the CBM wells must be dewatered to allow removal of the gas. A landowner in southern Colorado agreed to utilize a part of his property to CBM production if the operation was completely integrated within the ranch setting and the dewatering.

A concept was developed to build a series of wetlands that could be supplied by CBM water. The wetlands were to be aesthetic features, which when planted would not only address water quality but would serve as habitat for the animals and birds in the area. Staff from AECOM, an international design, planning, and engineering firm, evaluated potential wetland sites, developed a water budget to understand stormwater runoff and CBM wetland dewatering supply to each site, sized and designed the wetlands, surveyed and staked them out on-site, checked precision grading and oversaw the construction process, and specified and supervised planting.

Federal Funding Sources for Wetland Projects

- **Five-Star Restoration Program.** Provides funds to support community-based wetland and riparian restoration projects.

- **National Coastal Wetlands Conservation Grant Program.** Provides matching grants for conservation and restoration of coastal wetlands.

(continues)

(continued)

- **National Oceanic and Atmospheric Administration Community-Based Restoration Program.** Provides financial assistance for community-based restoration of coastal wetlands.

- **Partners for Fish and Wildlife Program.** Provides financial assistance to private landowners to restore wetlands and habitat on their land.

- **Coastal Wetlands Planning, Protection, and Restoration Act.** Provides matching grants to coastal states to acquire, manage, restore, and enhance wetlands.

- **North American Wetlands Conservation Act Grant Program.** Makes grants available to states and private organizations for wetland conservation.

- **Wetlands Reserve Program.** Provides financial incentives to private landowners for wetland conservation and restoration.

- **Watershed Protection and Flood Protection Program.** Provides technical and financial assistance to local governments for wetland restoration projects.

Source: Kusler, 2003.

Types of Redevelopment and Infill Projects

- Historic preservation
- Waterfront development
- Brownfields
- Residential infill
- Adaptive reuse
- Downtown business district
- Multifamily
- Suburban commercial
- Mixed use development
- Roadway expansion

The primary objective for most conveyance stormwater systems is to improve flood protection. Systems are designed to handle peak runoff volumes and flow rates of a given design storm size. Most systems are designed to handle a 100-year flood, but some focus on a 500-year flood. Street drainage systems are typically designed for a 10-year storm, so it is not uncommon for stormwater to overflow the street.

An example of a conveyance system at a large scale is the Los Angeles River. The "river" is actually more of a giant concrete channel. Arnold Schwarzenegger's *Terminator* movies often include a chase scene in a big concrete canyon: That is the Los Angeles River. For most of the year, the river is almost empty, but when it rains somewhere upstream, the channel can fill in a matter of minutes, making it a very dangerous place.

The infiltration approach to stormwater management seeks to integrate water back into the landscape in an effort to mimic the natural hydrologic cycle. The idea is to slow down stormwater runoff and give it an opportunity to penetrate into the ground.

The best infiltration stormwater management systems rely on a few simple techniques, applied consistently over an entire project or site. As my father used to say, this isn't rocket science. The idea is to slow down water and direct it where it causes the least amount of damage and where it can be used in the most beneficial way.

Paved surfaces are the nemesis of stormwater infiltration. It has been estimated that a one-acre parking lot creates 16 times more runoff than a meadow of the same size (SELC, 2008). Stormwater running over paved surfaces increases in velocity and has no way to permeate into the soil. One approach is to provide cuts in the curb to allow water to be distributed into an area that can absorb it.

On-site practices that provide treatment of runoff from roofs include rain gardens, rain barrels, green roofs, cisterns, and stormwater planters. Ecoroofs are an effective way to slow down storm runoff that typically falls on roofs. These roofs include some type of vegetative cover instead of traditional paved roofing. Ecoroofs can also be helpful in filtering air pollutants, reducing the impact of the urban heat island effect, insulating a building and lowering energy costs, and improving the overall aesthetic quality of an area. An ecoroof initially costs more than a conventional roof but can last twice as long (about 40 years).

The city of Portland (OR) Bureau of Environmental Services uses green street facilities to manage stormwater. These

Figure 3.18 *The headquarters for the American Society of Landscape Architecture, which is located in Washington, DC, features a green roof. The society is monitoring the roof to determine successes and challenges. Image courtesy ASLA.*

green facilities involve curb cuts combined with rain gardens. Since 2003, the city has constructed more than 500 of these types of facilities. It is estimated that the low-impact development strategies use cost about $172 per square meter ($16 per square foot), which is very cost-effective, considering the alternatives.

Parks, natural areas, and open space are opportunities for stormwater detention, but there are concerns about safety in play areas for children, mosquito problems, and/or protection and enhancement of wildlife. Stormwater detention and retention basins used to be closed off from the public via fences because they were deemed unsafe. Today we are taking a different approach and using these areas as recreational and landscape areas during dry weather. Most cities in the United States have a shortage of parks and recreation facilities. (See Figure 3.18.)

3.8.1 State Procedures

Each state establishes its own procedures for addressing erosion and sedimentation issues. Most require that an

erosion and sediment control plan be prepared and implemented prior to land disturbance. Sedimentation is the process where soil particles settle out of suspension as water velocity decreases. Sediment basins, sediment barriers, and related structures can all help filter or trap sediment. Both temporary and permanent facilities can be used to help manage stormwater runoff and limit sedimentation and soil erosion problems.

For an erosion and sedimentation control program to be effective, provisions for sediment control need to be made in the early planning stages. Some states have specific requirements that must be included in plans while others focus more on developing a basic structure and then allow municipalities to develop their own plans.

The objective of these plans is to reduce soil erosion and contain stormwater runoff. Obviously there is more than one approach to minimizing erosion and sedimentation damages. Policies governing permit issuance, inspection, and enforcement may vary between each municipality and county.

In 1975, the Georgia General Assembly passed the Erosion and Sedimentation Act (O.C.G.A. 12-7-1 et seq.) to address the impact of unchecked and uncorrected erosion and sediment deposition on land and water resources in the state (Georgia Soil and Water Conservation Commission, 2000). The act, which has been amended several times, requires counties and municipalities to have erosion and sediment control ordinances or be covered under state regulations. The intent of the act is to strengthen and extend the present erosion and sediment control program to conserve and protect land, water, air and other resources of the state. The plan also specifies that the review process will be accomplished by the local Soil and Water Conservation District or its delegated authority. It was written for four specific audiences, including:

1. Land disturbers, including landowners, developers and their consultants, architects, engineers, land surveyors, and planners

2. Enforcers, including officials and employees of local units of government charged with administering and enforcing the law on a local level and the Environmental Protection Division when it is the issuing authority

3. Plan reviewers, including the soil and water conservation districts and local issuing authorities

4. Plan preparers

Figure 3.19 *This sequence shows changes in the Birdsfoot Delta of the Mississippi River in Louisiana. The changes cover three decades, and these images show how sediment deposits slowly reshape the delta. The dark areas indicate the sedimentation deposits. Image courtesy USGS.*

3.8.2 Minimizing Erosion

Erosion affects virtually all watersheds, although the source and degree of impact may differ significantly. Any activity that includes clearing, dredging, grading, excavating, transporting, and filling may result in soil erosion. Erosion control is based on two main concepts: (1) disturb the smallest area of land possible for the shortest period of time, and (2) stabilize disturbed soils to prevent erosion from occurring.

Any time we disturb soil, we increase the possibility of erosion. Potential sources of sediment pollution include agricultural erosion, deforestation, overgrazing, silvicultural erosion, urban runoff, construction activities, and mining activities. Agricultural uses that involve tilling the earth can leave the soil unprotected. New construction also results in soil disturbance. As a result, most water districts have strict regulations on how much of a site can be modified

at a time. An erosion and sediment control plan should be submitted as early in the planning stage as possible.

The timing of land-disturbing activities and installation of erosion control measures must be coordinated to minimize water quality impacts. Major construction, land clearing, and grading operations should be scheduled to occur during the drier times of year when stormwater runoff is less of a concern.

Efforts should be made to limit exposure of construction areas. Most permits minimize the size of the disturbed area. Erosion controls reduce the amount of sediment lost during dam construction and prevent sediment from entering surface waters. Erosion control is based on (1) minimizing the area and time of land disturbance and (2) stabilizing disturbed soils to prevent erosion. (FEMA, 2003). (See Figure 3.19.)

It is important to schedule construction projects so that clearing and grading are done during a period of time when erosion is less likely to occur. That means trying to limit construction during relatively dry periods.

If grading is conducted on a larger part of the site, the disturbed area needs to be stabilized to prevent erosion. In most states, mulch, temporary vegetation, or permanent vegetation must be added to exposed areas in a timely manner to avoid soil erosion issues. Many water districts require that exposed areas be treated within 7 to 14 days after disturbance.

Wherever possible, natural vegetation should be retained and protected since this is one of the best ways to minimize stormwater runoff and soil erosion issues. At a minimum, existing vegetation should be protected with fencing, tree armoring, and retaining walls or tree wells.

3.8.3 Controlling Pollution

Pollutant reduction is usually a major goal of most stormwater management efforts. Pollutants found in urban stormwater include sediment, nutrients, trace metals, hydrocarbons, bacteria, organic carbon, pesticides, and trash and debris. Once we determine which pollutants are causing the water quality problems, we can develop strategies for dealing with those particular pollutants.

Basic Principles of Soil Bioengineering

- Fit the soil bioengineering system to the site.
- Retain existing vegetation whenever possible.
- Limit removal of vegetation.
- Stockpile and protect topsoil.
- Protect areas exposed during construction.
- Divert, drain, or store excess water.

Source: USDA-NRCS, 1992.

In lakes, soil erosion and sedimentation are among the largest pollutants. Sediment decreases water quality for fish and other stream animals and plants. Sediment can also change flow, increase erosion, raise water temperature, lower dissolved oxygen, impact aquatic habitat structure, and result in the loss of fish and other aquatic populations.

Erosion can be a major problem for water quality because of the phosphorus that is transported to the lake attached to soil particles. Phosphorus can be carried into a lake from erosion and surface runoff. It causes algae growth, which contributes to a decrease in water clarity and water quality. Heavy algae blooms also can deplete the oxygen needed by fish and other aquatic organisms depleted as the algae decompose.

Methods to Control Runoff and Sedimentation from Construction Sites

- Build check dams.
- Construct runoff intercepts.
- Locate potential land-disturbing activities away from critical areas.
- Preserve on-site vegetation.
- Build retaining walls.
- Create sediment basins/rock dams.
- Install sediment fences.
- Install sediment traps.
- Plant vegetated buffers.
- Plant vegetated filter strips.

One way in which stormwater runoff damages local waterways is by washing pollutants directly into rivers and streams. Stormwater runoff from roofs, driveways, and roads carries pollutants, such as oil, heavy metals, chemicals, and lawn fertilizers, directly to nearby waterways.

3.9 LAND USE PLANNING AND MANAGEMENT

Land use planning focuses on the physical layout of communities. Land use has a significant impact on water resources. It determines how streets, pipes, and water lines are laid out and where paving and greenspace are located. It also has a major impact on growth patterns and level of density.

In the United States after World War II, when the automobile became affordable, people moved out of the cities and into neighboring suburbs seeking the good life. Having a single-family home, a white picket fence, and a large yard was considered the American dream. The problem, though, is that over the years, this dream led to uncontrolled sprawl that has created some serious problems, including:

- Increasing traffic congestion and commute times
- Air pollution
- Inefficient energy consumption and greater reliance on foreign oil
- Loss of open space and habitat
- Inequitable distribution of economic resources
- Loss of a sense of community

Four Processes of an Erosion and Sediment Control Program

1. Ordinance development and implementation
2. Plan preparation and review
3. Inspection and enforcement
4. Information, education, and training

Land use patterns and the types of development permitted are determined by a planning process that incorporates social, political, institutional, natural, and other factors. The process occurs at the local level. Local governments typically are responsible for land use and growth management, and their decisions are vital in managing water resources. Through land use plans and ordinances, local governments can set development standards that conserve and minimize water use. Water management districts do not have the authority to change local comprehensive land use plans or land use designations.

Land use types influence the hydrologic and physical nature of the watershed. The implementation of land use policies can help communities and regions balance the demands of growth with the health of environmental resources. Land use is a major contributor to water quality. Increasing coordination of environmental planning can help reduce the adverse effects of land use and stormwater on water quality.

The type of land use can have a major impact on stormwater runoff and water quality. Industrial land uses potentially have the greatest negative impact. For example, on a project in Cobb County (GA), one of the biggest issues is the industrial development along the Chattahoochee River. In the county's future land use plan, industrial uses along the river are shown to remain in place. The comprehensive plan states that "there needs to be a concentrated effort by Cobb County to protect these remaining undeveloped /underdeveloped industrial areas from residential and commercial incursion," as there are no other places in the county suitable for such development. The desire to maintain industrial land in this location, however, must be balanced with the need to create a high quality of life for people in what is essentially a residential area. Because much of the industrial development in this area consists of junkyards and auto salvage yards, and the land is on the banks of the environmentally sensitive Chattahoochee River, the appropriateness of retaining all industrial land use should be evaluated.

Land use practices causing indirect wetland impacts can be managed at the local level through zoning, subdivision ordinances, stormwater criteria, and other development regulations (Cappiella et al., 2006). Wetland protection historically has been the domain of federal and state permitting authorities, but these agencies have no control over local land use decisions, so their ability to protect wetlands at site level is limited.

3.9.1 Land Use and Zoning

Land use planning and zoning practices have a significant impact on development patterns within a watershed. Smart water management is key to sustainable growth, allowing both economic development and conservation to exist side by side (www.garivers.org/gawater).

In some states, such as Florida, land use and zoning are required to be consistent. That means if land use changes, zoning changes with it. In Georgia, that is not the case. Land use is considered to be a vision of how a city or county wants to grow while zoning defines the legal rights and uses for a piece of property. Zoning determines where particular land uses are located, requirements for parking, sizes of roadways, permitted impervious land coverage, and the requirements for other physical elements.

Zoning is the classification of land into districts. Under the guise of protecting citizens' health, safety, and welfare, governing bodies used zoning to separate land uses into numerous single-use zoning districts. Many say that this application of zoning has led to sprawl and bland communities. There is a current trend to allow for multiple-use districts where commercial, retail, and housing can all occur together, as in a traditional city.

Regulations for each zoning district establish the size of structures, floor area ratios, amount of impervious surface, setbacks, and permitted uses. The trend in zoning is to move toward flexible zoning or form-based codes that allow designers more opportunity for creativity without rigid guidelines. The existing or by-right zoning provides a developer with clear guidelines for what criteria must be met to gain approvals. If the by-right zoning does not achieve the desired outcome, usually measured by profitability, it is possible to pursue a rezoning of the property.

3.9.2 Ordinances

One concern is that conventional planning and zoning applications do not always protect water resources. Land use planning needs to determine the pattern of development, what type is permitted, and its relationship to streams and other natural features.

A number of different zoning ordinances are being used to protect water resources, including farmland preservation ordinances, performance-based zoning, conservation ordinances, and overlay zones.

Farmland preservation ordinances seek to prevent agricultural land from being developed. These ordinances help preserve open space and wildlife habitat, and these lands are directly linked to water resources such as streams

and wetlands. Performance-based zoning, which is also referred to as bonus or incentive zoning, allows developers to increase density in some areas in order to preserve sensitive land in other areas. Overlay zones provide a greater level of restrictions in specific areas. Such zones may occur where we want to influence a specific type of development or protect sensitive environmental resources.

Land use ordinances must contain technical principles as provided in the law and procedures for issuance of permits. Minimum standards are included in the law, but local ordinances may be more stringent. In the 1990s in the state of Georgia, municipalities that fail to enact a comprehensive erosion and sediment control program were required to follow rules and regulations developed by the Environmental Protection Division of the Georgia Department of Natural Resources (Georgia Soil and Water Conservation Commission, 2000).

Conservation land use focuses on using cluster development that concentrates density in selected areas and maintains open space and agricultural land in others. The overall density for an area is the same, but there is a much greater level of undisturbed areas. Clustering allows the design of more effective urban runoff management systems and reduces surface runoff. Another benefit of cluster development is that it reduces infrastructure costs because fewer roads and utilities are needed.

3.9.3 Land Use Data

Land use data are produced at a local, state, and national level. At the local level, each major municipality is required to have a land use to guide future development. In Cobb County (GA), where I live, there is a county-wide land use plan, and each city in the county produces its own land use data. Each generates a new land use map every five years as part of a comprehensive planning process. Most states also provide a clearinghouse of geospatial data that includes land use data. Land use surveys typically are performed using aerial photos and satellite imagery to define boundaries.

For example, the Minnesota Land Use—Agricultural and Transition Areas document was produced to update Minnesota's 1969 land use inventory. The project was funded by the state legislature and features 17 different categories of land use. The mission of the Georgia Land Use Trends Project is to track and analyze the changes in Georgia's land use. These data will provide valuable information for planners and decision makers. GIS databases for the entire state are generated using LandSat data, and databases have been produced for 1974, 1985, 1991, 1998, 2001, and 2005.

In California, the state's Land and Water Use Program of the Department of Water Resources collects land use data and develops water use estimates that are used for statewide water planning (www.water.ca.gov/landwateruse).

At the national level, a number of agencies are involved with making land use data available. USGS's Land Use and Land Cover (LULC) data consist of historical land use and land cover classification data based primarily on the manual interpretation of aerial photography from the 1970s and 1980s. The LULC includes 21 different categories of cover type.

The U.S. Department of Agriculture's Economic Research Service has been a source of major land use data since 1945. Data on agricultural land uses, including U.S. cropland, were first produced in 1910. The Major Land Uses (MLU) series provides information on all major uses of public and private land in the United States. The MLU data summarize cropland, forest, pasture and range, and miscellaneous and special uses, such as urban, recreational, and parkland.

3.10 SHORELINE MANAGEMENT

A shoreline management plan (SMP) is a comprehensive plan to manage the multiple resources and uses associated with a lake or reservoir. The objectives of an SMP typically are to:

- Manage and protect the shoreline

- Establish and maintain acceptable fish and wildlife habitat, aesthetic quality, and natural environmental conditions

- Promote the safe and healthful use of the lake and shoreline for recreational purposes

Protecting the shoreline is critical for ensuring the health of a body of water.

Three General Types of Shoreline Use Classifications

1. Preserving natural resources and minimizing or prohibiting shoreline development

2. Allowing limited development along the shoreline

3. Allowing more intense levels of development within the project shoreline

---

Creating shoreline management policies, permitting systems, and development guidelines is an important part of the SMP development process. These policies help ensure there is a consistent vision for protecting existing resources. Once policies are in place, development guidelines and a permitting system make sure the policies are followed. The SMP planning process also allows project stakeholders to provide input and to express their concerns.

Development guidelines define appropriate design decisions, construction methodologies, protection measures, and maintenance practices that will help meet policies established for a lake. The guidelines have a lot to do with the overall character of the development around a lake, and they provide guidance for architects, landscape architects, engineers, and other designers, giving form to the places where we live, play, and gather.

The U.S. Army Corps of Engineers is responsible for managing the shoreline, and its adjacent public lands and waters, for many lakes across the United States. The Corps do this in a manner promoting safe and healthful public use. The objective is to maintain a balance among permitted minor private uses, long-term resource protection, and public recreational

---

Data to Track in an SMP Monitoring Program

- Amount of undisturbed shoreline
- Undisturbed shoreline that is developed
- Number of new docks constructed
- Number of boats launched at specific project ramps
- Number of permit violations
- Changes in land uses adjacent to or near the project

---

opportunities. The Corps uses shoreline use classifications, which are areas designated for specific uses that are consistent with the goals and objectives of the SMP.

The Lake Seminole (FL) Shoreline Management Plan is one example of how shoreline is protected. The plan provides guidance and information for effectively managing the shoreline at Lake Seminole, including its adjacent public lands and waters. The plan was prepared in accordance with U.S. Army Corps of Engineers requirements specified in 1992 Engineering Regulation 1130-2-406, titled "Shoreline Management at Civil Works Projects" (USACE, 1985. http://corpslakes.usace.army.mil/employees/policy.cfm?Id=shoreline&Code=All).

3.10.1 Stabilization and Protection

One of the primary goals of shoreline management is to protect a lake's shoreline. Shoreline erosion, which is the wearing away of material along the bank, is a major problem. It occurs in large open water bodies as a result of waves and currents that cut away at banks. Although shoreline erosion is a naturally occurring process, it causes havoc on human settlement.

Bank stabilization often is required to protect the shoreline and prevent erosion. One way to stabilize banks is with hardscape elements, such as walls, riprap, or other engineering approaches. Some shorelines need these types of structural stabilization because of the energy of the waves that hit the shore. Riprap, gabions, and sloping revetments are common approaches used to stabilize slopes.

Vegetative plantings and wetland enhancements or preservation of existing vegetation can be the most effective means of protecting shorelines and filtering pollution from stormwater. The use of native herbs and grasses, wetlands, and aquatic vegetation can help protect shorelines, dissipate wave energy, filter pollution, and provide wildlife habitat. Vegetative buffers are used to protect specific resources, such as wildlife, aesthetics, recreation, or cultural resources.

One goal is to provide an environment that supports native aquatic plant species while at the same time minimizing problems with exotic species. Unwanted plants often are

present when the water temperature changes, the water becomes polluted, or the chemical composition of the water changes. In contrast, native aquatic plants are found in healthy streams.

Often a combination of techniques may be necessary to control erosion. Concrete revetments can be designed with open areas that allow vegetation to reestablish along the shoreline. An integrated approach using structural systems, bioengineering techniques, and vegetative plantings can be an effective way to stabilize slopes.

3.10.2 Shoreline Ownership and Access

The ownership along the shoreline of a lake varies depending on the lake. The majority of the shoreline along many lakes in the United States is privately owned, so access is limited. One reason that so much of the shoreline is privately owned is that waterfront property is worth a premium. On many lakes, private lots on deep water can be worth well over $1 million.

Along Lake Allatoona (GA), for example, a U.S. Army Corps of Engineers lake located just north of Atlanta, the entire shoreline is publicly owned. The Corps has control of the entire water's edge, a fact that has helped maintain the lake's water quality. For a recent project, plans were developed for a new 4,000-acre development surrounded by 5,000 acres of Corps land.

In addition to lands purchased in fee title, which means buying the property outright, the Corps also often purchases easements on some private land surrounding lakes. Flowage easements can be acquired to provide the government the perpetual right to flood privately owned land, if necessary.

Ownership also controls access to the lake. Generally, legal access to the shoreline is considered within 200 feet or a reasonable distance a person could carry a motor, fishing tackle, and other related gear. Some protected shoreline areas are designated to maintain or restore aesthetic, fish and wildlife, historical, cultural, physical limitations, or other environmental values. These areas are typically off limits. In addition, prohibited access areas are also closed. These areas typically include hazardous zones near dams, spillways, hydroelectric power stations, and water intake structures. Public access is not allowed in these areas for health, safety, and security reasons.

3.10.3 Shoreline Use Permits

Shoreline use permits are used to authorize private structures or activities of any kind affecting project lands or waters of a lake. The permits are issued for private floating recreation facilities, access paths, mowing, and landscaping activities that do not in any way involve a disruption to or a change in landform. All of these permits are nontransferable.

Shoreline use permits typically are issued for a specific period of time but are subject to revocation if it is determined that the public interest requires such revocation. For a project at Lake Lanier (GA), the shoreline use permits were set not to exceed five years. A charge is typically made for shoreline use permits to help defray expenses associated with issuance and administration of the permits.

Examples of Facilities for Which Shoreline Development Permits Are Issued

- Individual docks and piers (private and commercial)
- Common (or group) docks and piers
- Boathouses
- Excavation and dredging
- Erosion control
- Riprapping
- Water removal from reservoir
- Effluent discharge
- Retaining walls, bulkheads
- Fences
- Walkways
- Landscape plantings
- Hunting blinds

3.11 NATURAL RESOURCE PROTECTION

All across the United States, organizations and agencies are trying to protect natural resources. Growth and development pressures have raised questions about how to preserve rivers, wetlands, prairies, and woodlands. One problem is that it becomes more difficult to conserve natural lands as they become more expensive and less available with each passing year. Land around water in particular becomes more in demand, and these are often areas where water management is critical.

Protecting natural resources typically also results in protecting water resources. For example, remaining natural areas in an urban subwatershed are important pockets that provide habitat, green space, and some stormwater treatment. At the same time, they are often fragmented, compacted, and stressed by stormwater runoff, poor soils, invasive plant species, and human disturbance. Municipalities often own or manage natural areas, and many of these parcels are prime candidates for reforestation, wetland restoration, and land reclamation. Natural resource programs typically seek to expand watershed benefits by systematically restoring and increasing natural areas at the subwatershed level. It also may involve working with the community to convert vacant land to beneficial uses, such as community gardens (Rowe and Schueler, 2006).

It is important to manage the natural areas in a subwatershed comprehensively, including urban forests, wetlands, stream corridors, open space, and vacant lands. These areas can be used to control flooding and address stormwater runoff issues.

3.11.1 Local to Federal

Efforts to protect natural resources occur at all levels in the United States, from local cities and counties seeking to protect what they have, to federal agencies establishing broader policies that have the same objective. In Albemarle County (VA), for example, the fundamental goal of the county's environmental team is to protect the natural resources for

---

future generations. This is done through the implementation of programs that manage surface and groundwater, protect and restore stream corridors, and generally preserve the integrity of the natural environment (www.albemarle.org/department.asp?department=planning&relpage=5720).

In Minnesota's Twin Cities region, residents support the increased protection and preservation of important natural resource areas. In the Metropolitan Council's 2001 Survey of Metro Area Residents, 93% of respondents agreed or strongly agreed that "as areas develop, governments should do more to protect natural features" (www.metrocouncil.org/planning/landuse/NRProtectionStrategy.pdf).The council is making efforts to protect the resources in the region. Its overall regional plan, the *2030 Regional Development Framework*, is directed at meeting the needs of current and future residents, using land sensibly, and protecting the region's prized natural environment. The plan identifies one of its goals to be "preserving vital natural areas and resources for future generations." The corresponding policy states: "work with local and regional partners to reclaim, conserve, protect and enhance the region's vital natural resources."

For the U.S. Forest Service, the stewardship of water, soil, and air resources is a basic requirement for national forest land management. The Forest Service has developed a state-of-the-art stream inventory system that is used to get a better understanding of the health of a stream and its surrounding habitat. This system measures fish habitat, fish population, macroinvertebrates, channel stability, valley segment types, and riparian vegetation, among other factors. The Forest Service also is involved with rehabilitating watersheds to protect water quality. This includes the development of constructed wetlands and other activities.

Environmental organizations, such as the Sierra Club, are actively involved in protecting natural resources. The Sierra Club was founded in 1892, and its mission is to "explore, enjoy and protect the planet." The club has over 750,000 members in 65 chapters and over 400 local groups nationwide, and its grassroots approach makes it one of the most powerful and influential environmental organizations in the country.

Ecosystem Issues to Consider during the Watershed Planning Process

1. What are the sensitive habitats and their buffers, both terrestrial and aquatic?

2. Where are these habitats located in the watershed? Are there any fragmented corridors?

3. What condition are these habitats in?

4. Are these habitats facing any of the following problems?
   a. Invasive species
   b. Changes associated with climate warming
   c. Stream fragmentation and/or in-stream flow alterations
   d. Changes in protection status

5. On what scale are these habitats considered (e.g., regional, watershed, subwatershed, or site-specific)? Are these scales appropriate for the biological resources of concern? Does the variability, timing, and rate of water flow hydrologically support indigenous biological communities?

Source: EPA, *Handbook for Developing Watershed Plans to Restore and Protect Our Waters*, www.epa.gov/owow/nps/watershed_handbook.

3.12 URBAN HYDROLOGY

The world is undergoing the largest wave of urban growth in history. In 2008, for the first time in history, more than half of the world's population lived in towns and cities (UNFPA, 2007). It is expected that 60% of the world's population will be urban by 2030 and that most urban growth will occur in less developed countries. Over 75% of the U.S. population lives in cities. With so much of the world's population in urban areas, it is no surprise that water demand in urban areas is extensive.

Houston's Urban Forests

American Forests conducted a study of a 3.2 million-acre area in Houston to document urban forest cover (American Forests, 2001). It also analyzed 25 individual sites with aerial photography using a software program called CITYgreen to map and measure tree cover and to calculate the benefits of Houston's trees. Study results show that trees provide significant benefits in stormwater runoff reduction, energy savings, and pollutant removal. The study found that Houston's tree cover reduces the need for stormwater management by 2.4 billion cubic feet per peak storm event, saving $1.33 billion in one-time construction costs.

Source: National Management Measures to Control Nonpoint Source Pollution from Urban Areas. Management Measure 2: Watershed Assessment, (November 2005).

Impervious land coverage is a fundamental characteristic of urban and suburban areas. *Impervious surfaces* can be defined as any material that prevents or reduces the infiltration of water into the soil. *Effective impervious area* (EIA) is a term used to describe the total impervious cover that is directly connected to the storm drain network. This includes streets, driveways, parking lots, sidewalks, and other paved areas. EIA is usually expressed as a percentage of the total watershed or subwatershed area. The higher the number, the greater the amount of paving.

One of the environmental consequences of impervious land coverage is stream degradation. Even in higher-density developments, the impact of impervious land coverage can be mitigated by a variety of site planning and design techniques.

The percentage of impervious cover in a watershed is a pretty good indication of water quality. The calculation is simple: The more paving you have, the lower the quality of water. The level of stream degradation increases as the amount of impervious cover increases. An urban watershed typically has a total impervious cover of greater than 10%. Research has shown that there is a decline in water quality when watershed impervious cover exceeds 10%, with severe degradation expected beyond 25%. By definition, then, urban watersheds have water quality issues. Even

most of the pervious areas in urban landscapes are highly disturbed and require some level of restoration.

Humans have done a great job of mucking up streams in urban areas, and we simply do not have the financial resources to repair the damage that has been done. For that reason, we must pick and choose the best ways to protect and restore water resources.

Streams in urban watersheds are fundamentally different in character from streams in more rural watersheds. In general, urban streams are typically shallow, wide, and straight as a result of development. The stream corridor in urban areas is typically much smaller than those in less developed areas because of encroachment that occurs along stream edges. In some urban areas, smaller streams have been paved over and now are restricted to underground pipes.

Natural stream channels are dynamic systems that are constantly changing. This causes some significant conflicts because in urban areas, there is a tendency to try to confine streams into fairly tight areas. Stream channels seek to maintain equilibrium by changing their alignment and physical layout. A stream meanders, straightens out, and meanders again, cutting into adjacent banks as it seeks the path of least resistance.

It is extremely difficult to maintain healthy water resources in urban areas. Healthy streams generally have stable channels, good water quality, and good stream biodiversity. A healthy channel will not degrade or aggrade, and it has the capacity to handle normal water flow and sediment loads. Urban watersheds are often degraded, do not meet water quality standards, and as a consequence are subject to many regulatory drivers that are complex, costly, and confusing to implement (Rowe and Schueler, 2006). The biggest problem with many stream restoration projects in the past is that they have been reactive, focusing on solving an individual problem rather than helping address the larger issues within a watershed.

Some problems associated with urban watersheds include:

- Changes in flow

- Increased sedimentation

- Higher water temperature

- Lower dissolved oxygen

- Degradation of aquatic habitat structure

- Loss of fish and other aquatic populations

- Decreased water quality due to increased levels of nutrients, metals, hydrocarbons, bacteria, and other pollutants

Sediment deposition gradually raises the elevation of the streambed in a process called channel aggradation. The *National Water Quality Inventory: Report to Congress,* 2002, identified urban runoff as one of the leading sources of water quality impairment in surface waters.

Structural solutions for restoring urban watersheds have not proven very successful in the past, at least not in terms of improving natural processes. Often a combination of nonstructural and structural practices is the most cost-effective approach. Because most urban streams are already impacted, much effort focuses on restoring and retrofitting these streams. The problem is that these types of projects are almost always more complex, expensive, and time consuming than new stormwater practices.

Four groups of restoration practices often are applied for urban streams:

1. Stormwater retrofits
2. Stream restoration
3. Riparian management
4. Discharge prevention

Other types of restoration practices are more typically applied in more rural areas. These include pollution source control, pervious area management, and municipal stewardship.

Most urban stream repairs involve some form of bank stabilization. *Hard bank stabilization* involves the use of structural bank protection practices to protect stream banks from further erosion or potential failure. *Soft bank stabilization* involves utilizing slope control, vegetation, and biodegradable fabrics to stabilize a bank.

3.12.1 Existing Systems

In most of our major cities, stormwater runoff is a major concern, and the systems that have been installed are seriously outdated and in need of repair. In urban areas, it is particularly difficult to maintain stormwater pipes. Gaining access to these pipes typically involves tearing up streets, which can be expensive and disruptive to traffic and day-to-day business activities.

There are a variety of standards and approaches for quantifying how to manage stormwater for water quality protection. Many municipalities utilize an 80% to 90% annual capture rate as a standard of practice for the water quality volume. Some jurisdictions focus on reducing impervious land coverage rather than emphasizing a specific water quality volume.

Approaches for cleaning up a stream corridor include routine stream cleanups, stream adoption programs, citizen hotline reporting, discharge and dumping prevention, bank stabilization, reforestation, and pollution source controls.

One of the best ways to reduce the generation of urban runoff or nonpoint source pollution is through planning and design. Land use approaches to stormwater management are effective for reducing runoff, improving infiltration, providing wildlife habitat, and enhancing aesthetics. Reducing the runoff generated from urban rooftops can reduce pollutant loads, flooding, channel erosion, and many other stream impacts (Rowe and Schueler, 2006). Current efforts focus more on better stormwater practices, stream buffers, green space and forest conservation, and integrating water management with land use planning and other long-term planning efforts. Since 1991, EPA has promoted the watershed approach as the key framework for dealing with problems caused by urban runoff and other sources that impair surface and groundwaters (EPA, 2002).

Once an urban area reaches build-out, the watershed starts to stabilize to some degree. This can take decades, though, and in our cities, we seem to want to tear up something and start over, don't we?

3.12.2 Impervious Cover Model

The impervious cover model (ICM) is one method for determining the current and future quality of streams and other water resources. The ICM predicts the nature and extent of habitat degradation. It focuses on the *average* behavior of a group of indicators over a *range* of impervious cover.

The ICM classifies four types of urban streams, according to their current health and repair potential (Schueler and Brown, 2004):

1. **Sensitive streams** have less than 10% subwatershed impervious cover and have the potential for "good" to "excellent" stream indicator scores. Even when sensitive streams do not attain high quality, they often have good to excellent potential for restoring channel stability and/or aquatic diversity.

2. **Impacted streams** have between 10% and 25% subwatershed impervious cover and show clear signs of declining stream health. Most indicators of stream health fall in the "fair" range.

3. **Nonsupporting streams** range between 25% and 60% subwatershed impervious cover and no longer support their designated uses, as defined by hydrology, channel stability habitat, water quality, or biological indicators.

4. **Urban drainage** refers to streams or channels with subwatersheds that exceed 60% impervious cover and where the stream corridor has essentially been eliminated or physically altered so that it functions primarily as a conduit for flood waters.

The ICM makes predictions for five major types of urban stream impacts:

1. Changes in stream hydrology
2. Alteration of the stream corridor
3. Stream habitat degradation
4. Declining water quality
5. Loss of aquatic diversity

3.12.3 Sewage and Septic

Sewage is the most common type of illicit discharge in most communities, and this can result in severe health and water quality issues. In particular, sewage discharges are a huge problem in urban areas. The storm sewer systems in most urban areas are underground, and many have been in place for decades. It is difficult to determine the condition of some systems, but many are in need of repair. The number, type, and distribution of stormwater hot spots vary enormously between subwatersheds.

Sewage and other pollutants get into our streams and other water resources in several ways. Occasionally sewage is illegally dumped into storm drains from recreational vehicles and into lakes from houseboats and lakeside homes. Some companies have illegally dumped sewage directly into the water. Sewer lines often follow the stream corridor; when they leak, overflow, or break, they send sewage directly to the stream. The frequency of failure depends on the age, condition, and capacity of the existing sanitary sewer system.

Believe it or not, sometimes sewage is intentionally dumped into water by municipalities or private companies. The city of Atlanta (GA) is frequently fined by EPA for dumping sewage directly into the Chattanooga River. It seems it is cheaper to pay fines than it is to fix the problem.

Septic systems are a huge problem, especially in rural areas, where no storm sewer systems exist. According to EPA, approximately one in four American homes is on a septic system. Septic systems have a failure rate of 5% to 35%, depending on soil conditions and other factors. EPA estimates that the average life span of a septic system is 20 years, yet a survey conducted in the Chesapeake Bay watershed found that the average age of septic systems in the area was about 27 years (MDE Accomplishments Report, 2002–2006).

Wastewater treatment is the process of improving the quality of wastewater. Wastewaters include septic tank effluent, primary effluent, pond effluents, and secondary effluents from overloaded or poorly controlled systems (EPA, 1999). Municipal systems may serve hundreds of residential, commercial, and industrial properties, while on-site systems may serve a single home. Wastewater treatments typically consist of primary, secondary, and tertiary treatment.

3.12.4 Trees in Urban Watersheds

One of the biggest changes in many urban watersheds is the loss of forests and other natural areas. Conserving existing forests is the best approach to protect a watershed's health from the impact of urbanization. On average, forests produce 30% to 50% less runoff than do grass lawn areas. In addition, plants take up water from the soil and release moisture in the air via a process called *transpiration*. A mature tree can transpire up to 100 gallons per day. *Evapotranspiration* is the combined loss of water from evaporation via soil and plant surfaces and transpiration by plants.

Most urban areas have a shortage of parks, green space, and areas with natural vegetative cover that could allow water to percolate into the soil and underground aquifers. Most urban "forest" has less than 50% canopy coverage. A study by the national conservation group American Forests revealed that more than 60% of the natural tree cover and vegetation in the Atlanta area has been lost since 1972 (American Forests, 2001).

Unfortunately, what is happening in Atlanta is similar to what is happening all across the United States. Urban trees are being eliminated at an alarming rate, and the potential impacts may be devastating. Researchers with American Forests discovered that every city they studied had at least a 30% decline in urban trees over the last 10 to 15 years. The areas once covered with trees and understory plants typically are developed into residential, commercial, and industrial areas or used for highways, parking areas, or other types of infrastructure needed to support all the people living in an urban area (American Forests, 2001).

The loss of urban forests and associated green space means there is more stormwater runoff and fewer places to absorb runoff and lessen the impact of flooding. As a result, interest in urban watershed forestry, which combines the fields of urban and community forestry and watershed planning, has increased.

For city-wide or regional analysis, the amount and spatial distribution of tree canopy cover is important. Changes in tree canopy cover due to tree removal can be measured by comparing images from different periods. Any georeferenced high-resolution images can be used as reference data to analyze urban forests as long as the tree canopy can be reliably separated from noncanopy surfaces.

Cities can get accurate, up-to-date information to evaluate changes in an urban forest. High-resolution aerial and satellite imagery is widely available and has become very affordable. Many cities are also implementing field studies to find out more about their urban forests and their impact on water resources. In Boston (MA), for example, hundreds of volunteers conducted an inventory of street trees in the city. They used aerial imagery to identify approximately 500,000 trees along streets and in public areas, such as parks and open spaces.

American Forests has developed a process called Urban Ecosystem Analysis (UEA) to help assess urban forests. With UEA, a Regional Ecosystem Analyses process uses LandSat imagery to compare land cover over time, and Green Layer Analysis uses data from high-resolution satellites to model tree canopy layers. This information can help users to understand larger issues within an urban watershed.

A number of groups and organizations focus on increasing the number of trees in their communities by combining high-tech analytical and management tools with old-fashioned fieldwork. American Forests used a combination of satellite data, field surveys, and GIS technology to assess changes in the forest canopy of the Portland (OR) metropolitan region from 1972 to 2000.

In San Francisco (CA), a partnership between Friends of the Urban Forest, the city and county of San Francisco, and Autodesk has significantly enhanced urban forest planning in the city. The three are creating an Urban Forest Map that geospatially locates each tree in the city, maintains tree data in a consistent database, and provides Web-based access to this information for maintenance, planting efforts, and other planning activities.

The city of Chicago (IL) has a "Green Infrastructure Mapping" Program that is intended to support numerous green initiatives, including stormwater runoff monitoring and modeling, evaluation and assessment of pollution control measures, studies of energy savings from green roof initiatives, carbon sequestration studies, and valuation of urban trees.

TreeVitalize is a group that is working on addressing the loss of tree cover in the five-county southeastern Pennsylvania region. Its goal is to plant 20,000 shade trees, restore 1,000 acres of forests along streams, and train 2,000 citizens to plant and care for trees. Tree-planting activities began in fall 2004 and continued through fall 2007. Part of the project was to develop maps and tables showing tree cover by local municipality, by census tract, and by watershed.

Urban forests provide a wide array of benefits to society and the environment, and many communities are actively involved with maintaining and restoring these precious resources. These forests have a significant impact on the water quality in urban areas, and we are starting to realize that by protecting trees, understory, and groundcover plants, we can reduce water resource problems.

3.12.5 Landscape in Flux

The urban landscape is in a constant state of flux. The next time you drive through a major city, pay attention to all of the construction going on and all of the areas that need some type of repair. Planners typically determine policies and procedures, and designers work within this structure to give physical form to cities. The design and planning process typically starts by identifying a problem and conducting a thorough inventory and analysis to find out more about a place. The program for a project and subsequent design decisions are based in large part on this analysis. Urban designers need to have a thorough understanding of a site in order to ensure a successful project. The more detailed, complete, and comprehensive the data, the better the analysis will be.

The goal of the USGS Urban Dynamics Program (http://landcover.usgs.gov/LCI/urban/intro.php) is to provide a greater understanding of land use changes that occur in urban areas. The program analyzes land use change, provides a historical perspective of these changes, and helps assess the impacts of the changes. USGS scientists use historic maps, aerial photographs, and LandSat satellite data to create urban land use databases that reflect several decades of change. These databases are then used to analyze the effects of urbanization on the landscape and to model urban growth and land use change under alternative growth scenarios. Methods for land use reconstruction, geographic analysis, modeling, and impacts assessment also are developed and refined.

For the Upper Cahaba Watershed Study (AL), EDAW identified areas in a 550-square-mile urban watershed that needed to be guarded to protect water quality. The watershed includes the suburban spread from the city of Birmingham, Alabama, and subdivisions are being developed at an alarming rate. The first part of the study focused on how to work with such a large area and how to identify the natural land conditions that made it susceptible

to development. By identifying which areas were the most sensitive, options, such as cluster development that would preserve these areas or making sure that any development met very strict standards, could be explored. The study was submitted to local governments, who then decided how best to implement its recommendations.

In urban design and planning, one difficulty is that a "community" is made up of a mixture of people of different ages, races, religions, interests, and values. Urban design and planning decisions need to address the concerns of all of these people. Urban design is a highly collaborative process because it has to address this diverse constituency.

Urban Runoff Pollution Mitigation Ordinance

In 1995, the city of Santa Monica (CA) passed an Urban Runoff Pollution Mitigation ordinance in an effort to minimize impacts on its water resources. The ordinance required new developments to implement management practices to collect precipitation, increase infiltration, and manage urban runoff on-site rather than after it enters the storm drain system. Since the ordinance was initiated, hundreds of new developments have implemented management practices, resulting in a 1.2 million gallon decrease in stormwater runoff for each storm of 0.1-inch rainfall or greater (Shapiro, 2003).

Source: Tom Richman & Associates and Bay Area Stormwater Management Agencies Association, *Start at the Source*, *Design Guidance Manual for Stormwater Quality Protection. San Francisco, CA,* 1999.

3.12.6 Watershed Scale

Watersheds are defined based upon size. Larger watersheds are classified using the Hydrologic Unit Code (HUC), which is a system of hierarchical codes. The HUC system divides the country into 21 regions based on the watersheds of 21 major river basins, and there are 222 watershed subregions that are further broken down into 2,262 smaller watersheds called cataloging units. The system is typically used by federal agencies, states, interstate commissions, tribes, and organizations involved with watershed issues.

USGS has developed the National Hydrography Dataset, which is a comprehensive set of digital spatial data derived from USGS and EPA information about surface water features. It includes information on specific watersheds.

Impacts of Urbanization

Streams and Wetlands

- Increased runoff volume, peak discharge rate, and bankful (channel-forming) flow
- Decreased base flow
- Stream channel enlargement
- Stream temperature increase
- Loss of large woody debris
- Increased bank erosion
- Increased embeddedness
- More frequent stream channel alterations (crossings, dams) and barriers to fish migration
- Increased inputs of sediment, nutrients, metals, hydrocarbons, bacteria, pathogens, organic carbon, methyl tertiary butyl ether (MTBE), pesticides and deicers
- Reduced abundance and diversity of aquatic insects, fish, and amphibians

Wetlands

- Increased ponding and water level fluctuation
- Downstream flow constrictions from road crossings with undersized culverts
- Decreased groundwater recharge and hydrologic drought (in floodplain wetlands)
- Sediment deposition
- Pollutant accumulation in wetland sediments
- Nutrient enrichment
- Increased chloride inputs from road salt application
- Reduced abundance and diversity of wetland plants, aquatic insects, amphibians, and birds

Source: CWP (2003).

3.13 GROUNDWATER PROTECTION

Protecting groundwater resources will be a major challenge in coming years because of increased development pressures and water demands, climate change, and the uncertainty of surface water availability.

Groundwater is a hidden resource, and to learn more about this resource we have to rely on more than our five senses. Fortunately, we do not have to resort to dowsing to gain a better understanding of groundwater. Groundwater mapping and modeling helps us make decisions about how to manage water resources in terms of both water quality and water quantity.

Groundwater is one of the nation's most critical natural resources. It is the largest source of usable water storage in the United States, containing more water than all reservoirs and lakes combined, excluding the Great Lakes. According to scientists, an estimated 1 million cubic miles of groundwater is located within one-half mile of the land surface. Only a very small percentage of groundwater is accessible and can be used for human activities. Most cities meet their needs for water by withdrawing it from the nearest river, lake, or reservoir, but many depend on groundwater as well.

Water is already in short supply in many parts of the United States, and the situation is only going to get worse. According to a 1999 United States Geological Survey, groundwater is the source of about 40% of the water used for public supply and provides drinking water for more than 97% of the rural population in the United States. Between 30% and 40% of the water used for the agricultural industry comes from groundwater. We need to understand groundwater if we are going to continue to make good decisions about sustainable water resources.

In recent years, people have begun to understand that groundwater and surface water are fundamentally interconnected and are integral components of the hydrologic cycle. Nevertheless, most laws governing groundwater issues are based on this notion that groundwater and surface water have nothing to do with each other. In most parts of the country, surface water is governed by doctrines of riparian law or prior appropriation. Groundwater traditionally has been treated as a common resource, with virtually no restrictions on accessing the water. If you can afford to pay someone to drill a well and you happen to hit water, you can do whatever you want with it.

The unregulated pumping of groundwater is no longer a viable option. In many parts of the country, groundwater is being withdrawn at rates that are not sustainable, and the result is a degradation of water quality and quantity. The water level in aquifers is being lowered, and because we keep digging deeper and deeper wells to access the water, the water quantity is further depleted. In coastal areas, intensive pumping of fresh groundwater has caused saltwater to seep into freshwater aquifers.

Groundwater is also critical for the environmental health of rivers, wetlands, and estuaries throughout the country. Groundwater withdrawals can result in reduced flows to streams and alter wetland hydrology. Changes in stream flow have important implications for water and flood management, irrigation, and planning.

There are hundreds of examples across the country where groundwater is threatened. The California Department of Health Services reported in 2008 that more than 300 public supply sources and an equally large number of private homeowner wells were contaminated and should not be used. In portions of the Southwest, Northeast, and Midwest, arsenic occurs naturally in groundwater at levels that exceed drinking water standards, and many municipalities are now debating whether to build treatment plants or reservoirs. Either will cost hundreds of millions of dollars.

According to the Arizona Department of Environmental Quality, approximately one-third of Arizona water systems exceed the level set for arsenic poisoning. One long-term impact of the 1988 drought in the Midwest is that many aquifers were overpumped by farmers seeking to save their crops and their way of life. Arkansas residents use groundwater to meet approximately 93% of their water needs.

In many parts of Florida, the existing aquifer system is not sufficient to meet the needs of the state's growing population and the needs of the environment, agriculture, and industry. Florida is one of four states in the country that uses more groundwater than surface water.

3.13.1 A Sustainable Approach

Sustainability of groundwater resources entails four basic premises:

1. Surface water and groundwater should be considered a single resource.

2. Groundwater is a finite resource and is part of a larger natural resources system.

3. Groundwater recharging is influenced by natural processes, including climate variability.

4. Communities need to share and manage groundwater resources.

The Ground Water Protection Council (2007) has defined a broad vision of what it would take to maintain a sustainable source of groundwater. It wrote that the nation needs to:

> [C]ontinue to conduct research and provide information—at a scale that is useful to states and local entities—about such matters as the safe, or sustainable, yield of aquifers (and methods for determining that yield); water-use data; and delineating boundaries and water budgets of three-dimensional watersheds, including scientifically based and cost-effective methods of quantifying interactions between ground water and surface water.

3.13.2 Data at the Local Level

In the United States, groundwater management decisions are made at a local level, not at the federal level. State and local agencies manage water resources and collect and analyze local data. Each state produces a report about groundwater within its borders. For landscape architects, the best source of groundwater information is from state, counties, or regional water districts.

Many states are using interactive maps for sharing groundwater information. For example, the Kentucky Geological Survey (KGS) Interactive Groundwater-Quality Data Map (www.uky.edu/kgs/gis/intro.html) displays groundwater-quality data for Kentucky. Users can choose from a list of 32 layers to display including geology, watershed boundaries, roads, orthophotography, and sinkholes. There are seven types of information about groundwater, including:

1. Water well and spring record search
2. Water well and spring location map service
3. Groundwater-quality data search
4. Graphical groundwater-quality comparison service
5. Groundwater-quality data map service
6. Karst potential index map service
7. KGS water research home page

Counties across the United States are also implementing their own groundwater policies. For example, in 2001, the King County (WA) Council created the Groundwater Protection Program to provide management, policy, and technical expertise to help protect the quality and quantity of the groundwater resources in the county. One objective of the program is to help local communities identify groundwater protection needs and to integrate groundwater issues with other local planning efforts, such as growth management plans. King County uses an interactive map that enables visitors to select and query groundwater information through Web-based maps and geographically based software.

3.13.3 Data at the National Level

Data about groundwater has been collected in the United States for decades. One responsibility of the USGS is to assess the quantity and quality of the nation's water supplies. The National Water-Quality Assessment Program was developed by the USGS in 1991 to determine the condition of our nation's streams, rivers, and groundwater. NWIS contains water data for the nation. USGS has offices around the country, which collect local data and conduct studies in a particular area as part of NWIS. The groundwater database contains records from about 850,000 wells, and data have been collected for more than 100 years. Measurements are commonly recorded at 5- to 60-minute intervals and transmitted to the NWIS database every 1 to 4 hours.

The Ground-Water Database includes more than 850,000 records of wells, springs, test holes, tunnels, drains, and excavations. Each well location includes information such as latitude and longitude, well depth, and aquifer. This information is available online through USGS's NWISWeb Interface (http://nwis.waterdata.usgs.gov/nwis). The Regional Aquifer-System Analysis Program was initiated in 1977 as a response to droughts during that year. Computer models were used to develop estimates of current and future water availability for aquifers and provide a baseline for future studies.

The Ground Water Atlas of the United States, developed by the USGS, includes the location and the hydrologic and geologic characteristics of the principal aquifers throughout the 50 states, Puerto Rico, and the U.S. Virgin Islands. It consists of an introductory chapter and 13 descriptive chapters, each covering a multistate region. The atlas is useful for providing information in a regional and national context but not for design or planning projects. The data provided is useful for landscape architects working on regional planning projects.

USGS also has geospatial information on aquifers and other water resources for use with GIS programs. The GIS data include information on:

- Aquifers
- Dams
- Groundwater climate response network
- Hydrologic units
- Surface water sampling sites
- Stream-flow stations
- Water use
- General hydrography data

Groundwater maps primarily are defined using geologic contacts and hydrogeologic divides. Groundwater maps typically use USGS topographic maps as a base and include significant natural and man-made features, such as roads, streams and rivers, lakes, and buildings. These maps are generated from well log and drilling reports, bedrock information, and geologic and hydrogeologic data.

3.13.4 Groundwater Modeling

Landscape architects need to understand the basic fundamentals of groundwater modeling to know what these models show and how we should use the information. A groundwater model represents a simplified version of the processes and characteristics of a groundwater system. Only recently have scientists developed modeling techniques for estimating the amount of groundwater stored underground. Groundwater models can be used in all phases of the design and planning process.

The first step in the modeling process is to construct a conceptual model that describes the groundwater system. This model can be used to understand the extent of a groundwater system. The next step is to take this description and express it mathematically. The two models contain the same information, but the mathematical model expresses the information as a set of equations. The ability to measure specific parameters of a groundwater system via mathematical models means that changes that occur can be calculated.

Analytical models can be used to evaluate the physical characteristics of a groundwater system. These types of models can be used to better understand the impact that design and planning decisions have on the groundwater. The real key to effective analytical models is to ensure there are sufficient data to predict accurately what will happen in a given situation. Different sets of simplifying assumptions will result in different model results. At a master plan level, groundwater modeling helps us understand where to plan for green spaces to help protect and recharge aquifers.

If the United States plans on continuing to promote sustainability, this country needs to take a holistic view of freshwater that recognizes that surface water and groundwater are connected and should be treated as a single resource.

Many of the digital tools used to model groundwater have been developed over the years by the United States Geological Survey. Most modules for groundwater modeling can be downloaded free of charge (http://water.usgs.gov/software/lists/groundwater), but many of these programs were written in the FORTRAN computer language and are not user friendly. Fortunately, many of the newer modeling programs have graphic interfaces that make them much easier to use. MODFLOW, developed by the USGS, is currently the most widely used numerical model for analyzing groundwater flow problems in the country. Flow from wells, recharge zones, evapotranspiration, drains, and riverbeds and creeks can be simulated. MODFLOW-2005 can be used to address such issues as water availability

and sustainability, interaction of groundwater and surface water, seawater intrusion, and remediation of contaminated groundwater. ModelMuse is a graphical interface for MODFLOW-2005.

WhAEM 2000 is a groundwater flow model designed to delineate zones and map protection areas. The program was developed by EPA and is used to support many of EPA's water planning and management initiatives. Pulse is used to estimate groundwater recharge and discharge, while STRMDEPL08 is used to calculate stream-flow depletion from wells. The Department of Defense's Groundwater Modeling System (GMS) is one of the most sophisticated groundwater modeling programs available. It is a comprehensive software package for developing computer simulations of groundwater problems. It provides tools for every phase of a groundwater simulation, including site characterization, model development, postprocessing, calibration, and visualization. The current version of GMS provides an interface for popular programs such as MODFLOW, MODPATH, MT3D, RT3D, FEMWATER, and SEEP2D.

The GMS interface is separated into several modules, which contain tools that allow manipulation and model creation from different data types. Of these, the Map module provides a suite of tools that are probably of most interest to landscape architects. The Risk Analysis Wizard is another tool that should be beneficial to landscape architects. It is used to quantify the risk of a contaminant exceeding critical levels in groundwater or the risk of a capture zone. Many groundwater models are starting to incorporate Geographic Information Systems data since the technology helps create more accurate and robust models, and GMS can use GIS or computer-assisted design data.

3.14 WATER OUTREACH EFFORTS

The more people understand the issues involved with water resources, the better prepared they will be to make the best decisions to ensure that the most sustainable solutions are employed. At the federal, state, and local level, water resource agencies and organizations have introduced outreach efforts to inform the public about sustainable water solutions.

EPA maintains a Web site called *Surf Your Watershed* (www.epa.gov/surf) that allows individuals to find the watershed where they live as well as information about that watershed. Input your county name, zip code, or city, and the site will return an 8-digit HUC identifying your local watershed. Clicking on the link will provide access to an Environmental Profile that includes maps, total maximum daily loads and impaired water bodies, restoration efforts, toxic releases and Superfund sites, and links to USGS water data for your watershed.

The Florida Water Star certification program was initiated by the state in 2006. It is a voluntary certification program for new and existing homes that encourages water efficiency in household appliances, plumbing fixtures, irrigation systems, and landscapes in new home construction.

Many organizations, cities, and water districts produce brochures on water conservation, water-wise landscaping, and designing and maintaining irrigation systems and distribute them to the public. Some also offers a speaker's bureau to coordinate water conservation presentations to community groups.

The St. Johns River Water District, which includes northeast Florida, provides information to school and community groups and at seminars, exhibits, and other community events. Specific district education programs include Project WET (Water Education for Teachers), WaterWays, the district's Watershed Action Volunteer Program, and a Water Conservation Public Awareness Campaign that has been highly successful in generating public awareness (http://sjr.state.fl.us/waterprotectsustain/index.html).

The Great Water Odyssey is an interactive, multidisciplinary, computer-animated educational software program that introduces elementary school students to water resource and conservation issues. The program was also developed by the St. Johns River Water District with the assistance of a panel of award-winning educators and experts from the fields of science and water management.

The Florida Lake Management Society is a 501(c)(3) nonprofit organization that promotes, protects, enhances, conserves, restores, and manages Florida's aquatic resources. It also serves as a forum for education and information exchange and advocates environmentally sound and economically feasible lake and aquatic resource management in the state. The society has created a cost-sharing program called "Love Your Lake" that funds lake, pond, and shoreline demonstration projects (http://flms.net).

Florida Water StarSM provides criteria to improve a home's water efficiency both indoors and outdoors. A Florida Water StarSM-certified home could reduce outdoor water use by 40% or more and indoor water use by 20% or more. If only 500 homes were built to Florida Water StarSM standards and saved 95,000 gallons each, 47.5 million gallons of water would be saved every year (http://sjr.state.fl.us/waterprotectsustain/index.html).

Michigan Council of Governments published *Opportunities for Water Resource Protection in Local Plans, Ordinances and Programs: A Workbook for Local Governments*, as a guide for local communities to protect water resources (www.semcog.org/PrinterFriendly.aspx?id=498).The workbook provides checklists that guide users through the process of establishing a water resource protection program, and it covers a wide range of topics, including land conservation, erosion and sediment control, public education, and pollution prevention.

The Environmental Protection Agency launched its WaterSense program in 2007 to help consumers and businesses identify products that meet the program's water-efficiency and performance criteria. EPA estimates that the average household could save more than 11,000 gallons of water by installing more efficient utilities (www.epa.gov/watersense).

Watershed Plan Builder is another EPA tool designed to help users produce a customized outline of their watershed. The tool walks users through a series of pages where you can input information about your watershed. The resulting customized outline can then be used to develop a watershed management plan (EPA, 2008).

EPA's *Handbook for Developing Watershed Plans to Restore and Protect Our Waters* (2008) is intended to help communities, watershed organizations, and state, local, tribal, and federal environmental agencies develop and implement watershed plans to meet water quality standards and protect water resources. The handbook is more specific than most other guides in terms of quantifying existing pollutant loads, developing estimates of the load reductions for water quality standards, developing management measures, and tracking progress.

3.14.1 Demonstration Projects

Many communities implement demonstration projects that highlight stormwater management alternatives. These projects are intended to let the public know how their tax dollars are being spent. Demonstration projects also are a great way to help people understand what they can expect from master plans in the long run.

Most demonstration retrofits are sized to treat the water quality volume and introduce new stormwater technologies. Well-designed and highly visible demonstration retrofits are a good tactic to garner greater support to finance more widespread retrofitting efforts in the future.

Austin, Texas Outreach

Austin's watershed outreach and education programs are unique and diverse, ranging from Earth-wise gardening to school and community programs. Outreach activities are specifically aimed at empowering people to adopt practices and change behaviors to reduce stormwater pollution problems. The city has successfully targeted education efforts to reach specific audiences and demographic groups. For example, stormwater outreach efforts include school and camp programs, a watershed Web site, bilingual maps and brochures, storm drain marking, watershed cleanups, citizen monitoring, and a xeriscaping program. The city provides convenient access to services that enable residents to become good watershed stewards, such as hazardous waste and recycling drop-off sites, regular yard waste collection, pet waste collection stations, discounted compost, and used oil collection. In addition, the programs are regularly evaluated and adapted to reach the greatest number of people (www.ci.austin.tx.us/watershed/).

Smart Watershed Program

In Maryland, the Center for Watershed Protection has developed the Smart Watershed program. Education is an important part of the program since it increases public awareness about important behaviors that produce or reduce stormwater pollution. Recent experience has shown that carefully targeted campaigns can be very effective in changing watershed behaviors. Community programs are also the most direct conduit to services that make it easier for residents to practice better watershed stewardship on their own patch of ground. Public involvement is critical to enlist long-term support for local watershed restoration efforts. Early public involvement in the planning process can provide important feedback on restoration goals and priorities. Communities that establish a positive relationship with residents during each step of the restoration planning process can gain support for project and program funding (Rowe and Schueler, 2006).

The Smart Watershed benchmarking tool comes with a detailed questionnaire to measure activity and integration with municipal watershed restoration programs. Points are awarded based on answers to 56 individual benchmark questions with a total of 100 points possible. Communities that exceed the national average level of restoration activity in a program area can earn 15 extra credit points.

3.15 CASE STUDIES

Lake Okeechobee, Florida

Lake Okeechobee is a critical water resource for South Florida. It is one of the largest lakes in the United States, having a surface area of 730 square miles and a drainage basin covers more than 4,600 square miles, and is a key component of the Kissimmee-Okeechobee-Everglades ecosystem. Lake Okeechobee is the headwaters of the Everglades, and the health of this entire ecosystem is dependent on the water quality in the lake. The lake provides habitat for a wide variety of migratory waterfowl, wading birds, and wildlife. The lake is also a source of drinking water for the region and is used for irrigation water for the Everglades Agricultural Area. (See Figures 3.20 and 3.21.)

With the settlement of South Florida, the demands on the water from Lake Okeechobee increased significantly. In an effort to tame Mother Nature, the Herbert Hoover Dike was constructed in the early 1900s. The earthen dike system is about 140 miles in length and has numerous water control structures to provide flood protection, navigation, recreation, freshwater for the communities of South Florida, water for agriculture, prevention of saltwater intrusion, and enhancement of environmental resources. The dike has certainly helped grow the region, but this growth has also increased demands on Lake Okeechobee. As a result the overall health of the lake has declined over the years.

Conflicts

Discussions about how to divide water between environmental needs and South Florida's agriculture and communities can quickly become heated. Agricultural representatives warned the district that Lake Okeechobee water rights must be protected to keep growers south of the lake in business (Reid, 2008). Communities in the area are experiencing severe water shortages, and they argue that the highest priority should be for drinking water. (See Figure 3.22.)

Lake water is directed into the Caloosahatchee River to help protect Florida's west coast fishing grounds and drinking water supplies by keeping out saltwater.

Environmentalists are adamant that the water from Lake Okeechobee should be used to maintain existing ecosystems. Sixteen species known to occur in the vicinity of Lake Okeechobee currently are listed as threatened or endangered by the U.S. Fish and Wildlife Service.

Preserving water for fish and wildlife in the Kissimmee River is important, but that could have effects on supplies for the Everglades. The Kissimmee River was straightened and channeled in the 1960s for flood control, and reshaping the river and restoring its marshes returns water flows to the Everglades (Reid, 2008).

Recent droughts in the Southeast have increased the debate. One big issue in the region is that the Corps has been keeping Lake Okeechobee at a foot lower than normal because of concerns for the existing dike. Apparently,

Figure 3.20 *Lake Okeechobee is often referred to as the heart of South Florida's regional water management system. At its capacity, the lake holds 1 trillion gallons of water and varies in depth from 1 to 13 feet. Image courtesy USGS.*

Figure 3.21 *Lake Okeechobee is so large that it is clearly defined in this satellite image of South Florida. Image courtesy USGS.*

Figure 3.22 *There are a lot of competing uses for Lake Okeechobee, including boaters and sailors who want to take advantage of the warm weather and crystal blue waters. The U.S. Army Corps of Engineers manages five boat ramps along the Okeechobee Waterway: the St. Lucie South Recreation Area, Ortona North Recreation Area, W.P. Franklin South Recreation Area, W.P. Franklin North Campground, and Port Mayaca. Image courtesy U.S. Army Corps of Engineers.*

when Lake Okeechobee reaches high water levels, the dike system leaks, and the risk of dike failure increases significantly. At a time when there is such a shortage of water, though, intentionally keeping the lake level lower is a source of irritation for many water users in the region.

Planning Efforts

A number of planning efforts strive to restore the lake and its watershed. The Florida State legislature passed the Lake Okeechobee Protection Act (LOPA) during the year 2000 session. LOPA takes a watershed-based approach to restoring and protecting the lake, and its overall objective is to help meet state water quality standards by reducing the total phosphorus total maximum daily load (TMDL). In 2007, the Florida Legislature expanded the Lake Okeechobee Protection Act to restore and preserve the lake's watershed and the Caloosahatchee and St. Lucie estuaries.

Since 2000, Florida has invested more than $70 million to improve farming practices, construct wetlands, and implement phosphorus reduction technologies. In 2005, the state initiated a comprehensive plan to accelerate restoration and recovery of Lake Okeechobee. The $200 million the Lake Okeechobee and Estuary Recovery project focused on expanding water storage areas, constructing treatment marshes, and expediting environmental management initiatives to enhance the ecological health of the lake and downstream coastal estuaries (Reppen, 2005). The idea was that the plan would reduce pollution and better manage the flow of water while meeting our flood control and water supply responsibilities.

The goal of the Comprehensive Everglades Restoration Plan is to capture freshwater and redirect it to critical areas, with most of the water being used for environmental restoration. The $8 billion project includes the implementation of several watershed improvement projects as well as the construction of aquifer storage and recovery wells.

The Lake Okeechobee Watershed Construction Project Phase II Technical Plan is a requirement of the Northern Everglades and Estuaries Protection Program. It identifies facilities to achieve Lake Okeechobee TMDL, provides measures to increase water storage and reduce excess water levels, and identifies storage goals to achieve desired lake levels and inflow volumes to estuaries while meeting other water related needs. To meet water quality objectives, the plan recommends utilizing 42,000 acres for treatment wetlands, implementing 1.7 million acres for agricultural best management practices, and utilizing innovative "green" nutrient control technologies.

In 2008, the South Florida Water Management District proposed guidelines to protect water resources in the Kissimmee River and in Lake Okeechobee. The district proposes to keep water in the newly restored Kissimmee River marshes off-limits to farms and growing communities, and that has upset a lot of people in the agricultural industry (Reid, 2008).

The one given is that planning efforts for Lake Okeechobee and its watershed will continue to explore options for improving farming practices, strengthening permitting criteria for new development, implementing growth management incentives, reducing pollution, and improving water quality.

Client: South Florida Water Management District, www.sfwmd.gov.

Louisiana's Comprehensive Master Plan for a Sustainable Coast

Louisiana's Comprehensive Master Plan for a Sustainable Coast seeks to incorporate hurricane protection projects with those that focus on rebuilding coastal wetlands within the state. The master plan serves as the guide for all coastal restoration and hurricane protection efforts in the state. The document states: "We must begin creating a sustainable

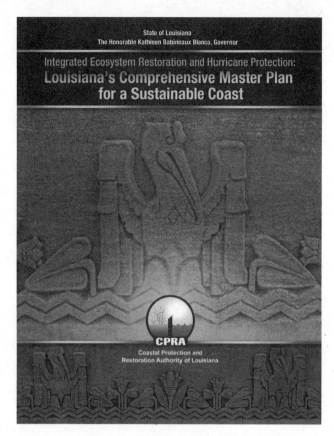

State of Louisiana
The Honorable Kathleen Babineaux Blanco, Governor

Integrated Ecosystem Restoration and Hurricane Protection:
Louisiana's Comprehensive Master Plan for a Sustainable Coast

CPRA
Coastal Protection and
Restoration Authority of Louisiana

Figure 3.23 *Louisiana's Comprehensive Master Plan for a Sustainable Coast provides guidance for the state as it decides how best to protect existing water resources. Image courtesy Louisiana Coastal Protection and Restoration Authority.*

coast without delay, using methods that we know can work, while also field testing new concepts and learning as we go. Given the magnitude of the task at hand, a stepwise process based on sound science and engineering is the only way forward."

Louisiana's Comprehensive Master Plan for a Sustainable Coast was initiated in November 2005, when the state legislature enacted a law creating the Coastal Protection and Restoration Authority (CPRA). The CPRA was mandated to coordinate efforts to achieve long-term, comprehensive coastal protection and restoration.

(See Figure 3.23.) The goals of the master plan, as outlined by CPRA, were to:

• Present a conceptual vision for a sustainable coast.

• Be a living document that changes over time as our understanding of the landscape improves and technical advances are made.

• Emphasize sustainability of ecosystems, flood protection, and communities.

• Integrate flood control projects and coastal restoration initiatives to help both human and natural communities thrive over the long term.

• Be clear about what we don't know.

Measures in the Plan

The measures contained in the plan can be broken down into three categories.

1. **Restoring sustainability to the Mississippi River Delta.** The master plan stresses the need for reconnecting the Mississippi River to the wetlands by restoring the flow of water through the wetlands. Among the objectives of this approach are: implementing land building and sustaining diversions; restoring marshlands by using dredged material; stabilizing and restoring shoreline barriers; and closing the Mississippi River Gulf outlet.

2. **Restoring sustainability to the Atchafalaya River Delta and Chenier Plain.** The master plan emphasizes the importance of the Atchafalaya River Delta, which is the only region of coastal Louisiana that is building land naturally. The plan also recommends the creation of a freshwater and sediment plan for the Chenier Plain. In the plain, navigation channels and canals have allowed saltwater to penetrate inland, destroying fragile marshes and impinging on freshwater lakes. The plan offers alternatives for managing river and surface freshwater supplies to ensure the availability of freshwater.

3. **Hurricane protection.** Hurricane protection is important to protect the communities in southern Louisiana. The master plan contains a series of recommended hurricane protection and coastal restoration measures, and offers strategies for implementing these measures. In the fall of 2005, Hurricanes Katrina and Rita had battered the Louisiana coast, destroying approximately 200 square miles of marsh, damaging over 200,000 homes, killing 1,400 Louisianans, and displacing more than 1 million more. The impact on the state's economic base was significant.

The hurricane measures included both structural and nonstructural alternatives. The master plan specifically states that all hurricane protection structures must be built and maintained in such a way that the natural ecosystem remains functional. Levees or some other form of flood control structure are recommended for areas with high flood and storm surge risk. These areas include Lake Pontchartrain, Barataria Basin and West Bank, Plaquemines Parish, Terrebonne Parish and Atchafalaya Delta, LA 1 Highway Corridor, Acadiana, and Chenier Plain.

One major concern with building levees is that they may result in the loss of wetlands along the Louisiana coast. According to the U.S. Geological Survey, Louisiana loses about 35 of its 4,600 square miles of wetlands every year. Another option is to use nonstructural measures to reduce the risk of flooding. Restoration and nonstructural measures can reduce the risk from storm surge in parts of Louisiana that have a lower level of risk.

Integrating the Plan

The master plan is intended to provide guidance and continuity for other planning efforts within the state. Changes in laws and policies are required in order to implement all of the recommendations in the plan. The plan also recommends that a coastal assessment group and an applied coastal engineering and science program be implemented as part of the state's management structure.

Key principles of the plan are being included in other plans, including Louisiana Recovery Authority's Louisiana Speaks, the state's annual plan, Ecosystem Restoration and Hurricane Protection in Coastal Louisiana. and the U.S. Army Corps of Engineers' Louisiana Coastal Protection and Restoration Report.

Implementation of the Master Plan

The state is undergoing a number of projects that incorporate the principles from the master plan. On August 1, 2008, Louisiana Governor Bobby Jindal announced plans to invest more than $1 billion in coastal protection and restoration projects in the state. Another $15 billion is being invested in New Orleans and other areas for coastal restoration and hurricane protection projects. The projects focus on strengthening the existing levee system as well as restoring wetlands and coastal areas that serve as natural hurricane barriers.

According to the U.S. Army Corps of Engineers, it spends about $200 million each year to dredge navigation channels in Louisiana. Traditionally, the sediment has been dumped into the deep waters of the Gulf of Mexico, but a better approach would be to use the sediment to restore coastal areas. A sediment pipeline is being proposed to help restore wetlands and barrier islands in Plaquemines, Jefferson, and Lafourche parishes. The project is expected to cost about $37 million to construct.

For shoreline restoration of Caminada Headlands and Barataria Basin to provide a buffer against storm surges, $70 million has been allocated. The barrier islands function as the first line of protection against hurricanes and act as a speed bump for storm surge and wave energy, so protecting and restoring these islands is important.

Client: State of Louisiana.
"Environmental News Service," 2008, www.lacpra.org/.

2002 Olympic Village

Barcelona, Spain

The 2000 Olympic Games, which were held in Sydney, Australia, are often referred to as Australia's Green Games. The Olympic Park was constructed on a 1,581-acre site that was initially intended for a major urban renewal project for Homebush Bay. Homebush Bay is a suburb of western Sydney located about 16 kilometers west of the central business district. Much of the original site was an industrial brownfield that had been used for a variety of military and industrial activities. Part of the site had even housed one of Sydney's trash dumps. (See Figure 3.24.)

The Olympic Village is part of a 90-hectare development called Newington, which is near Homebush Bay. The Olympic Village is located on the northwest part of the Olympic Park. The initial goal of the Olympic Village was to provide temporary housing for more than 15,000 athletes. That is no trivial task. After completion of the Sydney Olympics and the Paralympic Games, which occurred two years later, the idea was to sell the residential properties to the public and transform the village into a vibrant community that was a part of Newington. (See Figure 3.25.)

The village consisted of residential precincts, a retail center, a business park, adjoining wetlands, and a nature reserve. Energy is conserved by using natural ventilation, efficient zoning systems, renewable energy, solar power, photovoltaic panels, and two gas cogeneration engines that are more environmentally friendly than traditional electricity. This development allowed the village to make the transition from a public to a private development. The long-term plan is that the village will become home to 16,500 residents, and another 24,500 workers and students will commute to the site each day.

The idea behind the Olympic Village was to utilize known technology in an environmentally friendly and sustainable way instead of developing new technologies. One of the benefits of this approach is that it enabled the village to serve as an example for other communities to follow. Development of the village showed that it was possible to be environmentally sustainable, and to do so in a way that is also economically and commercially viable.

Figure 3.24 *A series of walkways and trails connect the Olympic Village to passive recreation opportunities along the wetlands and nature preserve. Image courtesy EDAW.*

Sustainable Planning Approaches for Water Resources

Figure 3.25 *Over the years, the vegetation has grown around the former Olympic Village, creating a parklike setting. The housing units were converted to private use after the end of the Olympics. Image courtesy EDAW.*

Figure 3.26 *Constructed wetlands are used to capture and filter stormwater runoff from the Olympic Park. Image courtesy EDAW.*

Water is reclaimed, managed, and reused across the entire Olympic site. There were a number of efforts to utilize water effectively. A dual water supply system was used for the Olympic Village. Although this approach was commonplace in other parts of the world, including the United States, it was very new for Australia. Water for human uses is supplied through one set of pipes, and recycled stormwater and sewage effluent runs through a second set of pipes.

There were efforts to minimize the use of stormwater drains and instead to take a more natural approach to stormwater management. Runoff from residential areas and parklands are also filtered and then directed into the wetlands. Water is then put back into a filtration station and treated a second time, then used by the City of Newington for residential and commercial uses, and for parks and open space. (See Figures 3.26 and 3.27.)

Figure 3.27 *The housing units in the Olympic Village stair-step down the hill to take advantage of natural ventilation and southern exposure and to offer views of the wetlands and nature preserve. Image courtesy EDAW.*

Water-efficient toilets, showers, and valves were used, as were rainwater harvesting systems and native plants and drip irrigation systems. Efforts were also made to reduce waste by working with existing buildings, incorporating recycled material into construction, and building with recycled materials. As much as 90% of the hard waste was recycled on-site. Most of the temporary facilities built for the Olympics will be reused rather than torn down.

Client: International Olympic Committee
Landscape Architects for the Olympic Village: EDAW

Landscape Architects for the Olympic Park:
Peter Walker and Partners, USA
Hassell,
Bruce Mackenzie Design
Hargreaves Associates, USA
Martha Schwartz, USA
Clouston
Scahaffer and Barnsley
EDAW
Denton Corker Marshall
Johnson Pilton Walker

Ducks Unlimited

Parts of the United States

Ducks Unlimited (DU) was founded in 1937, when a small group of conservationists got together to raise money for waterfowl conservation. DU's mission is to conserve, restore, and manage wetlands and associated habitats for North America's waterfowl, and over the years it has conserved more than 11.6 million acres of waterfowl habitat.

DU is the world's largest private waterfowl and wetlands conservation organization, with more than 1 million supporters. The original founders were waterfowl hunters, and today 90% of DU members are hunters. In 2008, DU raised $261 million, and 88% of that was utilized for conservation. (See Figure 3.28.)

The group has conservation projects throughout the United States, Canada, and Mexico, and in parts of Latin America and the Caribbean. The Level 1 Conservation Priorities for DU include the Prairie Pothole Region, Western Boreal

Figure 3.28 *Ducks Unlimited has had a significant impact on preserving wetlands and enhancing wildlife habitat over the years. Image courtesy Ducks Unlimited.*

More than 20% of the Boreal Forest is comprised of wetlands, and these, combined with thousands of lakes, make this region critical breeding, staging, and molting habitat for many waterfowl and waterbirds. In recent years the wetlands have started to be impacted by environmental pressures, including forest management; agriculture; climate change; hydroelectric development; and oil, gas, and mineral extraction. DU's current activities focus on land cover inventory and mapping, waterfowl surveys, wetland/waterfowl productivity research, and hydrologic/wetland risk mapping. (See Figure 3.30.)

Central Valley/Coastal California. California's Central Valley is considered to be one of the most important and threatened waterfowl habitats in North America. The area extends from Bodega Bay south to northern Mexico, and includes San Francisco Bay, San Diego Bay, and the Salton Sea. One issue is uncertainty about the availability of sufficient water for the wetlands in the region. DU has completed or is working on more than 1,500 projects in the Central Valley and the adjacent San Francisco Bay area, and has been involved with restoring more than 60,000 acres of wetlands and in protecting another 56,800 acres.

Gulf Coastal Prairie. The Gulf Coast Prairie includes an area from the Mississippi–Louisiana state line and extends to the mouth of the Rio Grande River. The marshes and bays along the Gulf of Mexico were once among the most productive wetland systems in North America, but these areas have been significantly impacted over the years, primarily because of increased development, agricultural uses, and construction of levees and other flood control measures.

Mississippi Alluvial Valley. The Mississippi Alluvial Valley consists of the floodplains and valley of the lower Mississippi River and includes parts of Louisiana, Mississippi, Arkansas, Tennessee, Kentucky, Illinois, and Missouri. These states have lost over 20 million acres, or 57%, of their wetlands over the years.

Forest, Central Valley/Coastal California, Gulf Coastal Prairie, and Mississippi Alluvial Valley.

Prairie Pothole Region. The Prairie Pothole Region includes parts of five states: North Dakota, South Dakota, Iowa, Minnesota, and Montana. It also includes the Canadian provinces of Alberta, British Columbia, Manitoba, and Saskatchewan. The region includes more than 100,000 square miles of what was formerly a mixture of tallgrass prairie, mixed grass prairie, shortgrass habitat, and thousands of wetlands dispersed throughout the region. More than half of the potholes have been drained and converted to agriculture, and the impact on migratory waterfowl and other wildlife has been significant. Researchers estimate that nearly 194,000 acres of native grasslands have disappeared in the region since 1984. The habitat provided by the wetlands supports more than 50% of North America's migratory waterfowl. (See Figure 3.29.)

Western Boreal Forest. The Western Boreal Forest in Canada is the world's largest land-based ecosystem.

Conservation Methods

Ducks Unlimited utilizes a wide array of methods to conserve wetlands and valuable habitat for North American

Figure 3.29 *The Prairie Pothole Region is one of the regions where Ducks Unlimited is involved with restoration projects. Image courtesy Ducks Unlimited.*

Figure 3.30 *The Western Boreal Forest consists of an extensive number of wetlands. Image courtesy Ducks Unlimited.*

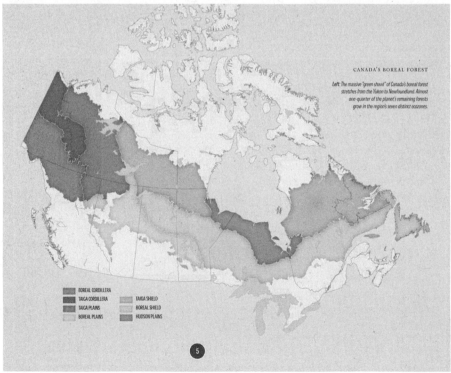

waterfowl. One of the most effective tools is the Wetland Reserve Program (WRP), which gives DU, the U.S. Department of Agriculture (USDA), private landowners, and other program partners the ability to restore, manage, and conserve wetlands across the nation. The WRP is a voluntary, incentive-based conservation program authorized by the Farm Bill. The primary intent of WRP is to provide financial and technical assistance to landowners who want to restore and protect wetlands on their property. According to the USDA, more than 1, 275,000 acres of wetlands and associated habitats have been conserved as a result of WRP. A landowner sells or leases a conservation easement to the government that protects the wetlands from development. The landowner retains ownership of the land.

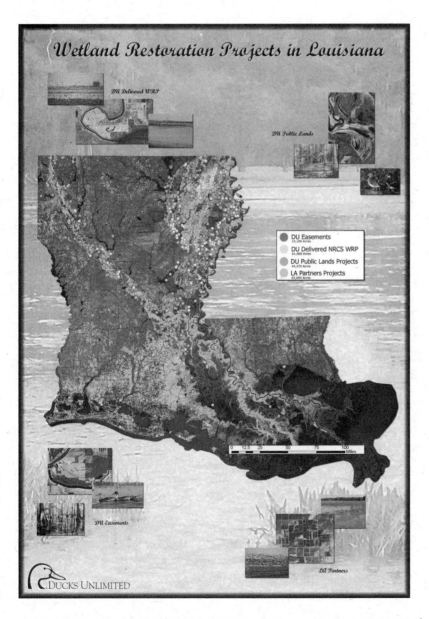

Figure 3.31 *This map shows Duck Unlimited's restoration projects in Louisiana. Image courtesy Ducks Unlimited.*

The Natural Resources Conservation Service manages WRP, and it has a goal of restoring 250,000 acres annually. In the last couple of years there have been more landowners interested in participating in the program than there are funds available. In the Mississippi Alluvial Valley alone, the WRP has conserved and restored over 400,000 acres of land.

Innovative Funding

One thing that makes Ducks Unlimited so effective at what it does is the innovative approaches it takes to preserving and protecting wetlands.

Virtually all of DU's projects are done in cooperation with a number of partners, including state and federal agencies, private corporations and foundations, and individuals. These partners work together to provide the cost-share funding needed for wetland conservation. In some situations, DU purchases property in order to restore habitat and then sells or donates the property to an organization or agency to manage the site.

There is also a new market where landowners can supply environmental credits that can be sold in a voluntary trading market to meet conservation practice requirements on their land. These types of trading programs have been used for environmental issues such as greenhouse gas emissions, water quality, and mitigation banking.

Ducks Unlimited has been an active support of the North American Wetlands Conservation Act (NAWCA), which provides challenge grants for wetlands conservation projects in the United States, Canada, and Mexico. The money provided through NAWCA requires a local match, and DU has played a major role in providing the funding for this match. NAWCA and DU signed an agreement on May 8, 2007, to collaborate on promoting the preservation, restoration, and management of wetlands. (See Figure 3.31.)

Ducks Unlimited signed a memorandum of understanding with the U.S. Fish and Wildlife Service that expanded DU's historic partnership with the federal duck stamp program. This program is important, because since 1934, the federal duck stamp program has raised more than $700 million, money that has been used to conserve more than 5.2 million acres of migratory bird habitat across the United States.

Client: Ducks Unlimited

Saint Paul on the Mississippi Design Center Best Management Practice Cards

The Saint Paul on the Mississippi Design Center is a multi-agency, multidisciplinary team that seeks to improve the quality of life in the city. The center received a grant from the McKnight Foundation to focus on expanding water quality capacity in the area.

The Design Center is a program of the Saint Paul Riverfront Corporation, and it has four objectives:

1. Provide stormwater design expertise
2. Increase Design Center staff capacity
3. Develop a stormwater best practices manual
4. Organize and present the material at a seminar

The Design Center wanted to find a way to let the public know about water resources. It developed a series of water quality Method Cards, intended to guide various best management practices (BMPs) specific to Saint Paul at four development scales: individual, block, neighborhood, and citywide. The center decided to use the cards because most existing water quality manuals were cumbersome and difficult to use.

1. **Block.** At this scale, BMPs focus primarily on the best ways to capture and treat stormwater. Space is limited, so solutions typically are fairly small and straightforward.

2. **Site.** At a site scale, emphasis is on small-scale projects that seek to manage stormwater runoff. These types of BMPs can include rainwater harvesting, reducing surface runoff, and other small, affordable solutions.

3. **Neighborhood.** There are more opportunities to implement a wider range of BMPs at the neighborhood scale because more space is available. Neighborhood BMPs may be constructed in parks, utility easements, street rights-of-way, urban plazas, or other public spaces. New developments have an opportunity to implement BMPs in a holistic, integrated approach that can be a very effective way to manage water resources.

4. **City.** BMPs at the city scale typically utilize citywide initiatives, programs, maintenance activities, and resources.

The BMP cards are intended to be used at the beginning of the design process in order to explore which stormwater management approaches would be most appropriate for a given project. One of the benefits of using cards instead of a typical book or manual is that the cards can be unbound, sorted, or prioritized.

Obviously some BMPs are better suited for specific problems than others. The BMPs in the Method Cards generally can be classified as meeting one of these outcomes:

- Prevent pollution
- Filter pollutants from runoff
- Promote biological processes
- Control soil erosion and sedimentation
- Slow peak discharge
- Promote infiltration into groundwater
- Reduce water temperature

Client: City of Saint Paul, Minnesota

Consultant: SRF Consulting Group, Inc.

A free copy of the *Water Quality Manual* is available by e-mailing marroquin@riverfrontcorporation.com.

Orange County Water District

Orange County, California

The Orange County Water District (OCWD) was formed in 1933 to protect Orange County's rights to water in the Santa Ana River. OCWD's primary responsibility is to manage the groundwater basin under northern and central Orange County. This groundwater is used by more than 20 cities and water agencies serving more than 2.3 million county residents.

The Santa Ana River Watershed is southern California's largest watershed, covering more than 153 square miles. There are about 40 groundwater basins in the watershed, with Orange County being one of the largest. The Santa Ana River Watershed has a long, rich agricultural history, but in recent years expanding industrial and commercial uses and a growing population have increased demands for water. The watershed has one of the fastest-growing populations in the state, and is expected to be home to more than 10 million people by 2050. It is estimated that approximately 2.1 million acre-feet (687 billion gallons) of water will be needed to meet demands. Southern California usually receives fewer than 11 inches of precipitation a year, so there is little natural perennial surface water in the Santa Ana watershed.

Most of the needs have to be met via groundwater resources. In 1936, OCWD began purchasing portions of the Santa Ana River channel for recharge. Over the years, this recharge system has been expanded, and it now includes more than two dozen facilities that cover over 1,000 acres.

Groundwater Management

Protecting groundwater is the highest priority for the OCWD. OCWD monitors the groundwater taken out each year to ensure that the basin is not overdrawn, refills the basin, and is in charge of implementing programs.

The district estimates that it saves approximately $16 million to $19 million a year by collecting stormwater and recharging it into the basin. River water is routed through a series of constructed wetland ponds to reduce nitrate levels. Within OCWD property and adjacent lands are approximately 465 acres of constructed wetlands, consisting of a system of 50 shallow ponds. The ponds are most effective during the summer months because of the warmer temperatures. These ponds currently remove around 20 tons of nitrates per month.

OCWD has made a number of infrastructure improvements, including inflatable rubber dams on the Santa Ana River, pumping stations, pipelines, valves, flow meters, water level sensors, and a computerized control system. To create a more water-efficient natural habitat, OCWD is removing invasive nonnative grasses. OCWD has also implemented a water resources management system (WRMS), which integrates geographic information and groundwater management systems. Data are collected from more than 3,500 wells throughout the basin, and that information is used to make better decisions about water resources.

OCWD has one of the most sophisticated groundwater protection programs in the country, and its Groundwater Replenishment (GWR) System is the world's largest water purification project of its kind. The GWR System produces enough near-distilled-quality water for 500,000 people. The system processes treated sewer water, achieves near-distilled-water quality, and then puts the water back into the groundwater basin. Seventy-five percent of the recharge operations use gravity instead of pumping stations. Over the years, more than $178 million in regional, state, and federal grants and subsidies has been invested in the GWR System.

The GWR System uses two filtration processes to treat the water: microfiltration and reverse osmosis. Microfiltration is used to remove small suspended particles, bacteria, and other materials out of the water. Reverse osmosis forces water through several sheets of thin plastic membranes to filter out minerals and contaminants. Microfiltration typically is used as a first pass to process the water, and reverse osmosis provides a greater level of treatment. The water produced by the GWR process is so clear that when it is mixed with existing groundwater, it actually lowers the overall mineral content of the county's water.

The treated water from the GWR System is injected into an expanded underground seawater intrusion barrier along the coast. One of the big advantages of the GWR System is that it provides a source of water that is not susceptible to drought. (See Figures 3.32, 3.33, and 3.34.)

Figure 3.32 *One of the Orange County Water District's responsibility is to monitor groundwater in the area. This map shows the groundwater levels as of November 2004. Image courtesy OCWD.*

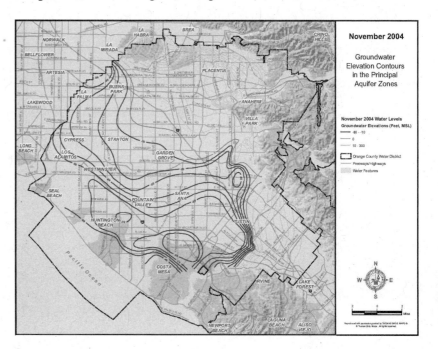

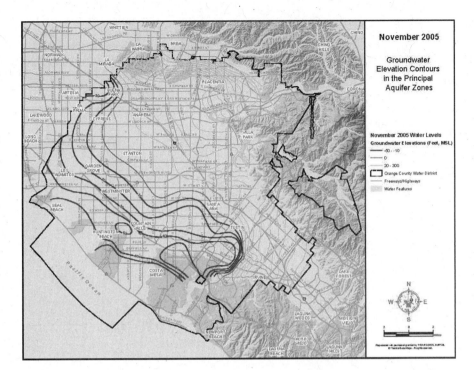

Figure 3.33 *This map shows the groundwater levels in November 2005. Image courtesy OCWD.*

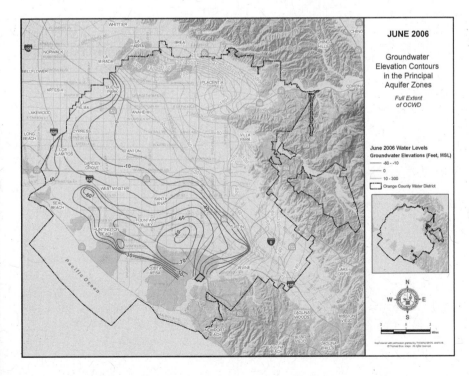

Figure 3.34 *This map shows the groundwater levels in June 2006. Image courtesy OCWD.*

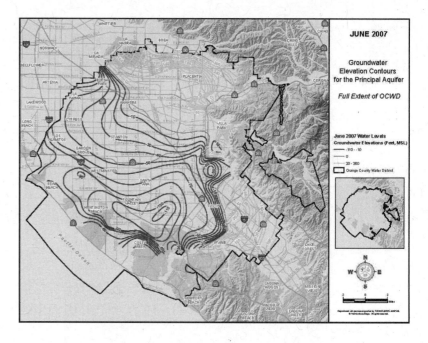

Figure 3.35 *This map shows the groundwater levels in June 2007. Image courtesy OCWD.*

Research

OCWD's groundwater protection policy includes water quality monitoring, cleanup of contaminants, regulatory agency support, toxic residuals removal, and hazardous waste management. Ongoing research seeks to find more efficient ways to manage these water resources. The OCWD has a Research and Development Department that focuses on three primary research areas: water reclamation, groundwater recharge, and microbial water quality. A number of programs focus on each area.

The Advanced Water Quality Assurance Laboratory, which was completed in Spring 2009, houses enough researchers and equipment to analyze 18,000 water samples each year. OCWD uses more than 700 wells with a total of over 1,400 sampling points to take the water samples. The samples are monitored and analyzed for more than 330 constituents, which greatly exceeds the 122 required by regulatory agencies.

The OCWD is exploring groundwater management and water quality activities, such as expanding the wetlands above the Prado Dam, analyzing the effectiveness of different groundwater treatment techniques, and enhancing the conservation of endangered or threatened species. The Green Acres Project is a water recycling effort that provides reclaimed water for landscape irrigation at parks, schools, and golf courses as well as for industrial uses, such as carpet dying. The project has the capacity to purify 7.5 million gallons of reclaimed water per day.

Environmental concerns are also a concern in the basin. More than 100 species of wildlife are found on district lands, and OCWD is working to preserve natural habitat in these areas.

Recognition

OCWD has a reputation of being an international leader in groundwater management, seawater intrusion barriers, and water reuse and purification. This reputation is well earned. The Environmental Protection Agency (EPA) awarded the district its 2008 Clean Water State Revolving Fund "Pisces" award, which showcases projects that advance clean and safe water through exceptional planning, management, and financing. The district also received the 2008 Stockholm Industry Water Award, 2008 U.S. EPA Water Efficiency Leader Award, Water Agency of the Year from the International Desalination Association, and Water Agency of the Year from WaterReuse Association.

Client: Orange County, California

The Oregon Garden

Silverton, Oregon

The Oregon Garden is a perfect example of the expression "form follows function." In the mid-1990s, the Oregon Association of Nurseryman (OAN) was looking for a site to build a botanical garden that would highlight the native plant material grown in the state. (See Figure 3.36.) About that same time, the city of Silverton was having problems associated with its wastewater system. The city failed to meet its National Pollutant Discharge Elimination System permit requirements for treated wastewater, and Silver Creek was listed on the state's 303(d) list of water bodies not meeting water quality standards.

Instead of purchasing land to create wastewater wetlands to treat the water, the city of Silverton worked out an agreement with the OAN to construct the wetlands as part of the botanical garden. The city provided $5 million toward the purchase of the land, and in exchange, it located its wastewater wetlands on the site. The wetlands were originally intended to mitigate wetlands destroyed in the development of an industrial project, but that project did not move forward.

The master plan for the garden was developed in 1996 through a collaborative design process with landscape architects and architects leading the effort. Groundbreaking for the site was in June 1997, and since then the gardens have been built one piece at a time. More than two dozen designers have been involved with various projects over

Figure 3.36 *The Oregon Garden is a joint effort between the Oregon Association of Nurseryman and the city of Silverton. Image courtesy OAN.*

Figure 3.37 *The Japanese Garden is one of the highlights of the garden. Image courtesy OAN.*

the years, and the results have been spectacular. Oregon Garden is now a world-class public botanical garden that attracts more than 200,000 visitors a year. (See Figure 3.37.) It includes more than 20 specialty gardens and features, including a pet-friendly garden, visitor center, sensory garden, rose garden, 400-year old Signature Oak, a children's garden, a grass amphitheater for events and concerts, and four major water features, including a waterfall and a water garden.

Wetlands

The 240-acre site has several distinct ecosystems, including wastewater wetlands, oak woodland, mixed conifer/deciduous forest, and an upland prairie. During the summer months, about 700,000 to 800,000 gallons a day run through a series of three terraces that make up the wetlands, which provide a natural filtration system for the recycled water. There are 16 shallow ponds in the upper terrace,

and when these are full, the water flows into a large pond at the second terrace level. The lower terraces consist of eight large, deep ponds that serve as the final filter. The wetlands are not regulated as a treatment process, but they do lower temperature and nutrient load.

The wetlands are a little over 17 acres in size, and they are used to treat the city of Silverton's wastewater. (See Figure 3.38.) Once the wastewater is treated, nutrients are removed, and the temperature is reduced, the water is sent back into the watershed. Approximately 42 acres of the garden's plant collections are irrigated by treated wastewater. A holding tank is used to capture some of the water so it can be used for the irrigation system. Original plans were to use the treated water for the freshwater fountains, but restrictions have prevented that from happening so far.

One issue was that the water collected from the city's wastewater system did not match the garden's irrigation needs because there is too much flow in the spring and fall

Figure 3.38 *Water is an integral part of the Oregon Garden. Image courtesy Wikipedia.*

Figure 3.39 *One goal of the Oregon Garden is to become a major research center, with a focus on sustainability. Image courtesy Wikipedia.*

and not enough in the summer, when irrigation demands are the highest. Another problem is that the wetlands do not go dry in the summer like natural wetlands. Instead, they stay wet year-round. Among other things, this has led to an explosion in the local bullfrog population. Perhaps frog-gigging (a popular sport in Kentucky) would be something worth looking into.

A-Mazing Water Garden and Gordon House

Landscape architect Carol Mayer-Reed designed the A-Mazing Water Garden, a one-acre garden near the entrance to the garden that includes an 80-foot-long water wall and a display of colorful ornamental aquatic plants. Visitors explore bog gardens and other plantings along the water's edge by walking through a maze of small pathways. The lowest pond features water lilies, lotus, iris, cannas, and rushes. The A-Mazing Water Garden—yes, that is really its official name—is a separate water feature, not connected to the constructed wetlands. A floating wetland has been

added to the garden in order to enhance the role that plant roots play in filtering the water.

The Gordon House was designed by architect Frank Lloyd Wright in 1957 and is the only building he designed in the state. In 2001, the house was donated to the Oregon Garden and moved to its current site. The house was restored and dedicated as a public museum in March 2002. It is currently the only Wright-designed building in the Pacific Northwest open to the public.

Research Focus

The Oregon Garden wants to become an international research center for sustainability. One area of research the garden is interested in is how to improve the functionality of replacement wetlands. (See Figure 3.39.) One of the biggest reasons that these types of wetlands fail is because plant material is not properly established, and invasive grasses and weeds have a tendency to take over. To aid in research endeavors, the Sustainable Plant Research and Outreach (SPROUT) Center, located in the Oregon Garden, focuses on promoting the garden's mission through environmental education and research on environmental sustainability. SPROUT's stated mission is to develop the use of plants and plant material for environmental sustainability purposes, through the development of new techniques, new plants, and new propagation methods. SPROUT's larger purpose is to make Oregon an international center for the research and development of plants for environmental purposes.

"The Silverton Oregon Garden: Explore a Garden Oasis Located Near Silver Creek Falls," http://oregon-travel.suite101.com/article.cfm/the_oregon_garden#ixzz0Au3KkcPl.

Yolanda Wilson, "Oregon Garden—A Lesson in Sustainability," September 9, 2008. http://vanveenbulbs.blogspot.com/2008/09/oregon-garden-lesson-in-sustainability.html.

GO TO 2040 and Northeastern Illinois Regional Water Supply/Demand Plan

The Chicago Metropolitan Agency for Planning (CMAP) is the official regional planning organization for seven northeastern Illinois counties that includes the metropolitan Chicago area. One of CMAP's responsibilities is to develop a comprehensive regional planning for the area, which is expected to have up to 2.8 million new residents by 2040. To fulfill this mission, CMAP developed GO TO 2040. The purpose of this plan is to provide better transportation, increased economic development, cleaner air and water, more-accessible jobs and housing, and other quality-of-life improvements in the seven-county region.

A six step process was utilized to develop the GO TO 2040 plan.

- Step 1. Develop a regional vision
- Step 2. Understand existing conditions
- Step 3. Evaluate potential planning strategies
- Step 4. Develop a preferred future scenario
- Step 5. Choose major capital projects
- Step 6. Communicate final plan

This process took two years to complete and was highlighted by extensive research, analysis, and public input. The result is a preferred Regional Scenario that clearly defines policy directions to guide growth in the region. The GO TO 2040 plan was approved in June 2008 by the Board of CMAP, and the final plan is expected to be implemented in October 2010

Recommendations of the plan include the following:

- Creating more livable communities with compact, mixed-use development

- Investing more effectively in education and work-force development, while fostering a business climate that encourages job growth and private sector innovation

- Improving the region's system of parks and open space and reducing consumption of energy and water.

- Planning multi-modally for transportation and target transportation investments to achieve outcomes such as economic growth, environmental protection, or congestion reduction, while finding more sustainable ways to finance infrastructure improvements.

- Tracking the region's performance to assess where to make improvements

If the preferred Regional Scenario becomes reality, it is expected to improve quality of light in the region. The environment will be healthier, the economy will be stronger, infrastructure will be more effective, and the region will be a better place to live and work. The preferred Regional Scenario offers specific recommendations that

Figure 3.40 *The Preferred Regional Scenario was one of the products of the GO TO 2040 PLAN.*

Figure 3.41 *A variety of options were used to give the public an opportunity to participate in the planning process.*

Figure 3.42 *The Northeastern Illinois Water Supply/Demand Plan is expected to help manage water resources for the Chicago metropolitan area.*

Northeastern Illinois
Regional Water
Supply/Demand Plan

L O O K I N G   O U T   T O   2 0 5 0

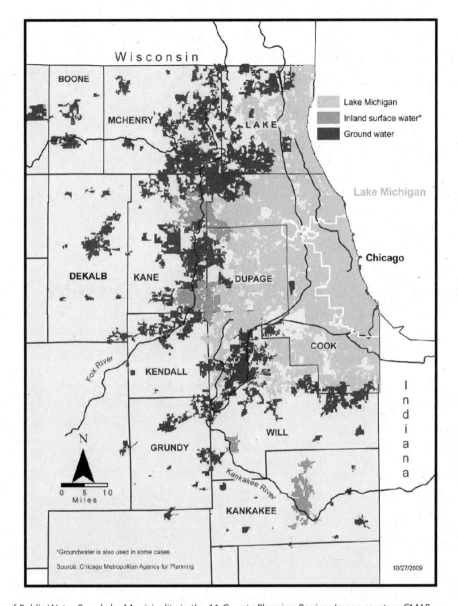

Figure 3.43 *Source of Public Water Supply by Municipality in the 11 County Planning Region. Image courtesy CMAP.*

are intended to address areas of concern, including: including: land use and housing, energy/water conservation, food systems, open space, transit improvement, freight, transportation finance, education/workforce, economic innovation, tax policy, data sharing and transparency, and coordination between federal, state, and local programs.

Northeastern Illinois Regional Water Supply/Demand Plan

One of the major issues to be addressed in the Chicago metropolitan area is water. You might assume that the Chicago area has plenty of water because of its proximity to Lake Michigan, but the state is limited by a U.S. Supreme

Court Consent Decree that restricts the amount of water that can be pulled from the lake. There is concern that the rapid growth in the area and limited available water could lead to severe shortages in the near future.

To address water resource issues, the Northeastern Illinois Water Supply/Demand Plan was developed. The plan was developed with funding from the Illinois Department of Natural Resources (IDNR) and is coordinated by CMAP. The plan was approved in early 2010 the Regional Water Supply Planning Group, which oversees 11 counties in northeastern Illinois, and it is intended to ensure that clean water will be available in the region for both household and commercial uses in the future.

One major focus of the plan is to emphasize conservation measures, reuse water, and improve how water is managed.

Programs as ambitious as GO TO 2040 and the Northeastern Illinois Water Supply/Demand Plan take years to implement, and difficult choices have to be made in order to meet the goals. It will also take years before the plan is fully implemented, and it will have to be tweaked and updated along the way.

Client: Chicago Metropolitan Agency for Planning (CMAP)
www.cmap.illinois.gov

Singapore Deep Tunnel Sewerage System

Public Utilities Board (PUB) of Singapore is nearing completion on its Deep Tunnel Sewerage System (DTSS), which is considered one of the most innovative and visionary water projects in the world. The DTSS is considered to be a major step toward ensuring the long-term sustainability of Singapore's water resources. It is designed to collect, treat, and reclaim used water.

PUB is a statutory board under the Ministry of the Environment and Water Resources and is the water agency that manages Singapore's water supply, water catchment, and sewerage. PUB promotes water conservation, keeping water catchments and waterways clean, and taking a sustainable approach to water resources.

Like many other major cities, Singapore has had to come up with solutions for its waste problems. The city decided the best approach was to replace the nation's entire sanitary sewer system with one designed to meet its needs for the next 100 years. What makes the DTSS so unique is that it is a complete conversion to a new infrastructure.

Singapore has been aggressively pursuing innovative approaches in part because it has to. The size of the island, the lack of available land, and continued growth means that traditional approaches do not work there. The basic concept for the DTSS was developed in the late 1990s when Singapore began asking serious questions about how it was going to develop a comprehensive wastewater system. All of Singapore is on a sewer system. That is one of the benefits of the island being the size that it is.

The DTSS uses cross-island deep tunnels to intercept all wastewater and convey it by gravity to two new centralized water reclamation plants. The DTSS is expected to have a total cost of approximately $3.65 billion.

DTSS

Singapore's Deep Tunnel Sewerage System has been described as a superhighway for managing water resources. It includes four major components:

1. **Link sewers** that intercept flows from existing sewers, pumping stations, and water reclamation plants. Wastewater is collected in sewers and conveyed to the main deep tunnel sewer.

2. **Deep tunnel sewers** that convey flows by gravity to the two centralized water reclamation plants at the two ends of Singapore.

3. **Water reclamation plants** that provide a high standard of treatment prior to discharging the treated effluent via the outfalls.

4. **Outfalls** that convey treated effluent for deep-sea discharge via diffusers.

Figure 3.44 *The Singapore Deep Tunnel Sewerage System utilizes cutting-edge technology to address the city's sanitary sewer problems. This image shows one of the two large tunnels that are each more than 80 kilometers (30 miles) long and up to 6.5 meters (7 yards) in size. Image courtesy Public Utilities Board of Singapore.*

The DTSS was constructed in two phases, with construction starting in 2000. Phase One of the DTSS was completed in 2008 and comprises a 48-kilometer-long (30-mile) deep tunnel, a centralized water reclamation plant, a network of link sewers, and a deep-sea outfall. The water from the tunnels is directed to the centralized water reclamation plant in Changi. Phase One cost approximately $2.5 billion and involved 49 main contractors and consultants and more than 300 subcontractors and suppliers. The second phase, which is expected to start in 2012, will consist of a deep tunnel to a water reclamation plant in Tuas that includes a sea outfall into the Straits of Singapore. This phase also will include additional link sewers and an extension to the Changi water reclamation plant. (See Figure 3.44.)

The project consists of two large tunnels that have a total length of 80 kilometers (49 miles), and smaller sewers that are a total of 170 kilometers (106 miles) in length. The treatment system uses gravity to convey wastewater through the deep water tunnel. This eliminates the need for pumping stations and reduces the chance for sewage overflows.

The large tunnels have diameters up to 6.5 meters (21 feet) and are located 50 meters (164 feet) below the surface. The route of the tunnels was selected in order to minimize the impact on existing structures. In many cases, the tunnels follow major expressways. Eight earth pressure balance tunnel-boring machines were used concurrently to dig the 48 kilometers (30 miles) of deep tunnels.

Changi

The Changi Water Reclamation Plant is a state-of-the-art used water plant capable of treating 800,000 cubic meters (176 million gallons) of used water a day. The treated water is then discharged into the sea through deep-sea outfalls or channeled to the Changi NEWater factory for further purification into NEWater, Singapore's own brand of highly purified reclaimed water. Much of the plant is built underground, and it requires less than a third of the area needed for a conventional plant. Singapore's prime minister officially opened the Changi water reclamation plant on June 23, 2009.

One big benefit of the DTSS approach is that it does not take much space. Singapore has only about 700 square kilometers (1730 acres) of land, so land is at a premium. A benefit of the DTSS is that old pumping stations and wastewater treatment plants will be decommissioned, and this will free up much-needed land for future development. Since the mid-1940s, Singapore has expanded its land area by filling in shallow coastal areas. The DTSS offers a better, more environmentally friendly way to obtain usable land. More than 290 hectares (717 acres) of land will be freed up for development as a result of DTSS.

The project has received numerous awards for its innovative approach to sewage management. DTSS Singapore's deep tunnel sewerage system was awarded Water Project of the Year at the Global Water Awards 2009. (The annual Global Water Awards is considered to be one of the most prestigious achievements in the global water industry.) Organizers of the Global Water Awards said, "Singapore's Deep Tunnel Sewerage System is a visionary project whose value will be appreciated well into the next century." The DTSS also received a Project Innovation Award in the Planning Projects category of the International Water Association, and Singapore's approach to reclaiming water received the Environmental Contribution of the Year award in 2008. PUB won the Stockholm Industry Water

Award in 2007, one of the highest accolades in the international water sector.

In the long run, this project will result in significant savings for Singapore. In the last 20 years, for example, the Singapore government has spent $2 billion on sewerage infrastructure alone. The new sewerage system will also improve the water quality across the island as well as in the straits of Johor and Singapore.

Project Engineers: CH2M Hill and Parsons Brinckerhoff

General Contractors: Lum Chang Building Contractors Pte. Ltd.;

Koh Brothers Building and Civil Engineering Contractor Pte. Ltd.;

Sembcorp Engineers and Constructors Pte Ltd.;

Keppel Engineering Pte., Ltd.; and

United Engineers Ltd./Voltas

Cowichan Basin Water Management Plan

Vancouver Island, Canada

The Cowichan River Basin includes a 307-square-mile area located on the southern end of Vancouver Island in British Columbia, Canada. The Cowichan River is known for its rich biological diversity and is considered to be one of the finest trout-fishing streams in the province. (See Figure 3.45.) The Cowichan River is a designated Heritage River and is important for cultural First Nations, recreational, and commercial fisheries.

The basin provides important habitat to major runs of Chinook, Coho, and chum salmon. Because water levels in the Cowichan River are low, the salmon population is threatened.

The Cowichan Basin Water Management Plan was initiated in December 2005 and was completed in March 2007. It was intended to help ensure there is enough water for both people and the environment. There are serious conflicts over water use in the basin, with fewer water resources available to meet the needs of the growing population as well as demands for other clean water supplies. The management plan is a regional initiative that attempts to balance costs and benefits and to ensure that community, ecological, and economic values are protected.

Focus of Plan

One of the major questions was how to balance the use of water for salmon resources, economic activities, drinking water supplies, water quality, and recreational interests.

Most water for agricultural irrigation and domestic supplies come from groundwater sources, and withdrawals from the existing system exceed inflow during the summer. In recent years, extended drought has caused water levels to fall, and that has had a negative impact on salmon and trout populations, recreation and tourism, treatment for sewage effluent discharges, and water availability for local businesses. The anticipated population growth in the province will put an even greater burden on the already threatened water resources in the basin. (See Figure 3.46.)

The Water Management Plan focuses on five objectives. The plan:

1. Identifies current water consumption and supply issues.

2. Identifies trends that may influence future water supply and demand.

3. Identifies management alternatives for meeting current and future water needs.

4. Recommends best strategies and operational methods in response to identified issues.

5. Recommends an implementation plan.

The Water Management Plan is intended to meet water demands for a 1:20-year drought, meaning that there is sufficient water to fulfill requirements for 19 out of 20 years on average. To meet this criterion, the basin needs a total of 110 million cubic meters of water; this will require an additional 50 million cubic meters of storage. Five alternatives were

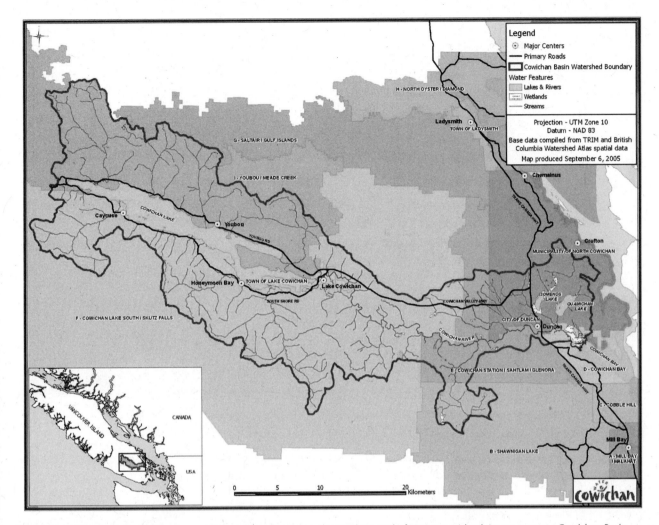

Figure 3.45 *The Cowichan Basin covers a 307-square-mile area on the southern end of Vancouver Island. Image courtesy Cowichan Basin Water Advisory Council.*

compared to each other and to a base-case scenario using a multiple accounts evaluation, an analysis method that uses both quantitative and qualitative indicators.

Improvements

The Cowichan Basin Water Management Plan recommends a wide range of soft and hard infrastructure approaches to managing water resources. The plan recommends the installation of water meters that allow individuals, businesses, and industry to monitor their water consumption.

It also recommends demand-side management tools and pricing signals to improve availability of water supplies. Metering provides valuable data collection that can be used to help develop water resource policies.

One of the most pressing problems is to balance supply and demand for water, especially in the summer months. Catalyst Paper is the primary water license holder on Cowichan Lake. The company employs approximately 1,000 people and makes a very significant contribution to the local economy. Catalyst Paper has implemented water conservation and monitoring programs in recent years, and

Figure 3.46 *The Water Management provides information about how water resources are interlinked. Image courtesy Cowichan Basin Water Advisory Council.*

in 2003, the mill began using seawater, instead of river water, for effluent cooling at the treatment plant.

The Water Management Plan calls for improvements to the way existing weirs along the river are managed. A weir and control gates were built in 1957 and 1965 to ensure an adequate summer and fall supply of water for the paper mill. When lake levels drop in the spring, the weir's control gates are gradually closed to keep the lake level up. When lake levels are high, "pulses" of water are released in early fall for the Chinook salmon migration.

Moving Forward

Funding for the project will come from grants, in-kind contributions, and potentially water user fees. There is also a possibility that property taxes will be used to cover some of the costs of water management.

The management plan has strong support from the public because of an extensive public participation process. A 26-member Water Management Forum represented the community of users in the basin. Some of the agencies involved in the process include the Cowichan Valley Regional District, Fisheries and Oceans Canada, British Columbia Ministry of Environment, Catalyst Paper Corporation, Pacific Salmon Commission, and the Cowichan Tribes. The final plan has been adopted by the local, provincial, and regional governments, First Nations, and industry.

One result of the Water Management Plan is the creation of the Cowichan Basin Water Advisory Council, a multi-party organization that works with all of the stakeholders in the basin in order to achieve plan goals. The council is in charge of implementing the Water Management Plan. The council is also involved with exploring ways to pay for water management. As part of the plan, costs were estimated for major capital items and for demand management actions. Expectations are that a detailed capital and operating budget will be developed for different water management tasks.

Planners: Westland Resource Group Inc., Victoria, BC
Cowichan Basin Water Management Plan, www.cvrd.bc.ca/index.asp.

Hay Lake Project

Hay Lake, Arizona

In January 2000, the Hay Lake property was purchased by the U.S. Forest Service, becoming the largest wetland restoration project in Arizona history. The Hay Lake wetlands provide important waters for migratory birds and other local wildlife.

The Hay Lake complex is made up of five different lakes: Hay, Long, Tremaine, Soldiers, and Soldiers Lake Annex. The National Resource Conservation Service (NRCS) developed and restored the Hay Lake wetlands under a 30-year easement that covers approximately 1,517 acres. In addition to the NRCS, other organizations involved in the project include the Arizona Game and Fish Department, U.S. Forest Service, Grand Canyon Trust, Audubon Society, Coconino Rural Environmental Corps, and the Wildlife Society.

The project was funded through the Land and Water Conservation Fund (LWCF). The LWCF was established by Congress in 1965 and uses funds from offshore oil and gas leases for state and local conservation projects. The NRCS purchased the conservation easement for Hay Lake from a local sod farm, which has a water-sharing agreement that determines how the water is allocated.

The focus of restoration efforts has been on converting the land back to an ephemeral wetland ecosystem and reestablishing habitat for migratory birds and other wetland-dependent species. About half of the acreage serves as a buffer to the wetland.

The water delivery system in the area includes man-made irrigation ditches, natural channels, and a series of outlet structures that divert water primarily for irrigation uses. There is a minimal road network in the Hay Lake wetland easement to access different properties as well as the railroad in the area. The roads also needed to ensure that the channels in the area can be accessed when necessary.

The area is used primarily as wildlife habitat and for recreational uses. Traditionally there have not been enough areas designated specifically for wildlife viewing at Hay Lake. There is also a lack of interpretative opportunities.

Client: State of Arizona

Rio Salado Habitat Restoration Project

Phoenix, Arizona

The Rio Salado Habitat Restoration Project includes 595 acres along a five-mile stretch of the Salt River just south of downtown Phoenix (AZ). The goal of the project is to restore the native wetland and riparian habitats that were historically associated with the Salt River. The area was once a dumping ground and was considered an eyesore.

At one point the Salt River flowed year-round through what is now Phoenix, but disruptions associated with urban growth put an end to this.

The Rio Salado project seeks to balance water conservation and the use of water to sustain wildlife habitat. Original discussions about creating a park began more than 40 years ago, but projects of this scale sometimes take a while to implement. The project became a reality through the joint efforts of the Phoenix Parks and Recreation Department, the Army Corps of Engineers, and the Flood Control District of Maricopa County. (See Figure 3.47.)

The project includes a flood control feature, five miles of trails, and a wildlife habitat. There are future plans to develop an additional eight miles of Rio Salado downstream. The restoration includes the riparian areas, wetland areas, trees, native plantings, and desert grasslands. The project includes:

- 140 acres of mesquite Bosque habitat
- 43 acres of cottonwood/willow habitat
- 65 acres of lower Sonoran habitat (paloverde and mesquite association)
- 80 acres saltbush/quail bush/burro brush
- 51 acres of aquatic strand
- 200 acres of open space
- 16 acres of wetland marsh

Planting trees was a big part of the project, and native trees were grown from seeds and cuttings. Cottonwood-willow gallery forests occur along the lower elevation rivers of the Southwest, and large areas of cottonwood and willows are being restored along the lower terraces. Mesquite bosques are also another common southwestern riparian habitat, but most have been destroyed over the years, and it is now considered one of the rarest plant communities in the country.

Water for the vegetation and wetland areas within the project comes from five wells that pull water from underground aquifers. Much of the water that comes into the Rio Salado comes from stormwater runoff from nearby Phoenix city streets. Pumps, pipes, and canals were developed to help distribute water from the wells in the area. Small reservoirs on the site store water, which is then used to support vegetation along the banks of the river. Nearly 60% of the water used in the project returns to the aquifer.

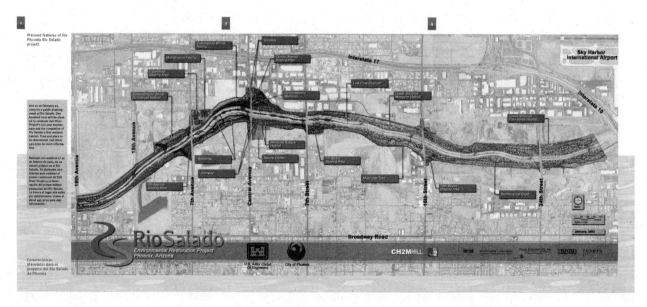

Figure 3.47 *The Rio Salado Habitat Restoration Plan is a green ribbon that follows the Salt River near downtown Phoenix. Image courtesy EDAW.*

Central Avenue includes a staging area that is used for educational activities provided by park personnel and volunteers. These activities include interpretive walks, birdwatching walks, bike rides, and arts and craft fairs. There are also plans to construct the Rio Salado Habitat Restoration Area headquarters and an Audubon Arizona Nature Center in this area. Other future features here include an equestrian staging area that also includes water treatment facilities. There is expected to be a strong focus on educational programs since this is an opportunity to let visitors learn more riparian systems.

A number of trails, seating areas, and trailheads have been developed, and they provide great access to the different ecosystems. Some trails are paved, while others are more informal. The area has become a birdwatchers' paradise, and it attracts a lot of visitors. More than 200 species of birds have been spotted along the various habitat areas.

The Rio Salado Habitat Restoration Area officially opened to the public in November 2005.

Client: City of Phoenix, Arizona

Jackson Bottom Wetlands Preserve

Hillsboro, Oregon

The Jackson Bottom Wetlands Preserve is a 725-acre wildlife preserve located in Hillsboro (OR), just west of the city of Portland. (See Figure 3.48.) Jackson Bottom consists of the lowland area with the floodplain of the Tualatin River, which meanders through the bottom area, and is between 40 to 60 feet wide in places. (See Figure 3.49.)

The city of Hillsboro, Oregon Department of Fish and Wildlife, U.S. Soil Conservation Service, and the Portland Audubon Society, among others, have worked together to preserve and enhance the natural resources of the area. Jackson Bottom Wetlands Preserve provides valuable habitat to a wide variety of wildlife, and the site is viewed as one of the city's most valuable resources. The preserve is the home of a wide array of wildlife, and restoration efforts have significantly improved the quality of the habitat. It is part of the Tualatin River wildlife corridor and the Pacific

Flyway, so it is a popular place for migrating birds and mammals.

Wetland Utilization

The Jackson Bottom Wetlands Preserve is recognized as one of the region's leaders in utilizing wetlands to improve the

Figure 3.49 *The Jackson Bottom Preserve is known worldwide for its rich floodplains and wetlands. Image courtesy Jackson Bottom Wetlands Preserve.*

Figure 3.48 *The Jackson Bottom Wetlands Preserve logo is used to help "brand" the Bottom. Image courtesy Jackson Bottom Wetlands Preserve.*

Figure 3.50 *This photograph shows a wetlands area after the flood waters of the previous winter have receded. Image courtesy Jackson Bottom Wetlands Preserve.*

quality of our water. One of the goals of the preserve was to create an exemplar of wetlands preservation and development that would serve as a model for other areas around the country. For example, experiments at Jackson Bottom have shown that wetlands serve an important function in the reduction of pollutants, such as phosphorus. Treated wastewater is used in a series of constructed wetlands and marsh enhancement projects to significantly improve both water quality and wildlife habitat.

After significant winter or spring rains, the Tualatin River typically overflows across the Jackson Bottom. The floodplain covers approximately 3,000 acres, so it will hold a lot of water. During the floods of January 2006, Jackson Bottom held over 10 billion gallons of water, and this greatly reduced flooding threats downriver. The wetlands at Jackson Bottom are able to accommodate the water, and the end result is good for the environment too. As the water slows down, sediment is dropped, and this helps bring in organic matter to the bottom area. (See Figure 3.50.)

One of the partners is the Unified Sewerage Agency, and a major goal of the preserve is to utilize the large amounts of water from the sewerage agency to maintain water levels in wetlands and ponds. The wetlands in the preserve are also used for biofiltration treatment of the wastewater.

The preserve has a wetlands monitoring system that is used to collect information on weather, water quality, habitat, and wildlife. Water quality monitoring probes measure several parameters, including temperature, pH, dissolved oxygen, electrical conductivity, turbidity, and water level. The data are used for environmental education and to help inform resource management decisions. Researchers and wetland experts from around the world come to the preserve to learn about how these types of water-related programs work. (See Figure 3.51.)

Improvements

In the 1970s, efforts were initiated to improve the wetlands and restore wildlife habitat. Much of the wetlands had been drained for agriculture and grazing. Over 170 acres of wetlands have been restored over the years, and there are plans for more improvements. A strategic plan for the preserve was completed in 2002, and it is used

Figure 3.51 *Camas plants, which hold a cultural significance to Native Americans in the region, are frequently found in Jackson Bottom. Image courtesy Jackson Bottom Wetlands Preserve.*

Figure 3.52 *This viewing shelter on the north end of the preserve provides opportunities to see parts of Jackson Bottom. Image courtesy Jackson Bottom Wetlands Preserve.*

to guide design, planning, and educational programming decisions.

The Jackson Bottom Wetlands Preserve has long been recognized as a leader in education, habitat restoration, and community partnerships, and it is a model that other communities have emulated. One of the most popular facilities on the preserve is the Wetlands Education Center, which offers a number of award-winning education programs. The 12,000-square-foot center was opened in September 2003. The preserve has on display the only rescued, genuine American Bald Eagle nest, a very popular exhibit. The center includes an exterior 3,000-square-foot deck that wraps around the building. (See Figures 3.52 and 3.53.)

Education programs focus on subjects related to wetlands, wildlife and education, and they attract thousands of people every year. Funding from the Governor's Watershed Enhancement Board was used to develop learning opportunities within the Preserve. The Oregon Legislature created the enhancement board to promote public awareness about the need for restoring watersheds.

One nice problem that the preserve has had is that the popularity of the educational programs has been more than the small staff and volunteers can handle. Most centers

Figure 3.53 *The Wetlands Education Center is a popular facility on the preserve. Image courtesy Jackson Bottom Wetlands Preserve.*

would like to have that kind of problem. The preserve used funding from the Hillsboro School District to hire a recreation program supervisor. This new position has enabled the preserve to provide more natural resource education classes.

Client: City of Hillsboro, Oregon
Jackson Bottom Preserve, www.jacksonbottom.org.

Raritan Basin Watershed Management Plan

North Central New Jersey

The Raritan Basin is located in north central New Jersey. The basin consists of a 1,100-square-mile area that includes 11 subwatersheds and is home to 1.2 million people. (See Figure 3.54.) The Raritan Basin Watershed Management Plan was developed by stakeholder participants from the Raritan River Basin. The New Jersey Water Supply Authority provided staff and project management services to the stakeholders, and funding was provided by the Water Supply Authority as well as the New Jersey Department of Environmental Protection (NJDEP).

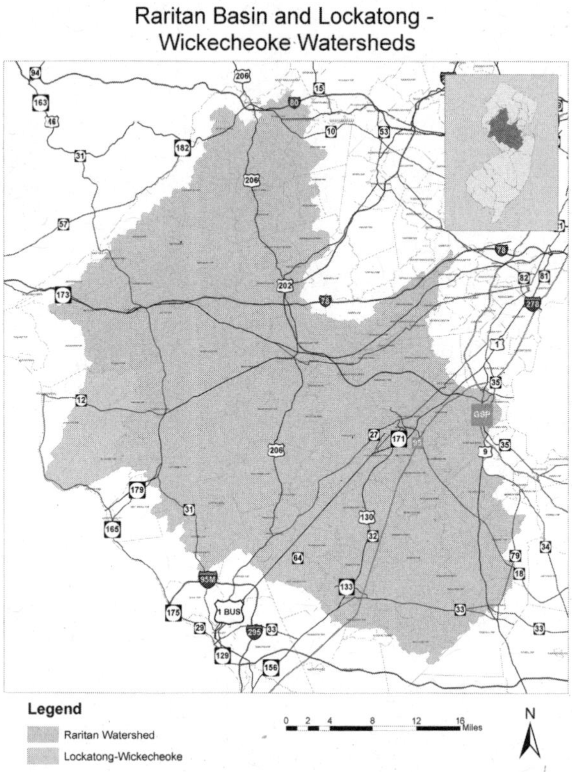

The Raritan Basin Watershed Management Plan currently focuses on stormwater management, pollutants from land runoff, wastewater treatment plants, development approaches, open space plans, and many other issues. There are a lot of competing uses for water within the basin. Some of the current uses include drinking water; irrigation water for farms, nurseries, and golf courses; water for industries; environmental requirements; and water for recreational activities, such as boating, fishing, and hiking. (See Figure 3.55.)

Six major issues were identified in the Raritan Basin. They are:

1. **Surface water pollution.** The two biggest problems are phosphorus and fecal coliform bacteria, primarily from nonpoint sources.

2. **Loss of riparian areas.** There have been significant losses of riparian areas within the basin. Most riparian losses initially were caused by agricultural uses, but many recent losses are due to increased development and urbanization.

Figure 3.54 *The Raritan Basin covers a 1,100-square-mile area in north central New Jersey. Image courtesy Raritan Basin Organization.*

Figure 3.55 *The Raritan Basin Watershed Management Plan is intended to help protect water resources in the region. Image courtesy Raritan Basin Organization.*

3. **Biological impairment of streams.** Studies from NJDEP and watershed associations indicate that the number of severely and moderately impaired streams has increased in recent years.

4. **Loss of groundwater recharge.** Studies show that there were significant losses in available water resources due to a loss of groundwater recharge. Two subwatersheds showed losses of over 20% in the last 10 years, and others showed losses between 15% and 20%.

5. **Water supply limitations.** There is a safe yield of approximately 225 million gallons per day from surface water and about half that from groundwater supplies.

6. **Stormwater impacts.** Much of the basin is urbanized, and one of the major impacts of urbanization on streams is disrupted stream hydrology. One problem is that stormwater has not been managed on a watershed basis.

Figure 3.56 *The Raritan Basin is home to a variety of land use patterns, with agriculture being one of the most common. Image courtesy Raritan Basin Organization.*

Major Components

The plan includes four major components: (1) a vision statement, (2) goals, (3) measurable objectives, and (4) implementation strategies.

The management plan recommends a number of major changes for the Raritan River Basin. These include:

- Protection and preservation of critical lands that protect water resources

- Maintenance and restoration of groundwater recharge

- Improved control of stormwater

- Management of water supply resources on a subwatershed, watershed, and regional basis

- Restoration of damaged streams and riparian areas, and protection of high-quality streams and riparian areas

- Restoration and protection of ground- and surface waters that are impaired by pollutant loads

The plan includes a number of recommendations for achieving these changes. One of the stated recommendations is to "establish and carry out a coordinated, watershed based, governmental and private sector effort to plan and implement restoration activities that will improve the function and quality of headwater streams." Another recommendation focuses on developing an integrated water budget system that includes both ground- and surface water. For water quality, recommendations focus on addressing both point source and nonpoint source discharges to treat key pollutants. The effectiveness of existing and proposed stormwater management systems needs to be improved to protect and restore watershed health through restored base flows and controlled storm flows.

The plan also identifies a series of "transformational" strategies that focus on making major changes within the basin. These types of changes occur over time, but the Raritan plan seeks to make these changes within a generation. These transformational changes have the potential to significantly alter the entire basin. (See Figure 3.56.)

Stakeholders and Partners

The Raritan Basin Watershed Management Plan is not a regulatory document; it requires voluntary actions at some level before it is implemented. It is important, then, for stakeholders in the basin to support the plan's recommendations. These stakeholders were actively involved in the development of the plan.

The plan emphasizes education, outreach, partnerships, and stakeholder involvement. The basic idea is to help address basin issues through increased training of teachers in existing programs, such as Project WET, New Jersey Audubon Society's WATERS curriculum, and programs offered by watershed associations.

To ensure that stakeholders stay involved in the planning process, the Raritan Basin Watershed Alliance was formed. Its mandate is to:

- Keep the Raritan plan current and continually improving—track progress, update, adapt, ensure that the strategies are scientifically defensible, and react to new circumstances, policy changes, and environmental conditions.

- Create public and official support for plan implementation.

- Create coalitions/partnerships for plan implementation, and assist with acquisition of financial and other resources where requested.

- Encourage and support implementation efforts and assist with project planning.

- Maintain and enhance technical knowledge and capabilities of the basin and ensure dissemination to those who need it.

- Do the above with the minimum resources necessary.

The plan received an award from New Jersey planning officials in May 2003.

Client: State of New Jersey

Norwalk River Watershed Initiative

Parts of Connecticut and New York

The Norwalk River Watershed is approximately 40,000 acres or 64.1 square miles. The watershed has a length of approximately 20 miles, and approximately 66,000 people live in it. It encompasses portions of six municipalities in Connecticut (New Canaan, Norwalk, Redding, Ridgefield, Weston, and Wilton) and one in New York (Lewisboro). The watershed is bounded by the Housatonic River watershed on the north and east, the Hudson River watershed on the west, and Long Island Sound on the south. It is defined by three main drainages: the Norwalk River, Comstock Brook, and the Silvermine River. It includes the Norwalk inner harbor and the area extending to the mouth of the Norwalk River.

In 1997, federal, state, and local government agencies, environmental groups, and concerned citizens formed the Norwalk River Watershed Initiative (NRWI) to address degradation of water resources and to promote water quality recovery. The NRWI developed the Norwalk River Watershed Action Plan, which describes specific objectives and action items for four key issues: (1) habitat restoration; (2) land use, flood protection, and open space; (3) water quality; and (4) stewardship and education.

One purpose of the NRWI was to build local capacity to protect and restore the Norwalk River Watershed. Another was to integrate recommendations in the Long Island Sound *Comprehensive Conservation and Management Plan* into local land use planning and regulatory programs.

Two-thirds of the households in the watershed obtain their water from public water supply systems, and the rest get water from private wells. Fifty-six percent of the homes in the watershed use public sewage disposal systems. Most of the private septic systems are in rural and suburban areas.

The Norwalk River Watershed Action Plan includes action items for restoring habitat for fish and wildlife, for addressing flood-prone areas, and for restoring water quality. Some recent projects that focused on improving water quality include the removal of invasive vegetation, dam removals, and stream bank restoration. More than 6,000 linear feet of stream corridor in the watershed has been restored over the years. Structural habitat enhancements, such as conifer tree revetments, stream bank soil bioengineering, instream and bank-placed boulders, and large woody debris and rock deflectors, were installed.

To address the issues of habitat loss, the Norwalk River Watershed Association, cooperating partners, and volunteers have been working on a number of habitat restoration projects.

The NRWI developed an outreach program to educate residents about the watershed. There is also a 20-person advisory committee that provides leadership for implementation of the action plan. To encourage private landowners within the watershed to address water resource issues, a watershed improvement loan is available to those wanting to make specific improvements on their land.

Client: Norwalk River Watershed Association, Inc.

Restoration Planning Process for the Gulf Coast

On August 29, 2005, Hurricane Katrina slammed into the Gulf of Mexico. (See Figure 3.57.) At landfall, it had winds of 140 miles per hour and a storm surge of more than 30 feet, and it affected an area that covered 108,000 square miles. (See Figure 3.58.) When levees and floodwalls failed, parts of New Orleans were inundated with more than 20 feet of water. By the time it dissipated, Hurricane Katrina had left a million people without homes, jobs, or schools, and resulted in more than $250 billion in damage. A few weeks later, Hurricanes Rita and Wilma also ripped through the area. By late December, the Federal Emergency Management Agency had taken 2,530,657 claims from hurricane victims seeking financial help. (Steiner, Faga, Sipes, and Yaro, 2006).

On September 15, the president pledged to rebuild the Gulf Coast and do whatever it took to bring back New Orleans and southern Louisiana. Before rebuilding, there were a lot of questions that needed to be addressed.

Some of these questions included the following:

- Do we strengthen the levee system and build more levees, focus on restoring barrier islands and wetlands, or perhaps both?

- Can we design new communities that can withstand the impacts of hurricanes while still protecting our natural resources?

- Do we need to stop development along all or part of the Gulf Coast?

- How do we protect and restore the natural resources in the region?

Understanding the Problem

A number of issues associated with the Gulf Coast needed to be addressed before rebuilding. More than 10 million people currently live in coastal counties along the Gulf of Mexico—3.5 times the population that was there in the 1950s. Barrier islands, marshes, and wetlands once served as buffers that absorbed the impact of high winds and storm surges, but over the past 50 years, more than 900,000 acres of coastal land have been lost. Louisiana's 3 million acres of wetlands have borne the brunt of human activity, population increases, and natural processes for decades. (See Figure 3.59.)

Sediment carried by the Mississippi River historically has been deposited at the mouth of the river, creating a complex system of deltas. The Mississippi has been straightened, tributaries have been dammed and channels dredged, wetlands have been filled, areas that were originally part of the floodplain have been cut off, and hundreds of miles of levees, dikes, and pumps have been built in the region

Figure 3.57 *Hurricane Katrina slammed into the Gulf Coast on August 29, 2005. This Category 4 hurricane caused severe destruction along the Gulf Coast from central Florida to Texas, mostly due to storm surge. Image courtesy NOAA.*

Figure 3.58 *It affected an area that covered 108,000 square miles. Image courtesy FEMA.*

Figure 3.59 *This map shows all major hurricanes that have hit the Gulf Coast since 1851. Image courtesy EDAW.*

to accommodate development. Collectively these systems have changed the natural flow of water.

The Gulf Coast has been battered by major hurricanes for as long as human beings have lived there, and the results have been devastating. Katrina is just one example. As a result of environmental damage and land loss, the Gulf Coast is more exposed, and minor storms that had little impact 20 years ago cause significant flooding today. Unless development patterns along the Gulf Coast change, this trend is going to continue, and future damages will continue to set records for level of destruction.

Modeling Sustainability

Being able to determine which areas are most likely to be impacted by hurricanes, storm surges, flooding, and other natural disasters will assist decision makers in preparing for and minimizing their impacts. EDAW worked with the National Consortium to Map Ecological Constraints to develop a Sustainability Analysis Model that can be used to map environmentally sensitive areas of the Gulf Coast region and to classify potential risks associated with natural disasters. This model, which takes a holistic approach founded on the idea of sustainable resilience, provides guidance for today's rebuilding and tomorrow's land development (Steiner et al., 2006).

EDAW's Sustainability Analysis Model integrates and expands the work being done from the Environmental

Protection Agency (EPA), FEMA, National Hurricane Center (NHC), National Oceanic and Atmospheric Administration (NOAA), NOAA Coastal Services Center, and Coastal Data Development Center. Among the factors being addressed in the process are historic hurricane tracks, high-wind risk areas, storm surges, flooding, significant flooding events, rise in sea elevation, loss of wetlands, marshes, and barrier islands, economic impacts, demographic vulnerability, and growth patterns. By combining these factors into one comprehensive model, the resulting analysis can be used to create public and private sector policies that reduce impacts from future hurricanes and severe storms. (See Figure 3.60.)

Models for Evaluating Impacts. With all of the available data, the key is to assess the data and determine how it should influence decisions about rebuilding the Gulf Coast. By using computer-based modeling procedures that utilize the best available data, we can help ensure that design and planning decisions have a strong scientific foundation. Landscape architects can integrate several modeling programs into the design process.

Wind-Impact Models. To forecast and track hurricanes and severe storms, the NHC uses a variety of mathematical models that simulate the characteristics of a storm and the potential impacts it will cause. These include the Inland High-Wind Model, which was developed by researchers at NOAA, and is used to estimate how far inland strong winds will extend. This model is used by the NHC to map high-wind risk areas.

Sea-Level Models. The Sea-Level Affecting Marshes Model is used to evaluate the impact that a rise in sea level has on marshes and wetlands. NOAA publishes a Sea Level Trends report, and EPA produces maps of lands vulnerable to sea-level rise on the Gulf Coast that identify areas in danger of being inundated.

Storm-Surge Models. Being able to predict storm surges along the Gulf Coast is critical because the greatest potential for loss of life related to a hurricane is from storm surges. One of the most common software packages used to model storm surges is Sea, Lake, and Overland Surges from Hurricanes (SLOSH). This model was developed by the National Weather Service to

Figure 3.60 *A bathymetry map shows the topography beneath the water. The bathymetry has a major impact on how storm surges occur along the coast. Image courtesy EDAW.*

calculate potential surge heights from hurricanes. The SLOSH model can:

• Compute surge heights for the open coast.

• Simulate the routing of storm surge into sounds, bays, estuaries, and coastal river basins.

• Calculate surge heights for overland locations.

SLOSH models also can take into account the impact that natural and man-made barriers would have on surge heights. This means that we can have a better understanding of the impacts of design decisions such as constructing a levee, restoring wetlands, or rebuilding barrier islands. Hurricane Evacuation Studies combine the results of SLOSH models with traffic flow information. (See Figure 3.61.)

Loss-Prediction Software. HAZUS-MH is a powerful risk-assessment software program for analyzing potential losses from floods, hurricane winds, and earthquakes. HAZUS-MH, which was developed by FEMA, can be useful to landscape architects involved with long-range planning along the Gulf Coast. The model combines scientific and engineering data with GIS to produce estimates of hazard-related damage

Figure 3.61 *Most deaths associated with hurricanes occur because of storm surge. This map shows the areas along the Gulf Coast that are more vulnerable to storm surge. Image courtesy EDAW.*

before or after a disaster occurs. The Hurricane Wind Model can help estimate direct economic loss, damages to buildings, tree blow-down, debris, and even poststorm shelter needs.

Societal Risk. Some members of society are more vulnerable than others. High-risk populations include a high percentage of people over the age of 65, single parents with children, people living in poverty or on public assistance, those with no vehicle, and those who live in rental units or in older structures built before 1970. These factors are combined to create a societal risk map using data from the Coastal Risk Atlas (EDAW, 2006).

Final Vulnerability Mapping. By combining these factors into one comprehensive model, the resulting analysis can then be used to create public and private sector policies that reduce impacts from future hurricanes and severe storms. This mapping approach allows us to create a scientific base from which to make design and planning decisions. The goal is not to create science but to employ data-driven environmental analysis to minimize future loss of life and property and protect public health, safety, and welfare. With all of the available data, the key is to assess the data and determine how it should influence decisions about rebuilding a sustainable Gulf Coast. (See Figure 3.62.)

Figure 3.62 *This map shows the areas along the Gulf Coast that are most vulnerable when combining risks such as wind, storm surge, sea rise, and societal risk. Image courtesy EDAW.*

Client: National Consortium to Map Ecological Constraints to Develop a Sustainability Analysis Model
Planning: EDAW, University of Texas, RPA

Big Darby Accord Watershed Master Plan

Columbus, Ohio

The Big Darby Accord Watershed Plan provides a comprehensive long-term land use plan for protecting the Big Darby Watershed in Franklin County, which is just west of the city of Columbus (OH). The Big Darby Accord planning area is 56,000 acres, or roughly 84 square miles in size.

The watershed is considered to be one of the most biologically diverse aquatic systems in the Midwest. Big and Little Darby creeks have been designated as State and National Scenic Rivers, and approximately 38 state and federally listed endangered aquatic species have been identified. (See Figure 3.63.)

The mission of the accord is to "cooperatively develop a multi-jurisdictional plan and accompanying preservation and growth strategies, capable of implementation, oversight, and enforcement." The plan identifies supporting policies that each jurisdiction should adopt to ensure the watershed is protected. These major policy recommendations focus on environmental concerns, conservation development, the town center, open space, water quality, best management practices and sewer service. The Big Darby Accord Plan is intended to serve as a multijurisdictional guide for development and conservation. It was prepared collaboratively among 10 jurisdictions within the Franklin County portion of the watershed.

Figure 3.63 *The Big Darby Accord watershed includes a variety of different land uses, including natural areas that need protection from development. Image courtesy Big Darby Accord.*

Principles

The accord plan tales a proactive approach to managing development and ensuring the protection and improvement of water quality and aquatic habitat in the watershed. Three alternative plans were developed for the area, and these were analyzed to determine which was best at balancing human needs with the environmental requirements. Hydrological modeling was used to evaluate the potential impacts of potential land use changes on natural resources. The final plan recommends promoting new development in areas that already have the highest-density since this approach can utilize existing utilities and centralized sewer. Conservation practices are encouraged in the more rural areas that typically lack this kind of infrastructure.

The accord developed a set of plan principles that shaped the planning process. They are:

- Protection of environmentally sensitive areas (see Figure 3.64)

- A general land use plan that balances environmental protection and responsible growth (see Figure 3.65)

- A general land use plan that recognizes existing sewer and wastewater treatment capacities

- Growth areas served by adequate public facilities, particularly central sewer

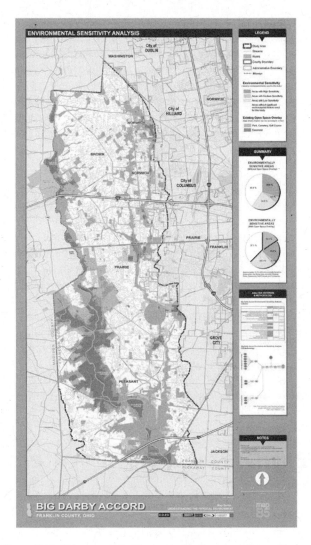

Figure 3.64 *This map shows the level of environmentally sensitive areas in the watershed. Image courtesy Big Darby Accord.*

The planning process included opportunities for public feedback, including stakeholder interviews, small focus groups, four public meetings, a project Web site, e-mail notifications, press releases, a hotline number, and mailings.

Land Use

The land use plan identifies three key goals to protecting water quality:

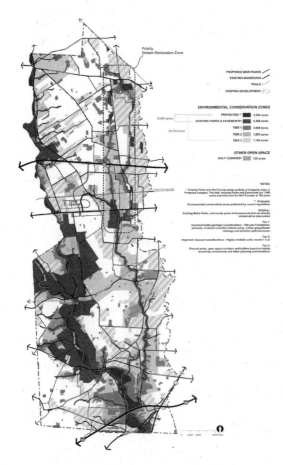

Figure 3.65 *This map shows the open space in the Big Darby Accord. Image courtesy Big Darby Accord.*

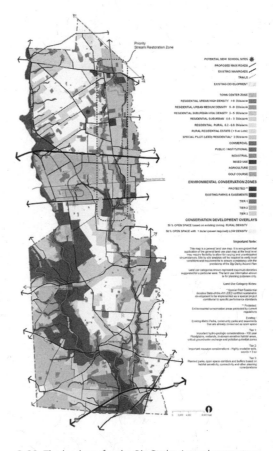

Figure 3.66 *The land use for the Big Darby Accord promotes a sustainable town center and cluster development in order to protect open space. Image courtesy Big Darby Accord.*

1. Preserve large, continuous areas of open space.

2. Preserve critical ecological areas, such as wetlands, floodplains, and riparian corridors.

3. Minimize overall land disturbance and direct connection of impervious surfaces associated with development.

Proposed general land use plan categories were developed with consideration of current types of development in the watershed. The land use plan protects environmentally sensitive areas in a green infrastructure of approximately 20,000 acres that includes floodplains, wetlands, groundwater and surface flow exchange areas, special habitat areas, wooded areas, and areas with groundwater pollution potential.

Development is managed and focused in a sustainable town center and cluster development that will promote conservation and the preservation of open space.

The Town Center zone is mixed–use area that includes residential, retail, office, public uses, and open space. At 2,500 acres, this zone is large enough to handle much of the anticipated growth in the area. Central sewer service is planned for the more dense parts of the development, while most areas of the watershed will work with existing sewage and treatment systems. (See Figure 3.66.)

The general land use plan identifies an area of about 350 acres for residential development to develop using LEED (Leadership in Energy and Environmental Design) techniques.

For the Darby Accord, the focus is more on community and site planning and uses LEED ND (Neighborhood Design), a system that focuses on elements that bring the buildings together into a neighborhood.

Water Quality

The main goals of the Big Darby Accord planning effort are to preserve and protect areas that contribute to water quality. Stormwater management policies are tied to maintaining and improving water quality and aquatic life. All development site plans must include a stormwater pollution prevention plan that contains details and specifications for runoff, erosion, and sediment control measures that will meet the requirement of the permit.

The application of best management practices (BMPs) help address water quality issues as well. BMPs for the accord were adapted from the state of Minnesota's *Stormwater Design Manual* (2005). Information on mitigating water

quality impacts was derived from the Northern Virginia BMP Handbook, prepared in 1992 by the Northern Virginia Regional Planning Commission and Engineers Surveyors Institute.

Implementation

Implementation of the Big Darby Accord will require the efforts of the many stakeholders that exist within the watershed. The planning process was initiated in April 2005. It is expected to take 20 to 30 years for the plan to be implemented. Funds to implement the accord will come from a variety of sources, including: a new community authority, tax increment financing, contributions from developers, and other options. Planners for the project estimate that these sources could generate up to $430 million over time.

Client: Big Darby Accord
Planning: EDAW

The Menomonee Valley Community Park: Transforming the Menomonee River Valley

Milwaukee, Wisconsin

The Menomonee Valley is a 140-acre site that manages storm runoff from over 1 million square feet of light industrial development in a series of parks. It is a project that bridges between site and system scales. (See Figure 3.67.) The park is a major amenity within the valley and is at the heart of the redevelopment of the area.

The park amenities include: playing fields; multi-use building; central green; plaza and chimney restoration; walkways; public art; landscape plantings; and miscellaneous site improvements, such as benches, lighting, and signage. (See Figure 3.68.) One major benefit of the park is that it connects the north and south sides of the city to the valley.

Park Areas

Five park subareas were defined. They are:

1. **Chimney Park.** This area includes playing fields, court games, trails, parking, informal lawn areas, and picnic areas. The park will also include a major community gathering here. The two large smokestacks from the rail yard that was originally located on the site have been left standing and serve as a visual landmark that is also a reminder of Milwaukee's industrial heritage. (See Figure 3.71.)

2. **River Lawn.** A large lawn opens up onto the river and gives people access to the Menomonee River. This area

Figure 3.67 *The Menomonee Valley Community Park is intended to manage storm runoff for a neighboring light industrial development. Image courtesy Wenk Associates.*

also includes a series of small dikes that extend into the river, creating aquatic habitat. (See Figures 3.69 and 3.70.)

3. Airline Yards. This narrow 23-acre piece of land along the river will include native areas and trails. A primary objective is to restore the natural areas at Airline Yards.

4. Parkway. Developed as part of the shops redevelopment, the parkway includes streetscape plantings, walking paths, and seating areas.

5. Potential Park Expansion. These areas, not in the original master plan, include River Lawn West and the former Wheelhouse Property. The River Lawn includes a river theater, gathering space, river access, trails, picnic areas, and a stormwater management area that includes meadows, wetlands, and ponds. The former Wheelhouse Property is a 1.8-acre site planned for an environmental education facility, a police equestrian facility, and parking to support these uses.

Stormwater Treatment

The design of Stormwater Management Areas was a critical part of the park. The park provides flood detention

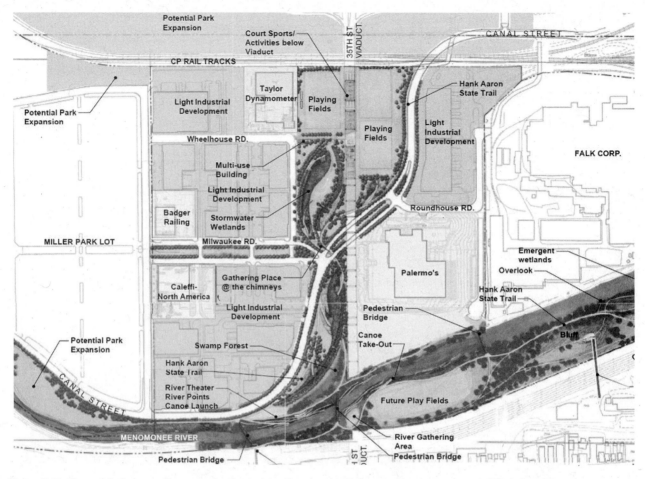

Figure 3.68 *The park includes a wide range of active and passive recreational opportunities. Image courtesy Wenk Associates.*

Figure 3.69 *The River Lawn area opens up the site to the river. Image courtesy Wenk Associates.*

Figure 3.70 *Park visitors have access to the river. Image courtesy Wenk Associates.*

Figure 3.71 *The Chimney Park is named after two large smokestacks from the rail yard that was originally on the site. Image courtesy Wenk Associates.*

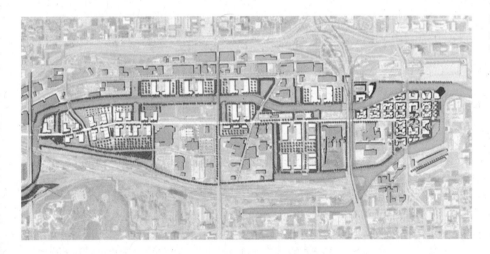

Figure 3.72 *Stormwater collection is a major goal of the park. Image courtesy Wenk Associates.*

and water quality treatment for the shops site and the Canal Street extension. (See Figure 3.72.) The Stormwater Management Areas and the Swamp Forest treat water in three steps:

1. Stormwater is collected and piped from surrounding developments to storm outfalls in the park and settles in small pools.

2. Storm flows spread out across broad shallow wetland meadows, allowing stormwater to infiltrate.

3. Infiltrated storm flows are collected and transpired through the plant material in the Swamp Forest.

Stormwater management areas include a 9-acre area and a 5.25 acre area of ponds, wetlands, wet meadows, and turf that treat and store stormwater. There is also a

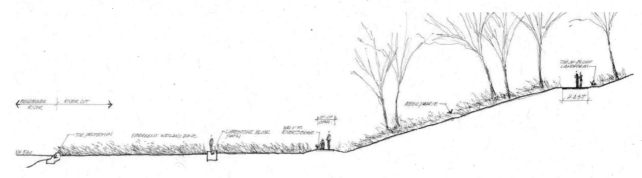

Figure 3.73 *Airline Yards is a narrow 23-acre piece of land along the river, and natural wetlands are part of the stormwater management system. Image courtesy Wenk Associates.*

0.3-acre sodium absorption area for runoff from a neighboring street. Natural wetlands located within the park are integrated with the stormwater management system. (See Figure 3.73.)

The planning team made an effort to elicit input from local stakeholders, including local businesses and landowners, government officials, and local associations and organizations.

Client: Milwaukee Department of City Development, and Menomonee Valley Partners, Inc.

Planning Team: Wenk Associates, Inc.

HNTB

Applied Ecological Services, Inc.

Wetlands at Richland Creek Wildlife Management Area

Tarrant County, Texas

The Richland Creek Wildlife Management Area (WMA) consists of approximately 14,000 acres located within the Trinity River flood plane in central Texas, about 80 miles southeast of the Dallas/Fort Worth Metroplex. Within the Wildlife Management Area is a 243-acre wetlands area that was constructed specifically for water treatment.

The Texas Parks and Wildlife Department acquired Richland Creek WMA in 1987, and it was used by the Tarrant Regional Water District as a mitigation property when the Richland Chambers reservoir was constructed. The reservoir provides drinking water for Tarrant County residents.

In the late 1990s, the Water District built a small pilot wetlands project that consisted of a couple of acres, and they tested it by running about 100,000 gallons a day through it for several years. (See Figure 3.74.) When tests indicated the process was effective for treating water, a larger project was initiated. The Richland Creek WMA is the first water recycling wetland in the nation.

Figure 3.74 *Texas Parks and Wildlife Department built the first wetlands at Richland Creek in the late 1990s. Image courtesy Texas Parks and Wildlife Department.*

How It Works

The Richland Creek WMA wetlands project functions as a large filter that pulls water from the Trinity River. The water flows into a sediment lake, then through a winding route that slows the water down even further, and then through a man made marsh. Once the water is filtered, it then flows into Alligator Creek and the Richland-Chambers Reservoir. Bypassing the wetlands and pumping the water straight from the Trinity into the reservoir does not work very well because the river water is much more polluted than the lake water. An estimated 70% of the used and treated Metroplex water goes to the Trinity River.

The wetlands were researched and analyzed for 10 years before officials felt that the system was to a point where the water treatment process was sufficient for the water flowing through the wetlands to flow into the reservoir.

One major benefit of wetlands is that they remove pollutants and suspended sediment, and they do it quickly and affordably. During the pilot study, the Water District determined that it would take seven days to run the water through the wetlands in order to treat it appropriately. Recently, the Richland Creek WMA wetland removed 99% of suspended solids, 63% of total nitrogen, and 54% of total phosphorus from water flowing through the system.

Wildlife Habitat

The WMA was created to compensate for habitat losses associated with the construction of Richland-Chambers Reservoir. One mission of Richland Creek WMA is to develop and manage indigenous and migratory wildlife species and their habitats and to provide public use in a sustainable way.

The bottomland soils support a number of bottomland- and wetland-dependent wildlife and vegetation communities. The wetlands may be artificial, but they simulate natural wetlands as closely as possible. Constructed wetlands are not intended to replace natural wetlands, and they do help in filtering stormwater and improving water quality.

The wetlands area is on the path for migrating birds, and it attracts a lot of birdwatchers. In spring, water levels are

Figure 3.75 *The wetland areas serve as important habitat for migrating birds. Image courtesy Texas Parks and Wildlife Department.*

flow level of the Trinity River has decreased in recent years. Because of existing allocations, if there is a drought and the river level is low, water will not be diverted into the wetlands.

Next Steps

The Richland Creek WMA has been heralded as an environmentally friendly model for developing public water supply. Plans are to eventually expand the WMA to include more than 2,000 acres. Once the project is completed, it is expected to be able to absorb up to 100 million gallons a day of brown river water from the Trinity and clean it enough to then flow into the Richland Chambers Creek without additional treatment needed. If this happens, the Richland-Chambers Reservoir will help augment the city of drinking water supply for the city of Fort Worth. Before that happens, however, a number of issues will need to be addressed.

lowered. This allows the vegetation in the lowlands to germinate, creating food for wildlife. Mudflats may not be the most aesthetically pleasing landscape features, but they do provide important habitat for migrating shorebirds. (See Figure 3.75.)

Texas Parks and Wildlife helps manage the site, so it is open to the public.

One concern is that there are a number of new reservoirs coming on line in North Texas, and with the Dallas–Fort Worth Metroplex pulling more water from the river, the

The Tarrant Regional Water District has provided funding for the wetlands project. It is expected to cost about $50 million when completed. The most expensive portion of the project to date was the construction of a pumping station and intakes on the Trinity River, which cost $9 million. One cost benefit is that much of the project is fairly low-tech, and as one administrator noted, "Is mostly about moving dirt."

Client: Tarrant Regional Water District

South Bay Salt Pond Restoration Project

San Francisco, California

The South Bay Salt Pond Restoration Project is the largest tidal wetland restoration project on the West Coast. When complete, the restoration will convert commercial salt ponds at the south end of San Francisco Bay to a mix of tidal marshes, mudflats, and other wetland habitats. (See Figures 3.76 and 3.77.) The project includes 15,100 acres, and restoration of these types of wetlands will significantly improve the physical, chemical, and biological health of

the bay. In addition, 1,400 acres of salt crystallizer ponds on the east side of the Napa River were also acquired.

The South Bay Salt Pond Restoration Project was needed because San Francisco Bay has lost an estimated 85% of its historic wetlands over the years. The impact of this loss of wetlands has resulted in a significant reduction in water quality, a decrease in tidal marsh habitats that are

Figure 3.76 *The San Francisco Bay is the largest estuary on the West Coast. Image courtesy USGS.*

Figure 3.77 *The tidal marshes and habitat areas are some of the most valuable natural resources in the region. Image courtesy USGS.*

important to fish and wildlife, and increased flooding in some areas.(See Figures 3.78, 3.79, and 3.80.)

Developing the Project

The goals of the project are to restore and enhance a mix of wetland habitats, provide wildlife-oriented public access and recreation, and improve flood management. In particular, the project will provide much-needed flood protection for the region. One proposed feature is an inboard levee system to reduce the hazards of coastal flooding.

Key agencies involved in the project include the California State Coastal Conservancy, California Department of Fish and Game, U.S. Fish and Wildlife Service, Santa Clara Valley Water District, Alameda County Flood Control and Water Conservation District, and U.S. Army Corps of Engineers.

The project is also expected to improve water circulation and water quality in the San Francisco Bay. Overall, environmental impacts of the project are a major concern. The project has to meet the California Environmental Quality

Act and the National Environmental Protection Act. Tidal marshes are vegetated wetlands that regularly receive some tidal action. They provide critical habitat for a number of wildlife species. One benefit is that the restoration of tidal marshes can be phased over a number of years as funding becomes available. Funds for acquisition and the implementation of the restoration, flood management, and public access plan come from a mix of local, state, and federal funds, as well as private funds.

Public Involvement

Public involvement is critical for a project like this. The California Department of Fish and Game, U.S. Fish and Wildlife Service, and California Coastal Conservancy, along with a coalition of scientists and stakeholders, conducted a four-year public process that led to the development of a restoration plan for the property. This plan, which is currently being implemented, serves as a blueprint for habitat restoration, flood protection, and the construction of new trails, viewing platforms, and other public access amenities along the bay.

Figure 3.78 *The South Bay Salt Pond Restoration Project is intended to help protect wetlands in the bay area. This map shows initial restoration actions planned for the project. Image courtesy EDAW.*

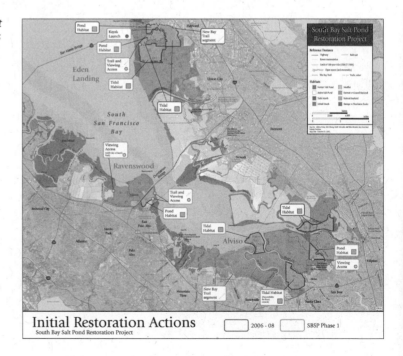

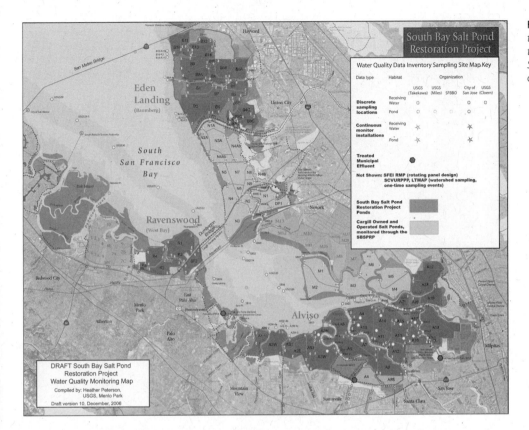

Figure 3.79 *This map shows the water quality monitoring that is occurring in the South Bay Salt Ponds. Image courtesy EDAW.*

Figure 3.80 *The restoration project will improve water quality and recharge groundwater. Image courtesy EDAW.*

Figure 3.81 *The salt ponds will be open to the public during the restoration process. Image courtesy USFW.*

One important component of the restoration is to minimize the potential habitat for mosquitoes. As a general rule, tidal marshes do not provide good habitat for mosquitoes.

The area will be accessible to the public. Locations for public access will be determined during the restoration planning process. Sensitive wildlife habitat areas are closed to public access year-round or during breeding seasons. (See Figure 3.81.)

Phasing out the salt production is estimated to take up to eight years. All state and federal regulatory agencies involved in the project signed a memorandum of understanding to help ensure long-term coordination. Long-term planning for restoring the bay area is expected to cost hundreds of millions of dollars. The exact cost is not known at this time.

Client: City of San Francisco
www.southbayrestoration.org

Brays Bayou

Houston, Texas

The Brays Bayou Flood Damage Reduction Project, commonly referred to as Project Brays, is a cooperative effort between the Harris County (TX) Flood Control District (HCFCD) and the U.S. Army Corps of Engineers, and it is designed to reduce the risk of flooding. The Brays Bayou watershed, with a population of more than 700,000 people, covers approximately 128 square miles. (See Figure 3.82.)

The HCFCD was created in 1937, and its primary purpose was to work with the Corps on local projects. The HCFCD began acquiring property along the upper reaches of Brays Bayou in the mid-1980s to create stormwater detention basins to help reduce the impact of floods. In 1988, the Corps conducted a study of Buffalo Bayou and its tributaries and determined that there were significant benefits to constructing a flood reduction project along Brays Bayou.

Figure 3.82 *The primary purpose of the Brays Bayou Flood Damage Reduction Project is to reduce flooding. Image courtesy U.S. Army Corps of Engineers.*

In 1996, the Federal Water Resources Development Act gave local nonfederal sponsors authorization to take the lead in federal flood damage reduction projects. The HCFCD took the lead on the Brays Bayou Flood Damage Reduction Project, with the Corps as a partner in the project. The Corps provides oversight and monitoring of planning, design, and construction according to federal rules, regulations, and guidelines.

Initial Work

The Brays Bayou project was designed to reduce the risk of future flooding in the area. This cooperative effort consists of more than 70 individual projects along the 31 miles of Brays Bayou.

The majority of these projects are aimed at reducing flood risks, but others focus more on protecting and enhancing environmental resources and providing recreational opportunities. Some of the recent projects include the development of a stormwater treatment wetland at Mason Park. One benefit of the wetland is that it lowers the new channel elevations for Brays Bayou. This would create a significant amount of wetlands without increasing the proposed cost very much.

Some of the initial work on Brays Bayou focused on the construction of the four stormwater detention basins. The four stormwater detention basins for Project Brays will collectively hold around 3.5 billion gallons of stormwater. According to the public relations folks at Project Brays, this is the equivalent of seven Astrodomes full of water. (See Figure 3.83.)

Arthur Storey Park

The Arthur Storey Park Stormwater Detention Basin is one of four Project Brays' stormwater detention basins. The 210-acre basin holds approximately 1.1 billion gallons of stormwater during high flow, and at other times of the year it provides much needed greenspace for neighboring communities. This project is a great example of taking a multiuse approach to stormwater management. The park includes recreational and aesthetic amenities such as picnic areas, a gazebo, tails, a learning center, native plantings, and wildlife habitat areas, and it also helps meet objectives for stormwater management. (See Figure 3.84.)

The detention basin will greatly reduce the risk of flooding for thousands of residents and businesses along Brays Bayou.

Figure 3.83 *Brays Bayou uses multiple techniques to address flood risks, including channel modifications, bridge modifications, and the construction of regional stormwater detention basins. More than 70 individual projects have been implemented along the bayou. Image courtesy U.S. Army Corps of Engineers.*

Figure 3.84 *The restoration process has improved habitat for birds and wildlife. Image courtesy U.S. Army Corps of Engineers.*

Results

Total project cost for Project Brays is estimated at $450 million, with the federal government and the district splitting the cost. Project Brays is scheduled for completion in 2014, but even then, various projects will continue. Project Brays will reduce the risk of flooding along Brays Bayou, but it does not eliminate the problem altogether.

Client: City of Houston, Texas

ProjectBrays.org

Wild Duck Lake Wetland Park Conceptual Master Plan

Beijing, China

In recent years, the Chinese government has invested a lot in protecting and restoring wetland resources. The China National Wetlands Conservation Action Plan was adopted in November 2000, and four years later wetland protection was added to the national agenda. Some local authorities have achieved progress in wetland protection legislation. Several provinces and autonomous regions, including Heilongjiang, Liaoning, Inner Mongolia, Hunan,

Figure 3.85 *The protected wetlands area at Wild Duck Lake help filter water and air pollutants for Beijing while also providing valuable habitat for birds. Image courtesy EDAW.*

Guangdong, Shaanxi, Gansu, and Ningxia, have approved legislation to protect wetlands.

The city of Beijing seems to understand the importance of Wild Duck Lake and other wetlands in the area. The Beijing Forestry Prospect and Design Institute initiated a detailed inventory and analysis of wetlands in the area in 2007. They have recently developed a database that includes all of the data collected during the study. This information is helpful for creating detailed plans for each wetland area. (See Figure 3.85.)

By the end of 2008, China had built 80 wetland parks, more than 550 wetland nature reserves, and 36 internationally important wetlands. All total, China has more than 38 million hectares (14.67 million acres) of wetlands, with

these wetland parks close to half of that total. One of the most important wetland parks for the capital city of Beijing is a Yeyahu, which means Wild Duck Lake. Beijing's suburban wetlands and reservoirs are particularly rich in birdlife and attract many different species, and Wild Duck Lake is the largest wetland bird nature preserve in north China. The lake itself has more than 1.5 million square meters (11.22 million gallons) of water.

The Wild Duck Lake Nature Reserve is Beijing's first wetland park and only wetland reserve for birds. One of the major goals for the lake is for it to become the first National Wetland Park in northern China. The protected wetlands area at Wild Duck Lake started with 3,400 hectares and has now increased to more than 10,000 hectares. It accounts for almost 20% of all the wetlands in and around

Beijing. The lake is located in Yanqing County, northwest of Beijing.

EDAW worked on a plan to raise water levels, improve water quality, improve habitat for birds, and create a recreational opportunity and educational destination for tourists as well as residents. Plans for the 3,400-hectare (8,400 acres) site included the renovation of an existing wetlands complex as well as the development of new wetlands and facilities. The new wetland facilities include a wetland visitor center, a wetland school, and other park amenities. A 45-hectare (111 acres) treatment wetland is located between the wetland school and the visitor center. (See Figure 3.86.)

In addition to Wild Duck Lake, other wetland areas around Beijing include Guanting Reservoir, Sahe Reservoir, and Bahe Wetland Park. These wetlands are important because Beijing lies on a major migration route for raptors, and all are endangered in China. The wetlands are viewed primarily as conservation areas, and although they are also viewed as recreational areas, the number of visitors is restricted.

One reason that Beijing has been building wetland parks is to address some of its environmental problems. One of the greatest benefits of Wild Duck Lake is that it helps purify the city's atmosphere. In particular, sand and dust are a

Figure 3.86 *A series of boardwalks allow visitors to experience the wetlands and natural resources in the park. Wild Duck Lake is expected to be one of the world's top birdwatching sites. Image courtesy EDAW.*

major problem in Beijing. When wetlands were greatly reduced in the early 1990s, sand storms and dust storms became a serious issue. The wetlands at Wild Duck Lake absorb this sand and dust and have helped improve the air around the city.

Client: Wild Duck Lake Nature Reserve Office
Landscape Architects: EDAW

Choctaw County Lake Development

Choctaw County, Mississippi

The Choctaw County Mississippi Board of Supervisors was interested in the possibility of constructing a new lake in the northeast part of their county. The intent of a master plan for the project was to determine the viability of this proposed lake and to develop initial concepts for what the lake would look like, and how it could be developed. The goal of the plan was to develop a clear and implementable vision that promotes an economically viable, environmentally sustainable development that provides housing and mixed uses for Choctaw County. (See Figure 3.87.)

The lake development has been supported by the Mississippi Department of Environmental Quality, which was interested in alternative sources of water to relieve demands on the shallow aquifers in the area.

Background

The idea of developing a new lake in Choctaw County was first considered in the late 1990s, and several studies have

Figure 3.87 *The study area for the Choctaw Lake Development Project included all of the watershed as well as the lands extending to adjacent roads. Image courtesy EDAW.*

been conducted over the years. Development of a lake was initially envisioned as a source of water for the burgeoning Red Hill Power Plant and other potential industrial uses in the county. (See Figure 3.88.)

In 2001, the Choctaw County Board of Supervisors developed the criteria for selecting a reservoir, and out of this came a concept plan identifying a site on Besa Chitto Creek as the preferred option. Subsequent studies completed in January 2008 concluded that from an engineering standpoint, a proposed lake location in the Sand Creek watershed was the most viable. It would fill with water in a relatively short period and remain full even in drought conditions. Several reservoir areas with different dam

alignments were identified in the Sand Creek watershed, ranging in size from 318 to 2,223 acres. A range of surface elevations were considered, from 400 to 430 feet above sea level. With the larger lake alternatives, a wide variety of recreational uses would be possible. The lake is expected to take years to complete, and even a smaller lake would take years to fill with water. Two fundamental concerns regarding lake capacity arose out of the engineering studies: Is the sediment that will make up the proposed lake lining fine and compact enough to hold water, and will it remain full, despite fluctuations in environmental conditions?

An economic impact study completed by Mississippi State University (MSU) identified assets that can be used to

Figure 3.88 *The existing site has been harvested for timber, so much of the vegetation is fairly new. Image courtesy EDAW.*

attract appropriate development for the lake. MSU estimated that Choctaw County requires 5.5 million gallons per day of water and that the lake would be able to accommodate this demand.

Planning Process

The planning approach for the proposed lake development explores a variety of alternatives and strategies for creating viable communities. The key to good design and planning is to take a holistic approach to all resources. Development that uses land efficiently and protects undisturbed natural areas allows a community to grow and still protect its water

resources. To best protect water resources, the lake development plan needs to consider local factors and employ a wide range of land use strategies, including: building a range of development densities, incorporating adequate open space, preserving critical ecological and buffer areas, and minimizing land disturbance. The planning process integrates stormwater management into the overall fabric of the master plan, so that water is considered an essential element during each phase of the process.

The master plan is intended to create a framework that guides future development in the study area. This plan provides a broad vision for the area and defines an achievable and cost-effective strategy for implementation. Although conceptual in nature, the design and land use plans are drawn from a thorough and careful understanding of the land, the community, and the history that has shaped both.

EDAW drafted an initial program for lake development and then used this program to develop three preliminary concepts for the master plan, including conceptual engineering. These concepts were evaluated to determine the pros and cons of each. Based on feedback from county representatives, the design team revised concepts and selected a preliminary preferred master plan that combined the three original alternative concepts. This preliminary preferred plan was reviewed with county representatives, and changes were incorporated in the final concepts for the master plan.

Opportunities Analysis

Economics Research Associates (ERA) conducted an opportunities analysis that takes a broad assessment of market and economic conditions and identification of real estate opportunities related to the development of a new lake in Choctaw County. The planning team examined demographic and economic characteristics of three man-made lakes in Mississippi: Okatibbee, Dalewood Shores, and Ross Barnett.

ERA examined the supplies for lodging and likely candidates for recreational development around the lake—golf courses, campgrounds, marinas, and hotels—in Choctaw County study area and the state of Mississippi. ERA's goal was to understand the proximity of supply and the pricing parameters within which the market operates. ERA determined that housing would predominantly be primary homes for those living in the area, and although demand will initially be slow, it will increase over time.

Funding is expected to be a combination of direct payments by the municipality as well as a temporary tax increase. Real estate development opportunities will likely be relegated to supporting ongoing operational and upkeep costs. Water sales are expected to be a significant source of revenue when the lake is fully operational.

Development of Alternative Concepts

Based on an analysis of the site, the programming needs, and the market analysis, EDAW developed a series of planning concepts for the proposed lake development. The study looked at three potential dam locations. Dam Alternative B would form the smallest of the lakes being considered in this study, measuring approximately 1,750 acres with a shoreline of about 194,000 linear feet. It would also require construction of the longest dam of the three options, however, at 5,500 feet. Dam Alternative A creates a lake 1,900 acres in size, with a shoreline of approximately 197,500 linear feet (or about 3,500 more feet than Dam B). The extra acreage adds more deep water, good for boating and enhancing the visual quality of the lake, and more shoreline to develop prime residential property. In addition, this dam would be 4,200 feet in length, and this would be a significant savings in construction cost. (See Figure 3.89.)

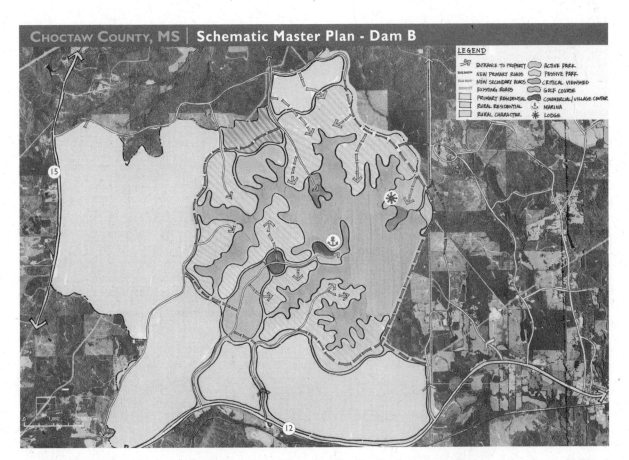

Figure 3.89 *The concept plan for the proposed lake explored different locations for the dam to create the lake. Image courtesy EDAW.*

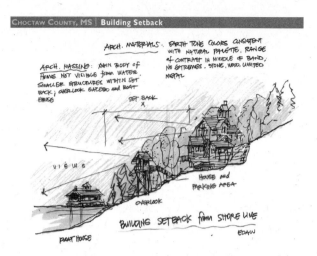

Figure 3.90 *One major concept for the plan was to locate buildings and community structures up the hill to take advantage of views and to protect the shoreline. Image courtesy EDAW.*

Dam X would result in the largest lake being considered, measuring approximately 2,500 acres in size with a shoreline of about 223,000 feet. The lake would also have the most abundant deep water, so its aesthetic quality would be significantly higher. The dam would be approximately 4,900 feet in length. A significant proportion of the lake would extend into Oktibbeha County. (See Figure 3.90.)

The Choctaw County Board of Supervisors made the decision to go with Dam A since it provides the best balance of cost to lake size, and it did not require the participation of Oktibbeha County.

Program Elements

After reviewing site carrying capacities and the market analysis, EDAW developed a preliminary list of program elements for the proposed lake development. These

Figure 3.91 *A pattern board defines the basic architectural character that is intended for development around the new lake. Image courtesy EDAW.*

program elements include the physical features that will be included as part of a master plan. (See Figure 3.91.)

Each alternative concept included various locations and arrangements of these elements:

- Marina
- Lodge/hospitality center
- Primary and rural residential
- Rural character area
- Active and passive recreation
- Trails
- Camping
- Swimming beach
- Golf
- Fishing
- Limited commercial services

Land Acquisition Strategies

Because the majority of the land in the study area is privately owned, land would have to be acquired to construct the lake. There are several different scenarios for the acquisition of the land that will be inundated by the lake. The difference in the land acquisition scenarios is how much land around the lake will be acquired and owned by a new lake board. There are four basic options for acquiring land:

Option 1. Acquire the entire study area.
Option 2. Acquire a ½-mile buffer around the lake.
Option 3. Acquire a ¼-mile buffer around the lake.
Option 4. Acquire the lake and public areas.

The county is still evaluating which land acquisition strategy would be most appropriate.

Current Status

The Choctaw County Board of Supervisors is proceeding with plans for the proposed lake. It has decided on the Dam A location, which would create a 1,900-acre lake, and is in the process of obtaining the appropriate funding, conducting additional engineering studies, and submitting a 404 permit to the Army Corps of Engineers. As one supervisor said, "This lake project will take years to implement, and it is more for our kids and grandkids then it is for us. Creating a legacy takes patience."

Client: Choctaw County Board of Supervisors
Land Planners: EDAW
Engineers: Crowder Engineering
Economic Analysis: ERA

Ross Barnett Reservoir

Jackson, Mississippi

Ross Barnett Reservoir, located in Jackson, Mississippi, was created in the early 1960s through a multiyear process that began in the mid-1950s. The primary purpose of the reservoir is to provide drinking water for the City of Jackson. (See Figure 3.92.) The enacting legislation that led to the development of the lake created the Pearl River Valley Water Supply District, a state agency whose purpose was to construct and manage the 33,000-acre reservoir and the 17,000 acres surrounding the lake. The physical boundaries for the district were defined by the 300-foot contour line, plus all lands within one-quarter mile of the line. In addition, the legislation allows the district to annex lands within an additional mile, a provision that has proven an effective way to spur development in off-lake areas that utilize the district's sanitary sewer infrastructure.

Because of the existing topography, the average depth across the entire reservoir is just 10 feet, so it is very shallow in many locations. This may not be the prettiest lake in the South since it·lacks deep water, but it has the reputation for being a great place to fish.

The Pearl River Valley Water Supply District maintains and operates a water treatment plant and regional water distribution system that is the primary supply for the city of

Figure 3.92 *Ross Barnett Reservoir serves as the primary water source for the city of Jackson, Mississippi. Image courtesy Pearl River Valley Water Supply District.*

Jackson. Interestingly enough, the residential development along the lake gets its water from wells, not the reservoir.

The district was established to promote the balanced economic development of the state and to aid in flood control, conservation and development of state forests, irrigation of lands needing irrigation, and pollution control. The district does not receive any state or local tax dollars; operational funding is provided through the leasing of the landholding to resident homeowners and businesses. Land is not sold to homeowners. The district regulates almost all activities within its boundaries: development plan approval, signage, design standards, usage of land and water, hunting, fishing, and boating. Fire and police are provided by each of the five counties, though a force is still maintained by the district. (See Figure 3.93.)

Leasehold development was a new idea when introduced in the mid-1960s. The district decided to go with a leased land offering primarily because eminent domain was used to acquire land for the reservoir. One initial flaw in the program was the offering of 50-year fixed-fee leaseholds that contained no escalation provisions. As a result, there are a number of 60-year leases in place for $350 per year. The general consensus is that the land is greatly undervalued.

Development around Ross Barnett Reservoir is tightly controlled by the district. Landholdings are released in a

Figure 3.93 *The lake is used to control flooding as well as provide drinking water for Jackson. Image Courtesy Pearl River Valley Water Supply District.*

considered fashion that seeks to maintain a healthy supply and demand balance. The district acts as the master developer, releasing parcels to developers as the economy permits. Once agreement is reached between the district and the developer, a third-party appraiser assigns values to each of the parcels identified by the developer's subdivision plan. The developer pays approximately 50% of the land value, with the remaining 50% paid for through the issuance of leaseholds as each home is sold.

Development of homes began in 1965, soon after the dam was complete. Through the early 1970s development was described as extremely slow, and it was not until prime residential lots in Jackson were almost completely developed that the area around Ross Barnett Reservoir began to develop quickly. Today, Ross Barnett Reservoir is essentially a primary residential bedroom community for Jackson, attracting a mix of families and empty-nesters. Homes along the lake are almost exclusively single-family detached units.

The trend in the Ross Barnett market has been to offer fairly limited packages, with community clubhouses, perhaps tennis, and in some instances a community marina. More recently, as the market evolved, amenity offerings are becoming more substantial in terms of activity programming, but physical developments (e.g., golf courses, clubhouses, etc.) continue to be modest at best. Instead, the reservoir, its views, array of water-based activities, and array of public parks and commercial venues continue to be the primary amenity selling point for real estate.

Client: Pearl River Valley Water Supply District

Village in the Forest

Lake Allatoona, Georgia

A Village in the Forest is a proposed 4,300-acre master planned community in Cherokee County, Georgia. Lake Allatoona and land owned by the U.S. Army Corps of Engineers surrounds the site to the south, east, and west. (See Figure 3.94.) This is one of the largest planned communities ever proposed for the state of Georgia. When constructed, A Village in the Forest would include a town center, 5 villages, a marina, 500,000 square feet of commercial space, 12,000 housing units, 40 miles of trails, and 2,200 acres of greenspace. Because of the sheer size of the project, there has been a lot of interest from state and local officials, federal agencies, environmental organizations, local residents, and other stakeholders who want to know more about the project.

The basic concept was to embrace and maximize the natural beauty of the property and create an opportunity for people who truly want to connect with the forested environment around them. The natural features of the property provide an opportunity for the new community to serve as a national model of green, sustainable development. During an envisioning charrette, the design team established a vision for the project that says: "Come live in a village where art, architecture and landscape are one and beauty is celebrated. Where opportunities abound for social interaction or private reflection. Where the forest, streams and lake are protected and cherished. Where the heart is nurtured, the spirit inspired and the soul is free to soar." (See Figures 3.95 and 3.96.)

The proposed project was complex because of its size, diversity of uses, uniqueness of the concepts, large number of stakeholders involved, and the short timeline. The design team had to develop a detailed land use plan, complete with village plans, road layout, densities, trails, and amenities, for the entire development in less than three months. Because of the controversy surrounding a project of this size, it was critical that all concepts associated with the project be communicated in a clear and understandable format.

Growth Control

Growth is inevitable, growth is necessary, but how growth is accommodated can be good or bad. One of the major

Figure 3.94 *A Village in the Forest is a 4,300-acre development on Lake Allatoona, Georgia. It is surrounded by 5,000 acres of U.S. Army Corps of Engineers land. Image courtesy EDAW.*

Figure 3.95 *Phase I of the development was determined in large part by county lines. The decision was to limit initial development in Cherokee County because of political issues. Image courtesy EDAW.*

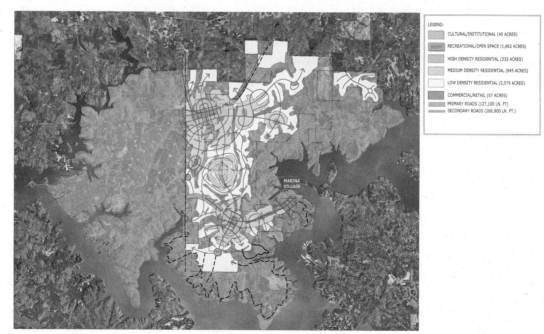

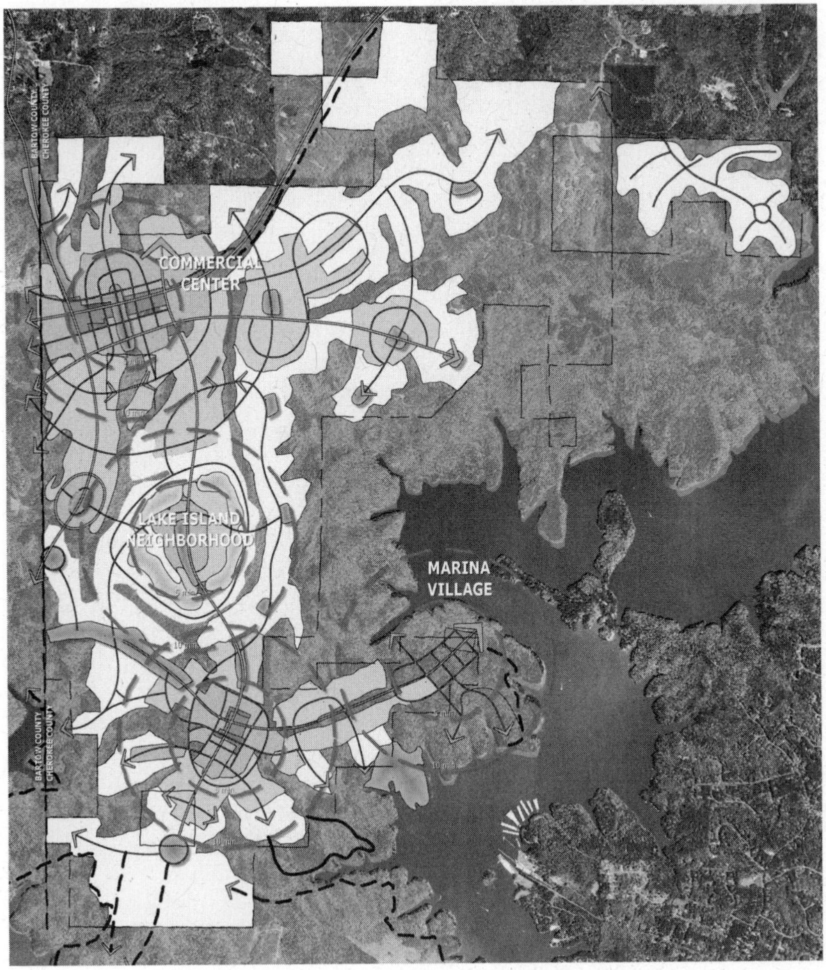

Figure 3.96 *The Phase I development included three villages and a town center. Image courtesy EDAW.*

problems in Cherokee County (GA) is that growth is uncontrolled, and sprawl is commonplace. The solution to sprawl is to increase densities in areas that are best suited for development and preserve agriculture and open space in other areas. A Village in the Forest does just that.

Although large lot zoning reduces the total number of homes that can be built, it spreads out development in a way that leaves little land usable for farming, forestry, or even recreational trails. The approach used in A Village in the Forest concentrates development in six villages, each with a commercial center within walking distance for most

pedestrians. By clustering development in the areas best suited to accommodate it, much of the site can be preserved as green space. (See Figure 3.97.)

Green Space

Within A Village in the Forest, 1,686 acres, or 40.9% of the site, will be green space consisting of undisturbed areas, active and passive parks, open space, and civic space. (See Figure 3.98.) Impacts to streams, vegetation, and steep slopes will be minimal, and much of the existing site will not

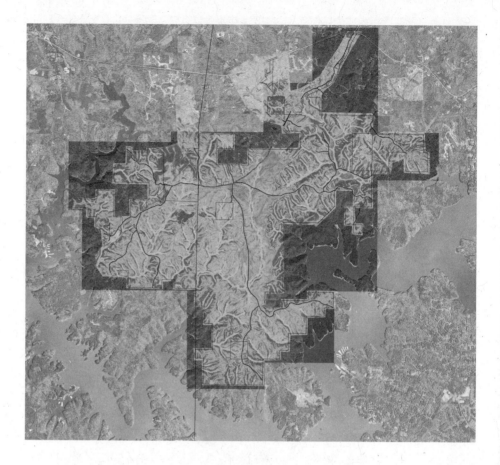

Figure 3.97 *One major site limitation was the existing topography. A slope analysis map identifies the best places to build. Image courtesy EDAW.*

Figure 3.98 *The town center is intended to be a gathering space for socializing and is a key part of the public domain. A town center is often the heart and soul of a community. Image courtesy EDAW.*

be disturbed. As a result, A Village in the Forest will maintain much of the natural character of the existing site.

Public green space is broken down into five categories:

1. Stream buffers/wetlands
2. Open space
3. Civic space
4. School sites
5. Civic building sites

Stream Buffers/Wetlands. Almost 540 acres—13.1% of the site—is designated protected buffers for streams. These buffers extend 50 feet on each side of the stream, and are intended to help protect the character and quality of those streams. These buffer areas will be largely undisturbed, and existing vegetation will be preserved.

The various neighborhood developments are designed to fit around this pattern of streams. (See Figure 3.99.)

Open Space. *Open space* refers to undisturbed areas outside of stream buffers. In A Village in the Forest, 22.8% of the site will be open space that preserves existing vegetation, so the natural character of these areas will be maintained. A series of trails will extend through the open spaces and connect to parks, schools, churches, and other public gathering areas.

Because of the proximity to the U.S. Army Corps property, which abuts three sides of A Village in the Forest, the perceived amount of undisturbed open space will be very high. Trails will connect the Corps' property to Village property, and there will be numerous opportunities to hike along trails in a natural setting.

Civic Space. *Civic space* consists of areas reserved for parks, playgrounds, ballfields, and other types of public use. These spaces are dispersed throughout the neighborhoods so they are within walking distance for most residents. These civic spaces serve as public gathering areas, and they are an integral part of the different villages and neighborhoods. Of the site, 123 acres, or 3%, is set aside for civic spaces. These spaces are also an important part of the overall water management strategy for the project and are useful for stormwater retention.

School Sites. In A Village in the Forest, sites for four elementary schools, each approximately 25 acres in size, are planned. The four elementary schools are located to best serve all six villages. All four school sites are connected to a larger network of trails, walkways, and open space that help make this a walkable community. The idea is to integrate these schools into the neighborhoods so that children can walk to school, children will be taking classes with their friends, and parents will have an opportunity to become more actively involved in the schools. (See Figure 3.100.)

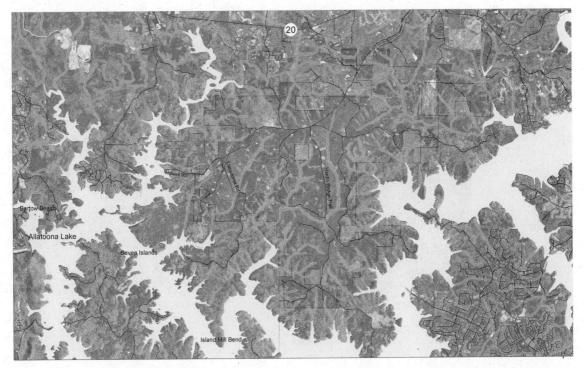

Figure 3.99 *The plan was developed to protect existing streams on the site. A 50-foot buffer was established. Image courtesy EDAW.*

MACAULEY

SCALE 1"=1200'
0   600   1200   2400

NORTH

Potential School Sites

Four elementary school sites are proposed as part of this development. The basic idea is to create schools that are an integral part of the neighborhoods they serve. We want to create an environment where kids can walk to school, where the kids are from the same neighbors and have classes with their friends, and parents know all of the other parents. Each elementary school site is approximately 20 to 25 acres in size, and is linked to parks, open spaces, civic spaces, and public gathering areas via a network of trails. A proposed high school and middle school would be located off site.

October 16, 2006

A Village in the Forest
Cherokee County, Georgia

EDAW | AECOM

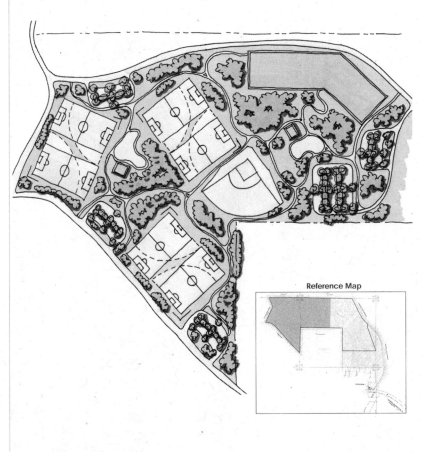

Recreation Complex

A major recreation complex will be part of a joint high school/middle school site located outside of A Village in the Forest. The recreation complex will be approximately 30 to 40 acres in size, and will include multipurpose sports fields that can accommodate football, baseball, soccer, and other sports-oriented activities.

November 16, 2006

A Village in the Forest
Cherokee County, Georgia

EDAW | AECOM

Reference Map

Based on a market analysis, the design team did not anticipate needing four elementary schools to meet the immediate needs of the village, so two of the sites were to be used as public parks for the immediate future. Of the other two schools, approximately half of each site will be used as open space to accommodate playfields, trails, playgrounds, and other recreational uses. This means that 75 acres of land allocated for schools, approximately 1.8% of the site, will be available as green space. (See Figure 3.101.)

Civic Building Sites. *Civic building sites* are reserved for uses such as churches, community centers, and other structures intended for public use. Most of the civic building sites are located in or near the six village centers since this puts them within walking distance

MACAULEY

Stormwater management recommendations

1. Micromanage stormwater:
   * Develop detailed stormwater management concept plans.
   * Refine and micromanage the stormwater using detailed modeling.
   * Require builders and future homeowners to meet the plan.
   * Each neighborhood should be self sufficient in meeting stormwater management requirements.
   * Develop HOA documents that protect stormwater management efforts.
   * Develop stormwater training programs for new residents

2. Micromanage relationship of stormwater and soil:
   * Perform percolation tests and locate stormwater infiltration facilities.

3. Control runoff close to the source:
   * Decentralize stormwater management efforts.
   * Control impervious runoff starting at the home, building, or road.

4. Create water features, such as lakes and wetlands:
   * Create water features to help control surface runoff.

5. Use progressive site design guidelines:
   * Limit traditional pervious surfaces.
   * Limit curb and gutter, while preferring road side swales and ditches.
   * Limit road widths and separate lanes to minimize road grading impacts.
   * Use medians for stormwater management features.
   * Use pervious trail surfaces and sidewalks.
   * Use cisterns and dry wells to collect runoff from homes.
   * Incorporate rain gardens and swales in all lots and developed areas.
   * Create planting strips adjacent to impervious surfaces.
   * Minimize number and size of cul-de-sacs; use vegetated islands in cul-de-sacs.
   * Use rooftop planters on commercial facilities.
   * Minimize excess parking, and incorporate sharing parking and drivers where possible.
   * Create bioretention areas.
   * Use Low Impact Development (LID) techniques.

Commitment to Excellence

Macauley is committed to making "A Village in the Forest" a national leader in regards to stormwater management.

Stormwater Management

An initial review of hydrology and water quality requirements is used to determine the best design and planning approaches for meeting water quality objectives. Our plan meets all of Cherokee County's current Stormwater Management Development Regulations. The plan also meets stormwater management standards in the Etowah River Habitat Conservation Plan (HCP). This site is a Priority 3 Area, meaning there are no runoff volume limits. Macauley supports decisions made by the Army Corps of Engineers that Lake Allatoona not be used for stormwater detention, and all stormwater will be contained on site.

September 7, 2006

A Village in the Forest
Cherokee County, Georgia

EDAW | AECOM

---

of most residents. There are approximately 16 acres of civic building sites throughout the development. It is estimated that approximately half of each site would be devoted to a building, parking, and other infrastructure requirements, and the other half would be available as public open space.

Conservation Subdivisions. Approximately 51% of the site is designated as conservation subdivisions. In these areas, a minimum of 40% of the area is designated as open space, meaning that roads, infrastructure, and private lots can take up no more than 60% of the subdivision. Better site design practices, such as conservation subdivisions, help retain a site's natural hydrology and infiltrate stormwater within the boundaries of the development project.

Stormwater and Habitat. Preserving approximately 41% of the site as green space will help us address potential stormwater runoff issues. This type of compact development, which uses land efficiently and protects undisturbed natural lands, allows for growth to occur while still protecting water resources. According to EPA,

higher densities better protect water quality, especially at the watershed and individual lot levels. Reducing the amount of land consumed by development can also help preserve habitat for many species. Compact development leaves more open ground that can filter rainwater and more open space for birds, animals, and people to enjoy. (See Figure 3.102.)

Client: Macauley Company
Planner: EDAW
Engineer: Lowes Engineering

"Think Water First" Program

Lake Allatoona, Georgia

Lake Allatoona, located just north of Atlanta (GA), is situated on the Etowah River, a tributary of the Coosa River. The lake itself is just over 12,000 acres in size and is one of the most frequently visited U.S. Army Corps of Engineers lakes in the nation with more than 6 million visitors a year. For over 50 years, Lake Allatoona has provided the community

with hydroelectric power, flood control, public water supply, recreational opportunities, and wildlife habitat. (See Figure 3.103.)

The Lake Allatoona Preservation Authority (LAPA) was created in 1999 to protect and preserve the lake. LAPA

Figure 3.103 *Lake Allatoona is an Army Corps of Engineers lake. Image courtesy USACE.*

instituted its "Think Water First" educational campaign to inform elected officials about the benefits of stormwater management and land use controls on the overall health of Lake Allatoona.

Once the short-term and long-term goals are confirmed in the next two to five years, the Think Water First educational campaign will be designed around these goals. Following a goal-setting workshop with LAPA, the planning team drafted concepts to share with LAPA regarding the development of the Think Water First educational program.

One objective of the Think Water First campaign was to change how people thought of the lake. Three steps were defined to achieve this change in behavior: awareness, understanding, and action.

1. **Awareness of Lake Allatoona water quality challenges.** This phase educated elected officials about the existing conditions of Lake Allatoona, the location of critical areas around the lake, and the extent of drainage area and political jurisdictions that flow into the lake.

2. **Understanding of Lake Allatoona water quality issues.** This phase focused on the potential sources of chlorophyll-a and ways that elected officials can influence water quality in Lake Allatoona.

3. **Action to protect water quality in Lake Allatoona.** This phase focused on specific actions that can be taken to protect water.

Awareness of Lake Allatoona

Lake Allatoona is an important resource for the region as a drinking water supply source, economic engine, recreation destination, and an aesthetic amenity. The recent "State of the Lake" report shows that water quality is better than it has been in the past several decades. However, without diligent efforts of Lake Allatoona and the communities in the watershed, these improvements can fade. The lake has over 6 million visitors annually, making it one of the most frequently visited Corps lakes in the United States. Associated with the large number of visitors, Lake Allatoona has a significant impact on the local economy. Protection of the lake from stormwater runoff that leads to periodic chlorophyll-a exceedances should be a concern of

Figure 3.104 *An important aspect of the project was to develop educational information about Lake Allatoona. Image courtesy USACE.*

elected officials in the watershed. Specific facts about the lake's health and regional significance can build awareness for the Think Water First educational campaign. This fact-based approach was used in the video produced for the City of Atlanta Department of Watershed Management to support its public involvement efforts in promoting water conservation measures to its consumers. As part of the department's Everything Water campaign, the video helped to explain rate increases and the new conservation rate; highlight eligibility requirements for discounted senior rates and the Care and Conserve program; show consumers how to read their water meters; and educate the public on different measures to reduce water consumption overall. The tone of the video is upbeat and positive, and also emphasizes the money that can be saved by consumers by employing a variety of conservation methods. In addition to use in a public education forum, the city aired the video on its cable access station and incorporated it into an interactive kiosk. (See Figure 3.104.)

Understanding of Lake Allatoona Challenges

Elected officials have a large role to play in the protection of Lake Allatoona; they approve comprehensive land use plans and zoning maps, development and redevelopment requirements, acquisition of open space, and local funds for stormwater and watershed management activities. All of these decisions affect water quality in Lake Allatoona. Most elected officials will support the protection of the lake but may not understand how their decisions may impact water quality. The challenge is providing a deeper sense of understanding of the complex interactions among land use decisions, policy decisions, and water quality in Lake Allatoona.

The planning team worked with the LAPA board, educational committee, and scientific advisory committee on making these relationships clear to elected officials. The team has experience through the Upper Cahaba Watershed Study in Birmingham (AL) working with elected officials and the public to establish watershed protection strategies.

The primary source of drinking water for metropolitan Birmingham, the Cahaba River is also nationally recognized for its biodiversity and recreational value. Population growth and associated land development in the Upper Cahaba Watershed was a growing concern for everyone in the Birmingham region. EDAW staff provided a coordinated approach to guide future development while protecting the Upper Cahaba River and its tributaries. The process engaged elected officials, and staff from several jurisdictions worked together on the Upper Cahaba Watershed Study.

Actions to Protect Lake Allatoona

Once elected officials are compelled to protect the lake, the educational campaign should provide clear and specific actions for elected officials and their staff to implement. To maintain momentum, AECOM recommended that the educational campaign include short-term and long-term actions, as success with the short-term actions will promote long-term actions. The AECOM team developed a number of short-term actions built off of the "Think Water First" campaign. These short-term actions were vetted with the educational committee and scientific advisory committee.

First Mile. LAPA has appropriately identified the first mile perimeter around the shore of Lake Allatoona as sensitive land areas. A number of tools and techniques are available to protect and preserve this sensitive area.

First Question. Lake Allatoona is such an important resource that all development processes should recognize their impact on water quality in the lake. The local development review checklist can be modified so that the first question is "How will this development project protect water quality in Lake Allatoona?"

First Plan. Comprehensive local land use plans and zoning decisions set the foundation for future development and can significantly impact water quality in Lake Allatoona. Planning for watershed protection is an integral part of the Think Water First campaign. As these elements are added to the land development process, additional "first" elements may be added. The AECOM team felt it best to establish a limited number of "first" initiatives to increase the local effectiveness. Longer-term actions include the implementation of sound land use planning and stormwater management. The team has developed a number of comprehensive local land use plans and greenspace plans, including those for the city of Brunswick, Glynn County, and Columbia County in Georgia. The team also brings LAPA stormwater management and low-impact design (LID) expertise including stormwater projects for the city of Atlanta and the city of College Park and an LID feasibility project for San Francisco, California. The technical staff at M&E and EDAW will provide LAPA and the elected officials in the watershed with sound recommendations for protecting Lake Allatoona.

Develop Think Water First Multimedia Elements

Once the Think Water First educational campaign goals and program were developed, the multimedia elements were customized to LAPA's needs.

Video. A short video on the lake is used to generate excitement for the Think Water First campaign. A documentary-style video takes the viewer through the journey as the project unfolds to address environmental impacts to the watershed, homeowner issues, and other community concerns as well as the technical and engineering challenges involved.

Presentation. A presentation covering recommendations for improving the health and well-being of Lake Allatoona was developed for LAPA board members and volunteers to take into local communities to gain support for the Think Water First educational campaign.

Toolboxes and Fact Sheets. The program includes two toolboxes: one for Engineering and Stormwater staff and one for Community Development and Planning and Zoning staff.

Multimedia Options

The LAPA Web site is a tremendous resource and could include interactive tools and information to support the Think Water First educational campaign.

Content developed both now and in the future as part of the Think Water First educational campaign can be easily hosted on the LAPA Web site. The Web site provides unlimited access for elected officials, local government staff, and the public. The synergy created by the Think Water First educational campaign may encourage new visitors to the Web site. The team envisions the LAPA Web site as the first stop for anyone interested in Lake Allatoona. Another effective tool for communicating an evolving educational campaign is the use of interactive media. As the project unfolds and new materials are created to support its mission, interactive material can be quickly updated to reflect the most current information available. This information can be incorporated into an interactive DVD; however, a better vehicle for the interactive media component would be the LAPA Web site. A Web-based interactive approach allows the piece to expand as the project expands, to be continually updated and always current, and also represents a green alternative.

Client: Lake Allatoona Preservation Authority

Sorrento Creek

San Diego, California

The Sorrento Creek Channel Maintenance Redesign Project seeks to control flood risk in the Sorrento Valley area by implementing a maintenance dredging and vegetation management program. One objective was to reduce the amount of dredging that occurred along Sorrento Creek and Los Peñasquitos Creek. Among other things, the dredging helps protect the downstream Los Peñasquitos Lagoon. The lagoon is on the State of California's Section 303(d) list of impaired waterbodies for siltation/sediment, so minimizing sediment transport was important.

The project consists of an eight-acre site in the city of San Diego, and it includes waters and wetlands under jurisdiction of both the U.S. Army Corps of Engineers and the California Department of Fish and Game. The site is located in a narrow, urbanized floodplain in Sorrento Valley, where Los Peñasquitos Creek, Sorrento Creek, and Carroll Canyon Creek all converge. The city of San Diego wanted Sorrento Creek to be redesigned in order to reduce potential water quality and biological impacts, decrease dredging time, and increase cost effectiveness. (See Figure 3.105.)

The project was initiated as a result of a lawsuit by surrounding businesses that argued that flood protection was inadequate. The project area was originally dredged in the 1970s, but this activity was not conducted on a regular basis. As a result, the stream would get overgrown, silt would build up, and flooding problems would arise. During 1997, the city conducted an extensive dredging operation to clean up the channels. The first dredging event removed 67,000 cubic yards of accumulated silt, sediment, and vegetation and had 10 trucks lined up for 10 hours a day for five months to move all the debris. In addition, 20,000 cubic yards of clean fill material had to be brought in to construct temporary roads.

The project incorporates a new dredging approach that is intended to reduce water quality and biological impacts to the creek while at the same time improving sediment

Figure 3.105 *The purpose behind the Sorrento Creek Channel Maintenance Redesign Project was to reduce the image of dredging and improve water quality as well as create a more sustainable natural environment. Image courtesy USACE.*

Figure 3.106 *New dredging techniques minimize environmental impacts. Image courtesy USACE.*

capture capacity. The new approach uses a floating dredge to remove sediments from the creek hydraulically. Sediment was dredged and vegetation removed to maintain flood capacity for a 10-year return storm.

The process is also much more cost effective than the traditional bucket-dredging approach, saving the city hundreds of thousands of dollars each year. By eliminating the bucket-dredging approach, temporary roads no longer had to be constructed. These roads have had a significant negative impact on the natural resources around the creeks in the past. This approach also eliminates temporary filling within Sorrento and Los Peñasquitos creeks. (See Figure 3.106.)

Prior to any site work, ambient water quality measurements (e.g., turbidity, pH, conductivity, dissolved oxygen, temperature, salinity) were collected at 12 locations throughout the project footprint to document preconstruction conditions A water quality protection plan was developed to increase monitoring effectiveness and to help reduce environmental impacts.

The project has multiple objectives and reporting requirements, and part of the land impacted by the project is classified as being environmentally sensitive. The project had to comply with environmental permit conditions authorized through the San Diego Regional Water Quality Control Board, the city of San Diego, the U.S. Army Corps

of Engineers, the California Department of Fish and Game, and the U.S. Fish and Wildlife Service. The redesign and its planning components were critical to negotiating permits from local, state, and federal agencies.

Potential impacts to water quality and related resources have been reduced as a result of the project. A variety of best management practices (BMPs) were implemented to minimize impacts to natural resources. Some of the types of BMPs that were utilized include:

- Check dams
- Sealed dewatering enclosures
- Discharge scour protection
- Storm drain inlet protection
- Straw bale barriers
- Silt fences
- Construction entrances
- Scheduling

Water bags have been introduced to the site, and they can be inflated on location to help control flooding.

Client: City of San Diego
Planning Team: EDAW
Contributing Consultants: EDAW, Inc., JND Thomas Dredging, Kilmer-Horn and Associates, Inc., Konecny Biological Services

Mississippi River/Gulf of Mexico Watershed Nutrient Task Force, Gulf Hypoxia Action Plan 2008

In January 2001, the Mississippi River/Gulf of Mexico Watershed Nutrient Task Force issued the Action Plan for Reducing, Mitigating, and Controlling Hypoxia in the Northern Gulf of Mexico. In 2004, the task force completed *A Science Strategy to Support Management Decisions Related to Hypoxia in the Northern Gulf of Mexico and Excess Nutrients in the Mississippi River Basin*. In 2006, the task force completed the Management Action Review Team report, a compilation of information on point sources and programs for reducing nutrient loadings, which offers recommendations for how to utilize those programs in the Mississippi River Basin.

In 2008, the task force updated the initial plan and generated a *2008 Action Plan.* This plan lays out the steps needed to meet long-term goals. The plan was initiated because, in the Gulf of Mexico, there is a large area of low oxygen (hypoxia) in which most marine life is absent and is threatening to change the biology of the region off the coasts of Louisiana and Texas. The hypoxia is primarily caused by excess nutrients, which lead to extensive growths of algae, which deplete the oxygen in the water when they die and decompose. If the hypoxia is not addressed, the impact to the Mississippi River and the Gulf of Mexico could be devastating.

The hypoxic zone in the Northern Gulf of Mexico forms each summer. It can extend up to 80 miles offshore and stretch from the mouth of the Mississippi River westward to Texas coastal waters. In 2007, the hypoxic zone was 7,900 square miles. The goal of the *2008 Action Plan* is to reduce the five-year running average size of the zone to less than 1,900 square miles.

The project is important because the watershed of the Mississippi River drains 41% of the contiguous United States. It includes waters from several major river systems, including the Missouri/Platte River Basin, the Ohio/Tennessee River Basin, and the Arkansas/Red/White River Basin.

The Mississippi River Basin includes two functionally distinct zones: the Mississippi watershed with its tributary network, and the deltaic zone at the lower end of the river system.

The Mississippi River/Gulf of Mexico Watershed Nutrient Task Force has reaffirmed six overarching principles as guidance to reach the three major goals of the 2008 Action Plan:

1. Encourage actions that are voluntary, incentive-based, practical, and cost-effective.

2. Utilize existing programs, including existing state and federal regulatory mechanisms.

3. Follow adaptive management.

4. Identify additional funding needs and sources during the annual agency budget processes.

5. Identify opportunities for, and potential barriers to, innovative and market-based solutions.

6. Provide measurable outcomes as outlined below in the three goals and 11 actions.

The task force revised and reaffirmed three goals that are intended to be consistent with these principles. They are:

1. **Coastal goal.** To reduce or make significant progress toward reducing the five-year running average areal extent of the Gulf of Mexico hypoxic zone to less than 4,000 square miles by the year 2015.

2. **Within-basin goal.** To restore and protect the waters of the 31 states and tribal lands within the Mississippi/Atchafalaya River Basin through implementation of nutrient and sediment reduction actions.

3. **Quality-of-life goal.** To improve the communities and economic conditions across the Mississippi/Atchafalaya River Basin through improved public and private land management and a cooperative, incentive-based approach.

4.0 SUSTAINABLE PRACTICES FOR SITE PLANNING, DESIGN, AND IMPLEMENTATION

4.1 DEVELOPING GOALS AND OBJECTIVES

What are we trying to accomplish when it comes to water resources? The answer, of course, varies from one water resource project to the next. For example, one fundamental question is what each lake association wants its lake to look like 20 years from now, and what steps need to be taken to achieve that vision.

Goals related to water resources often start off very broad. Virtually every city wants to have clean, safe, and available drinking water. That is pretty much a given. Water resource goals and objectives are defined early on in the watershed planning process to help ensure the plan will meet expectations. Many of these goals are greatly influenced by federal and state policies. In the United States, the Clean Water Act, for example, has guided many goals from the state level to the local level. State water plans typically outline basic goals that can be applied by water districts, counties, and municipalities.

Lincolnville, Maine, Comprehensive Plan Goals and Implementation Strategies for Water Resources

Water Resources Goal #1
To improve water quality in Lincolnville's lakes and ponds. The water quality in Lincolnville's lakes and ponds is a valuable and threatened resource.

Implementation Strategies
- Encourage the formation of a water resources subcommittee that would work in conjunction with the Land Use Committee to develop appropriate performance standards for construction adjacent to Lincolnville's lakes and ponds such as septic systems to be designed at a greater than minimum design factor.
- Encourage frequent visits by the chief executive officer to waterfront construction sites to assist contractors and owners in proper siting and erosion control measures.
- Educate Lincolnville residents in methods of maintaining satisfactory water quality in lakes and ponds.
- Encourage permanent erosion control measures on existing roads and driveways.
- Encourage the voluntary correction of malfunctioning septic systems on waterfront property through education and a town application to the Small Community Development Grant Program.
- Require developers to adhere to best management practices for erosion, sedimentation, and stormwater control.

Water Resource Goal #2
To maintain the water quality in Lincolnville's streams and brooks. The water in Lincolnville's streams and brooks serves an important function as the main water source for Lincolnville's lakes and ponds.

Implementation Strategy
- A yearly perambulation should be made of the major streams serving their water bodies.

(continues)

(continued)

- Consider the inclusion of other streams in the Shoreland Zone Ordinance.

Water Resources Goal #3

To ensure that the groundwater resources of Lincolnville are adequately protected. An adequate supply of pure uncontaminated groundwater is the most important natural resource in Lincolnville.

Implementation Strategies

- Develop a database of information on wells in the center that would assist in an analysis of hydrocarbon infiltration into the groundwater and to determine the extent, type, location, and source of pollution (Town Office Staff, CEO—Ongoing).

- Develop a database of information on wells in the beach area that would assist in the quantitative analysis of the saltwater infiltration issue (Town Office Staff, CEO—Ongoing).

- Encourage the identification of suitable land that might serve as sites for community wells in or adjacent to densely developed areas such as the beach or Lincolnville Center. Explore sources of funding such well development (Town Administrator, CEO—May 1994).

- Develop a plan for the protection of identified acquifiers (Conservation Commission, Planning Board, CEO—May 1994).

Water Resources Goal #4

To develop a phosphorus control management program in great pond watersheds.

Implementation Strategies

- Research methods of including phosphorus control measures in Town ordinances.

- Encourage individual lake associations to keep current on phosphorus mitigation and to research phosphorus problems.

- Develop broad-based community support for the 604-B program to be implemented in 1993. This grant, which has been awarded to Lincolnville, will assist our town to better understand and manage phosphorous buildup in our lakes and ponds.

Initial goals typically are developed by an oversight organization or agency, and are based on a review of existing conditions within a watershed. These goals usually start out broad but are then refined through a stakeholder process that seeks input from people who will be impacted by changes within a watershed. For example, White Pine County, Nevada, identified two primary goals for management of its water resources: maintaining the quality of its environment and maintaining the quality of life for its citizens. These goals probably apply to most communities around the world. (See Figure 4.1.)

The more specific we can make our goals, the easier it will be to refine these and make them measurable. For each goal that is defined, specific management objectives should be developed. A wide range of specific objectives should be developed and implemented to support each aspect of the goal.

It is critical that key stakeholders be involved with developing the goals and objectives for a particular watershed or water resource project. During the public participation process, people normally get involved because they have specific concerns. These usually involve personal issues, such as the availability of water for agriculture uses, watering the lawn,

---

Brazos River Bacteria Assessment

For the Brazos River Bacteria Assessment, the Texas Water Resources Institute established a series of goals to assess contact recreation use impairments and support watershed planning for five tributaries of the river. They are:

- Facilitating public participation and coordinating stakeholder involvement in decision making

- Developing a comprehensive Geographic Information Systems (GIS) inventory and conducting a watershed source survey

- Collecting water quality monitoring data

- Conducting bacterial source tracking

- Analyzing data using load duration curves and spatially explicit modeling

---

Figure 4.1 *Environmental education is often a goal of water-oriented projects. Image courtesy EDAW.*

Figure 4.2 *One goal of the National Museum of the American Indian, located in Washington, DC., was to utilize forms and materials that reflect Native American culture. Image courtesy EDAW.*

or having clean drinking water. There is an old joke that the best way to get people interested in water is to raise their monthly bill. It is hoped, though, that people will get involved for other reasons. There should be a strong educational component involved with every set of goals so the public can make informed decisions about what is important.

There are obvious conflicts when it comes to establishing goals for how to deal with water resources. Not all stakeholders may agree that wetlands are important, and

there are constant disagreements about what should be priorities for water use during times of drought or limited water availability. Some strongly support the preservation of wetlands, wildlife habitat, and undisturbed natural areas, while others are advocates of economic growth and development. (See Figures 4.2, 4.3, and 4.4.)

All states, districts, and municipalities in the United States have established goals for protecting water quality. Water quality standards define the goals for a water body by

Figure 4.3 *The series of waterfalls is supposed to be reminiscent of the natural falls found out west. Image courtesy EDAW.*

designating its uses, setting criteria to protect those uses, and establishing provisions to protect water bodies from pollutants. They are the foundation of the water quality–based pollution control program mandated by the Clean Water Act.

Figure 4.4 *The falls appear to be part of the building itself. Image courtesy EDAW.*

Compilation of Water Quality Goals

The California Environmental Protection Agency's Central Valley Regional Water Quality Control Board developed "A Compilation of Water Quality Goals" to introduce the state's water quality standards and to outline a system for selecting numerical water quality limits consistent with these standards, The standards are designed to protect beneficial uses of groundwater and surface water resources. These are consistent with the state's water quality standards, which are outlined in the *Water Quality Control Plans* adopted by the California State Water Resources Control Board and each of the nine Regional Water Quality Control Boards.

www.swrcb.ca.gov/water_issues/programs/water_quality_goals/docs/cover_text_aug_2007.pdf.

4.2 WORKING WITH LOCAL STAKEHOLDERS

At the same time that water resource issues are becoming more complex, citizens are no longer willing to let water resource managers, planning professionals, and hydrologists make all of the decisions about their community. The days of planning in a black box are gone, and concerned citizens want to know not only what decisions are being made but also how and why they are being made. Although it may take longer to make design and planning decisions, the likelihood of these decisions being implemented is much greater because of public involvement.

Nworie River

Nworie River is a first-order stream that runs about a 5-km course across Owerri metropolis in Imo State, Nigeria, before emptying into the Otamiri River. A first-order stream is the smallest tributary that makes up a stream system, and is typically referred to as a "headwater" stream. Its watershed is subject to intensive human and industrial activities resulting in the discharge of a wide range of pollutants. The river is used for various domestic applications by inhabitants of Owerri. When the public water supply fails, the river serves as a source of direct drinking water, especially for the poorer segment of the city. Studies of water quality parameters are therefore necessary to determine the extent of pollution so as to monitor likely danger, not only to the human population but also to the aquatic life. A total of 11 water quality parameters were investigated during January 2007, which fell within the dry season in Nigeria. The parameters investigated were:

1. Dissolved oxygen
2. Carbon dioxide
3. pH
4. Chloride
5. Nitrate-nitrogen
6. Nitrate
7. Ammonia-nitrogen
8. Hardness
9. Orthophosphate
10. Sulfide
11. Silica

With the exception of dissolved oxygen and carbon dioxide, other chemical parameters did not exceed the water quality standards, suggesting that the river was relatively unpolluted chemically when surveyed. However, the low dissolved oxygen concentrations and high carbon dioxide concentrations strongly indicate pollution by organic wastes. Further, the study demonstrated significant longitudinal variations in the water quality parameters along the course of the river, reflecting differences in quality and quantity of pollutants at various locations. It is recommended that further studies be conducted that include the biological profile of the river.

Nworie River, a typical freshwater resource under high urban pressure, is of enormous economic importance to inhabitants of Owerri metropolis as it serves as a water source and also as a channel of sewage disposal. The river also supports a substantial recreational and part-time fishing for youths.

Nworie River is potentially vulnerable to a variety of polluting influences. All through its course, there is a steady input of large quantities of detergents from laundry activities. At several points, the river receives large quantities of sewage and solid wastes, especially plastic water bottles. Further, when it rains, large volumes of runoff carrying agricultural and human wastes are discharged directly into the river.

It is recommended that Nworie River be dredged, but by experienced professionals who do such work. It may do more harm than good if improperly conducted by raking up pollutants that settled at the bottom of the river. Such actions may increase or cause the resurgence of waterborne diseases, such as typhoid, cholera, dysentery, and some intestinal parasitic diseases. The former river course deserves to be reestablished and its esthetic beauty and cleanliness restored. Any bridge crossing the river that impedes its free flow, as is currently the situation in some areas, needs to be reconstructed.

Figure 4.5 *Local stakeholders show up for a meeting to discuss possible plans for southern Cobb County, Georgia, and the Chattahoochee River. Image courtesy EDAW.*

One of the keys to effective water resource management is to involve as many stakeholders as possible during the planning process. The term *stakeholders* is often defined as any individual, agency, or organization involved in or affected by decisions made to water resources. Since we all need water, virtually everyone has some vested interest in water resources. The difference, though, is that if you live in Florida, you probably are not too concerned with the water situation in southern California, or if you live in China, you are not worried about water problems in Canada.

Frequently when we talk about stakeholders, we are talking about those people who are willing to step forward and express an opinion during the design, planning, or implementation process. In 1996, the Center for Watershed Protection (www.cwp.org) conducted research that showed that implementation of a plan that impacts water resources has the greatest chance of success when stakeholders are actively involved in the planning process from the start. (See Figure 4.5.)

It is not unusual for stakeholders to have conflicting concerns about what happens to water resources. Some want to use the water to grow crops, some to provide safe drinking water, and others to ensure that the environment is protected.

Stakeholder involvement is important in the development of comprehensive plans to help ensure that relevant issues are addressed. The level of stakeholder involvement varies from project to project. If people are okay with a project, they often do not get involved. Likewise, the more people who are upset about a design that involves water resources, the more they want to have their voice heard.

There are a number of ways to get stakeholders involved in a project. Most projects include well-advertised public meetings and workshops to give people an opportunity to get involved. Some projects include one-on-one interviews with key stakeholders. Surveys are also a great way to reach people. These can include traditional surveys sent through the mail or picked up at a public place, or online surveys that allow people to share thoughts while sitting at their computer in their own homes.

4.2.1 Types of Stakeholders

Water resources projects involve a multitude of players, each with a unique perspective and its own process to accomplish its ends. To understand how technology fits into these processes, it is important to first understand the perspectives and motivations of each player and how each relates to the other's process. In land planning, the key players include developers, professional consultants, public agencies and organizations, nongovernmental organizations and nonprofit interest groups, the public, and financiers.

Developers

Developers are the people who take the risk and conceive the vision for a land development or water resource project and typically see it through to its completion.

Professional Consultants

Professional consultants are the people hired by the developer to bring an idea to fruition. Many different consultants enter the project at various phases, including market analysts, planners, landscape architects, surveyors, civil engineers, environmental consultants, architects, urban designers, and attorneys.

Public Agencies and Organizations

Water resource management is a highly regulated enterprise. Much of the information prepared by professional consultants is in direct response to these regulations. In the public sector, planners review a proposed development to ensure that it meets all zoning and subdivision regulations and contributes to the community and its character. There is a public planning process that must be understood by those involved with water resource management, along with a review process for subdivisions and other developments on the land. In the United States, federal agencies often represent the general public in water resource projects. The U.S. Fish and Wildlife Service, U.S. Army Corps of Engineers, National Park Service, Bureau of Land Management, Environmental Protection Agency, and Bureau of Indian Affairs may all be involved in various water-oriented projects. Each state has its own agencies that address statutory roles and responsibilities. State agencies are responsible for parks and recreation, fish and wildlife, water quality, historic preservation, cultural resource management, and other activities. Local government has primary responsibility for urban watershed restoration. Local jurisdictions and agencies involved in water resource projects may include regional councils, county agencies, and municipal departments.

Nongovernmental Organizations and Nonprofit Interest Groups

Nongovernmental organizations (NGOs) and nonprofit interest groups are concerned with preserving parcels of land from development for other uses and activities such as open space, wildlife, protection of sensitive natural resources, drinking water and flood protection. NGOs include homeowners' associations; environmental groups; chambers of commerce; builders and contractors; recreation organizations; and individual property owners. Other groups, such as trade associations, research and academic institutions, sporting groups, and individual citizens, might also be involved.

NGOs and nonprofit interests groups exist all across the United States. Lake Homeowners Alliance is a nonprofit organization formed to unite Georgia's lake community associations. The Bay Area Stormwater Management Agencies Association is an association of several stormwater programs representing a dozen municipalities. The North Carolina Lake Management Society was formed in 1994 to bring together individuals and groups with shared interests in lakes. Its members include lake homeowners, scientists, agency representatives, and citizens. Members of the Lake Hartwell (GA) Coalition are concerned with the U.S. Army Corps of Engineers' decision to take more water out of Hartwell Lake because of the impact it would have on the local economy. The coalition is made up of a group of business owners on both the Georgia and South Carolina sides, and they are concerned because the low lake levels in the summers of 2006 and 2007 have all but killed tourism. Fewer people are visiting the lake for vacation, and that has had a negative effect on the local economies around the lake (Kneiser, 2008).

At the national level, the Nature Conservancy (TNC) is a conservation organization working to protect ecologically important lands and waters for nature and people. TNC has developed an Aquatic Ecosystem Classification Framework that helps establish priorities for freshwater areas. TNC also

Figure 4.6 *Many of the decisions we make about water resources are intended to ensure we allow future generations to have sufficient water. Image courtesy EDAW.*

has a Sustainable Waters Program that focuses on how water flows can be managed to meet human needs while sustaining ecosystem health.

Public

The public is a major stakeholder in every watershed restoration effort. People in the community typically are impacted by any changes to water resources. One big issue with water resource projects is to find a way to reach out to the public and ensure they have an opportunity to participate in the process. (See Figure 4.6.)

Financiers

Land development projects are funded in numerous ways since typically they are very expensive. Financiers include private investors (pension funds, wealthy individuals, joint ventures); real estate investment trusts, mortgages, construction loans, public redevelopment loans, public grants such as those for affordable housing or historic preservation, or equity financing using cash flows from the developer's other projects.

4.2.2 Web-Based Communication Technologies

The Web's pervasiveness makes it an ideal platform for increasing the level of collaboration on design and planning projects. Web-based applications can enable better coordination among design team members and can also help increase the level of public participation in civic decision making. Secure logins, public and private interfaces, correspondence tracking, and database integration are useful features, as are digital-based mapping and graphic products.

Web-based communication technologies are also frequently used to encourage stakeholder participation in water resource decisions. These Web-based tools are inexpensive, easy to access, and easy to use. The Internet can be accessed anytime, day or night, and participation for a design or planning project on the Web can be run for months or even years. In addition, Web-based tools can offer greater access to groups that have difficulty reaching public participation meetings, such as the physically handicapped or the elderly, and can also allow individuals living in rural areas to participate in the decision-making process without traveling long distances to do so.

With a Web-based system, it is important to ensure that a diverse audience reflects the concerns and values of a community. Participants at public meetings do not always reflect community views, and the loudest participants frequently dominate a meeting. Individuals who are hesitant to express their opinions at a public meeting may find it more comfortable to post on a Web site because of the anonymity this approach provides.

But Web-based participation tools also have their limitations. One of the biggest concerns with using Web-based systems for public participation is that they lack the face-to-face interaction, deliberation, and exchange of ideas that should be part of traditional town meetings. Another concern is that this type of system discriminates against citizens who cannot afford or do not have ready access to the appropriate computer technology. Traditional points of public access to computers, such as libraries and schools, help minimize this concern, and new Web-access locations, such as Internet cafés, are becoming more popular in many communities.

The Department of Energy is using Internet sites in an effort to increase public participation in the National Environmental Policy Act process for both the Savannah River (GA) site and the Peconic River (NY). The project Web site contains the project status and description, technical resources available for the project, baseline information, and opportunities for stakeholder involvement. The discussion forum for both projects allows participants to discuss topics of interest through the Web site. There is no registration required to participate in the discussion forum.

For Web-based public participation to be effective, Web sites and scheduled discussions need to be regularly publicized through the media and brochures distributed in the community, such as in libraries, community and neighborhood centers, and other appropriate locations. In addition, these Web-based communication technologies must be looked at simply as another set of tools that may help get the right people involved in the decision-making process for design and planning projects.

Community-based online mapping is also a popular way to share information with citizens because the information is so easy to access and to modify. The objective behind online mapping is to share data across organizations, platforms, and formats in order to enhance the community planning process. One of the real benefits of this approach is that as citizens become more involved in making decisions about their neighborhood, they also get a better understanding of where they live and what is important to their neighbors. This process of discovery helps lay the foundation for discussions involving design and planning projects.

4.2.3 Public Involvement Plan

One of the first tasks on a water resource planning project is typically to work with the client to prepare a public involvement and communications plan. The plan confirms how many public meetings will be conducted, as well as timing, general locations, and other variables to ensure that all stakeholders are aware of and have access to the planning process. It also identifies potential additional strategies for communicating via the press, Web-based communications, e-mail list serves, and other communication strategy enhancements deemed applicable to the project.

The design and planning team meets with residents, individuals involved in development finance, those with knowledge about community and historic assets, and other people in an effort to understand and quantify realistic development and preservation potential for the study area. Meeting with these groups and individuals provides a better idea of what opportunities and constraints are associated with each project or site.

4.3 DESIGN PROCESS

The design process is intended to outline the steps needed to ensure that a project has clearly defined objectives, that sufficient analysis is conducted, and that design decisions take into account all considerations in order to lead to a sustainable solution. An effective design process should lead to better design and planning decisions. For example, some of the environmental benefits of this process could include protection of ecologically significant natural resources, reduction of runoff, and preservation of open space and wildlife habitat.

There are many different approaches to the planning and design process, but they can all be simplified into five major steps.

1. **Research.** Define what the project will be.

2. **Inventory/Analysis.** Determine if the land will support the proposed use.

3. **Synthesis.** Develop a concept and design for the land use.

4. **Implementation.** Adopt a plan or build the design.

5. **Evaluation.** Determine if the project works as intended.

Knowing where you are in the process will influence the scale of thinking, the data that you require, and the application you use to process the data (Digital Land). (See Figures 4.7, 4.8, 4.9, 4.10, and 4.11.)

Figure 4.9 *An aspect map shows the direction the land is facing. South- and west-facing slopes receive the most sun. Image courtesy EDAW.*

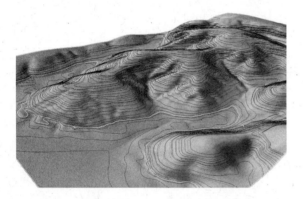

Figure 4.7 *Slope analysis looks at the existing topography to determine the best places to build. The dark areas on the map have the steepest slopes at Liberty Hill Farms at Lake Wateree, South Carolina. Image courtesy EDAW.*

4.3.1 Research

One of the initial steps in the design process is to determine what the project is and how best to approach a specific site or issue. This involves understanding the issues and stakeholders involved, and opportunities and concerns that need to be addressed.

For a project to meet its stated goals, it needs to be considered within a broader context. This involves understanding local and regional trends and patterns and the changes that are expected to occur that could influence water resources. Local, regional, and national growth trends need to be evaluated in natural recreational activities, and other communities must be surveyed to see what has been successful. Stormwater quality requirements should be considered early in the design process to prevent water quality BMPs from being an afterthought. (See Figure 4.12.)

4.3.2 Inventory/Analysis

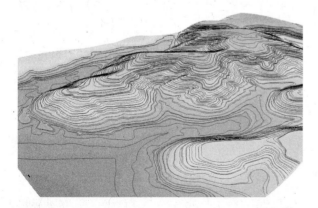

Figure 4.8 *This elevation map shows the changes in height of the existing landform. In order to make maps easier to read, symbols and colors are used to represent various natural and man-made features. The darker areas are typically inundated by water. Image courtesy EDAW.*

Effective strategic planning always begins with a sound base of information. For every project, designs and planners conduct an initial inventory and analysis of the site and

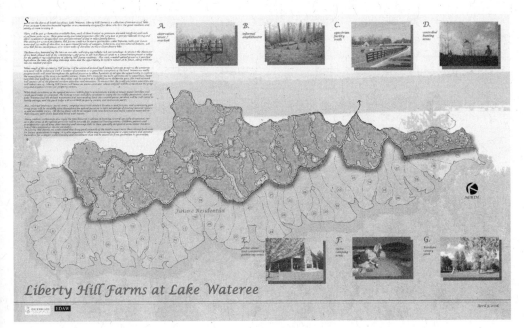

Figure 4.10 *The master plan for Liberty Hill Farms at Lake Wateree, South Carolina, consists of large estate lots in order to reduce the impact on natural resources. Image courtesy EDAW.*

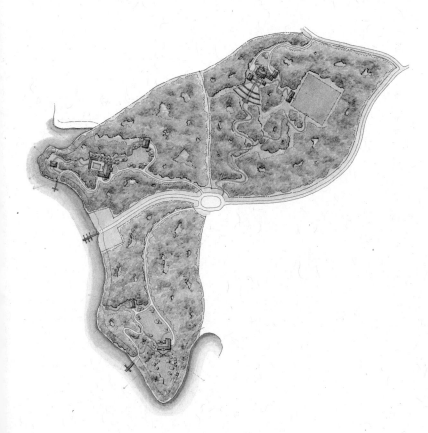

Figure 4.11 *The estate lots allow for the preservation of large expanses of green space. Image courtesy EDAW.*

adjacent areas, and this information serves as the foundation from which decisions are made. Designers and planners use geospatial data, satellite photos, computer-assisted design data, and site visits to identify key existing conditions and opportunities. The process includes documenting existing facilities and amenities, thoroughly analyzing the implications of the existing site, and then

starting the synthesis process to determine the most appropriate design and planning decisions. The inventory phase includes identifying all significant cultural, natural, historic, and aesthetic resources and evaluating them as part of the planning process. (See Figure 4.13.)

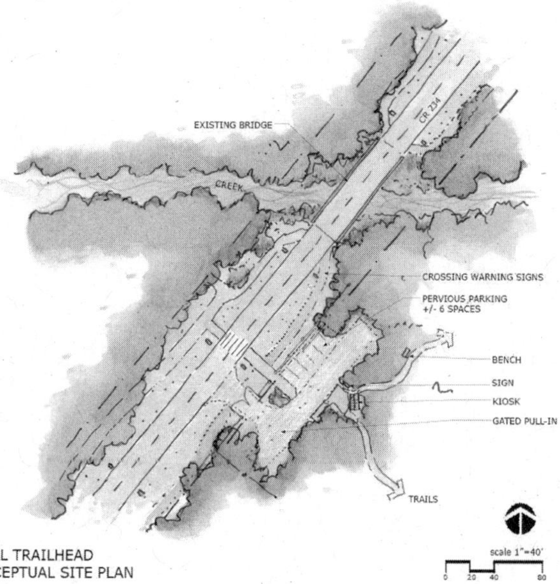

Part of understanding local needs is to listen to residents and other stakeholders. While accurate facts are essential, it is the public's vision, trust, and support that truly drive the effort. Stakeholder involvement will be paramount in generating enthusiasm and building the broad community support for innovative parks, recreation, and open space planning in the years ahead.

4.3.3 Synthesis

Synthesis involves building on the research and inventory/analysis and generating plans that meet the stated goals of a project.

A master plan is intended to create a "framework" that guides the future development of a project. The objective of the synthesis process is to develop a master plan that provides clear design guidance for a cohesive series of implementation projects.

This master plan identifies future, discrete improvement projects and lays out an achievable and cost-effective strategy for their implementation. Although conceptual in

Figure 4.12 *This plan for Camp Canal, in central Florida, allows access to the river Styx. Image courtesy EDAW.*

Figure 4.13 *Bubble diagrams are developed to represent potential design alternatives. Image courtesy EDAW.*

Sustainable Practices for Site Planning, Design, and Implementation

nature, design concepts should be drawn from a thorough and careful process that determines the best solution for a given problem. Conceptual plans compare and contrast a property's existing resources with identified community needs, preferences, and associated service requirements. Emphasis is on designs that are sustainable, from both an environmental and an economic standpoint. For example, site designs that emphasize sustainability and green practices can also result in cost savings by reducing the size of runoff detention structures and eliminating catch basins and pipes.

The plan evaluates potential sites on a property and determines the best location for specific program elements. In addition, adjacent properties are evaluated to determine the impact they have on the overall goals of the project.

Based on a review of the alternative concepts, feedback from the city, stakeholders, and other appropriate participants is incorporated into the design. Public meetings give citizens and stakeholders an opportunity to share their thoughts on the master plan. The result of this process is the development of a preliminary preferred master plan, which may be one of the original alternative concepts or some new concept that perhaps has elements of each. This preliminary preferred master plan typically is reviewed by the client, and any changes are incorporated in the final master plan. (See Figures 4.14, 4.15, and 4.16.)

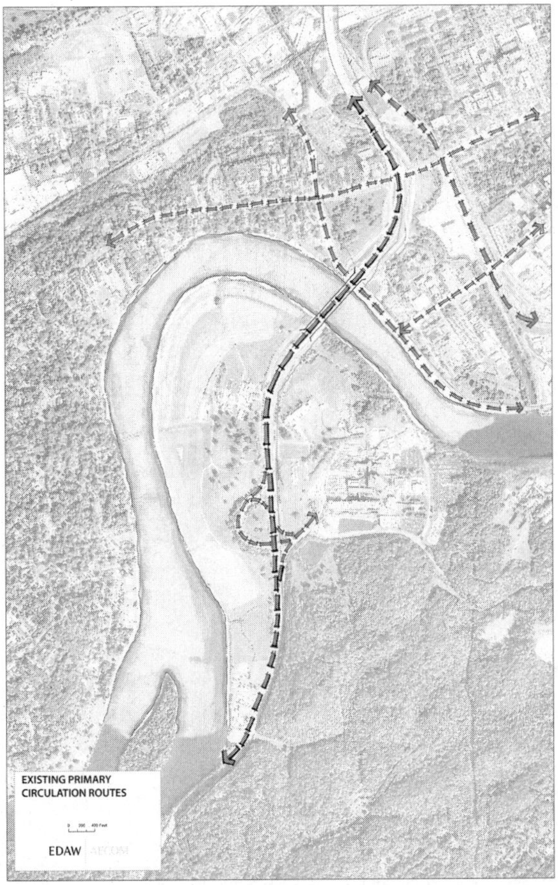

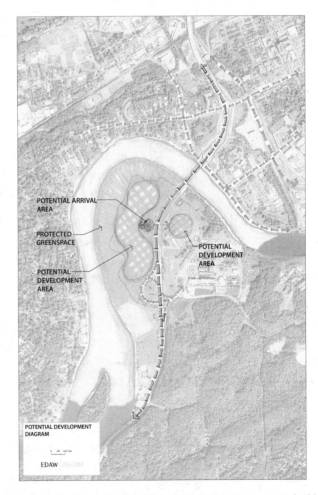

Figure 4.14 *The start of any design project is to understand existing site conditions. This map shows existing transportation infrastructure at the University of Tennessee (UT) at Knoxville, which wanted to explore alternatives for a new research campus. Image courtesy EDAW.*

Figure 4.15 *One alternative for the UT research campus was to build facilities on both sides of the road. Image courtesy EDAW.*

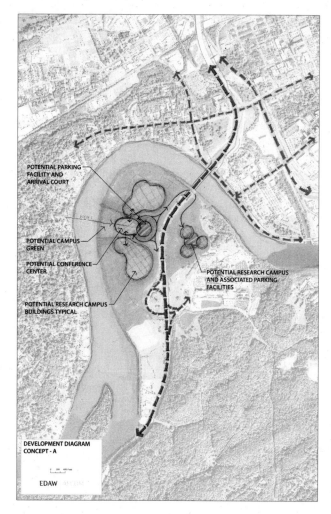

Figure 4.16 *Each alternative is evaluated to determine which is the best fit in terms of program goals. Image courtesy EDAW.*

4.3.4 Implementation

The final measure of any plan is whether its recommendations are implemented. For a given project, a design team will recommend the regulations, policy changes, intergovernmental agreements, public-private partnerships, capital investments, tax incentives, and other measures that can help support a coordinated, sustainable, and appropriate development program.

The objective is to develop a plan that is achievable and sustainable, balancing the vision of the community and the fiscal responsibility of a municipality. Doing this includes understanding the constraints of public sector funding and the need for phasing strategies that are flexible, cost effective, and opportunistic in response to funding successes.

Following adoption of a master plan by a municipality, an action plan and implementation strategy is developed that notes tasks, responsibilities, and timelines for moving the project forward. The implementation strategy also describes the organizational structure and process that will be used, analyzes maintenance and operations, and addresses management needs. (See Figures 4.17, 4.18, and 4.19.)

At an overview/conceptual level, strategic recommendations address such issues as organization and management, operations and maintenance responsibilities, and possible funding for development and operations.

The key to any master plan is creating a strong vision and then finding a way to make that vision a reality. One approach is to develop a multiyear funding plan for development that will cover both the initial stages of construction as well as later stages when development may be more supportive and incremental.

Figure 4.17 At Baldwin Park, Orlando, Florida, a small lake was constructed to manage stormwater. Baldwin Park is a New Urbanism development that emphasizes smart growth principles. Image courtesy EDAW.

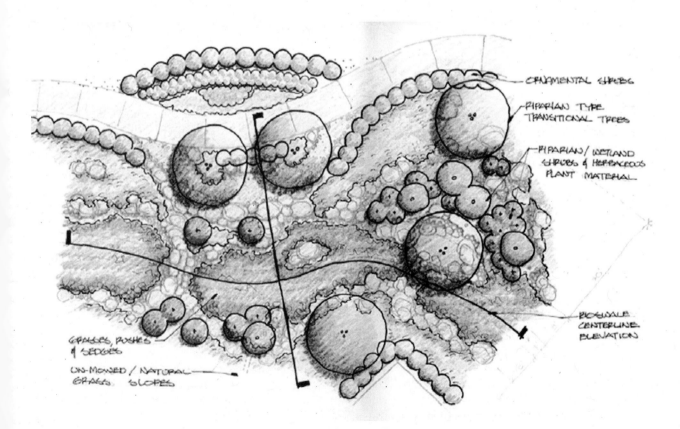

ORNAMENTAL SHRUBS

RIPARIAN TYPE TRANSITIONAL TREES

RIPARIAN / WETLAND SHRUBS & HERBACEOUS PLANT MATERIAL

BIOSWALE CENTERLINE ELEVATION

GRASSES, RUSHES & SEDGES

UN-MOWED / NATURAL GRASS SLOPES

Figure 4.18 Quarry Falls is a 230-acre sand gravel quarry in Mission Valley, California. Image courtesy EDAW.

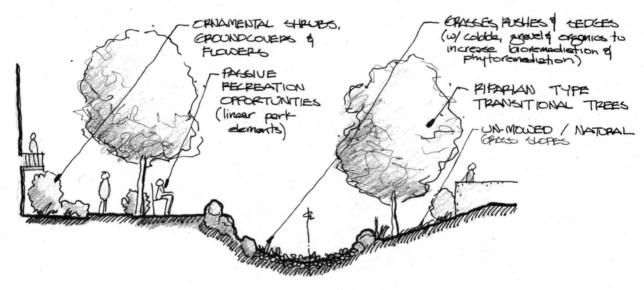

Figure 4.19 *Grasses, rushes, and sedges are combined with hardscape materials to help create a linear park. Image courtesy EDAW.*

Cobb County River Line Planning Process

The Cobb County Community Development Agency requested land use, preservation, recreation, and nonvehicular transportation planning services for the development of a master plan in southern Cobb County (GA). A key tenet of the plan was to get insight from a wide range of stakeholders who really knew the River Line area and who could report on its strengths as well as its challenges.

Review of Existing Studies and Data

A baseline analysis was undertaken to understand the context of the River Line study area. Plans addressing policy, transportation, open space, the Chattahoochee River, and historic resources were reviewed to ensure the consistency of the River Line Master Plan with their contents and to recommend potential amendments to these plans.

Inventory and Analysis

The AECOM design and planning team documented existing conditions, analyzed the implications of what is there, and then started the synthesis process to determine the most appropriate design and planning decisions. Specific issues assessed include the study area's current land use patterns, recreational opportunities, nonvehicular transportation options, preservation efforts, and urban design elements.

Development of Primary Planning Principles

Six primary planning principles were developed to guide development of a master plan. They are:

1. Enhance connectivity,
2. Reconnect to the river.
3. Enhance recreation opportunities.
4. Emphasize cultural and historic resources.
5. Create community-friendly character.
6. Develop strong sense of identity.

Sustainable Practices for Site Planning, Design, and Implementation

Alternative Planning Concepts

The design team developed three alternative planning concepts:

1. **Green/Community.** This concept places an emphasis on natural resources, pedestrian connections, new parks, and community facilities.

2. **Historic/Cultural.** This concept emphasizes the rich, diverse history of the River Line area.

3. **Village Center.** This concept focuses on developing an urban center that serves as the heart of the River Line neighborhood and making the transition from a bedroom subdivision to a true village center.

Preliminary Preferred Master Plan

Based on reviews of the alternative concepts, we incorporated feedback to create a preliminary preferred master plan. This plan incorporates the strongest features of the three alternative concepts and blends them into one plan.

Final Master Plan

The preliminary preferred master plan was reviewed and appropriate modifications were made and incorporated into the final master plan. The primary focal point of the preferred alternative is a mixed-use village center that would include commercial, residential, and public uses and would include public gathering spaces, walkways and trails, and strong visual and physical links to the river.

Implementation Strategy

The implementation strategy is intended to provide direction for how to make the recommendations in this plan a reality. The strategy and schedule are organized around the four guiding elements of the master plan: land use, preservation, recreation, and transportation. Environmental issues are a priority because there is a high probability that industrial sites along the river are contaminated. It is difficult to determine the type and amount of pollution that has occurred, and what remediation is required, until initial studies are completed.

4.4 LAKE MANAGEMENT PLAN AND ACTIONS

Each lake has unique characteristics that define it. The size, shape, mean and maximum depths, volume, and location of the lake are important, as is watershed size, watershed land use, soil types, climate, and water chemistry.

A sustainable lake management plan should start by establishing goals and should address shoreland development, lake uses, water management, and water quality. Once goals are established, data are collected and analyzed, and a plan of action is developed. Water monitoring is also critical for river basin planning so progress toward cleaner water can be measured.

4.4.1 Lake Water Quality

The water quality of a lake depends in large part on what happens in the watershed. Every watershed is unique, and several factors interact to define a lake basin's characteristics. Collecting water quality data is one of the best ways to determine the condition of water resources. Some of the data used to evaluate a lake basin include depth contour, high/low water maps, aquatic plant inventories, water quality data, and other information. The soil and water conservation district manager is a good source of information on lakes within a given area.

Water quality measurements are an indicator of the impacts of land-based activity on the lake. As development within a watershed increases, runoff, erosion, and sedimentation tend to increase as a result of the more impervious area that does not allow water to percolate into the soil. Often there also is an increased delivery of phosphorus, which is a major contributor to algal populations and decreased water clarity in a lake. Other water quality measurements that may be collected include dissolved oxygen levels, pH, chlorophyll-a, nitrates, and turbidity. (See Figure 4.20.)

Many lakeshore areas, because they are located in rural areas, depend on septic systems as their only feasible option for treating wastewater. Noncomplying septic systems are a concern because the threats they present to lake water quality. These types of septic systems can discharge

Figure 4.20 *At Lake Wateree, South Carolina, water quality is a major concern. One of the biggest culprits is agricultural uses along the lake. Image courtesy EDAW.*

nutrients and fecal bacteria into water supplies. Increased phosphorus levels, for example, can result from failing and nonconforming septic systems as well as from animal waste.

Aerial spraying of herbicides and pesticides, irrigation in sandy soils, and uncontrolled runoff of water from fertilized cropland or animal contaminant areas such as pens or other small, fenced spaces can also impact water quality.

Changes in water quality are primarily a reflection of what happens along the shoreland and within a watershed. The crucial areas for water quality include the land within one-eighth mile of a lake and the land use practices that take place there. Public lands adjacent to lakes need to be managed for the direct benefit of the lakes. Development along steep slopes and bluffs can lead to destabilization of slopes and significant erosion problems. Steep bluffs can be a significant problem if they are unstable and begin to erode.

Measures that could help improve water quality include vegetative buffer strips, conservation tillage, and erosion

mitigation practices along the lakeshore. (See Figures 4.21 and 4.22.)

4.4.2 Water Changes

For accurate watershed management, lake fluctuations for both high and low water also should be taken into account. Changing water levels impact real estate development, recreation, aquatic plant growth, and fish habitat. The depths of the lake identify where fish are likely to live and where aquatic vegetation is likely to grow.

Natural lakes typically stay at a fairly constant level, assuming that normal rainfall and stream flow occurs. The water levels of most lakes are susceptible to changes in precipitation, and during a drought, the lake level can drop significantly. Many lakes are also dependent on the amount of precipitation that falls within their watershed. Man-made lakes often are lowered to ensure there is an adequate amount of water flowing downstream. In addition, in northern areas, man-made

Figure 4.21 *At Lake Mecred, California, a water level assessment was conducted to get a better idea of water fluctuation in the lake. Image courtesy EDAW.*

Figure 4.22 *Lake Merced is known for its scenic beauty and is a popular tourist attraction. Several decades ago, the lake's water level continued to shrink, threatening the health of the existing lake ecosystem. Due to better management of the aquifer and occasional additions of water, the lake level has been rising since the 1990s. Image courtesy EDAW.*

lakes are intentionally lowered in the fall to allow for enough room for melting snow in the spring.

The littoral zone of a lake is the shallow part where light can penetrate to the bottom. It is typically less than 15 feet in depth and is the area where aquatic vegetation is able to grow. The clearer the lake, the larger the littoral area. The shallow water, abundant light, and nutrient-rich sediment in a littoral zone provide ideal conditions for plant growth.

Sustainable Approaches for Lake Development

There are several different sustainable approaches for lake development. The following was used for the master plan for a new lake in Choctaw County, Mississippi.

- Primary residential: one- to two-acre lots.
- Create an economically viable development.
- Protect cultural and natural resources.
- Utilize sustainable design practices.
- Emphasize rural character.
- Maximize visual quality.
- Ensure quality of water.
- Provide public and private development.
- Create a strong development framework.
- Provide public access.
- Create public recreation opportunities.
- Maintain integrity of the lake.
- Utilize smart growth principles, including mixed-use development.

Mapping historical water levels helps develop an understanding of potential changes in the lake environment. This information is particularly valuable when determining the viability of new development. Watershed managers and planners use historic lake level data to prepare local water management plans and to model lake water quality characteristics. Lakeshore owners use the data to better understand the impacts of water levels at their property, such as where to locate a new dock.

The key to measuring lake temperature is consistency. To get good standard readings of lake temperature, measurements should be made in five feet of water or more. The best time to take the temperature is in late afternoon or early evening.

4.4.3 Water Clarity Readings

Water clarity is measured using a secchi disc, an eight-inch white circular metal plate attached to a rope marked in half-foot intervals. It is lowered into the water, and the depth at which it is no longer visible is recorded. Water clarity, or transparency of a lake, is the most straightforward way to

---

Lake Management Plan

A recommended process for lake associations to create a unique lake management plan is presented next. The steps are general enough to cover the scope of topics that need to be addressed for a comprehensive lake management plan but also flexible enough to be tailored to the unique needs of a specific lake and its community.

1. Initiating Support for the Planning Process
   - Commit to the lake management plan.
   - Choose a planning method.

2. Data Collection and Information Gathering
   - Develop a case history of the lake with available data and anecdotal information from those who have lived on the lake for many years.
   - Create watershed maps.
   - Create a parcel-based database.
   - Collect water quality and lake basin data.
   - Conduct a property owners' survey.

3. Planning Your Lake Management Actions
   - Identify issues and concerns.
   - Develop a vision for the future.
   - Determine your management goals.
   - Create action steps you will take to meet your goals.

Source: *Sustainable Lakes Planning Workbook: A Lake Management Model*, Minnesota Lakes Association in cooperation with the University of Minnesota Center for Urban and Regional Affairs (May 2000).

'NEIGHBORHOOD' GROUPS OF HOMES (4-8) WITH COMMON CLUB FOR BOATHOUSE AND DOCK, BOARDWALK LINKING HOMES

HOMES BEHIND TREE SETBACK

COMMON DOCK AT NEIGHBORHOOD

BOARDWALK TO DOCK

COMMON BOAT/DOCK CLUB
5.27.03   LAC MEKINAC   EDAW

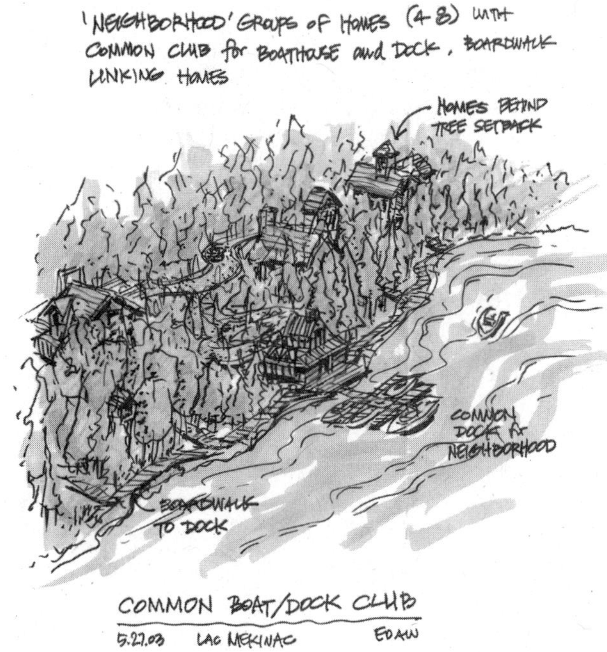

Figure 4.23 *The use of common docks is one way to help protect water quality. Image courtesy EDAW.*

evaluate water quality. Water clarity is influenced by several factors, including the amount of algae, aquatic plants and sediment present, and the natural color of the lake water.

Water transparency varies considerably in lakes across the United States. Many southern lakes have transparencies of no more than two or three feet for most of the year. In contrast, many lakes out West have much greater transparency. (See Figures 4.23 and 4.24.)

Mukhaizna Water Treatment Facility

The Mukhaizna Water Treatment Facility in Oman, an Arab country in southeast Asia, incorporates a process called mechanical vapor compression brine concentrator to generate treated water from oil and gas extraction. This water is then used to supply stream generation. The facility is the largest produced water reuse project in the world, with a capacity of almost 43,000 barrels of oil per day. Approximately 90% of water is reused, and this helps minimize the impact on other water resources.

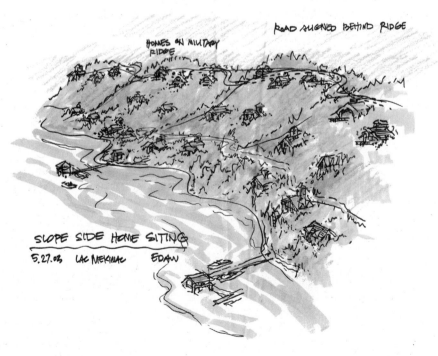

ROAD ALIGNED BEHIND RIDGE

HOMES ON MILITARY RIDGE

SLOPE SIDE HOME SITING
5.27.03   LAC MEKINAC   EDAW

Figure 4.24 *By pulling homes back from the edge of a lake, we can help protect the shoreline. Image courtesy EDAW.*

4.5 RIVER, LAKE, AND WETLAND RESTORATION

In just a few hundred years, Americans have done a great job of totally disrupting the natural processes associated with rivers, streams, lakes, and wetlands. Fortunately, we have also finally figured out how valuable these natural resources are, and efforts are being made to restore them to a point where they function as Mother Nature intended.

Water restoration traditionally has focused on the stream corridor, but many communities are expanding the scope of their efforts to include a larger part of the watershed. In many situations, specific solutions address more than one problem. Solutions range from site-specific solutions to those that address larger water resource issues. Stream repair techniques are limited by their in-stream location, and as a result, the solution may be treating the symptoms but not the underlying causes.

A common goal of stream restoration projects is to minimize erosion, but a certain amount of erosion occurs even

---

The Cost of Constructing Wetlands

The major items included in capital costs of constructed wetlands are

- Land costs
- Site investigation
- Clearing and grubbing
- Excavation and earthwork
- Liner
- Media
- Plants
- Inlet structures
- Outlet structures
- Fencing
- Miscellaneous piping, pumps, etc.
- Engineering, legal, and contingencies
- Contractor's overhead and profit

---

in healthy streams. Streams continuously meander, widen and narrow, and seek the path of least resistance in an effort to reach a stable equilibrium. The problem is that when the velocity and volume of water increases, it can destroy the natural balance of a stream and can significantly increase erosion.

4.5.1 Hydromodification

Hydromodification is one of the leading sources of impairment in U.S. waters. The U.S. Environmental Protection Agency defines *hydromodification* as the "alteration of the hydrologic characteristics of coastal and non-coastal waters, which in turn could cause degradation of water resources." Examples of hydromodification in streams include dredging, straightening, and, in some cases, complete stream relocation (EPA. www.epa.gov/nps/hydromod/).

EPA has grouped hydromodification activities into three categories: (1) channelization and channel modification, (2) dams, and (3) stream bank and shoreline erosion. Channelization can cause in-stream flow changes and result in the faster delivery of pollutants to downstream areas. Channelization modifications include widening, straightening, deepening, and clearing channels of debris and sediment. All of these activities increase water velocity and can result in higher flows during storm events, which potentially increases the risk of flooding.

Categories of channelization and channel modification projects include flood control and drainage, navigation, sediment control, infrastructure protection, mining, channel and bank instability, habitat improvement/enhancement, recreation, and flow control for water supply (EPA. www.epa.gov/nps/hydromod/).

Years ago, channel modifications were made to a river in Missouri in an effort to improve its navigation. The problem is that the modifications increased water velocity so much that barges had to run their engines in reverse when going downstream in order to maintain control, and traveling upstream was a slow process. (See Figure 4.25.)

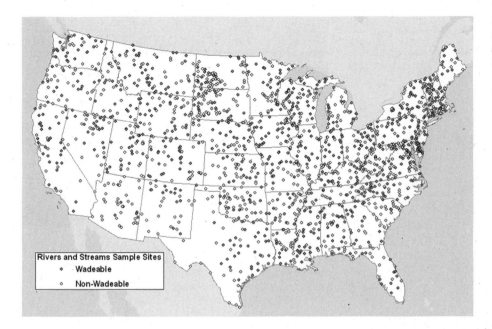

Figure 4.25 *EPA is conducting a detailed survey of all rivers and streams in the continental United States. Image courtesy EDAW.*

Rivers and Streams Sample Sites
- Wadeable
- Non-Wadeable

Tracking Changes in Stream Quality

Changes in stream quality can be tracked according to five broad indicators:

1. Changes to stream hydrology
2. Physical alteration of the stream corridor
3. Stream habitat degradation
4. Declining water quality
5. Loss of aquatic diversity

Source: Tom Schueler, Center for Watershed Protection, *Urban Subwatershed Restoration Manual Series—An Integrated Framework to Restore Small Urban Watersheds,* Manual 1, Version 2.0.Prepared for: Office of Water Management, U.S. Environmental Protection Agency (February 2005).

4.5.2 Stream Repair Practices

Stream repair practices are intended to enhance the functionality and appearance of streams. Stream repair techniques are designed to fix specific problems. The techniques include:

- Hard bank techniques to stabilize eroding banks
- Soft or deformable bank stabilization techniques
- Grade controls to stop channel incision
- Flow deflectors to concentrate the low flow channel
- Techniques to enhance stream habitat features
- Stormwater flow diversions
- Techniques to remove or mitigate fish barriers

Site preparation techniques include removal of trash and rubble, control of invasive plant species, restoration of urban soils, control of hill-slope erosion, and capture and distribution of stormwater evenly across the riparian zone. Riparian management practices focus on restoring the quality of forests and wetlands within a stream corridor. (See Figures 4.26 and 4.27.)

The goal of many restoration projects is to reintroduce characteristics that normally would be found in a natural, healthy stream. That means creating a more natural geometry to the channel that includes shallow slopes and elevation changes, restoring vegetation along the banks, and removing structural elements that impede channel flow. Stream corridor restoration practices are typically not feasible in the upper range of nonsupporting subwatersheds. Nonsupporting subwatersheds experience severe erosion and extensive habitat degradation, and often are impacted to the point where full ecological restoration is not a viable option (Konrad, 2003). Most urban streams have been

---

Figure 4.26 *A simple set of stepping-stones helps eliminate potential negative impacts of this stream. Image courtesy EDAW.*

Figure 4.27 *The Strangers Creek Restoration Project (KA) helps restore native grasses. Not only is it beautiful to look at, but it also provides ideal conditions for the ecosystem to thrive. Image courtesy Strangers Creek Stream Restoration.*

impacted to a point where opportunities for restoration are limited. For one thing, urban streams typically possess poor habitat conditions; as a result, they usually do not have healthy fish populations. The annual nutrient load produced by urban watersheds can be as much as six times higher than that produced by rural watersheds.

4.5.3 Fish Passages

Migratory fish passage throughout U.S. rivers and streams are obstructed by over 2 million dams and many other

barriers, such as blocked, collapsed, and elevated culverts (www.nmfs.noaa.gov/habitat/restoration/ORI). Migrating fish populations are also impacted by the turbines of hydro-electric dams. Fish ladders and bypass channels are just a few measures that are intended to help fish travel past dams. Some of the other approaches that have been used over the years to help improve fish passage are spill-and-water buckets, fish lifts, advanced hydroelectric turbines, transference of fish runs, and constructed spawning beds. Some of these approaches have worked and some have not. The difficult thing is that fish are unpredictable, and every stream and every dam or obstacle is unique.

4.5.4 Constructed Wetlands

Constructed wetlands are artificial wetlands built to provide wastewater treatment. Constructed wetlands employ ecological processes found in natural wetland ecosystems. They typically are made of shallow ponds or channels that include aquatic plants and rely on natural microbial, biological, physical, and chemical processes to treat wastewater. They are almost always regulated as wastewater treatment facilities and have been used to treat many types of wastewater at various levels of treatment. Constructed wetlands are well suited for wastewater treatment in small

Figure 4.28 *This restored wetlands is in Palo Alto County, in northern Iowa. Image courtesy NRCS.*

communities where inexpensive land is available, but they are not used very often in urban areas. They typically have impervious clay or synthetic liners and engineered structures to control water (EPA, 1999).

Constructed wetlands are an effective and reliable water reclamation technology if they are properly designed, constructed, operated, and maintained. They generally are designed to treat municipal or industrial effluents as well as stormwater runoff.

Constructed wetlands are complex systems in terms of biology, hydraulics, and water chemistry, and we still are learning the details of how they work. The treatment systems of constructed wetlands are based on ecological systems found in natural wetlands. Landscape architects often are concerned with the visual character of constructed wetlands and other engineering-oriented water resources. In the past, many of these types of projects were fenced off because they were considered to be safety hazards. Municipalities did not want to have to face the liability issues that would occur if someone accidentally got hurt. (See Figure 4.28.)

4.5.5 Unified Stream Assessment

A unified stream assessment (USA) is conducted by a person who walks the entire length of a stream and is intended to evaluate conditions and identify restoration opportunities along an urban stream corridor. The USA has been developed by the Center for Watershed Protection (www.cwp.org) and is designed to rapidly collect basic information needed to assemble a manageable list of potential restoration projects in the stream corridor. It assesses the most severe eroding banks along the survey reach. The data compiled from a USA survey is analyzed to evaluate the restoration potential of the stream corridor.

A USA consists of nine stream corridor assessments: eight impact assessments and a single overall reach level assessment. The eight impact assessment forms are:

1. **Outfalls**—all stormwater and other discharge pipes

2. **Severe erosion**—bank sloughing, active widening, or incision

3. **Impacted buffer**—lack of natural vegetation, width

4. **Utilities in the stream corridor**—leaking sewer, exposed pipes susceptible to damage

5. **Trash and debris in the stream corridor**—trash and illegal dumping

6. **Stream crossing**—culverts, dams, natural features, and so on

7. **Channel modification**—straightening, channelization, dredging, and so on

8. **Miscellaneous**—unusual features or conditions

The reach level assessment considers average bank stability, in-stream habitat, riparian vegetation, flood plain connectivity, access, flow, and substrate over the entire reach.

4.5.6 Bridging Solutions

There are a lot of opportunities for changing the physical layout of urban areas. According to the U.S. National Vacant Properties Campaign, vacant and abandoned properties occupy about 15% of most cities. It would be possible to covert some of this land to green space, or perhaps create constructed wetlands, retention basins, or wildlife habitat that can enhance a community's ability to address water resource problems.

One of the major objectives of the Ebey Island Viaduct Bridge, which crosses wetlands where the Snohomish River enters the Puget Sound north of Seattle, was to protect the surrounding riverine environment. Some of the environmental concerns included avoiding the disturbance of existing natural river features, such as logjams that form important local fish habitats as well as surrounding vegetation, steep terrain, and potential soil instability. Along a similar vein, when the Wes Smith Bridge was to be rebuilt, residents of Index (WA) wanted a bridge that was aesthetically pleasing and would have minimal environmental impact since it would span habitat for the endangered chinook salmon and bull trout. The 262-foot structure was constructed of steel arches because it allowed a long span with minimal structure depth, so piers did not have to be constructed in the river.

(continued)

the reservoir with the plastic balls across keeps out the sun, which triggers the formation of bromate. Bromate is a suspected carcinogen and is considered to be a serious public threat. The balls are black because that is the only color that is able to deflect UV rays.

The plastic balls cost around 40 cents each, and the Department of Water and Power ordered 6.5 million of them to use in other preserves. That means the city of Los Angeles spent almost $3 million for little plastic balls. Rumors that McDonald's had to close down all of their Playland playgrounds because of an inadequate number of small plastic balls apparently is not true.

Eventually there will be 3 million plastic balls in the Ivanhoe Reservoir, and they are expected to remain there for around five years, or until the underground water storage project is completed.

Source: "Water Projects Writ Large," *Southwest Hydrology* 7, no. 5 (September/October 2008).

The Vancouver Island (Canada) Highway Project consists of more than 90 bridges along 142 miles of highways, including two of the largest that span the Big Qualicum and Tsable rivers. Construction of the bridges was a concern because both rivers provide important habitat for coho, chum, and chinook salmon, as well as steelhead and cutthroat trout. Both bridges were also constructed of cast-in-place concrete because the weight of the structure could be greatly reduced, resulting in smaller bridge piers spaced farther apart. To protect fish habitat at the Tsable River Bridge, longer spans were used for the bridge, and the piers were set back a minimum of 30 feet away from the riverbank. Another big advantage is that the bridge surface could be built at the top of the piers almost 200 feet above the valley floor. Because the valley bottom was used only for the delivery of materials, most of the ancient Douglas firs were protected. And during construction of the bridge, work within the riverbank perimeter was restricted to the period between June 15 and September 15 so as not to damage fish stocks.

There is no shortage of examples of bridge projects that successfully address both aesthetics while minimizing environmental impacts. René Senos, a landscape architect

with Jones & Jones (Seattle, WA), is developing a series of bridge alternatives for the Ninepipe wetland complex in northwest Montana. "From an environmental standpoint, bridges are a better choice than culverts at stream and river crossings because they have less impact and also provide for the natural meandering inherent in all moving water," says Senos. "They also allow us to explore a wider range of possibilities for minimizing environmental impacts." Existing small bridges and culverts are being replaced with larger structures intended to improve hydrologic and ecological connectivity. For example, at the Ninepipe Reservoir, one of the options is to replace the existing 40-foot bridge with a 1,500-foot multispan bridge structure that would eliminate all fill within a wetlands area.

4.5.7 U.S. Gulf Coast

On the U.S. Gulf Coast, construction of massive levees that channel the Mississippi River, the dredging of canals and flood control structures, commercial and recreational boat traffic, forced drainage to accommodate development, and agriculture have all contributed to wetlands deterioration and loss.

Louisiana's 3 million acres of wetlands have borne the brunt of human activity, population increases, and natural processes for decades. As the barrier islands disintegrate, the formerly sheltered wetlands are then filleted like fish, exposing the soft underbelly of their forests, marshes, and ecosystems to the full force of open marine processes, such as wave action, wind, salinity intrusion, storm surge, tidal currents, and sediment transport, which then exponentially accelerate their death. Enhancement marshes are designed to benefit the community with multiple uses, such as water reclamation, wildlife habitat, water storage, mitigation banks, and opportunities for passive recreation and environmental education.

Critical for planners, landscape architects, and professionals in the industry of the built environment is an understanding of the life cycle of wetlands: They are not a stagnant land mass, and they will not automatically regenerate themselves like redividing cells; nor are they islands, or ruled by something as simple as predictable tides alone. Models and studies showing how nature intended the barrier islands/wetlands system to work and protect will help design

Figure 4.29 *A rise in sea level will change tidal patterns along the Gulf Coast. In LaCombe, Louisiana, much of the existing city will be inundated at high tide if the sea level rises 24 inches. Image courtesy EDAW.*

professionals take their cue from nature as to the evolution of the system rather than persisting in past engineering practices that have proven damaging and unsuccessful. Geologic and coastal reparation input regarding models for mitigation strategies should be a part of any planning process in the Gulf Coast.

There has been no shortage of plans for restoring the Gulf Coast. Discussions of how to rebuild it range from suggestions to just do it the way it was before, to more aggressive proposals that would take years to implement. For example, some proposals to restore coastal marshes and wetlands involve some combination of giant channels, valves, and sluice gates. One idea is to build a pipeline to carry 70 million cubic yards of silt to the coast, while another wants to divert one-third of the flow of the Mississippi River to start a new riverbed. Do we strengthen the levee system and build more levees, focus on restoring barrier islands and wetlands, or perhaps both? Can we design new communities that can withstand the impacts of hurricanes while still protecting our natural resources? Do we need to stop development along all or part of the Gulf Coast?

Previous planning efforts have had mixed results. The 1972 environmental movement resulted in requirements

that state governments develop comprehensive plans, and in the Gulf Coast region, these plans addressed specific requirements for coastal management. The State and Regional Planning Act of 1984 and the 1985 Omnibus Growth Management Act also were steps in the right direction in regard to addressing the impact of growth on natural resources. (See Figure 4.29.)

According to a report released by the National Research Council (NRC), the loss of wetlands in the United States has not stopped, despite more than 20 years of progress in restoring and creating wetlands. According to the NRC, the contiguous United States has lost more than 50% of its wetlands since the 1780s. Even though 1.8 acres of wetlands were created or restored for every acre lost during the past eight years starting in 1996, the United States still lost wetlands.

Section 404 of the U.S. Environmental Protection Agency's Clean Water Act requires those who want to discharge materials, such as soil or sand, into a wetland to get permission from the U.S. Army Corps of Engineers before doing so. Are Section 404 of the Clean Water Act and other efforts having a positive impact on reducing the loss of wetlands, or is the United States just running out of wetlands? The answer to that is debatable, but it is obvious that current efforts are not enough to help restore the kind of environmental balance that is needed to help stabilize the Gulf Coast region. One problem is that many of the created or restored wetlands are poorly constructed; as a result, they do not function as intended.

Previous attempts to help the state's wetlands led to passage of the 1990 Coastal Wetlands Planning, Protection and Restoration Act, which was sponsored by Senator John Breaux (D-LA). The Breaux Act currently funnels about $40 million to $50 million annually into the state for wetlands restoration projects.

Congress directed the Corps to develop options for a posthurricane rebuilding plan called the Louisiana Coastal Protection and Restoration Plan. In this plan, announced in the March 3, 2006, *Federal Register*, the Corps identifies four combinations of structural and nonstructural measures that would protect coastal Louisiana against a Category 5 storm. Central issues include: what role(s) restoration projects would play in such a plan; how restoration projects would be integrated with structural measures; and how projects to protect the New Orleans urban area and to restore coastal Louisiana can be integrated most effectively to minimize damage from future storm events (Zinn, 2007).

The Coast 2050 Plan is one of the most recent and ambitious series of coastal management and restoration plans proposed for the Gulf Coast. The plan, which was released in 1998, is led by the Corps. It provides recommendations for 77 "restoration strategies," to be completed over 50 years. The strategies would be distributed along the entire Louisiana coast but concentrated in the central coast. The anticipated result from fully implementing these strategies was to protect or restore almost 450,000 acres of wetlands. There have been numerous other studies in recent years that also focus on restoring wetlands in the region.

Under Coast 2050, Louisiana's barrier islands would be restored or maintained using the most cost-effective means. This would most likely include beach nourishment with dredged material combined with marsh creation projects on the bay side of the islands, although hard structures such as sea walls and groins are also being considered. But even under the best of circumstances, the array of projects in a complex program like Coast 2050

could not be completed for decades. In the aftermath of the 2005 hurricanes, the ecosystem restoration goals may be in competition with other demands for federal resources in coastal Louisiana. These demands include flood protection, economic development associated with navigation, and housing. It may be too expensive to fully support all these goals at the same time.

Too often in the past, insufficient attention was paid to the interactions between engineering structures, which extensively modified hydrologic regimes, and the physical and biological environment. One result was that extensive engineering efforts for managing the Mississippi River and numerous large-scale coastal navigation and storm-damage reduction projects caused widespread, ongoing changes in wetlands and barrier island stability, some say leading to the level of storm damages that were realized in the recent hurricanes. Many of these changes either were not foreseen or, if anticipated, were considered to be an acceptable cost of progress on other fronts (Dickey, 2005).

Some hurricane protection projects may have adverse effects on navigation access or on the coastal landscape. Restoration of the landscape in one area may claim river sediments that could have built land elsewhere in the coastal region. But there may also be project and program complementarities. A navigation channel may serve as an excellent conduit for moving sediment-laden water to areas where a wetlands restoration project is being proposed; in turn, that wetland area may help moderate storm surges and reduce storm damages (Dickey, 2005). (See Figure 4.30.)

4.6 LOW-IMPACT DEVELOPMENT AND SMART GROWTH

4.6.1 Low-Impact Development

Low-impact development (LID) involves using alternative development principles to minimize the potential impact of development on natural systems. LID helps communities

Figure 4.30 *Coastal salt marches in Everglades National Park are being restored. Image courtesy USGS.*

better protect water quality, habitat, and biological resources from the impacts of development and stormwater runoff (www.psp.wa.gov/stormwater.php). LID encourages the integration of treatment and management measures at the site level. Utilizing LID practices usually reduces the

Common LID Practices

- Bioretention cells or swales (also known as rain gardens)

- Pervious pavement

- Amending soil with compost

- Vegetated roofs (also known as green roofs or eco-roofs)

- Minimal excavation foundations

- Rooftop rainwater harvesting

- Dispersion

Source: www.psp.wa.gov/stormwater.php.

overall cost of a development project while increasing environmental performance.

The basic idea behind LID is to manage stormwater in a way that imitates the natural hydrology of a site. In a mature Pacific Northwest forest, for example, almost all the rainfall (or snowmelt) disperses along the forest floor, where it infiltrates into the ground and is taken up by the roots of plants and trees, or evaporates. Researchers estimate that about less than 1% becomes surface runoff (www.psp.wa.gov/stormwater.php).

LID projects can reduce the life-cycle costs associated with stormwater infrastructure and long-term maintenance. When combined with other key elements of a comprehensive local stormwater program, effective land use planning under the Growth Management Act and watershed or basin planning, LID can help communities more efficiently and effectively manage stormwater and protect their water resources. In the state of Washington, LID works with local land use planning under the Growth Management Act. Once growth areas are determined, builders and planners can use LID approaches on building sites to reduce the adverse effects of development.

11 Common LID Practices per the Natural Resources Defense Council

1. Impervious surface reduction and disconnection
2. Permeable pavers
3. Pollution prevention and good housekeeping
4. Rain barrels and cisterns
5. Rain gardens and bioretention
6. Roof leader disconnection
7. Rooftop gardens
8. Sidewalk storage
9. Soil amendments
10. Tree preservation
11. Vegetated swales, buffers, and strips

Many recommendations focus primarily on limiting runoff from new development, but cutting back on stormwater impacts from existing development is just as critical. One common goal of these strategies is to reduce the amount of impervious surface. Streets account for roughly half of the paved surfaces in many traditional neighborhoods.

One potential limitation is that many cities and counties do not allow the implementation of LIDs in their current codes. As a result, many designers, contractors, and clients avoid using LIDs because of the time it will take to get these features approved. This is changing, though, as local governments realize the benefits of LID standards. Many local governments update their ordinances and policies periodically to promote practices that allow more stormwater to infiltrate and be naturally managed on development sites.

Prior to World War II, traditional residential streets in the United States were more pedestrian friendly. Slow-moving traffic was intended to share the road with pedestrians and children playing on the street. A standard residential area had 24-foot-wide streets with concrete curbs and gutters, lined with broad 12-foot-wide parkway strips planted with trees (BASMAA, 1999). A standard two-way local street with parking on both sides requires two traffic lanes and two parking lanes plus curbs, gutters, and sidewalks on each side, for a total of 40 to 50 feet of pavement.

In the San Francisco Bay area, most municipal street standards mandate that over 80% of land coverage in the public right-of-way be impervious. This results in a significant amount of stormwater runoff. Alternative standards can significantly reduce impervious land coverage while meeting access needs of local, residential streets.

Key Strategies of Low-Impact Development

- **Preserving-clustering-dispersing.** Protecting or replanting a significant portion of a development site's vegetation; locating development on a smaller part of the site; and directing runoff to vegetated areas. In many cases, this is the most efficient and cost-effective way to manage stormwater.

- **Bioretention (rain gardens).** Shallow, landscaped areas composed of soil and a variety of plants. Bioretention cells are stand-alone features; bioretention swales are part of a conveyance system.

- **Soil amendments.** Compost added to soils disturbed during the construction process. Soil amendments restore soil's health and its ability to infiltrate water.

- **Pervious pavement.** Allows water to infiltrate and removes pollutants. Pervious pavement includes concrete, asphalt, pavers, and grid systems filled with grass or gravel. Concrete and asphalt are normally impervious, but the use of special aggregate mixes can allow water to move through them.

- **Vegetated roofs.** Roofs composed of a waterproof layer, root barrier, drainage layer, growth media, and plants. Vegetated roofs provide slower release of runoff, improve energy efficiency, extend roof life, and provide wildlife habitat and recreational amenities.

- **Rooftop rainwater collection.** Catchment systems or cisterns that collect rooftop runoff for irrigation, drinking water, gray water or other purposes. Rooftop rainwater collection reduces runoff and demand on groundwater supplies.

(continues)

(continued)

- **Minimal excavation foundations.** Alternative building foundations composed of driven piles and a connector at or above grade. These foundations eliminate the need for extensive excavation and reduce soil compaction.

Source: www.psparchives.com/publications/our_work/ stormwater/lid/lid_brochure/lid_brochure06_11x17.pdf.

4.6.2 Smart Growth

Communities around the country are adopting smart growth strategies to reach environmental, community, and economic goals. Environmental goals include water benefits that accrue when development strategies use compact development forms, a mix of different land uses, better use of existing infrastructure by limiting sprawl, and the preservation of critical environmental areas. At its core, smart growth is about improving the well-being of communities through high-density, walkable neighborhoods and interconnected street networks. There are 10 main principles of smart growth:

1. Create a range of housing opportunities and choices.

2. Create walkable neighborhoods.

3. Encourage community and stakeholder collaboration.

4. Foster distinctive, attractive places with a strong sense of community identity.

5. Make development decisions predictable, fair, and cost effective.

6. Mix land use.

7. Preserve open space, farmland, natural beauty, and environmental areas.

8. Provide a variety of transportation choices.

9. Strengthen and direct development toward existing communities.

10. Take advantage of compact building design.

Smart growth means better planning and more land preserved. One of the keys to smart growth is developing plans that "fit" the land. Geospatial data should be the foundation for all design and planning decisions. By identifying buildable areas and areas to protect, an opportunities and constraints map can be generated to guide future decisions. (See Figure 4.31.)

Figure 4.31 *The Smyrna Market Village, in Smyrna, Georgia, is an example of smart growth. Included in this new downtown area is a city hall, community center, and city library. Residents enjoy open streetscapes that feature over 40,000 square feet of retail space, 18,000 square feet of office space, 7 restaurants, and 16 town homes. Image courtesy J. Sipes.*

A common misconception is that low-density development protects water resources; water quality experts say this is simply not the case. According to an EPA study, higher densities better protect water quality, especially at the watershed and individual lot levels. Compact, mixed-use developments that efficiently use existing infrastructure are more effective, according to the EPA, for preserving critical environmental areas, such as streams and wetland areas.

"Growth is inevitable, growth is necessary, but how growth is accommodated can be good or bad. In setting the framework for land development and redevelopment, we must focus on practices that are environmentally sound, economically vital, and that encourage livable communities—in other words, smart growth."

—Jim Chaffin, ULI Chairman, Smart Growth Conference, Baltimore, MD, 1998

According to the Brookings Institution, between 1982 and 1997, the amount of urbanized land in the United States increased by 47% while the nation's population grew by only 17%. Sprawling land use, with large lots and disconnected street networks, encourages driving and has a negative effect on water quality. Low-density patterns of development result in a greater loss of sensitive environmental lands, including wetlands, floodplains, critical habitat, aquifer recharge areas, stream corridors, and steep slopes.

The environmental impacts of development can make it difficult for communities to protect their natural resources. According to the EPA (2004), where and how communities accommodate growth has a profound impact on the quality of their streams, rivers, lakes, and beaches. Development that uses land efficiently and protects undisturbed natural lands allows a community to grow and still protect its water resources.

Keys of Smart Growth

Key Components of Smart Growth
- Five-minute walk to center of neighborhood
- Streets that are interconnected with surrounding uses and developments
- Prominent civic sites
- Pedestrian-oriented streets; alleys, parking lots, and garages behind buildings are hidden from view
- Parks surrounded by streets and framed by buildings
- On-street parking on most streets
- Street trees to provide a canopy over streets and sidewalks
- Sidewalks on both sides of most streets
- Communities that are not walled off or gated
- Buildings that front onto arterial and collector streets

Key Components of Sprawl
- Consumptive use of land
- Segregated land uses
- Inefficient
- Socially polarized communities
- Auto-oriented streets
- Private, rather than public, open space
- Institutional uses not integrated into the neighborhood
- Gated communities

Some communities have interpreted water-quality research as suggesting that low-density development will best protect water resources. The EPA, however, argues that this strategy can backfire and actually harm water resources. To best protect water resources, communities should consider local factors and employ a wide range of land use strategies, including building a range of development densities, incorporating adequate open space, preserving critical ecological and buffer areas, and minimizing land disturbance. The EPA has concluded that increasing development densities is one community growth strategy to minimize regional water quality impacts.

The purpose of water quality management practices is to manage point and nonpoint source pollution on a watershed basis in order to protect clean waters, restore impaired waters, and manage assimilative capacity for current and future users (Georgia Comprehensive State-wide Water Management Plan, 2008). Communities need effective local programs to inspect and maintain existing stormwater and restoration practices. Stormwater facilities can lose their effectiveness over time without ongoing efforts to ensure their continuing function (Rowe and Schueler, 2006).

The generation of stormwater volume, as well as the pollutant load carried in that volume, is very much tied to how and where land is developed. Most stormwater that is collected from curbs and gutters flows untreated into local waterways. Preserving open space, farmland, and critical environmental areas is one of the 10 smart growth principles.

In 2004, EPA conducted a study to determine the impact that growth patterns had upon water quality (EPA, 2005). EPA modeled three density scenarios at three scales (acre, lot, and watershed levels) and over three different time periods to examine the assumption that lower-density development is better for water quality. Stormwater runoff was used to measure the effects of differing density scenarios. High-density scenarios generated less stormwater runoff per house at all scales and across all time series build-out examples. For the same amount of development, compact density produces less runoff and less impervious cover than low-density development.

Much of the pervious surface in low-density development acts like impervious surface for handling stormwater. Development practices can involve wholesale grading of a site, removing topsoil, and causing severe erosion during construction as well as compaction by heavy equipment. Research shows that the runoff from highly compacted lawns is almost as high as runoff from paved surfaces (EPA, 2005).

In the United States, over 40% of waterways (streams, bays, estuaries, and lakes) are impaired by pollutants, sediment, warming, and nutrients. Communities with smart growth management strategies are in a better position to control pollutant loadings from stormwater discharges, soil erosion, wastewater treatment systems, and other sources. Smart growth reduces the amount of land utilized for development, which can help preserve habitat for many species. Compact area development reduces car trips, air pollution, and the need for parking. With smart growth, less land needs to be paved for parking lots or garages. That reduces development costs, leaves more open ground that can filter rainwater, and leaves more open space for birds, animals, and people to enjoy (EPA, 2005). (See Figure 4.32.)

Better site design practices, such as low-impact development, emerged as mechanisms to retain a site's natural hydrology and infiltrate stormwater within the boundaries of the development project. The smart growth movement was established, in particular, as a way to create new communities that were more sustainable and make better use of the land (EPA, 2005).

Strategies to reduce stormwater runoff from individual lots and building sites include: bioinfiltration cells, rooftop rain capture and storage, green roofs, downspout disconnection, programs to reduce lawn compaction, and stormwater inlet improvements.

Infiltration requirements pose challenges in urban areas, where legacy pollutants remain and/or where land costs are high. They also pose challenges in the development of new town centers or other compact districts that are constructed in greenfields.

4.7 RECREATIONAL USE

People find something about water appealing. Most of the water resources in the United States can be used for some type of water-oriented recreation. Whether it is shorelines, beaches, estuaries, freshwater wetlands or lakes, saline lakes, reservoirs, rivers and streams, these resources attract

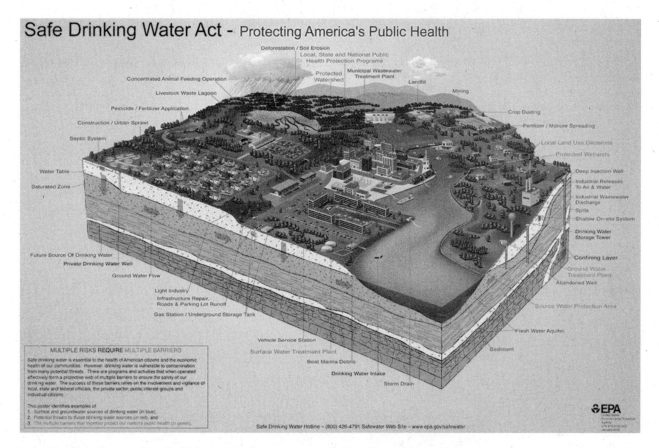

Figure 4.32 *EPA's brochure for Safe Drinking Water illustrates one smart growth approach to address water resources. Image courtesy EPA.*

a large number of people every year. Millions of Americans head for the nation's rivers every year to fish, boat, and swim. (See Figure 4.33.) For example, each year, more than 8 million people visit the 76 recreational areas surrounding Atlanta's Lake Lanier, which include 46 parks operated directly by the U.S. Army Corps of Engineers.

In the South, water-oriented recreation is part of the culture. One reason is that it is a great way to beat the summer heat, and this concept applies all across the country. (See Figure 4.34.)

Lakes are a major source of recreation in most parts of the country. Some of the recreation activities that occur on lakes include boating, water skiing, sailing, kayaking and canoeing, fishing, and swimming. There is something that encourages people just to sit, drink a cold beverage, and look at the water.

Some of the most common recreation facilities include boat moorage facilities (docks), swim docks and swim decks, ski jumps, courtesy docks, duck blinds, tramways, cable railways, boat mooring buoys, and other private floating recreation facilities. Many lakes no longer allow mooring buoys. A swim deck, a floating facility attached to a dock that has boat moorage stalls, is used for swimming or sunbathing.

Boats are at the heart of many lake recreation activities. Boat owners either bring in their boats on trailers and unload them via public boat ramps, or they park the boats

Figure 4.33 *Located in the Cherokee National Forest in the southeastern United States, the Ocoee River flows through a beautiful gorge surrounded by scenic wildlife and natural wonders. Millions of people enjoy recreational activities on the Tennessee River each year. Image courtesy J. Sipes.*

Figure 4.34 *Water is a great source of recreation, especially in hot summer months. As the weather heats up, splashing in water is the natural way for children to cool off and have fun. Image courtesy EDAW.*

on public or private docks at the lake. On most lakes, boat owners are encouraged to moor their boats at commercial marinas, utilize dry storage facilities off project lands, or trailer their boats to a public launching facility. Whether a dock is public or private, it should not extend out from the shore more than one-third of the cove width at conservation pool elevation. At many lakes, docks and other facilities that were once authorized by a permit would not be authorized now; and they are allowed under the grandfather clause. (See Figure 4.35.)

Even recreation opportunities that are land based have an impact on water resources. Traditionally, golf courses have required significant amounts of water to ensure that the fairways were green and lush. Today, most golf courses use reclaimed water and stormwater for irrigation of greens and tees. In most of the South, golf courses are required to reduce the amount of acreage irrigated, utilize efficient irrigation systems, and install soil moisture and rain sensors. Additional water conservation provisions typically are included in golf course irrigation permits.

Many cities and states are seeking to find the balance of how to use water for recreation while also meeting other demands. The city of San Diego (CA) has been using its reservoirs for public recreation since 1913, and it is known as a pioneer for this multiple-use approach. Some of the recreation activities that are associated with its lakes include fishing, boating, canoeing, kayaking, sailing, hiking, picnicking, waterfowl hunting, Jet Skiing, windsurfing, and other activities. The reservoirs serve as San Diego's public water supply, so protection of this resource is critical. The reservoirs and the recreation programs are operated by the Water Department's Water Operations Division.

The 2001 Texas Parks and Wildlife for the 21st Century report (Texas Tech University Studies, 2001), prepared by Texas Tech University, demonstrated the increasing need for outdoor recreation opportunities and for conserving natural resources within the state. A survey conducted as part of the study found that 52% of Texans felt that providing increased access for water-based recreational opportunities was a top priority. The study indicated that less consumptive recreational activities, such as nature hikes and birdwatching, are highly valued by Texans, even more so than consumptive activities, such as hunting, fishing, and boating. The study also indicated that there was a need for more state parks and that a ratio of 55 acres per 1,000

people should be adopted. In Texas, 14 of the 20 most-visited state parks provide water recreation opportunities, so the idea is that more state parks would equal more water-oriented recreation.

4.7.1 Marinas

Most major lakes and reservoirs have one or more marinas to provide the necessary services for the boating community. Marinas and community docks are an effective way to concentrate boating activities in one location. In contrast, on Lake Lanier in Georgia, the U.S. Army Corps of Engineers allows a maximum of 10,615 boat slips, and as of late 2008, just 150 were available (Duffy, 2008). If you are on the lake, you cannot help but notice all of the docks. They dramatically change the visual quality of the lake. Community docks are one way to minimize the impacts of private docks on a lake.

Water quality around a marina depends in large part on how well the basin is flushed. One problem with marinas is that they alter local wave and tidal flow patterns, and this can result in shoreline disturbance. The siting of a marina is critical. Marinas often are major sources of water pollution. Sewage management with marinas and shoreline development is an important issue. Raw or improperly treated boat sewage can result in a health hazard. Maintenance issues associated with marinas are also an issue.

Many watershed organizations around the country are implementing procedures to ensure that marinas are constructed and managed in an environmentally friendly manner. For example, the Tennessee Valley Authority has developed a Clean Marina Initiative, a voluntary program that is intended to promote environmentally responsible marina and boating practices. This program was established as part of the National Clean Boating Campaign, and it includes seven management measures that were identified by marina operators as priorities. These are:

1. Sewage management
2. Fuel management
3. Solid waste and petroleum recycling and disposal
4. Vessel operation, maintenance, and repair
5. Marina siting, design, and maintenance
6. Stormwater management and erosion control
7. Public education

Figure 4.35 *The Beech Fork Lake is located in Lavalette, West Virginia. The 720-acre lake has more than 31 miles of shoreline. Image courtesy U.S. Army Corps of Engineers.*

The *Tennessee Valley Clean Marina Guidebook (TVA, 2001)* is a reference tool complementing a self-assessment checklist used by the Tennessee Valley Authority to assess the quality of marinas.

One issue with marinas is that, like docks, many were constructed decades ago, and they do not follow current standards. Many have a "grandfather" clause that allows activities, structures, and facilities authorized under previous policies and prior permits to remain if they would not be permitting under existing policies. The grandfather status can be overridden when deemed necessary for public safety, for navigational use, or for flood control.

4.8 WILDLIFE MANAGEMENT AND HABITAT RESTORATION

Water is essential for maintaining a healthy, sustainable environment capable of supporting flora and fauna. Floodplains along rivers and streams are important habitats

for a variety of fish and wildlife. Riparian areas often occupy less than 1% of the landscape, yet they are among the richest and most diverse habitats on Earth. Riparian corridors are used by more than 70% of all land animals and are critical for wildlife connectivity to encourage migration. For example, more than 5 million migratory waterfowl spend the winter in Louisiana's marshes (LA Department of Wildlife & Fisheries, 2005). And of course rivers and their adjoining lands provide habitats for many types of plants, fish, and wildlife.

Wetlands provide a variety of habitats that support biodiversity. Almost half of all federally threatened and endangered species rely on wetlands directly or indirectly. It has also been estimated that more than 35,000 rare plants and animals are found in wetlands in the United States (Native Plant Conservation Campaign, 2003). (See Figure 4.36.)

4.8.1 Habitat Restoration Efforts

Habitat restoration projects often are accomplished through partnerships among a variety of federal, state, municipal, nonprofit, and private sources.

Figure 4.36 *Biologists conduct a stream survey of invertebrates in the Eightmile River, located in Connecticut. Image courtesy NRCS.*

Most states have developed comprehensive wildlife conservation strategies. A comprehensive habitat management program provides environmental protection and monitoring to assure that habitat is protected and preserved. Many state park systems and federal wildlife refuges were originally associated with U.S. Army Corps of Engineers lakes. Many still worked in partnership with the Corps to manage and operate the lands surrounding the lakes. States also have agencies responsible for issuing hunting and fishing permits, maintaining wildlife protection areas, protecting and managing wetlands, and protecting threatened and endangered species.

The Florida Fish and Wildlife Conservation Commission implemented a project to enhance the northwest littoral zone marsh of Lake Okeechobee. Lake Okeechobee covers 730 square miles with more than 100,000 acres of wetland habitats and is located in the center of the Everglades ecosystem. There were two objectives of this project: (1) enhance the fish and wildlife habitat by removing cattail and associated organics, and (2) conduct additional tussock removal.

In 2006, there were less than 3,000 acres of submerged aquatic vegetation in Lake Okeechobee. A year later, there were more than 30,000 areas of vegetation, a tenfold increase (www.ens-newswire.com/ens/nov2007/2007-11-26-093.asp). In 2006, the Audubon Society of Florida warned that the environmental health of the lake "has been degraded from decades of management that has placed the wants of some humans above the needs of wildlife and the environment."

In 1996, the Long Island Sound Study initiated the Habitat Restoration Initiative, a bistate, multiorganization effort to restore and enhance degraded coastal habitats in Connecticut and New York. The goals of the initiative are to:

- Restore the ecological functions of degraded or converted habitats

- Restore at least 2,000 acres of coastal habitat and 100 miles of riverine migratory corridors between 1998 and 2008

- Use partnerships to accomplish the restoration objectives and leverage limited, state, local, and federal funds

Figure 4.37 *The Yolo Bypass Area Land Management Plan helps preserve wetlands and wildlife habitat in the Sacramento Valley of California. Image courtesy NRCS.*

In 2003, the study published a manual entitled *Technical Support for Coastal Habitat Restoration*, (Long Island Sound Habitat Restoration Initiative, 2003) which includes a series of reports produced through the Habitat Restoration Work Group. Twelve priority habitats were identified as part of the study:

1. Beaches and dunes
2. Cliffs and bluffs
3. Estuarine embayments
4. Coastal and island forests
5. Freshwater wetlands
6. Coastal grasslands
7. Intertidal flats
8. Rocky intertidal
9. Riverine migratory corridors
10. Submerged aquatic vegetation
11. Shellfish reefs
12. Tidal wetlands

In Zimbabwe, the Lake Chivero Recreational Park is the home to a wide range of wildlife, including white rhinos, giraffes, zebras, wildebeests, impalas, ostriches, baboons, monkeys, duikers, jackals, porcupines, mongooses, and others. The park also has an impressive array of birds and fish. One reason that there is such an abundance of wildlife is that the park was formed in 1962 from the former Hwange game reserve. The park is almost 13,600 acres in size and the lake is approximately 22 square miles in size, making it an ideal wildlife refuge in terms of size.

A number of nonprofit organizations are involved with wildlife habitat restoration. The Wildlife Habitat Council (WHC) is a nonprofit group that focuses on restoring and enhancing wildlife habitat. Created in 1988, since that time the WHC has been involved in restoring more than 2 million acres in 48 states, Puerto Rico, and 16 countries. WHC helps large landowners manage their unused land in ways that preserves wildlife habitat. WHC is also working with the U.S. EPA to explore alternative ways to protect wildlife habitat, reduce the environmental footprint, and promote greater environmental stewardship at corporate facilities nationwide.

The U.S. Army Engineer Research and Development Center—Environmental Laboratory provides expertise on a variety of wildlife habitat restoration and management practices for civil works projects and Department of Defense installations. The center's current emphasis is on providing strategies for ecosystem-based habitat management that apply to a diversity of species occurring on Corps projects and military installations. The center has also developed the *U.S. Army Corps of Engineers Wildlife Resources Management Manual*, (1982) which is a collection of 70 technical reports published on species' natural history and habitat requirements, management practices and techniques, and census and sampling techniques, among other information (http://el.erdc.usace.army.mil/nrrdc/pdfs/wildlife.pdf). (See Figure 4.37.)

4.8.2 Federal Wildlife Programs

At the federal level, there are a number of programs intended to help preserve water resources for wildlife. The North American Wetlands Conservation Act is a federal grants program that funds wetland habitat conservation projects throughout North America. Projects funded by the act are intended to protect, restore, and enhance habitat for waterfowl and other wildlife that depend on wetlands. The program was passed by Congress in 1989, and since then more than 20 million acres of wetlands and associated uplands have been included as part of over 1,600 projects across North America.

Wildlife Habitat Incentives Program is a voluntary program authorized by the Farm Security and Rural Investment Act of 2002. The program provides cost-share assistance to landowners who want to enhance wildlife habitat areas on their lands. To be considered, landowners have to be willing to maintain their land to improve habitat areas for a minimum of 5 to 10 years. The National Resource Conservation Service administers the program.

Efforts to Restore Biological Diversity

Efforts to restore biological diversity may include:

- Preventing the introduction of urban pollutants to protect downstream waters
- Mitigating effects of development using biofilters, detention/infiltration basins, pervious pavements, and other strategies
- Retaining the natural riparian corridor and carefully applying measures to prevent or treat runoff
- Protecting and restoring creek bank vegetation
- Restoring the riffle/pool structure and meander length
- Preventing unauthorized diversions of water

The National Oceanic and Atmospheric Administration has developed the Open Rivers Initiative to focus on restoring fish habitat. The basic idea behind the initiative is to help communities address problems that restrict fish passage. It provides funds and technical support to pursue the removal of dams that serve as obstacles for fish, or the construction of fish ladders or other devices to help fish move around obstacles. (See Figure 4.38.)

Source: BASMAA, 1999.

Figure 4.38 *Step pools are used in this Iowan stream to improve fish habitat. The design allows fish to pass upstream more easily and helps expand the total amount of habitat available for fish. Image courtesy NRCS.*

The U.S. Fish and Wildlife Service's Partners for Fish and Wildlife Program provides technical and financial assistance to private landowners and tribes. The program was established in 1987 to assist with projects that conserve or restore native vegetation, hydrology, and soils associated with imperiled ecosystems. The overall goal of the program is to return sites to an ecological condition similar to what existed before they were disturbed.

The Marine Mammal Protection Act was enacted in 1972. It requires an ecosystem approach to natural resource management and conservation and prohibits harming marine mammals. The Fish and Wildlife Service, National Oceanic and Atmospheric Administration, and Marine Mammal Commission are all involved in the program.

Land-Water Corridor Characteristics

Land-water (or riparian) corridors have unique communities of plants and animals living near a river, stream, lake, lagoon, or other body of water. They serve a variety of functions important to both people and the environment:

- Preserving water quality by filtering sediment and pollutants from runoff

- Protecting stream banks and shorelines from erosion

- Providing a storage area for flood waters

- Providing food and habitat for fish and wildlife

- Preserving open space and aesthetic surroundings

Source: http://corpslakes.usace.army.mil/employees/vtn/pdfs/land-water.pdf.

4.9 NEW LAKES, RESERVOIRS, AND DAMS

According to EPA, there are more than 75,000 dams in the United States and a matching number of reservoirs. Many municipalities have invested in constructing new reservoirs as a way to ensure they have an adequate supply of water. (See Figure 4.39.)

The number of reservoirs being constructed in the United States has dropped significantly since the early 1970s in large part because of new environmental laws. Environmental constraints have made it all but impossible to build large reservoirs such as Lake Mead (NV) and Lake Powell (AZ). Historically, reservoirs often were built by damming up a stream. This is the simplest and most affordable method, but the environmental impacts are significant. Most new reservoirs are small because the larger reservoirs have too big of an impact, both environmentally and socially. They range from about 150 acres to 800 acres in size. Even smaller reservoirs are not being built on large streams because of environmental impacts. (See Figure 4.40.) One water manager said that in South Carolina, it is easier to permit a new nuclear power plant than a water supply reservoir because of the environmental restrictions. That may well be true, because the last few reservoirs in South Carolina took between 5 to 10 years to permit.

Cost is always a major restriction for building reservoirs. Building a dam costs something like $4,000 for every 1,000 gallons of water stored (Shelton, 2008). A new reservoir can cost well over $100 million, and many argue that there are other alternatives that are more fiscally and environmentally sound. Reservoirs are also much more expensive than the alternatives, especially if private land has to be acquired to create the reservoir. During the summer, it is common to see evaporation rates of a half inch per day for reservoirs in many Southwest states.

The responsibility of building and maintaining a dam rests solely with the owner, who is liable for the water stored behind the dam. Many states provide funding to expand existing reservoirs and construct new ones. For example, the state of Georgia will pay up to 20% of the cost to expand a reservoir and up to 40% of the cost to build a new one.

Georgia has developed more water reservoirs in the last 20 years than any other southern state. Its creation of large reservoirs began in the early 1900s, when the Georgia Power Company impounded waters for use as cooling structures for coal-fired electrical plants and hydropower. Additional

Figure 4.39 *The John W. Flannagan Lake is located in Dickenson County, Virginia. The 1,145-acre lake has almost 40 miles of shoreline. Image courtesy U.S. Army Corps of Engineers.*

Figure 4.40 *Union Grove Lake, located in Tama County, Iowa, is a 118-acre impoundment that is part of Grove State Park. Image courtesy NRCS.*

reservoirs were built in the 1930s by the Tennessee Valley Authority as part of a large flood control and power generation project in the Tennessee River Valley. The U.S. Army Corps of Engineers began constructing dams in Georgia for navigation and flood control in the 1940s and 1950s under the Flood Control Act of 1944 and the Watershed Protection and Flood Prevention Act of 1954 (*New Georgia Encyclopedia,* 2004).

After the severe droughts of 2007, Georgia passed the Water Conservation and Drought Relief Act, which fast-tracked state permitting for reservoirs. Water conservation can be the most economically efficient way of meeting water needs.

As of early 2008, a dozen new water supply reservoirs were under way in Georgia, seven of them in the metropolitan Atlanta area (Shelton, 2008). A new reservoir requires both an Army Corps of Engineers 404 permit and a state 401 permit. Although the Water Conservation and Drought Relief Act does not affect the 404 permitting process, it will speed up the state's 401 permitting process.

Typical of the new reservoirs being constructed is the 410-acre Hickory Log Creek reservoir in Cobb County (GA). The Cobb County–Marietta Water Authority and the city of Canton constructed a new water supply reservoir on Hickory Log Creek in Cherokee County. Construction of the dam was completed in December 2007, and filling the reservoir took another two years. At capacity, Hickory Log Creek can hold 6 billion gallons of water. Approximately 44 million gallons per day will be drawn from the reservoir ("Psst. South Carolina has a Secret," 2007). The reservoir is expected to meet the city of Canton's needs through 2050.

Concerns about water resources are not just about building new reservoirs either. States are going to have to find a way to rebuild reservoirs that are now 40 or 50 years old, and many are sorely in need of repair (Ricks, 2009). For example, Lake Murray is a 47,500-acre reservoir located near Columbia (SC). The lake is home to an estimated 30,000 residents. In the mid-1990s, it was determined that the Lake Murray dam would be vulnerable in the event of a major earthquake, so the decision was made to build a backup dam. The building of the backup dam was the largest active dam construction project in the United States for almost three years (Poindexter, 2005).

4.9.1 Tennessee Permitting Process for New Dams

Building a dam is not simple. Federal permitting of new reservoirs requires a defensible projection of the long-term water need for a specified service area and a thorough evaluation of all supply alternatives. The process varies from state to state, but typically a permit process is required, and the party wanting to build a dam is expected to prepare a detailed study on its potential impacts and benefits. Assessing the capacity of individual water sources, forecasting long-term water demand, and inventorying alternative sources of supply are all essential steps in the development of new reservoirs (Poindexter, 2005). Erosion control is required for construction of a lake and dam that will disturb one acre or more of land.

In Tennessee, an Aquatic Resource Alteration Permit (ARAP) must be obtained when a proposed dam will impound water on a stream or creek. Allowances must be made for the continuous flow of water downstream during and after construction of the dam. ARAP also monitors the long-term environmental impacts as well as the control of pollution during dam construction. The ARAP program is administered by the Natural Resources Section of the Division of Water Pollution Control.

Removing Dams

Removing a dam may require evaluations and permits from state, federal, and local authorities. Federal requirements may include:

- Rivers and Harbors Act Permit
- Federal Energy Regulatory Commission License Surrender or Non-power License Approval
- National Environmental Policy Act Review
- Federal consultations
  - Endangered Species Act Section 7 Consultation
  - Magnuson-Stevenson Act Consultation
  - National Historic Preservation Act Compliance
- State Certifications
  - Water Quality Certification
  - Coastal Zone Management Act Certification

Source: EPA 841-B-07-002 9-1 July 2007.

4.9.2 Dam Removal

In 1992, the National Research Council estimated that there were more than 2.5 million dams in the United States in 1992, and about 79,000 were large enough to be included in the National Inventory of Dams. Many of the other dams include small earthen berms to create farm ponds. Most of these dams are functional, but a number are being considered for replacement.

Congress authorized the U.S. Army Corps of Engineers to inventory U.S. dams with the National Dam Inspection Act of 1972. The Water Resources Development Act of 1986 authorized the Corps to maintain and periodically publish an updated National Inventory of Dams. The inspection of dams has led to an understanding that some dams are badly in need of repair, but the cost to do so may be prohibitive. Some dams have outlived their usefulness and no longer function as intended. Because regulations change, some hydropower dams that were licensed may no longer be in compliance with current regulatory standards (Powers, 2005).

One reason that removing a dam is so complicated is that many different agencies have some type of authority. The decision-making process required to get permission to remove a dam is lengthy and involves many different layers. Some of the priorities that need to be evaluated (EPA, 2007) when considering removing a dam are:

- Dam and public safety
- Economics
- Environmental concerns
- Risk
- Social values and community interests
- Scientific information
- Stakeholder participation

Types of Dams

- **Ambursen dam.** A buttress dam in which the upstream part is a relatively thin, flat slab usually made of reinforced concrete

- **Arch dam.** A concrete, masonry, or timber dam with the alignment curved upstream so as to transmit the major part of the water load to the abutments

- **Buttress dam.** A dam consisting of a watertight part supported at intervals on the downstream side by a series of buttresses

- **Crib dam.** A gravity dam built up of boxes, crossed timbers, or gabions, filled with earth or rock

- **Diversion dam.** A dam built to divert water from a waterway or stream into a different watercourse

- **Double curvature arch dam.** An arch dam that is curved both vertically and horizontally

- **Earth dam.** An embankment dam in which more than 50% of the total volume is formed of compacted earth layers that are generally smaller than 3-inches in depth.

- **Embankment dam.** Any dam constructed of excavated natural materials, such as both earthfill and rockfill, or of industrial waste materials, such as tailings

- **Gravity dam.** A dam constructed of concrete and/or masonry, which relies on its weight and internal strength for stability

- **Hollow gravity dam.** A dam constructed of concrete and/or masonry on the outside but having a hollow interior and relying on its weight for stability

- **Hydraulic fill dam.** An earth dam constructed of materials, often dredged, that are conveyed and placed by suspension in flowing water

- **Industrial waste dam.** An embankment dam, usually built in stages, to create storage for the disposal of waste products from an industrial process

- **Masonry dam.** Any dam constructed mainly of stone, brick, or concrete blocks pointed with mortar

- **Mine tailings dam (or tailings dam).** An industrial waste dam in which the waste materials

(continues)

(*continued*)

come from mining operations or mineral processing

- **Multiple arch dam.** A buttress dam comprised of a series of arches for the upstream face
- **Overflow dam.** A dam designed for water to flow over the top during times of flooding
- **Regulating dam.** A dam impounding a reservoir from which water is released to regulate the flow downstream
- **Rock-fill dam.** An embankment dam in which more than 50% of the total volume is comprised of compacted or dumped cobbles, boulders, rock fragments, or quarried rock generally larger than 3-inch size
- **Roller-compacted concrete dam.** A concrete gravity dam constructed by the use of a dry-mix concrete transported by conventional construction equipment and compacted by rolling, usually with vibratory rollers
- **Rubble dam.** A stone masonry dam in which the stones are unshaped or uncoursed
- **Saddle dam.** A subsidiary dam of any type constructed across a saddle or low point on the perimeter of a reservoir

Source: Powers, 2005.

4.10 LAND ACQUISITION

Several approaches can be taken to conserve land associated with important water resources. Conservation easements, land acquisition, and transfer of development rights are all ways to maintain natural resources.

Many state and local governments and private organizations have programs for purchasing land. A government agency or a nonprofit organization, such as a land trust, is often in a better position to acquire land for water resource management than are private parties because they are viewed as being unbiased and are not seeking to make a profit from the actions. One option for acquiring land is

a public/private partnership. A number of partnerships around the United States have proven to be very successful.

As part of the watershed planning process, key sites that are important for water resource management can be identified, and in some cases these sites can be acquired for the public good. The cost will depend on the value of the land. Land in urban areas, where water resource issues are often the greatest and where large-scale solutions are most needed, can be extremely expensive. One approach is to focus on acquiring critical pieces of property upstream in more rural areas where the land is more affordable in an effort to address water issues before they get to urban areas.

4.10.1 Fee Simple Acquisition

Land acquisition involves the acquisition of the title for a piece of property. It is by far the simplest and most direct way to obtain land for the protection or development of water resources, but it is also the most expensive. Some land is purchased outright, and some is donated.

4.10.2 Conservation Easements

Conservation easements are legal restrictions on the current and future use of land. You basically purchase the right to use land a certain way, but you do not own the land itself. Easements are an effective way to protect water resources since they restrict how a piece of land can be used. A conservation easement can be customized to include different restrictions depending on what is most appropriate for a given situation. Some landowners donate conservation easements to an agency or nonprofit group as a way to help protect environmental resources, but many do so because such a donation results in substantial tax benefits.

4.10.3 Leases, Deed Restrictions, and Covenants

One approach to protecting specific parcels of land is to lease the land on a long-term basis or to establish deed restrictions

Figure 4.41 *Ducks Unlimited works with landowners to protect wildlife habitat areas, and TDRs are one mechanism that can be used. Image courtesy Ducks Unlimited.*

or covenants. Sometimes landowners are not interested in selling their land, but they do not have immediate plans for the property and are willing to lease it to an agency or nonprofit group seeking to protect water resources. Leasing a piece of property is an effective approach in this situation to manage land for conservation. Deed restrictions and covenants limit the use of a piece of land by constraining how the land can be developed in the future.

4.10.4 Purchase of Development Rights

Purchase of development rights (PDR) is a voluntary land protection tool that allows landowners to voluntarily sell all or part of the development rights of their property. It is a way for landowners to protect their land from development and to get compensated for it. With a PDR program, a government agency or nonprofit organization buys the development rights for a piece of land from the landowner. A PDR program is particularly effective for helping farmers retain their land as active farmland. Often farmers sell the land because it is so valuable to developers. A PDR program

compensates farmers and makes up the difference in land value between farmland and developed land.

4.10.5 Transfer of Development Rights

Transfer of development rights (TDR) is a land use management technique that allows the development potential of a sensitive site to be transferred to another site that is better able to accommodate development. TDRs are based on a market-driven incentive program that involves selling the development potential of a site without actually buying or selling land. This approach typically is used to concentrate development density while preserving open space in other locations.

For landowners, TDRs offer an option for realizing the value of their land without having to actually sell or develop it. For example, if a piece of land is zoned to accommodate 10 houses, the landowner could build only one house, then sell the rights to build the other houses to a different landowner. That landowner then could build a denser development somewhere else. (See Figure 4.41.)

4.10.6 Land Trusts

Land trusts may be established by publicly or privately sponsored nonprofit organizations. The purpose of developing land trusts is to hold lands or conservation easements for the protection of habitat, water quality, recreation, or scenic value, or for agricultural preservation. In the United States, the Nature Conservancy and the Trust for Public Land are two national organizations that act as land trusts. They often acquire critical pieces of land and preserve them to protect important natural resources. For example, the organizations could acquire critical habitat areas or areas such as wetlands, old-growth forests, or aquifer recharge zones. These organizations often step in and acquire land that is a conservation priority when it becomes available, and then work with state or local agencies or nonprofit organizations later to determine the best way to manage the property.

General Steps for Setting up a TDR Program

- Provide education and outreach. The public should be familiar with the overall objectives of the program. Landowners and developers also need to be educated on how they will be affected.

- Conduct an analysis of market conditions.

- Identify and designate TDR "receiving areas" that have increased development rights.

- Identify and designate TDR "sending areas" that give up some or all of their development rights.

- Determine the nature of the program.

- Determine development potential and allocate TDRs.

- Consider a TDR bank. A TDR bank buys, holds, and sells TDRs. The bank can be either a government organization or a quasi-governmental entity.

Source: EPA, *National Management Measures to Control Nonpoint Source Pollution from Urban Areas* – Management Measure 3: Watershed Protection (November 2005, EPA-841-B-05-004), www.epa.gov/owow/nps/urbanmm/index.html.

4.10.7 Acquisition Programs

Land acquisition programs are available at the federal, state, and local levels. EPA provides funds through the Safe Drinking Water Act to protect public health by ensuring safe drinking water. The 1996 amendments to the act made it easier for communities to purchase land or conservation easements for the purpose of protecting public drinking water supplies by providing annual grants to each state.

Florida Forever is the state's primary source of funding for land acquisition. The program focuses on water resource development and restoration projects as well as land acquisition for nonstructural flood protection and conservation.

The Northwest Florida Water Management District established a land acquisition program in 1984. Over the years, the program has resulted in the acquisition of more than 207,000 acres of wetlands and recharge areas, and that number increases every year. The district has a Five-Year Plan that identifies specific areas that are important for preservation. If funding is available and landowners are willing to sell, the land is purchased and added to the district's green space.

In fall 1997, San Antonio (TX) Water System initiated a sensitive Land Acquisition Program to protect and preserve the quality and quantity of water in the city. The program specifically focuses on karst topography that is likely to have caves, sinkholes, and other geological features that are susceptible to pollution. The program is linked to San Antonio's Aquifer Protection Ordinance and the Water Resource Plan.

In May 1998 the Connecticut Legislature implemented an open space and watershed land acquisition that provided a matching grant program for municipalities, nonprofit conservation groups, and water companies. The South Central Connecticut Regional Water Authority has established a Watershed Fund Grant Program that is intended to help protect water quality throughout the region. One of the objectives is to acquire ecologically significant watershed land.

4.11 BEST MANAGEMENT PRACTICES

Best management practices (BMPs), as the name suggests, are site-specific applications that are recognized for their effectiveness in solving the problem at hand. A number of issues need to be considered when determining the most appropriate BMP for a given situation. These factors include, among others:

- Capital and maintenance costs
- Potential for removing pollution
- Potential for reducing and controlling stormwater
- Site considerations
- Opportunities for multi-use applications

Regulations regarding stormwater management drive most decisions about which BMPs are used on a given project.

To be effective, BMPs need to be selected to fit the specific demands of a site. One BMP may work in one situation and not in another. Some general principles apply to most sites, such as the need to stabilize soil and to prevent erosion, but the best approach to do so varies. In one situation, the use of native grasses and erosion fabrics may be the best approach, while in another, more structural materials such as gabions may be required.

In addition to meeting technical requirements, BMPs must also be sustainable, attractive, multipurpose, safe, and well designed.

4.11.1 BMP Databases

A number of databases provide information on BMPs. EPA provides a comprehensive list of BMP fact sheets that includes pricing information on construction and maintenance. (See Figure 4.42.) EPA's Engineering and Analysis Division conducted a study on stormwater BMPs

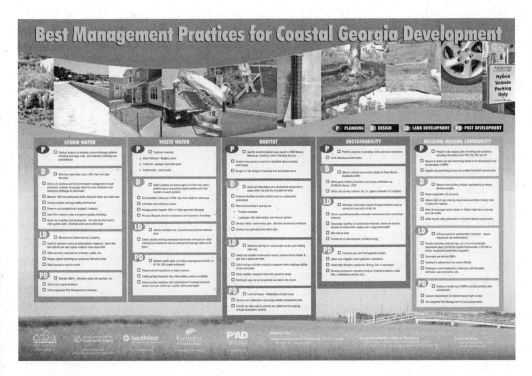

Figure 4.42 *This set of best management practices is geared toward projects along Georgia's coastal areas. Image courtesy Coastal Georgia Regional Development Center.*

during 1997 and 1998. This study provides information on the effectiveness of different BMPs as well as a range of anticipated costs and benefits (EPA, National Menu of Stormwater Best Management Practices).

Detailed design guidelines are available from stormwater BMP design manuals available from states, local governments and agencies, and other organizations. Some of the other EPA documents that include information on BMPs include: *Guidance Specifying Management Measure for Sources of Nonpoint Source Pollution in Coastal Water* (U.S. EPA, 1993); *Urban Runoff Pollution Prevention and Control Planning* (U.S. EPA, 1993); and *Municipal Wastewater Management Fact Sheets: Storm Water Best Management Practices* (U.S. EPA, 1996).

In 1992, the Northern Virginia Planning District Commission and Engineers Surveyors Institute produced the *Northern Virginia BMP Handbook: A Guide to Planning and Designing Best Management Practices in Northern Virginia*. This handbook is available for download at www.novaregion .org/pdf/NVBMP-Handbook.pdf.

The International Stormwater Best Management Practices Database features a database of over 300 BMP studies, performance analysis results and tools for evaluating BMP performance. The overall purpose of the project is to provide scientifically sound information to improve the design, selection, and performance of BMPs (http://bmpdatabase.org/).

The Transportation Research Board's *Environmental Stewardship Practices, Procedures, and Policies for Highway Construction and Maintenance* includes numerous management practices in highway construction and maintenance. The guidance was developed from the literature, state transportation agency manuals and procedures, and contributions of state departments of transportation and practitioners. The document serves as a guide to the development of environmental management systems and environmental strategic plans, both at the organizational level and in specific functional areas, such as road construction, vegetation management, materials recycling, winter road maintenance, and many other topics. The document can be downloaded in PDF format from TRB's Web site (www.trb.org/NotesDocs/25-25(4)_FR.pdf).

Many states have published BMP handbooks or guidance documents for in-state use. The California Stormwater

Quality Task Force's *California Stormwater Best Management Practice Handbooks* provide information on current practices and standards. The handbooks are sources of information on best management practices after construction (www.dot.ca.gov/hq/construc/stormwater/stormwater1 .htm). Louisiana is developing a program to reduce pollution from nonpoint or widely diffuse sources that may impact coastal waters. The program consists of menus of recommended BMPs or actions that can be taken to address specific problem issues as well as a plan to help bring about implementation of these practices.

Naiad is a Web-based repository that includes lessons learned from innovative urban water schemes. The project is part of the Sustainable Water Sources Program of the University of Queensland (Australia) (www.uq.edu .au/rsmg). The American Society of Civil Engineers has put together a National Stormwater BMP Database that focuses on stormwater BMP design and performance (www.asce .org/community/waterresources/nsbmpdb-extdesc.cfm).

In 1997, the Center for Watershed Protection developed a database for the Chesapeake Research Consortium titled "National Pollutant Removal Performance Database for Stormwater BMPs" (www.cwp.org/Resource_Library/ Controlling_Runoff_and_Discharges/sm.htm). This database provides BMPs that are geared specifically for removing pollution.

All development projects in Iowa must address water quality and comply with the stormwater policies and design criteria specified in Iowa's *Statewide Urban Design and Specifications Design Manual* (www.iowasudas.org/about .cfm). The manual includes standards for stormwater, sanitary sewers, water mains, and erosion and sediment control as well as other urban elements, such as roadways, utilities, and street trees.

In January 2004, Delaware Department of Transportation introduced the Delaware Urban Runoff Management Model, which provides a computational tool allowing designers and regulators to implement green-technology BMPs such as bioretention, bioswales, infiltration trenches, and filter strips (www.dnrec.state.de.us/dnrec2000/ Divisions/Soil/Stormwater/New/DURMM_UsersManual_01- 04.pdf). The program can be used to input more detailed and site-specific information for a particular BMP in order to determine how effective it would be.

4.11.2 Structural and Nonstructural Best Management Practices

According to EPA (1999), water resource BMPs can be organized into two major groups, structural and nonstructural:

Structural BMPs include:

- Infiltration systems, such as infiltration basins and porous pavement
- Detention systems, such as basins and underground vaults
- Retention systems, such as wet ponds
- Constructed wetland systems
- Filtration systems, such as media filters and bioretention systems
- Vegetated systems, such as grass filter strips and vegetated swales
- Minimizing directly connected impervious surfaces
- Miscellaneous and vendor-supplied systems such as oil/water separators
- Hydrodynamic devices

Structural practices to control urban runoff rely on four basic mechanisms:

1. Infiltration
2. Filtration
3. Detention/retention
4. Evaporation

Nonstructural BMPs include:

- Automotive product and household hazardous material disposal
- Commercial and retail space good housekeeping
- Industrial good housekeeping
- Modified use of fertilizers, pesticides, and herbicides
- Lawn debris management
- Animal waste disposal
- Maintenance practices such as catch basin cleaning, street and parking lot sweeping, road and ditch maintenance
- Illicit discharge detection and elimination
- Educational and outreach programs
- Storm drain inlet stenciling
- Low-impact development and land use planning

(See Figure 4.43.)

4.11.3 Vegetative Practices

Vegetative practices have gained in popularity in the last two decades and now are preferred to more engineering-oriented options. We have discovered in recent years that "soft" alternatives, such as vegetative practices, not only are effective for stabilizing slopes and helping minimize stormwater runoff problems, they also are very cost effective and are environmentally sound. The term *soil bioengineering* often is used instead of *vegetative practices,* since the practice involves the installation of plant materials to stabilize the soil.

Deep rooted plants help build soil porosity. Woody vegetation is particularly effective for stabilizing slopes because woody vegetation has more extensive root systems than do evergreens. Vegetative practices also provide valuable habit for wildlife and fish, and over time they can help restore environmental processes. (See Figure 4.44.)

Most vegetation BMPs specify that all disturbed areas be planted or at least covered with mulch or erosion fabrics within 14 days of disturbance. Some even go as far as shortening the period to seven days. Mulch can be effective for up to six months, but after that either temporary or permanent vegetation should be planted.

Plantings come in many forms, including bare root seedlings, container-grown seedlings, container-grown plants, and balled and burlapped plants. Of course, smaller plants are less expensive; as a result, they are often used for restoration efforts. Bare-root seedlings are often used for major restoration projects. Soil preparation is essential for establishing new plantings. Many restoration efforts have poor soils that have to be augmented with fertilizer or some type of soil mixture.

Figure 4.43 *For the Riverside Development Project in Roswell, Georgia, a combination of structural and nonstructural approaches were used along the Chattahoochee River. Image courtesy EDAW.*

Figure 4.44 *Deep-rooted plants were used to help stabilize this streambed in San Diego, California. Image courtesy EDAW.*

Sustainable Practices for Site Planning, Design, and Implementation

Newly planted vegetation needs time to get established, especially on steep slopes where erosion can be a problem. Erosion fabrics and mulch mats are often used to help establish vegetation on these types of slopes. Turf reinforcement mats combine vegetative growth and synthetic materials to help prevent soil erosion. Typically they are composed of interwoven layers of nondegradable geosynthetic materials, such as polypropylene, nylon, and polyvinyl chloride netting. Sodding is also an option for steep slopes because it provides immediate stabilization and helps minimize erosion problems. Running sod parallel to the contours of a slope is an effective way to reduce erosion and storm runoff.

One key emphasis of vegetative BMPs is that they are appropriate for specific sites. In South Florida, lawn irrigation counts for about 50% of drinking water used in the area. Simply turning off sprinklers is one of the best ways to conserve water. Of course, that is easier said than done, because people like their lawns to be green and healthy. In fact, most people in Florida overwater, which is not good for the grass because it results in shallow roots and makes the grass more vulnerable to disease.

BMPs for vegetation maintenance are also important. Mowing or underbrushing may be permitted for fire protection purposes only. In most situations, trimming of trees to obtain a view is prohibited, and trees larger than two inches in diameter may not be removed.

Americans spend large amounts of money seeding or sodding their yards, fertilize and irrigate the lawn so it will grow quickly, then spend innumerable hours mowing grass. In addition, overwatering wastes water, increases urban runoff, and increases pollution in rivers and streams. During times of drought, lawn irrigation is one of the first uses that is restricted. It is possible to greatly reduce the problems associated with inefficient irrigation systems. Some approaches include monitoring water usage, implementing drip irrigation systems, and installing sensors that prevent irrigation when it rains or when the soil is saturated.

4.11.4 Runoff and Sediment Control

During a high-intensity storm, often the soil is not able to absorb all of the water, and stormwater systems frequently overflow because of the volume of water. Slowing runoff helps reduce the erosion of stream banks.

There are a number of BMPs for reducing stormwater runoff. Wet and dry swales are constructed to handle stormwater runoff on the surface, unlike stormwater pipes, which are underground. A grass or vegetated swale slows down water and also helps reduce pollution carried by stormwater. Surface swales are often used in concert with curbless streets to allow stormwater from paved areas to run into the swales.

Recommended slopes for swales depend on a number of factors, including channel geometry, peak flows, soil types, base flows, and sediment load. As a general rule, vegetated slopes have a slope of between 2% to 6%. This allows positive flow but is not too steep to increase the flow of water to a level that would increase erosion. Paved channels can have a slope of as little as 1% since the hard surface presents little obstruction to water flow. One concern about paved channels is that they can significantly increase the velocity of water flowing down them.

Minimizing erosion and sedimentation is a major part of many BMPs. Sediment controls capture sediment that is transported in runoff. Filtration and gravitational settling during detention are the main processes used to remove sediment from urban runoff (Wenk, 2007). Sediment basins are constructed impoundment structures that are used to slow down stormwater runoff and allow sediment to settle out of the water. A sediment barrier is a temporary structure constructed of silt fences made of geotextile fabrics, straw or hay bales, brush, logs and poles, and gravel or other filtering materials. They are installed to prevent sediment from leaving the site or from entering natural drainageways or storm drainage systems. Sediment traps are small impoundments that allow sediment to settle out of runoff water.

4.11.5 Wetlands

BMPs for wetland restoration are among the most effective ways to manage stormwater and minimize the impact of pollution. Protecting existing wetlands is important, but new wetlands designed specifically for treating stormwater runoff can be constructed.

Figure 4.45 *Shallow wetlands can be useful for improving water quality. Image courtesy Wenk Associates.*

Among the different types of wetland designs are shallow wetlands, extended detention shallow wetlands, pond/ wetland systems, and pocket wetlands. Shallow wetlands consist primarily of marshes, and water treatment occurs in these shallow areas. Extended detention shallow wetlands are designed to hold stormwater and then release it over a period of time. With pond/wetland systems, the ponds trap sediments and reduce runoff going into the wetlands. Pocket wetlands are intended for smaller drainage areas and often are developed in areas with high groundwater as well as areas adjacent to natural open space.

Flow deflection practices place obstacles in the stream channel to alter the flow of water. A V-log drop is a stream repair practice used to provide grade control in urban streams. It consists of two logs joined at an angle with its apex pointing upstream. (See Figure 4.45.)

Figure 4.46 *Rain barrels can be used to help harvest rainwater at individual houses. Image courtesy NRCS.*

4.11.6 Rainwater Harvesting

Rainwater harvesting refers to the capture and storage of rainwater, with the water typically being used for landscape irrigation as well as potable and nonpotable indoor uses. Rainwater harvesting provides an opportunity to conserve and extend existing water resources. A rainwater harvesting system for a single-family home typically costs between $10,000 and $15,000. The storage tank is the most costly item. This may sound like a lot of money, but assuming a collection efficiency of about 80%, a typical 2,000-square-foot home in an area that gets about 60 inches of rain a year can collect over 55,000 gallons during that period. (See Figures 4.46 and 4.47.)

Figure 4.47 *The Chicago Center for Green Technology uses large cisterns to capture rainwater. Image courtesy Chicago Center for Green Technology.*

economic sense for homeowners, because the costs of collecting and treating rainwater are minimal, and utility bills can be reduced. Another big advantage is that less water flows into storm sewers, so less piping and infrastructure is needed to handle water. Rainwater harvesting also reduces potential flooding problems. One problem with rainfall harvesting is that at times there is not sufficient rain to depend on it as a drought-proof source of water supply.

The Lady Bird Johnson Wildflower Center, located in Austin (TX), is one example of successful rainwater harvesting. The center has a 70,000-gallon rainwater storage tank that supplies 10% to 15% of the water needed for the center's landscape.

The town of Bellingham (WA) is utilizing high-tech cistern/drywell systems that trap roof rainwater runoff. In the city, an average home dumps between 50,000 to 60,000 gallons of rain off the roof each year.

4.11.7 Rooftop Runoff Management

Rooftop runoff management practices can help conserve water and improve aesthetics. Examples of rooftop runoff management techniques include green rooftops, rooftop gardens, and rain barrels. The design, slope, and architecture of rooftops can reduce the volume of rooftop runoff as well (Rowe and Schueler, 2006).

A green roof is simply a roof that includes some type of vegetation instead of traditional shingles, tiles, or other roofing surface. The vegetation on the roof minimizes stormwater runoff by absorbing rainfall and promoting evaporation. This approach requires more planning, design, construction, and maintenance than a traditional roof, but the potential rewards can be significant. Green roofs can capture and retain 60% of the annual precipitation that falls on them. They can greatly reduce the amount of stormwater running into a storm sewer system, and that saves everyone a lot of money.

4.11.8 Filtering Systems

Filtering systems seek to capture and temporarily hold stormwater runoff and then run it through filters consisting of

In most states, rainwater harvesting systems are not subject to state building codes, and there are no clear construction guidelines to follow. Currently there are no national standards or regulations for rainwater harvesting systems, but many states and local governments offer tax breaks for installing rainwater harvesting systems. In many states, rainwater harvesting systems are exempt from state sales tax. In addition to tax exemptions, the city of Austin (TX) offers rebates and discounts for the installation of rainwater harvesting and condensate recovery systems.

There are a number of benefits to using water from rainwater harvesting systems. Collected rainwater is typically safe to drink and typically is of better quality than the treated water people get from their taps. Rain harvesting makes sand, gravel, organic matter, soil, or other media. This filtering process is effective for cleaning water and reducing the amount of pollution typically carried by stormwater runoff.

Infiltration systems are intended to contain stormwater and allow it to percolate through the soil into underground aquifers. A major benefit of these types of systems is that they reduce the total volume of stormwater runoff discharged from a particular site. With less water running off the site, there is less erosion, less sedimentation, and less pollutants. Infiltration planters are planter boxes that allow water to percolate into the soil below. They capture water from neighboring roofs, irrigate the plants, and allow water to percolate through the soil.

4.11.9 Erosion and Sediment Control Plans

Erosion and sediment control plans are an effective way to minimize problems associated with sedimentation. Most states and local governments require such plans to be developed for projects that involve water resources where there is a chance for erosion and sedimentation to occur.

EPA Case Studies

EPA has developed a series of stormwater case studies to help Phase II municipal separate storm sewer systems get started on or improve their stormwater management programs. Each case study is a two- to three-page description of how a Phase I or Phase II community has implemented a specific aspect of its stormwater program. The case studies all meet minimum standards of performance as defined by EPA, but they do not necessarily represent all the activities that a particular community could implement, but illustrate some of the possible solutions. Each case study description includes links to materials that further describe or were developed for the case study and the minimum control measure. The case studies can be found on EPA's Web site covering the National Pollutant Discharge Elimination System: http://cfpub.epa.gov/npdes/stormwater/casestudies.cfm.

Weirs and Check Dams

Check dams are small, temporary dams constructed across small streams, channels, or swales. They are intended to reduce the velocity of water flow, retain sediments, and in turn reduce potential erosion problems. A check dam can be constructed of a wide variety of materials, including rock or gravel, concrete, straw bales, or other materials that can withstand the water velocity. One limitation with using a check dam or weir is that this approach also changes stream flow, which may have an adverse impact on wildlife, water quality, and downstream water availability.

Maintenance is critical to ensure that a check dam or weir functions as planned. If the water velocity is too great, it can undercut or overflow the dam or weir. Sediment and debris typically need to be removed on a periodic basis, and the structure itself needs to be checked to ensure it is holding up well.

Best Management Practices for Stream Cleanup

- Boulder revetments
- Rootwad revetments
- Imbricated rip-rap
- A-jacks
- Live cribwalls
- Stream bank shaping
- Coir fiber logs
- Erosion-control fabrics
- Soil lifts
- Live stakes
- Live fascines
- Brush mattress
- Vegetation establishment
- Wing deflectors
- Log, rock, and "J" vanes
- Rock vortex weirs
- Rock cross vanes
- Step pools
- V-log drops
- Lunkers

(continues)

(continued)

- Boulder clusters
- Base-flow channel creation
- Parallel pipes
- Stream daylighting
- Culvert modification
- Culvert replacement and removal
- Devices to pass fish

Source: Tom Schueler, Chris Swann, Tiffany Wright, and Stephanie Sprinkle, Center for Watershed Protection, *Urban Subwatershed Restoration Manual* No. 8, Pollution Source Control Practices Version 2.0. 2004. http://water.montana.edu/pdfs/ELC_USRM8.pdf.

Streets and Parking

Some of the biggest culprits of stormwater runoff are the streets, driveways, and parking areas that are an essential part of human development. These transportation-related elements can comprise between 60% and 70% of the total impervious surface in an area. Driveways can account for up to 30% of the impervious cover in a typical residential neighborhood. The biggest problem is that these elements typically are constructed of impervious paving, such as asphalt or concrete, and this greatly exacerbates the stormwater runoff problem.

The best way to minimize stormwater runoff and potential sedimentation and erosion is to reduce the width of streets. Instead of using 12-foot 6-inch-wide streets, 10-foot- or 11-foot-wide streets can be used. Too often streets and parking areas are much larger than they need to be. For example, the Charlottesville (VA) City Code requires a minimum paved surface of 30 feet for a "local street," which is the lowest-volume residential streets addressed in the code. In contrast, the Center for Watershed Protection recommends a minimum of 18 to 22 feet of pavement for local streets (SELC, 2008). The use of rain gardens and bioswales instead of traditional curbs and gutters can have a significant impact on reducing stormwater runoff and water pollution. (See Figure 4.48.)

In the San Francisco Bay area, street standards mandate between 80% and 100% impervious surface coverage in the right-of-way for streets, curb, gutter, and sidewalk. If new standards are adopted for the most lightly traveled

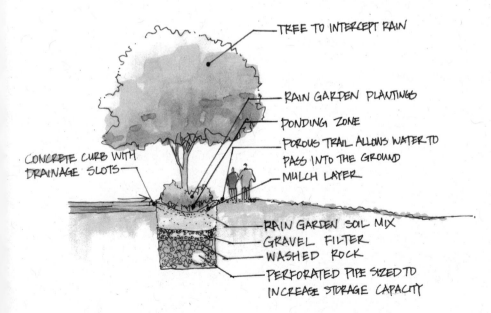

TREE TO INTERCEPT RAIN
RAIN GARDEN PLANTINGS
PONDING ZONE
POROUS TRAIL ALLOWS WATER TO PASS INTO THE GROUND
MULCH LAYER
CONCRETE CURB WITH DRAINAGE SLOTS
RAIN GARDEN SOIL MIX
GRAVEL FILTER
WASHED ROCK
PERFORATED PIPE SIZED TO INCREASE STORAGE CAPACITY

Figure 4.48 *Swales are used along the road to capture stormwater and allow it to percolate into the soil. Image courtesy EDAW.*

local streets, impervious surface coverage can be reduced by 25% to 60%.

Streets can be made narrower, and landscaped areas and/or trees can be incorporated into the street front so that they treat stormwater runoff. In addition, when tree pits are provided along with adequate soil and rooting space, street trees can provide additional stormwater capture and other numerous environmental benefits.

Cluster development encourages denser development that promotes walkability and requires fewer roads. Parking lots for commercial developments are often oversized and are intended for peak uses. For example, parking lots at shopping centers are often designed to accommodate Christmas shoppers. A better approach is to reduce the amount of paving and to encourage multiple uses of large parking lots. Older parking lots were designed to accommodate full-size cars, and as a result many use oversize parking stalls. Current standards specify smaller stalls more in keeping with compact cars. Adding planting medians and bioswales in large parking lots can greatly reduce stormwater runoff. A number of development codes specify that landscaped areas be included in parking lot designs.

Parking lots, especially surface lots, should be minimized and designed to reduce, store, and treat stormwater runoff. Where site limitations or other constraints prevent full management of parking lot runoff, designers should target high-use areas first.

Another way to reduce the impact of large paved areas is to use pervious materials that allow water to percolate into the soil. Stormwater can flow through the voids into grass, soil, or some other underlying material that can absorb and filter it. Where possible, provide planting spaces to promote the growth of healthy street trees while capturing and treating stormwater runoff. In arid climates, xeriscapes should be used to achieve similar benefits (Rowe and Schueler, 2006).

Permeable Paving

Permeable or porous paving provides the load-bearing support needed for roads, plazas, and other paved areas while also providing a more environmentally friendly alternative. Permeable paving contains enough void space to allow water to infiltrate runoff into the underlying soil. Porous pavement

helps recharge groundwater and removes up to 80% of pollutants such as sediment, trace metals, and organic matter. Permeable pavements allow the infiltration of rainwater and the treatment of runoff from adjacent impervious areas. Many government agencies are now implementing stormwater impact fees for all impervious areas.

The use of pervious concrete is among the EPA's recommended best management practices. Pervious concrete has been used since the 1980s, and it is being used in areas where stormwater runoff is a major issue. Pervious concrete is a mixture of cement, coarse-graded aggregate, and water, with little or no sand used in the mix. The lack of a fine aggregate allows water to percolate through the concrete and into the ground.

Pervious concrete also has other benefits, such as reducing heat in urban areas. It also is better around vegetation since it allows water to get to the roots of the plants. Pervious concrete also reduces the need for large detention ponds and stormwater infrastructure. Although the initial cost is higher, concrete pavement has a significantly lower life-cycle cost than asphalt.

Porous asphalt also has very little fine aggregate and a void content of up to 20%. It is often called a popcorn mix because of the size of the aggregate and the coarseness of the asphalt binder that holds it together. Other pervious materials include bricks and concrete pavers.

Weirs

Rock vortex weirs, also known as porous weirs, are an in-stream structure designed to provide grade control in smaller streams and create a diversity of flow velocities. The advantage of rock vortex weirs is that they can accomplish these functions while still maintaining bedload transport and fish passage; not many other grade controls can do the same. A rock cross vane is similar but differs in that the rocks barely extend above the stream invert. A vortex weir has a v-shaped channel that is used to control water movement.

Step Pools

Step pools are stream repair practices that consist of a series of low-elevation weirs and pools that dissipate stream energy along degraded or incising stream reaches. They are often used where a pinchpoint has occurred or in channels that have incised below a culvert or stormwater outfall. Step pools generally are made of very large rocks that alternate between short steep drops and longer low-gradient pools. In larger streams, step pools may also be constructed of sheet piles or poured concrete.

Street Drainage

The streetscape should be designed to minimize, capture, and reuse stormwater runoff. In many parts of the country, street drainage typically is handled by concrete curb and gutter along both sides of a residential street. The curb and gutter collects stormwater and orients it into underground pipes that are intended to get rid of the water as quickly as possible. Street design includes alternative stormwater collection strategies, such as linear biofilters and infiltration basins, rather than standard catch basins and storm drains. Where curb and gutter is used, efforts should be made to collect only the water that cannot be handled with rain gardens, bioswales, retention basins, and other stormwater management approaches.

A popular way to educate the public about the importance of their actions is to label storm drain inlets with messages about environmental concerns. For example, in Seattle (WA), the manholes indicate if the stormwater goes directly into Puget Sound or to one of the local streams.

Dry Wells and Cisterns

A dry well is a subsurface basin that is used to catch runoff for infiltration. A cistern is an aboveground storage container that is directly connected with a roof downspout. Water is diverted from the roof and stored for future use.

Biofilter Drainage Systems

Biofilters are vegetated slopes and channels that are intended to be a more environmentally friendly approach to managing stormwater than paved channels. Stormwater moving over the vegetation slows down, and pollutants can be dropped, not carried into a stream or river.

Stormwater biofiltration systems include bioretention systems, constructed surface-flow wetlands, and constructed subsurface-flow wetlands, among other systems.

In urban environments, small-scale treatment systems may be the most effective approach because of the limited available space. Bioretention filters, underground sand filters, dry swales, and other filter systems are effective for addressing water issues. The biggest issue with these kinds of systems is that they require a certain level of maintenance to minimize problems with sedimentation and other issues.

Rain Gardens

Rain gardens are basically small bioretention ponds that slow down stormwater and allow it to percolate into the soil. The basic idea of a rain garden is to capture stormwater runoff at the street level and divert it into vegetated areas instead of having it run off into the storm sewer system. This approach frequently takes advantage of the underutilized spaces in public rights-of-way and encourages adjacent property owners to participate in the process. Portland (OR) has been a big proponent of rain gardens. The city has found that this approach not only saves money but also is environmentally friendly and helps improve the overall aesthetic quality of neighborhoods. The biggest problem is that too many private landowners want the city to help them build their own rain gardens.

4.11.10 Controlling Runoff from Croplands

Several BMPs are available for controlling runoff from cropland areas, including contouring, strip cropping, conservation tillage, terraces, buffer strips, and grassed waterways. The state of Georgia estimates that it could potentially save $245 million a year by reducing soil erosion and improving water quality (Reeves et al., 2005). Depending on the severity of the problem, it may be necessary to combine BMPs to reduce runoff sufficiently.

Contour farming and conservation tillage are just two examples of ways to control runoff from croplands. Contour farming involves plowing parallel to the contours of the land instead of perpendicular to them. Doing this helps reduce soil erosion and runoff, and allows more water to be absorbed into the soil. Row crops are also planted along the contours.

One of the best ways to reduce runoff from croplands is to utilize conservation tillage, which focuses on limiting the amount of cropland that is disturbed or tilled. Conservation tillage reduces soil erosion and the damage that erosion causes to lakes, ponds, streams, recreational facilities, and other areas. The state of Georgia estimated that if all of the farmers in the state implemented conservation tillage, as much as 30% of agricultural-related runoff would be reduced. Conservation tillage can also increase agricultural production and improve water quality and quantity. Conservative tillage refers to the amount of residue that is left after a crop has been harvested. Any tillage system that leaves at least 30% of the soil surface covered with crop residue is considered to be a conservation tillage system.

4.12 CASE STUDIES

Golden Gate Park Green Roof

San Francisco, California

The California Academy of Sciences in San Francisco's Golden Gate Park is considered to be one of the most environmentally friendly museums in the world. The project was based on a number of "green" strategies, ranging from efficient water management to the use of sustainable materials, such as recycled steel and lumber harvested from sustainable-yield forests. In many ways the museum feels like part of the park because it is actually embedded into the site rather than sitting on top like most buildings. (See Figure 4.49.)

Construction for the new museum cost $400 million. Although that is a lot of money, most people think it was well spent. Some have called the new museum a "masterpiece of green design that displays nature and is also part of nature" (Reed and Loomis, 2008). One goal is to achieve Platinum-level LEED (Leadership in Energy and Environmental Design) certification.

The new academy is one of 10 pilot "green building" projects by the San Francisco Department of the Environment. The plan is for this to be the largest public LEED Platinum building in the world.

The museum is 410,000 square feet in size and houses the Steinhart Aquarium, the Morrison Planetarium, and the Kimball Natural History Museum. In addition, the building includes a four-story rainforest, three-dimensional theater, lecture hall, naturalist center, two restaurants, a garden and aviary, and a store. One unique thing about the museum is that it is transparent. Most museums strive toward creating a dark space where all light can be controlled, and natural light is considered a bad thing. (See Figure 4.50.)

One of the unique features of the California Academy of Sciences is the green roof that covers approximately 2.5 acres. The green roof is expected to absorb about 98% of all the rainwater that falls on it each year. The living roof reduces stormwater runoff by up to 3.6 million gallons of water per year. Thus there is no need for an expensive infrastructure of stormwater pipes and grates. The soil is able to absorb up to 4 inches of rain, and once it is saturated, the rainfall runs off into an underground recharge chamber. Gabion curbs intercept water runoff and allow water to better percolate into the soil. (See Figure 4.51.)

One significant issue was preventing the 6-inch soil base and plantings from eroding off the curved green roof during storms, especially in the winter months, when San Francisco gets most of its rain (Reed and Loomis, 2008). In order to help anchor the plants, more than 50,000 porous, biodegradable trays made from tree sap and coconut husks were placed along the roof.

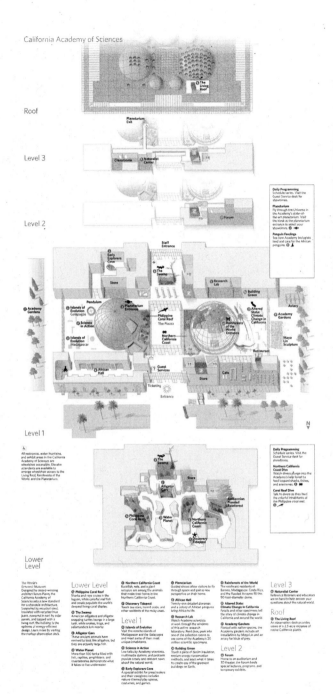

California Academy of Sciences

Roof

Level 3

Level 2

Level 1

Lower Level

Figure 4.49 *This map is an important tool to help guests chart their course through the California Academy of Sciences. Image courtesy California Academy of Sciences.*

Figure 4.50 *The interior of the academy includes a four-story rainforest. Image courtesy California Academy of Sciences.*

Motorized porthole windows in the roof can be open to allow more light and ventilation into the building. The roof also includes an observation deck where visitors can view the roof and the surrounding site.

The architects have estimated that the green roof helps reduce the building's energy needs by about a third. More than 60,000 photovoltaic cells along the glass canopy produce up to 10% of the academy's annual energy needs.

More than 1.7 million plants from nine different native species were used on the roof. The idea was not only to help minimize stormwater runoff but also to provide habitat for local wildlife. One objective was to develop habitat for the

Figure 4.51 *The green roof consists of a series of undulating "hills" that include skylights. Image courtesy California Academy of Sciences.*

Figure 4.52 *The academy's visitor map provides information about the various places for guests to enjoy, including the Planetarium, the Living Roof, the Philippine Coral Reef, and Rainforests of the World. Image courtesy California Academy of Sciences.*

endangered San Bruno elfin butterfly and the Bay checkerspot butterfly. (See Figure 4.52.)

Client: California Academy of Sciences

Design Architect: Renzo Piano Building Workshop

Project Architect: Stantec Architecture (formerly Chong Partners Architecture)

Landscape Architect: SWA Group

Engineer: Arup

Northfield Ponds Park

Denver, Colorado

The Northfield Ponds are part of the urban infill project to transform the Denver's former Stapleton International Airport into a mixed-used, new urbanism community. This is the nation's largest urban infill project. The project was initiated in 2001 and by the year 2020 is expected to have more than 25,000 residents. (See Figure 4.53.)

The Northfields Ponds Park is 35 acres in size. It was originally conceived as a stormwater detention and water quality facility. It can accommodate the runoff from 460 acres of commercially developed land. These types of facilities are usually closed to the public and are considered eyesores with no visual appeal. In 2004, EDAW was brought in to review the stormwater plans and to make design recommendations about enhancing the area. The decision was made to develop a parklike setting that also meets stormwater management goals. The intent was to develop a regional park that would provide much-needed green space while also addressing water management and construction concerns. Groundwater levels fluctuated significantly during the two years required for the design and construction process. That resulted in the need for

Figure 4.53 *The Northfields Ponds Park addresses stormwater runoff issues for development in the area. Image courtesy EDAW.*

Figure 4.54 *A series of walks and green spaces were developed around the Stapleton area. Image courtesy EDAW.*

some changes to previous design decisions. A number of adjustments also needed to be made to address specific site conditions. The surface stormwater system became an integral part of the community's parks and open space network. Plantings were located to follow groundwater contours so that plants will sustain themselves through typical Denver droughts. Native trees, shrubs, herbs, and grasses were planted in the wetland areas. (See Figure 4.54.)

Wenk Associates developed the Stapleton Water Quality Guidelines to provide best management practices addressing water resources. Bioengineering practices were used to slow down and spread out water runoff. Retention basins and pools, and drainage structures were designed as attractive architectural elements in the landscape. Sculpted concrete forms were used to add visual interest to pipes and culverts. The design team organized the facility into three "cells" for stormwater management.

Developer: Park Creek Metropolitan District and Forest City
Planner: EDAW
Landscape Architect: Wenk Associates

Water Wrapper

New York, NY

The Water Wrapper is a concept developed by architect Phu Hoang. It addresses a need for more ecologically sensitive building envelopes. It literally would produce a wall of water that helps define the building. Water particles would be released into a glass building envelope, and this process would help absorb solar heat and air pollutants. The idea behind the Water Wrapper is to use water to reduce the energy requirements of a building. (See Figures 4.55 and 4.56.)

The pattern and density of water in the envelope would be adjusted based on information collected from a network of sensors that detect solar heat and air quality levels. By utilizing collected rainwater and solar power, the Water

Figure 4.55 *The exterior of a building using Water Wrapper literally has a wall of water to help improve building performance. Image courtesy Phu Hoang.*

Sustainable Practices for Site Planning, Design, and Implementation

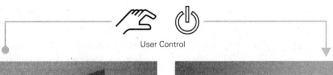

User Control

Housing Tower Prototype- Front (Global) and Rear (Local) Water Nozzle Arrays On

Housing Tower Prototype- Front (Global) Water Nozzle Array On

Figure 4.56 *The wall of water can be adjusted as needed to allow more sun in or to keep the sun out. Image courtesy Phu Hoang.*

Wrapper can generate dynamic visual effects that look like a wall of water while minimizing its impact on local water and energy supplies.

Credits: Phu Hoang, Hwa-Seop Lee, Dong

Contact information: Phu Hoang Office, LLC, 86 Walker Street, 4th Floor, New York, NY 10013, (t) 212.343.4203, (e) info@ phuhoang.com

Parc Diagonal Mar

Barcelona, Spain

Parc Diagonal Mar redevelopment came about as a result of the 1992 Olympic Games. The 84-acre site was once a dilapidated industrial zone next to one of the poorest neighborhoods in Barcelona. In 1987, developer Hines Interests began work on renovating the urban beachfront so that all construction would be completed in time for the 1992 Summer Olympic Games. After the games were over, the city was interested in continuing the renovation of the area. The site was acquired by Hines in 1996, and Hines and the city agreed to work together to implement a 10-year plan for the site. As a result, Parc Diagonal Mar became the first public/private agreement in Spain.

The public/private sustainability agreement between Hines and the city of Barcelona guided all major decisions about the design, construction, and operation of the project. The agreement called for sustainable development principles such as:

• Balancing human and natural resources

• Respecting interdependence of natural systems

• Respecting biological and cultural diversity

• Promoting social equity and economic development

- Balancing short-term and long-term needs and objectives

- Conserving natural resources to be incorporated in the design of the park

What was once a vacant brownfield has become a catalyst for redevelopment in this part of the city. The plan called for five residential phases, a retail center, three hotels, three office buildings, a convention center, and a public park. Construction of a new road extension and the park has helped spur the development in the area. Diagonal Mar now contains a super regional retail and entertainment center, three hotels with a total of 950 rooms, three Class A office buildings, and 1,400 apartments constructed in five independent phases. The regional shopping center, which was constructed in 2001, has more than 1.1 million square feet of floor space. The final residential phase of the development was completed in 2006. All total, the gross building area for the development is 4 million square feet.

The Park

At the heart of the Diagonal Mar development is a 34-acre park that was constructed in 2002. The park is the third largest in Barcelona. It serves as a gateway to the Mediterranean Sea for both tourists and locals. In particular, it helps connect surrounding working-class neighborhoods to the sea. In the past, these neighborhoods often were overlooked and neglected.

Many critics have praised the park for reflecting the architecture and patterns of Barcelona. The hardscaped, paved areas and the forms used around the lakes help create a strong, modern feel for the park. Among the creative features used in the park are: interactive elements, such as musical squares; a waterfall; sculptural mist fountains; exciting play areas; unique seating elements; and interaction with water. Porous pavement is used to minimize stormwater runoff and to allow the water to percolate into the soil. Native plants are used to minimize the need for irrigation, and any water needed to irrigate grass areas and plantings is pulled from one of the three lakes. The fountains in the park are time controlled and turned off to conserve water when the parks close. All buildings associated with the development utilize some type of rainwater collection system. One issue when designing the park was that all materials needed to be able to withstand the salty air from the Mediterranean. (See Figure 4.57.)

The park's three lakes help define the overall character of the space. Most photographs of the park include water in one

Figure 4.57 *The 34-acre park includes pedestrian spaces that focus on a series of ponds that provide visual interest for visitors. Today the park is one of the most visited tourist locations in Barcelona. Image courtesy EDAW.*

Sustainable Practices for Site Planning, Design, and Implementation

Figure 4.58 *The interaction of the strong architectural forms with the ponds and water features create an immersive experience. Image courtesy EDAW.*

form or another. The lakes that cut through the middle of the site serve as a major focal element. This is reminiscent of what Avenue Diagonal does; it cuts through Barcelona in the same fashion. The elevation and depth of the lakes was set so that groundwater serves as the primary source of water. The lakes also are used for stormwater retention for the surrounding development. (See Figure 4.59.)

The 2005 American Society of Landscape Architects Professional Awards Jury called the wetlands at Parc Diagonal Mar one of the best-constructed wetlands they had ever seen. The wetlands are used to collect and filter stormwater runoff.

While the park has been praised for its dynamic forms and spaces, there have also been criticisms. For example, the park does not appear to be very heavily used, and some of the design decisions have been criticized. As the park and the areas around it mature, the number of users may increase.

Today, Diagonal Mar is one of the most popular tourist destinations in Barcelona. The cost of the development was around $900 million, and much of this was paid for by private developers.

Owner/Developer: Hines Interests, Barcelona, Spain
Additional Owners: Habitat; Espais; Apex; Deka Immobilien; and DIFA Deutsche Immobilien Fonds AG.
Landscape Architects: EDAW, Inc., Atlanta, GA
Architects: Robert A.M. Stern Architects; Tusquets Díaz & associates; BST; Muñoz + Albin; Meeks + Partners; Carlos FerraterL Clotet y Paricio; GCA Arquitectes Associats; and EMBT Arquitectes.
Web site: www.diagonalmar.com

SW 12th Avenue Green Street Project

Portland, Oregon

The SW 12th Avenue Green Street Project is located in downtown Portland (OR) and is adjacent to Portland State University. In 2005, the city of Portland converted the underutilized area between the sidewalk and street curb into a series of landscaped planters to capture, filter, and hold stormwater runoff from the street. The project had three primary goals:

1. Be low cost in design and execution

2. Benefit the environment and enhance community livability

3. Provide a model for other jurisdictions to address stormwater (See Figures 4.59, 4.60, and 4.61.)

The 12th Avenue project disconnects the street's stormwater runoff from the system that feeds into the Willamette River. A 12-inch curb cut channels the street runoff into the first of four stormwater planters. Collectively, the four planters capture runoff from approximately 7,500 square feet of paved surfaces. They treat and infiltrate most of the runoff they receive. The water is collected up to a depth of 6 inches, and it then overflows into the next planter, and that continues until the fourth planter is full.

The majority of the runoff is managed on-site, instead of entering the storm drain system, which feeds directly into the Willamette River. The facility was tested twice in 2006 when the city simulated a storm with the equivalent to about 2 inches of rain. The four planters retained 50% to 72% of the 9,500 gallons of water used in the study. The planters are designed to intentionally overflow into the sewer system during intense storms with significant rainfall.

A couple of unexpected maintenance issues have had to be addressed. One is the amount of sediment load collected in the planters. In 2007, sediment was removed seven times, almost twice as often as was planned. Another is that the plants in the planters have grown much faster than anticipated, also requiring additional maintenance for trimming.

Figure 4.59 *The SW 12th Avenue Green Street Project captures stormwater and redirects it into a series of planters. Image courtesy City of Portland.*

Sustainable Practices for Site Planning, Design, and Implementation

Figure 4.61 *The planters are fairly simple, but they are effective at reducing stormwater runoff. Image courtesy City of Portland.*

The project was constructed in May and June 2005. The city of Portland and Portland State University have agreed to share responsibilities in maintaining the four planters. In 2006, the project received a General Design Award of Honor from the American Society of Landscape Architects.

According to the jury, the project "will be influential in the profession." The project also shows that sustainable design for water resources can be affordable. The entire project cost, including project management, was $38,850. Design fees were not included.

An interpretative sign has been placed on-site to provide information on how the stormwater facilities work. The more people understand what they see and how it works, the more they will appreciate these types of green solutions.

What makes the SW 12th Avenue Green Street Project successful is that several community partnerships have been developed to help maintain it. Representatives from the university were involved in the design and planning process. They also worked with local residents to ensure that their thoughts were considered during the process. Students and professors from Portland State's urban planning and environmental studies departments are expected to be involved with measuring the success of the project.

Client: City of Portland
Landscape Architect: Kevin Robert Perry, ASLA

NE Siskiyou Green Street Project

Portland, Oregon

The NE Siskiyou Green Street Project in Portland (OR) focuses on transforming how an 80-year-old residential street handles stormwater runoff. Traditional curbs and gutters had been used along the street, but all this approach does is get rid of the stormwater on this street and send it somewhere else for others to deal with. (See Figure 4.62.)

The NE Siskiyou Green Street Project had three primary goals:

1. Be low cost in design and implementation

2. Benefit the environment and enhance community livability

3. Provide a model for other jurisdictions to follow for similar projects

   These goals are basically the same as for the SW 12th Avenue Green Street Project since the City of Portland was the client for both.

When Portland made the decision to take a more sustainable look at urban stormwater management, it decided to look at approaches that allow the water to percolate into the soil rather than just putting it into pipes. The project basically disconnects the street's stormwater runoff from the city's combined storm/sewer pipe system. Instead, it manages all water within the neighborhood. One of the real strengths of this approach is that because the project is local, it is easier to get communities involved in the process.

The "green street" approach on NE Siskiyou Green Street is actually pretty simple and straightforward. It involves removing a small amount of paving that was used for parking and converting this space into a place that collects stormwater runoff. Two curb extensions were added, to capture, slow, clean, and infiltrate water runoff from the street.

The NE Siskiyou Green Street Project was constructed in the fall of 2003. The landscaped area is 7 feet wide and 50 feet long. Up to 7 inches of water can be collected in the landscaped area. If the water exceeds that level, it runs over a small check dam and flows into the landscaped area just downstream. The landscape system in place can infiltrate up to 3 inches of water per hour. For intense storms, the water

Figure 4.62 *The NE Siskiyou Green Street was one of Portland's first stormwater planters. Image courtesy City of Portland.*

Sustainable Practices for Site Planning, Design, and Implementation

Figure 4.63 *The planters can hold up to 85% of the rainwater from a 25-year storm. Image courtesy City of Portland.*

may overflow the landscaped areas and flow into the existing street inlets, but that is not expected to occur very often.

It has been estimated that the system can handle up to 225,000 gallons of water, which is enough to handle most storms. Simulations conducted by the city also predict that up to 85% of stormwater produced by a typical 25-year storm event can be absorbed by the landscaped areas. (See Figure 4.63.)

Because the NE Siskiyou Green Street Project was the first of its kind, it took almost a year for the project to get approved by the city. A big part of this process was an extensive public outreach effort to ensure that residents had an opportunity to share their thoughts.

Since its completion, the project has gained a lot of attention from communities that are seeking greener approaches to dealing with their own water resource issues. The project has been so successful that there is now a waiting list of neighborhoods wanting similar installations. After seeing the results of the NE Siskiyou Green Street Project, this approach to stormwater management seems to be a no-brainer. It is affordable, it works, it looks good, and residents like it.

www.asla.org/awards/2007/07winners/506_nna.html
Client: City of Portland, Oregon
Landscape Architect: Kevin Robert Perry, ASLA

Mount Tabor Middle School Rain Garden

Portland, Oregon

The Mount Tabor Middle School Rain Garden in Portland (OR) shows what is possible by exchanging paving for green space and harvesting the rain that is prevalent in the area. The city of Portland worked with Portland Public Schools to develop the project. It converted an asphalt parking lot and turned it into a rain garden that helps reduce stormwater runoff. What better place to build a project that teaches about sustainable stormwater management than at a school? An added benefit of the rain garden is that it can be used to teach students about water management. (See Figures 4.64 and 4.65.)

Figure 4.64 *The Mount Tabor Middle School Rain Garden took a small school parking lot and converted it into a garden where children can learn about sustainable water practices. Image courtesy City of Portland.*

Figure 4.65 *The existing site was an asphalt parking lot. Image courtesy City of Portland.*

Sustainable Practices for Site Planning, Design, and Implementation

Approximately 30,000 square feet of the asphalt parking lot was removed and replaced with the rain garden. A series of concrete runnels and French drains that allow water to percolate into the soil direct stormwater runoff into the garden. The garden can hold up to 8 inches of water, which is used to support the plants in the garden, and then soaks into the ground. Low-growing rushes and sedges provide interesting visuals in the garden. It certainly looks much better than a large asphalt parking lot.

The sewer system in the Mount Tabor neighborhood is inadequate to meet the stormwater needs of the community. As a result, efforts have been made to handle stormwater in a more environmentally friendly way by capturing the water instead of letting it run off. The Mount Tabor Middle School Rain Garden project disconnects part of the site from the neighborhood's sewer system.

Landscape architect Kevin Robert Perry has designed several sustainable water resource projects for the city of Portland's Sustainable Stormwater Management Program.

These include the NE Siskiyou Green Street, Mount Tabor Middle School Rain Garden, and SW 12th Avenue Green Street.

The Mount Tabor Middle School Rain Garden was completed in September 2006, and it has become a model for alternative approaches to dealing with stormwater. The rain garden is considered to be one of Portland's most successful sustainable stormwater management projects. The project has been applauded for its simple, cost-effective, and low-maintenance design approach.

Client: City of Portland and Portland Public Schools
Landscape Architect: Kevin Robert Perry, ASLA, Portland, Oregon
Brandon Wilson, City of Portland Environmental Services
Client: City of Portland, Sustainable Stormwater Management Program
Rain Garden Project Manager: Henry Stevens, Portland Bureau of Environmental Services
Portland Public Schools: Nancy Bond, Resource Conservation Specialist, and Chris Boyce, Environmental Specialist

Lagoon Park—University of California of Santa Barbara

Santa Barbara, California

Lagoon Park involves converting a 6-acre gravel parking lot into a natural setting that includes threatened habitat types, such as restored native California grasslands and vernal pools, meadows, and marshes. The University of California at Santa Barbara originally wanted to develop the site for university housing. The California Coastal Commission denied the university's planned residence halls because a wetland plant species was found in the area where the halls were to be constructed. The Coastal Commission required that these potential wetland areas be preserved.

Van Atta Associates, Inc. was the landscape architecture firm responsible for the restoration process. It focused on transforming the gravel parking lot into a restored wetland habitat. The university had a very small budget for developing the area, and it needed Van Atta Associates to come up with solutions quickly.

The plan for the project not only protects the existing resources in the area, it also provides opportunities for recreation and environmental learning. Pathways were established to connect UC Santa Barbara residence halls located nearby to key locations on the site.

These new wetlands and uplands provide habitat for a number of different flora and fauna. One objective was to create an environment that is good for all living creatures, including people. The wetlands and bioswales also help filter stormwater runoff before it makes its way to the lagoon. (See Figure 4.66.)

All of the plants in Lagoon Park were propagated from within the watershed. This helps ensure genetic accuracy for the plants. More than 80,000 native plants were propagated and grown at the university's greenhouses and nursery.

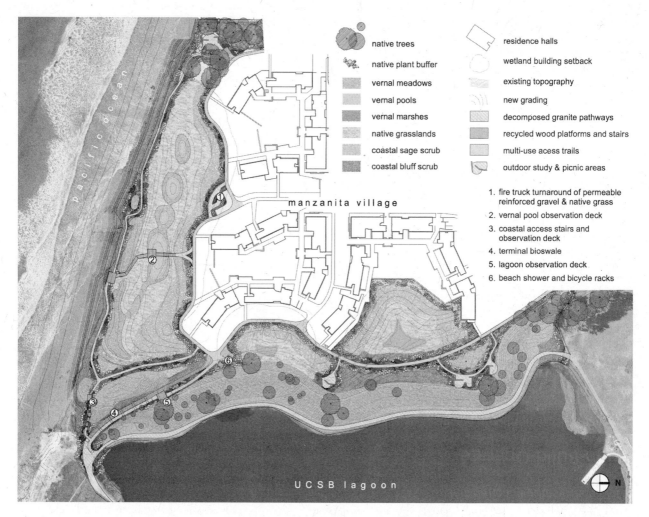

Figure 4.66 *The master plan for the lagoon included vernal meadows, pools, and marshes as well as native grasslands, native trees and plantings, and coast sage scrub and bluff scrub. Image courtesy Van Atta Associates.*

Twenty-seven species of local native wetland plants are growing in bioswales and shallow marshes.

The project is typically referred to as "Living at the Edge of Wilderness," and it addresses how humans interact with natural resources. The project received the 2008 American Society of Landscape Architects National Honor Award. The ASLA jury panel said Lagoon Park deserved recognition for successfully crafting an aesthetic and functional landscape. The jury said that the project was "Proof that you don't have to have a huge budget to do fabulous things."

Client: University of California of Santa Barbara
Landscape Architects: Van Atta Associates, Inc., Landscape Architecture + Planning, Santa Barbara, CA

Lake Pleasant Water Treatment Plant

Phoenix, Arizona

The Lake Pleasant Plant was developed to address the water needs of the city of Phoenix. The plant was a design-build-operate project, with construction beginning in 2003. The $336 million plant became operational in 2007. It is the most expensive capital improvement project to be undertaken by the Phoenix Water Services Department.

The project includes a raw water intake and pumping station, with 1.5 miles of large-diameter pipeline to deliver raw water to the 225-acre treatment plant site. The site was acquired from the Arizona State Land Department in 1998. A buried, 40-million gallon storage reservoir holds treated water, and a pump station supplies water to high- and low-pressure distribution systems.

Design-Build-Operate

At the time of its completion, it was the largest integrated design-build-operate project in North America. The plant currently has an initial treatment capacity of 80 million gallons per day (mgd), about 220,000 households, and is expandable to an ultimate capacity of 320 mgd, which would meet the needs of 880,000 households.

Under the design-build-operate concept, a company designs the project, builds it, and then operates it once it is finished. The bid from the American Water Enterprises and Black & Veatch team was $30 million less than the city's estimate. American Water is scheduled to operate and maintain the facility for 15 years, with an option for an additional 5 years. American Water is the largest investor-owned U.S. water and wastewater utility company. Black & Veatch is a global engineering, consulting, and construction company specializing in infrastructure development in energy, water, telecommunications, and management consulting for federal and environmental markets. The other member of the team was McCarthy, one of the oldest and largest privately owned construction firms in the United States The firm provides construction management, design/build, and general contracting services.

Innovation

One of the most innovative aspects of the plant is how it is blended into the desert landscape. Too often, water treatment facilities are industrial eyesores, and the city of Phoenix wanted to make sure that did not happen. Approximately 95% of the existing natural habitat was preserved. In addition, native vegetation was utilized to help the treatment facility further blend into the landscape.

The plant incorporates the latest developments in modern water technology and automation. The treatment process utilizes seven different filters for removing pathogens, viruses, and bacteria. Promoting conservation and recycling wastewater was an important part of the development because in the arid Southwest, precipitation can be less than 8 inches per year.

The project earned the 2009 Excellence in Public/Private Partnership Outstanding Achievement Award from the U.S. Conference of Mayors.

Client: City of Phoenix, Arizona

Project Engineers: Black & Veatch: www.bv.com; American Water: www.amwater.com; and McCarthy: www.McCarthy.com

---

Bonita Springs Water Reclamation Facility

Bonita Springs, Florida

Bonita Springs is located between Naples and Fort Myers, and is one of the fastest-growing coastal communities in Southwest Florida. The city has a population of a little over 42,000 people spread over a 41-square-mile area.

The East Water Reclamation Facility, which cost $58 million to construct, is located on a 165-acre site that includes a 10-acre wading bird habitat surrounding a 9-acre pond. The plant was completed in December 2006, and at the time it was the largest membrane bioreactor plant commissioned in the state. That plant also produces biosolids pellets from waste, and the pellets are sold as fertilizer. This benefits local agriculture uses, provides additional revenue, and eliminates the need for hauling off sludge.

Many water specialists consider membrane bioreactor systems as the best available technology for wastewater treatment applications. Membrane bioractor plants typically have very small footprints so they do not need that much land, and they are fairly simple to operate. The facility reclaims the water from wastewater to provide irrigation water, and has the capacity to treat 4 million gallons of wastewater per day. It can be expanded to handle 16 million gallons per day, which would meet the needs of Bonita Springs at build-out. Currently the facility processes the wastewater produced by more than 30,000 homes and businesses, helping maintain the integrity of the environment.

Because the Bonita Springs area is extremely vulnerable to hurricanes and other severe weather, it was important to ensure that the new treatment plant would have sufficient emergency power systems to keep running in any conditions. The system is set up so that operators can turn on the backup system even if they just suspect potential problems. This helps make sure there is always a consistent supply of energy.

The East Water Reclamation Facility was developed as a design-build project, meaning that one firm was responsible for every phase of the project. CH2M HILL, a full-service engineering firm, was responsible from conceptual to final design and then for overseeing construction and operation of the plant. The firm was awarded the 2008 National Design-Build Excellence Award by the Design-Build Institute of America for the project.

Design-build projects offer a number of benefits to plant owners. The process is typically simpler and more consistent since only one firm is in charge. There is no "passing the buck." This approach is also often less expensive because there are fewer misunderstandings in implementing a design concept and results in a shorter construction timeline. The design-build process also minimizes the project risk for an owner.

Bonita Springs Utilities is a not-for-profit water and wastewater utility.
Client: Bonita Springs Utilities, www.BSU.us
Planner: CH2M HILL

The Frontier Project

Cucamonga, California

The Frontier Project is a 14,000-square-foot demonstration building that features sustainable design, systems, and technologies. The project is intended to show that sustainable design can be very affordable and visually exciting. The building is open to the public, and it is intended to help inform builders, designers, environmental advocates, the general public, and others about sustainable practices in water, energy, and site conservation. Located in Rancho Cucamonga (CA), the Frontier Project will display and utilize sustainable innovations for southern California living and working environments. (See Figure 4.67.)

The Frontier Project Foundation is a nonprofit organization that focuses on environmental issues in southern California. Formed in 2005, the foundation quickly focused its energies on building a demonstration project that could be used to get others excited about sustainable practices.

The Cucamonga Valley Water District (CVWD) is the parent organization and guiding force behind the Frontier Project. It provides water treatment, water distribution, and sewer collection services for the city of Rancho Cucamonga as well as portions of other neighboring cities and counties.

Breaking Ground

Efforts are under way to achieve a LEED Platinum Rating, which is the highest rating available for sustainably designed buildings. The building includes sustainable features that

Figure 4.67 *The Frontier Project is intended to show that sustainable design can be very affordable and visually exciting. Image courtesy HMC Architects.*

are commercially available and some that are still in the research phase.

The Frontier Project includes several innovative technologies that are geared toward water conservation, including a green roof, a sustainable demonstration garden, and an on-site stormwater management cistern. The demonstration garden features low-water-use native plant materials and an efficient irrigation system. Stormwater runoff from the parking lot is captured, stored in a water cistern, and used to irrigate the plantings on the site.

The project is based on the premise that if commercial and residential builders and consumers are aware of the alternatives, the chance of changing current building practices goes up considerably. The technologies displayed are

available or in development for both residential and commercial consumers. The building includes a demonstration gallery for visitors to view and learn about new building technologies and materials. There is also a conference room for small workshops, classes, and seminars.

The Frontier Project broke ground on April 25, 2008, and was opened to the public in the fall of 2009.

On April 22, 2008, the American Institute of Architects Inland California Chapter and the Green Institute for Village Empowerment gave the project three awards.

Project Architect: HMC Architects
Builder: Turner Construction Company

Tingley Beach Restoration Project

Albuquerque, New Mexico

The city of Albuquerque, New Mexico, was built around the Rio Grande, and the river has much to do with the city's identity. One problem is that as the city grew, the riparian areas around the river were impacted. The riparian forest is locally referred to as a *bosque,* which is Spanish for forest.

The Tingley Ponds were originally constructed in the 1930s by the City of Albuquerque for recreational uses. (See Figure 4.68.) Tingley Beach became the first public swimming area in Albuquerque. It was a popular place to hang out in the hot New Mexican summer months. But in the 1950s, the beach was closed for swimming because of poor water quality. Fishing was still allowed. It took more than 30 years before there was a concentrated effort to do something about the water quality.

In 1987, a quality-of-life tax was implemented by the city of Albuquerque, and the funds were used to create a master plan for the Albuquerque Biological Park (BioPark) four years later. The park included the existing Rio Grande Zoo Tingley Beach and a new aquarium and botanic garden. The BioPark led design, planning, construction, and education development and manages the facility. Construction began in March 2004, and the grand opening ceremony was held October 15, 2005. The goals for the first phase of the project were to:

• Restore the lake to a sustainable aquatic system

• Create additional ponds

• Re-create wetlands

• Set up a natural filtration system for pond wastewater

• Plant native species

• Provide habitat for wildlife

• Increase outdoor recreational and educational opportunities

Figure 4.68 *The Tingley Ponds were originally constructed in the 1930s. Recently they have been restored to make them usable once again. Image courtesy U.S. Army Corps of Engineers.*

Figure 4.69 *Artistic sculptures add visual interest to Tingley Beach. Image courtesy U.S. Army Corps of Engineers.*

The U.S. Army Corps of Engineers is a major participant in the Tingley Beach Restoration Project. It designed and constructed the fishing ponds and wetlands, updated water quality operations, and contributed $6.5 million to construction for the project. (See Figure 4.69.)

Restoration

The primary goal of the Tingley Beach Restoration project was to restore and preserve habitat and enhance biodiversity along the Rio Grande. As part of the project, the

BioPark carried out a major construction project to restore degraded fishing waters, re-create wetlands, establish native plant species, and provide ways for visitors to interact with the restored ecosystem. The project has had a significant impact on improving water and habitat quality. The number of bluegill, catfish, bass, and other fish in the ponds has increased significantly in recent years, as has the number of water-oriented birds.

One major benefit of the restoration of Tingley Beach is that it provides an opportunity for a wide variety of activities, including day camps, fishing clinics, fishing derbies, guided hikes, bird and amphibian surveys, discovery stations, and more formal lectures.

The BioPark has developed interpretive programs that teach about the unique natural resources in the area, including the wetlands. Observation areas overlooking the wetland areas are used for environmental education programs and provide a great way to view the wetland ecosystems and wildlife.

Next

The total project cost was $16.5 million, with the city contributing $10 million and the rest from the Corps. The project was awarded the North American Conservation Award by the Association of Zoos and Aquariums.

Phase II improvements include additional office and classroom space, picnic areas, trails, an outdoor fitness course, and a swimming lagoon. A series of boardwalks will connect Tingley Beach with neighboring wetlands.

One of the real strengths of the project is that it is being monitored in order to determine which approaches were successful. Water quality staff monitors the ponds; local students monitor groundwater levels, water quality, precipitation, and surface activities; and the Corps monitors the plan. This monitoring process will produce important data that will be invaluable in helping make the best decisions about restoration activities at Tingley Beach and for other restoration projects around the country.

Client: City of Albuquerque, New Mexico
Media Contact: Terry Axline, (505) 764-6236, taxline@cabq.gov
Institution Name: Albuquerque Biological Park

Gilbert and Mosley Project

Wichita, Kansas

The Gilbert and Mosley Project in Wichita (KS) took an innovative approach to addressing groundwater contamination. The contamination was discovered during routine testing of the groundwater in the downtown area. A six-square-mile area was found to have high levels of tetrachloroethene, trichloroethene, dichloroethene, vinyl chloride, and additional contaminants associated with previous industrial activities in the area. (See Figures 4.70 and 4.71.)

The Environmental Protection Agency considered placing the site on its Superfund List until the city of Wichita agreed to accept responsibility. Superfund is the federal government's program to clean up the nation's uncontrolled hazardous waste sites. The impact on public health, environmental risks, and the local economy would have been devastating if the Superfund status had been assigned. Much of downtown Wichita would have turned into a ghost town. Unless the contaminated water was cleaned up, development in downtown Wichita was not feasible.

The city stepped in and accepted responsibility for the cleanup of the contaminated groundwater in 1991. It accepted responsibility for cleaning up the site and, in return, received funding commitments from both public- and private-sector partners. The city sued the businesses responsible for the contamination, and additional funding was generated by establishing a tax increment from the finance district.

The Gilbert and Mosley Project site encompasses approximately 3,850 acres that contain groundwater contamination. More than 8,000 parcels of land cover the areas with contaminated groundwater.

The project includes the construction and operation of a groundwater treatment system, an environmental education building, a plaza area, and other site improvements in Herman Hill Park. The name for the site comes from the fact that it is at the corner of Gilbert and Mosley streets. The project was constructed via a design-build process. Construction began in 2001 and was finally completed in early 2005.

Figure 4.70 *The Wichita Area Treatment, Education, and Remediation (WATER) Center serves as both a treatment system and an environmental education center. Image courtesy city of Wichita.*

Sustainable Practices for Site Planning, Design, and Implementation

Figure 4.71 *Water is an integral part of the WATER Center. Image courtesy city of Wichita.*

Treatment

Early on, the city recognized that it was not feasible to restore the aquifer to drinking water standards in a timely manner. Instead, the decision was made to focus on containing the contamination at higher levels and implementing more obtainable remediation goals. Extensive groundwater modeling was conducted in order to determine where to install extraction wells and develop the most efficient pumping system.

CDM, the designer/builder for the project, developed a comprehensive remedial solution that provided a complete strategy for the groundwater cleanup. The treatment facility was constructed in three phases. The first phase included the groundwater treatment building, extraction wells, influent and effluent piping sections, and air stripper. The second phase included the environmental education building and the adjoining plaza. The third phase focused on incorporating site improvements into an existing park—Herman Hill Park—and an emphasis was placed on aesthetics and environmental sustainability. (See Figure 4.72.)

The groundwater treatment system is designed to remediate large volumes of contaminated groundwater. It includes

Figure 4.72 *Treated groundwater is used on-site for both formal fountains and natural pools such as these. Image courtesy city of Wichita.*

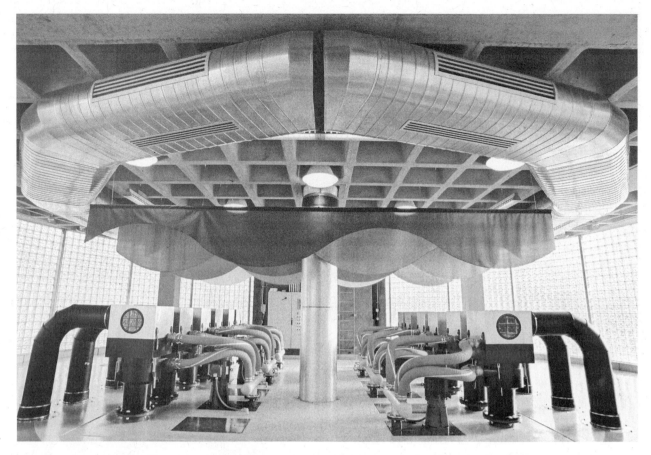

Figure 4.73 *The treatment facility is housed in a 3,000-square-foot space. Image courtesy city of Wichita.*

13 extraction wells, 5.5 miles of piping, and a hydraulic air stripper treatment system. The treated water is reused in fountains, aquariums, and other features in the new environmental education center.

WATER Center

The Wichita Area Treatment, Education, and Remediation (WATER) Center serves as both a treatment system and an environmental education center for the community. The project cost approximately $22.6 million to complete. The WATER Center consists of improvements to the park, educational displays, a covered public area, restroom facilities, and an 11,000-gallon outdoor aquarium featuring native aquatic plants as well as fish.

It includes a 3,000-square-foot groundwater treatment building and a 6,300-square-foot environmental education center. (See Figure 4.73.) The groundwater treatment building is circular in shape and features glass block walls and colored concrete columns and supporting sections. An aqueduct of colored concrete extends over the treatment building. The grand opening ceremony for the WATER Center was held on October 16, 2003.

The effluent from the treatment system is recycled and used in the many fountains around the plaza and for the site's irrigation system. The water is also used to supply a station where trucks can obtain water for nonpotable uses. Water from the fish observation area overflows into a constructed creek that meanders through the site before running into the Arkansas River.

The WATER Center offers a hands-on, interactive environmental center dedicated to the education and health issues caused by water and pollution. Visitors are intended to leave with an understanding of water resources, including groundwater, water pollution, and the water treatment process.

Next Steps

The city of Wichita was able to turn an environmental liability into a community asset. This project has numerous awards, including the Ford Foundation's Innovations in State and Local Government Award.

Since the groundwater treatment system began operating in December 2002, it cleans on average approximately 1.2 million gallons of contaminated water each day. Although this sounds as if a lot of water is being treated, experts estimate that at this rate, it could take up to 50 years to clean up the contaminated groundwater.

The project has also had a major positive impact on the area. According to the Wichita City Council, the project has resulted in more than $300 million worth of economic development in the downtown area.

Project Credits
Owner: City of Wichita, Kansas
Designer/Builder: CDM, Cambridge, Massachusetts, www.cdm.com
Architect: Gossen Livingston Associates, Inc., Wichita
Building Contractor: Dondlinger & Sons Construction Company, Inc., Wichita

Orange County Great Park Master Plan

Orange County, California

The Orange County Great Park is intended to do for Los Angeles what Central Park has done for New York City. The Great Park, at 4,700 acres, is almost twice the size of Central Park, and many expect that it will have the same kind of landmark presence once it is completed.

The site was once the home of the El Toro Marine Corps Air Station, which was closed on July 2, 1999, as part of the Federal Base Realignment and Closure process. (See Figure 4.74.) The property was purchased in 2005 by the Lennar Corporation for $649 million, and one of the conditions of the sale is that 1,347 acres be given to the city of Irvine for the Orange County Great Park. Lennar also agreed to pay $200 million for future development and maintenance of the park.

The Plan

On February 19, 2009, the comprehensive park design presented by Master Designer Ken Smith and the Great Park Design Studio was approved by the Orange County Great Park Board Corporation. Smith has been quoted as saying "One does not build a park, one grows a park." It will take many years to implement all of the ideas planned for the Great Park, which will include extensive natural areas and open space in addition to recreational and cultural areas.

Current thinking is that the park will contain a 2.5-mile canyon, more than 20 acres of lake, 974 acres of nature preserve, a wildlife corridor linking the Cleveland National Forest to the Laguna Coast Wilderness Park, miles of walking and biking trails, a cultural terrace, Orange County's largest sports park, a botanical garden, museums and other public facilities, and a tethered helium observation balloon that will be an icon for the Great Park. Approximately 3,885 areas are earmarked for open space, education, and other public uses.

The tethered helium balloon ride, called the Great Orange Balloon, was one of the first completed elements for the park. This is probably one reason you can find more bird's-eye-view photographs of the park than any other, with the possible exception of Central Park in New York City. (See Figure 4.75.)

Principles of sustainable development will guide all aspects of park design. Sustainability principles include renewable energy generation, efficient transportation system, water treatment system, and habitat restoration. Sustainable

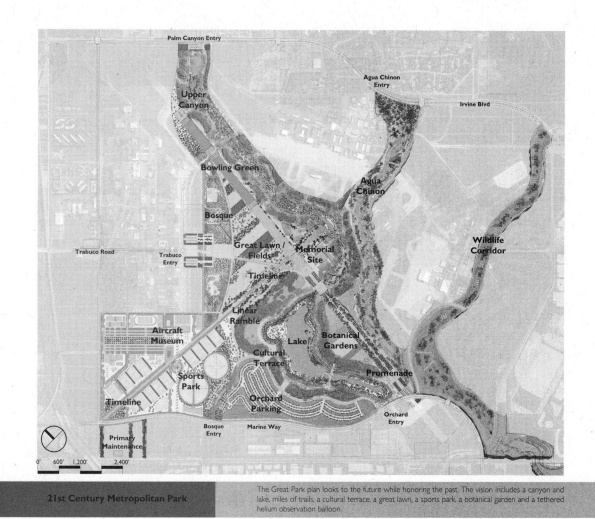

Figure 4.74 *The Orange County Great Park is located on the site of the former El Toro Marine Corps Air Station. Image courtesy Orange County Great Park Board Corporation.*

water measures include water conservation, water recycling in natural treatment wetlands, and runoff capturing. Twelve sustainability standards were developed to serve as a guide in the planning and operation of the park. These standards include: renewable energy, recycled materials, water conservation, biodiversity, air quality, inclusion, stewardship, heritage, health and transit. Future phases of the project will also explore different ways of harnessing solar power and using other energy sources.

The Great Park promotes alternative approaches to transportation. The idea is that visitors driving to the park can park their car and use shuttles or bikes or walk the many trails within the site. Walkers, hikers, and cyclists have the opportunity to select among easy or more challenging trails. (See Figure 4.76.)

Historic museum exhibits and a memorial will be constructed on site to commemorate the history of the military

Figure 4.75 *The helium balloon gives visitors a chance to get a bird's-eye view of the park as it develops. Image courtesy Orange County Great Park Board Corporation.*

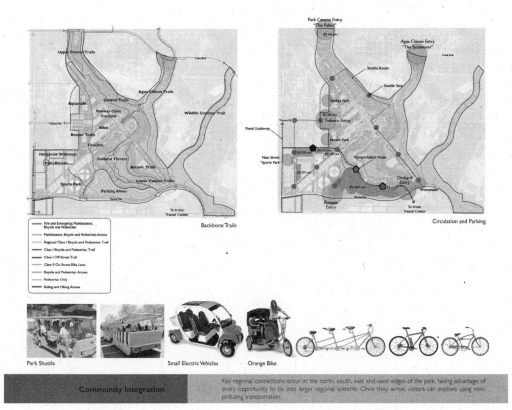

Figure 4.76 *Providing alternative modes of transportation was an important part of the project. Image courtesy Orange County Great Park Board Corporation.*

Key Plan

The Canyon

Section

Earthwork/Physical Form

The constructed canyon, up to 60-feet deep, will be a great oasis with one of the world's most impressive collections of palms, a diverse mosaic of natural habitats, and a sinuous-stream water feature with a string of small pools

Figure 4.77 *The Canyon is one of the major parts of the park. It will be as much as 60 feet deep in places. Image courtesy Orange County Great Park Board Corporation.*

base. The Museum District is expected to be one of the last areas to be developed.

Restoration

Restored native habitats are found in three major sections of the park: the Wildlife Corridor, Agua Chinon, and the Canyon. The Wildlife Corridor is off limits to the public. The corridor allows the animals to move from the mountains to the sea, and it links with nearby nature preserves.

Daylighting of the channelized stream, Agua Chinon, provides opportunities for natural water quality enhancements. The main feature of the Great Park is the man-made canyon that runs through its center. There will be more than a 60-foot change in elevation within the canyon. (See Figure 4.77.)

The plan includes the creation of wetlands, enhanced riparian habitat, and natural treatment systems that will help conserve and protect the area's water supply while providing additional habitat opportunities for wildlife.

Funding

The Orange County Great Park Corporation is responsible for developing and maintaining the park. The Great Park Corporation is a 501(c)(3) nonprofit organization established by the Irvine City Council in 2003.

The initial phase, which includes a visitor center, athletic fields, orchards, park entrance with fountains, reflective pools, café, and a 300-foot-wide rectangular steel gateway, is expected to cost about $450 million. The total cost, though, is expected to be well over $1 billion. A spokesman for the project was quoted as saying that cost estimates for the project "will change many, many times" as it moves forward (Reyes, 2007).

Funding is expected to come from fees and taxes from neighboring housing built along the edges of the park. This financing plan ensures that the Great Park will be developed at no cost to local taxpayers.

Water and Groundwater

One sustainable effort focused on cleaning existing stormwater and returning it into the groundwater table. One problem was that existing groundwater is polluted. Two large aircraft hangars on the site were the primary source of groundwater contamination. The Department of the Navy has the responsibility for contaminant cleanup at the base. Groundwater was modeled using computer software to determine the current problem, and the potential impact of the Great Park. There are currently more than 200 monitoring wells on the site that measure groundwater elevation and water quality. The Navy implemented a groundwater extraction system consisting of 39 shallow extraction wells with dedicated pumps, and a pipeline is used to send groundwater to a nearby treatment plant. Grading for the Great Park had to be revised so as not to disrupt the extraction system. In a future phase of the project, the pipeline eventually will be relocated.

Many of the impervious surfaces are being converted to more pervious land uses, and this means a greater level of groundwater recharge can be achieved.

Accolades

The American Society of Landscape Architects (ASLA), American Institute of Architects, and the American Planning Association all have awarded the park their highest honors. The ASLA jury referred to the project as "An innovative and sustainable approach to ecology, people and history on an amazing scale." In 2007, *Los Angeles Times* architecture critic Christopher Hawthorne cited the Orange County Great Park as one of the year's best designs.

Architect: TEN Arquitectos
Landscape Architect: Ken Smith Workshop West; and Mia Lehrer + Associates
Civil Engineer: Fuscoe Engineering
Urban Ecolot: Green Shield Ecology
Sustainability and Structural Engineer: Buro Happold
Lake and Streams Consultant: Aquatic Design Group
Water Feature Consultant: Fluidity

Cedar River Watershed Education Center

North Bend, Washington

The Cedar River Watershed Education Center is a regional education facility just east of Seattle (WA), near the town of North Bend. The watershed is the primary source of water for 70% of the people living in the Seattle area. There have been numerous efforts to protect the existing resources within the watershed, including the habitat for salmon, steelhead, and other fish and wildlife in the area. One of the primary focuses, though, is to ensure that Seattle's drinking water is protected.

The Education Center, which cost $6.08 million to construct, opened on October 2, 2001. Funding for the center

Figure 4.78 *The center was constructed of natural and recycled materials. Image courtesy Seattle Public Utilities.*

around the center was conserved. The center is used frequently by school groups. It hosts conferences, retreats, and environmental programs, but it is also open to the general public.

The different components of the project include:

- **Exhibit Hall.** This space is used for hands-on, interactive exhibits that tell about the watershed.

- **Loon and Lichen Learning Laboratories.** Provides space for students and visitors to learn more about the watershed. The lab includes microscopes, water test kits, and other equipment that is used for scientific studies.

- **Heritage Research Library.** The library includes a collection that focuses on the cultural and natural history of the watershed.

- **Auditorium.** The auditorium is used by school groups, environmental groups, tribal organizations, and other groups that need gathering space.

- **Heritage Court.** This outdoor space reflects the richness of the ecosystem within the watershed. It includes native plants, a meandering stream, and rain drums.

Fitting the Site

One of the best things about the Cedar River Watershed Education Center is that it practices what it preaches. The center is LEED certified, and it is often mentioned as an example of the type of sustainable design approach that the Pacific Northwest is known for. The site and building are integrated, and sustainable design solutions are evident at every turn. The final project takes advantage of every opportunity to educate visitors about the ecology of the watershed. (See Figure 4.79.)

The building is designed to be energy efficient and to take advantage of the site. Overhangs help control solar heat gain, windows are located to allow for cross-ventilation, and covered walkways help integrate interiors and exterior spaces while allowing visitors to stay out of the rain. The center also uses local materials, and when possible the materials are recycled. Wood, stone, and concrete are

was provided by a partnership between the city of Seattle and the nonprofit Friends of the Cedar River Watershed. Incorporated in 1996, the Friends of the Cedar River Watershed is dedicated to the protection and enhancement of the entire Cedar River Watershed. The center is operated by the Seattle Public Utilities. (See Figure 4.78.)

The Center

The Education Center is located on a ridge overlooking Rattlesnake Lake, and much of the existing vegetation

Figure 4.79 *Water on the site is used in a number of creative ways. This artistic feature collects rainwater from the roof. Image courtesy Seattle Public Utilities.*

the prevailing materials, and recycled plastic composite lumber was used for decking.

This part of Washington receives more than 60 inches of rain per year, and this was a big part of the design solution. Rain barrels are used to harvest this water, which is then reused on the site. Green roofs are used on some of the smaller structures, and a metal roof is used on the larger structures. (See Figure 4.80.) Soil and plants on the green roof help retain water by delaying runoff and naturally filtering rainwater. A new stream was constructed through the middle of the site, and it collects stormwater runoff. Bioswales are used to filter water from the parking areas. Native plants are added to reinforce existing plant communities. Among the other water-conserving features are waterless urinals that save over 45,000 gallons of water each year.

Computer-activated drippers drop water onto 21 drums that are covered with special plastic heads. The idea is that these "rain drops" will create music as they hit the drums.

Client: City of Seattle
Architects/Landscape Architects: Jones & Jones
www.cedarriver.org

Figure 4.80 *Green roofs are used on the smaller structures at the center. Image courtesy Seattle Public Utilities.*

Queens Botanical Garden Visitor Center

New York, New York

The Queens Botanical Garden is located on the site of the 1939 and 1964 World's Fairs. The site consists of 39 acres owned by the city of New York. The recent redevelopment project consists of a new LEED Platinum certified Visitor and Administration Center building, ornamental water features, and display gardens. The Visitor and Administration Center includes a reception area, an auditorium, a garden store, gallery space, meeting rooms, and administrative offices. The Queens Botanical Garden's stated mission is to demonstrate environmental stewardship, promote sustainability, and celebrate the rich cultural connections between people and plants. The building is the first publicly funded capital project in New York City to achieve LEED Platinum status. The 16,000-square-foot center is part of a $22 million infrastructure and landscape project. (See Figures 4.81 and 4.82.)

The new Visitor and Administration Center building builds on the Botanical Garden's Master Plan of 2001. (See Figure 4.83.) This plan addressed the addition of the Visitor and Administration Center as well as a new Horticulture/Maintenance Building; planting plan, stormwater system, water recycling systems; and transportation facilities. The center was completed in September 2007.

Green Solutions

It has been stated that one of the project's greatest successes has been to illustrate that "green" solutions can also be visually attractive and exciting. The Visitor and Administration Center includes such sustainable features as a green roof, solar panels, geothermal heating and cooling, gray-water recycling, and compost toilets. The compost toilets are intended for use by staff, and each uses 3 ounces of water with each flush instead of the 3.5 gallons used by conventional toilets.

The auditorium has a green roof that is planted with native species, and it helps absorb rainfall. The green roof also can

Figure 4.81 *The Queens Botanical Garden focuses on providing educational opportunities to learn about sustainability. Image courtesy BKSK Architects.*

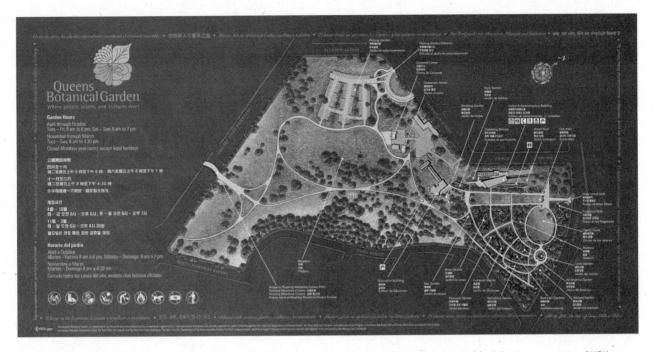

Figure 4.82 *The site for the Queens Botanical Garden is the same site used for the 1939 and 1964 World's Fairs. Image courtesy BKSK Architects.*

Figure 4.83 *The new Visitor and Administration Center is the first publicly funded capital project in New York City to achieve LEED Platinum status. Image courtesy BKSK Architects.*

Case Studies

Figure 4.84 *The building is constructed of green materials and is designed to accommodate a variety of uses. Image courtesy BKSK Architects.*

reduce heat, which is a serious problem in urban areas. The project also includes what is called a "cleansing biotope," a type of constructed stormwater wetland element. This system uses plant material and a gravel subgrade to help cool and filter water as it runs through it.

The center's long, narrow shape makes extensive use of natural light. This approach helps reduce energy use and is complemented by other approaches, such as the use of photovoltaic panels, natural ventilation, and a ground-source heat-pump system. (See Figure 4.84.)

Focus on Water

The gardens are open to the public for free and have become a popular recreation space for local residents. Meetings with these residents indicated that they had a desire for a prominent water feature on the site. Building on this thought, water was incorporated as the primary design principle for the project. Central to these efforts are features that address stormwater management, rainwater collection, and gray-water recycling.

Water is apparent in every part of the site, and the new building and surrounding site have been designed to work together in capturing and filtering rainfall. One of the project's goals was to handle 100% of stormwater management on-site. So far almost all of the rain that falls on the site is utilized, and very little finds its way into the city's storm sewers. The idea is to utilize a system similar to that of the natural hydrology of the site. All water associated with the Botanical Garden is treated with natural systems and maintained without any chemicals.

Rainwater is collected and recycled for use with irrigation and ornamental features, and the water-management cycle is displayed in the center. (See Figure 4.85.) Rainwater also feeds a water channel that falls from the roof and flows through the gardens. A constructed wetland is fed by water from the green roof, and that water is then treated and pumped back into the building to flush toilets in public restrooms.

Water was also used to help enhance the visitor experience. The Visitor and Administration Center and gardens are meant to demonstrate how to use green, sustainable

Figure 4.85 *Water is an intregal part of the site. Rainwater from the roof cascades down into a shallow pool. Image courtesy BKSK Architects.*

approaches. Water conservation and sustainable strategies have been incorporated into the garden's educational programming.

Innovation

A number of green techniques and materials were developed specifically for this project. Some plantings are experimental, and they are being monitored to determine which ones are successful. The benefit of being willing to try something that no one else has tried is that it helps expand our knowledge base of useful practices that meet sustainable objectives. One of the problems with trying something new, however, is that it can take a long time to get permits approved, and construction of these kinds of elements can be expensive.

The Queens Botanical Garden Visitor and Administration Center was also selected as an American Institute of Architects' Top Ten Green Project for 2008. It has been estimated that the center uses about 82% less water than a conventional building of the same size.

www.queensbotanical.org/103498/sustainable?o121454
Client: Queens Botanical Garden
Architect: BKSK Architects
Landscape Architect: Conservation Design Forum
Landscape/Water Design: Atelier Dreiseitl
Green Building Consultant: Viridian Energy Environmental, LLC
Specialty Construction Administration: Katrin Scholz-Barth Consulting
General Contractor: Stonewall Contracting Corp.

Tampa Bay Seawater Desalination Facility

Tampa Bay, Florida

The Tampa Bay Seawater Desalination facility is an integral part of the Tampa Bay region's drinking water supply. The plant uses a process called reverse osmosis membrane technology to remove salts and minerals from seawater to produce drinking water.

The Tampa Bay region has always relied on natural sources to meet its drinking water needs, but popula-tion growth and declining rainfall has led to a serious water shortage. In Tampa, all of the traditional water sources had already been tapped. The area had been impacted by a prolonged drought and diminishing underground water supplies, so the city had to come up with another alternative in order to meet its water needs. (See Figure 4.86.)

Figure 4.86 *Tampa Bay, like many coastal cities, can take advantage of available salt water if desalination is a viable alternative. Image courtesy NASA.*

In cities such as Tampa Bay, which are adjacent to large sources of saltwater, desalination has been a process that has been considered, but in the past the technology was not been cost effective. When Tampa Bay Water made the decision to build a desalination plant, most other attempts at building similar large plants in the United States were not successful. Tampa Bay believed its approach would enable it to produce affordable drinking water. Tampa Bay Water, which was formed in 1998, is a region's wholesale water supplier, and it is self-sufficient, meaning that all funding for the company is through the sale of water.

Decision to Go with Desalination

Proposals for the Tampa Bay desalination plant was first introduced in 1997, but the project was plagued with financial issues. The desalination plant originally went

online in March 2003 at a reduced capacity, but the plant failed several performance tests, and financial problems continued when the construction company working on the plant went bankrupt. The plant was shut down less than two years later because of problems. In late 2004, Acciona Agua and American Water Works combined forces to fix the problems associated with the plant and signed a long-term agreement to run the facility. Accsiona Agua is a unit of Acciona, one of Spain's largest contractors, and American Water Works is part of the German utility RWE. Acciona Agua specializes in building desalination plants, having constructed more than 70 plants worldwide.

The 30,000-square-foot seawater desalination plant cost $158 million to construct. Under a partnership agreement, the Southwest Florida Water Management District, the agency responsible for managing the public's water

Figure 4.87 *The Tampa Bay Seawater Desalination Plant cost $158 million to construct. Image courtesy Treehuggers.org.*

Approximately 1.4 billion gallons of warm water typically flow through the plant's cooling system daily. During posttreatment, chemicals are added to stabilize the water, and the water is pumped to other sites where it is blended with treated drinking water from other sources. This blending process with water from less expensive water sources is performed to make the final product more affordable.

Permitting and Monitoring

The permitting process for the Tampa Bay Seawater Desalination Plant was extensive. The Florida Department of Environmental Protection reviewed scientific research and public comments over an 18-month period before finally permitting the facility.

A number of monitoring programs are intended to ensure that environmental concerns are addressed. Operators continuously monitor the blending ratio of the seawater being returned to Tampa Bay to ensure compliance with environmental permits. Thousands of samples are collected as part of the monitoring, costing about $1.2 million annually.

Researchers determined that the desalination plant would not have a significant impact on the salinity of Tampa Bay. One big benefit of constructing the desalination plant is that it will deliver a drought-proof source of water, and the process for accessing this water is environmentally sustainable.

Results

The Tampa Bay Desalination plant produces 25 million gallons a day (mgd) of drinking water and is expandable to 35 mgd. The facility is able to meet more than 10% of the drinking water needs of the more than 2.4 million people in the Tampa Bay area. The plan was the largest seawater desalination facility in the United States when it was constructed, although there are plans to build a larger facility in California.

The success of the public-private partnership has garnered a lot of attention because of the cost of seawater desalination projects. The facility was named Desalination Plant of the Year in 2007 by Global Water Intelligence, a prestigious water industry publication in Europe.

Client: City of Tampa Bay, Florida

resources in the region, will reimburse Tampa Bay Water $85 million of the plant's eligible capital costs. (See Figure 4.87.)

Treatment Process

The Tampa Bay Seawater Desalination uses three main treatment elements in the desalination process: pretreatment, reverse osmosis, and posttreatment. Pretreatment removes sediment, organic matter, and other microscopic particles. With reverse osmosis, high pressure forces the pretreated water through semipermeable membranes and separates saltwater from freshwater. Reverse osmosis has been used successfully in nearly 200 water and wastewater treatment plants throughout Florida and produces some of the highest-quality drinking water in the world.

Shanghai Chemical Industrial Park Natural Treatment System

Shanghai, China

The Shanghai Chemical Industrial Park (SCIP) is located in the south of Shanghai, on the boundary between Jinshan and Fengxian districts, over 37 miles from the downtown area. In February 2002, the overall development plan of SCIP was approved by the State Planning Commission, which is authorized by the State Council. That same year, SCIP became one of the first industrial parks in China to undertake a regional environment assessment.

SCIP is one of the industrial projects with the highest investment in China. It is the first industrial zone that specializes in the development of petrochemical and fine chemical businesses, and also one of four industrial production bases in Shanghai. A goal of the park is to be one of the largest and the most integrated and advanced petrochemical hubs in the Far East. By September 2005, there were 54 companies registered in SCIP.

In 2004, SCIP started a process to make the development an eco-industrial park. To achieve this classification, SCIP planned to construct six infrastructure projects to enhance environmental performance, including a constructed wetland for the treatment of chemical wastewater. (See Figure 4.88.)

EDAW designed a water treatment system to purify industrial wastewater effluent for recycling within the industrial park. The treated water is then discharged into Hangzhou Bay. The 30-hectare Natural Wastewater Treatment System was designed to treat over 22,000 cubic meters per day of partially treated industrial wastewater. Innovative design components include a trickling filter mechanism for ammonia removal, followed by a shallow-water oxidizing pond for chemical oxygen demand, and two parallel free surface wetland systems.

Although improving water quality was a primary goal of the project, there was also an emphasis on improving aesthetics and improving wildlife habitat. The wetland research center that was developed was available for academic organizations in the Shanghai area. Construction on the SCIP Natural Wastewater Treatment System began in mid-2006 and was completed by spring 2007. At that time, natural water treatment systems were rare in China, and this project served as an example of what could be done. The wastewater treatment plant at SCIP employs new-generation concepts

Figure 4.88 *Initial concepts for the SCIP Natural Treatment System focused on improving water quality while also improving wildlife habitat and enhancing the visitor experience. Image courtesy EDAW.*

Sustainable Practices for Site Planning, Design, and Implementation

Figure 4.89 *Utilizing a natural water treatment system led to the creation of a park amenity where visitors can interact with the surrounding water. Image courtesy EDAW.*

of management and is used as a reference model by the Shanghai Environmental Protection Bureau. Effluents are checked by online monitoring systems. (See Figure 4.89.)

One goal at SCIP was to reduce industry's impact on the environment by preventing pollution. One source of groundwater pollution in the area is hazardous industrial waste, so an incinerator in the park handles all hazardous waste from Shanghai's petrochemical giants.

Reducing energy and water consumption are two specific goals for the SCIP. The efficient use of water is important in China in large part because so much of the country has water shortages. Official figures show that two-thirds of China's 660 cities have less water than they need and 110 suffer severe shortages.

SCIP is currently promoting ISO 14000 certification, which includes environmentally sustainable practices such as wetland water recycling systems and an ecological greenbelt. ISO stands for International Organization for Standardization and, as the name suggests, it ensures that processes such as pollution prevention are done in a manner that meets predefined standards. The recycling project is being implemented with the purpose of turning treated wastewater into demineralized water that is used for drinking. Surplus drinking water is automatically pumped into an underground water system.

Client: Shanghai Chemical Industry Park Administration Committee
Planners: EDAW

Heifer International Headquarters

Little Rock, Arkansas

The Heifer International Headquarters building is one of 45 LEED Platinum–rated buildings in the nation. It was completed in January 2006 and was the first Platinum-certified building in the state of Arkansas. The $17.5 million building was designed by the Little Rock architectural firm of Polk Stanley Rowland Curzon Porter.

Construction of the headquarters is the first phase of a three-phase development of the 22-acre Heifer campus. Phase Two is a 16,000-square-foot educational facility, the Polly Murphy and Christoph Keller Education Center. This facility will also include an expansion of the constructed wetlands and green space. The third phase will include the construction of a global village to educate the public about solutions to hunger and poverty.

The headquarters building was conceived as a series of concentric rings expanding from a central commons. This fits Heifer International's philosophy that providing an animal to a family has a far-reaching impact, much like the ripples created from a drop of water hitting the surface of a pool. Heifer's mission is to end hunger and poverty while caring for the Earth. For more than 60 years, the company has provided livestock and environmentally sound agricultural training to people in third-world countries.

The site for the 22-acre Heifer International Center campus is a reclaimed brownfield that is adjacent to the Clinton Presidential Library. (See Figure 4.90.) Both buildings are in Little Rock's revitalized central River Market District, which is located downtown next to the Arkansas River. President Clinton attended the grand opening of the Heifer International Headquarters.

Innovations

Taking a sustainable approach to designing and constructing the building makes sense, considering the type of work that Heifer does. The building features a number of "green" solutions, including low-flow fixtures and waterless urinals to conserve additional water. Electrical energy for the building is provided by wind power through an energy exchange program. This results in a structure that uses 55% of the energy of a building using conventional construction methods.

The long, curved shape of the building, which is 62 feet wide at its widest point, is designed to capture sunlight for passive solar heating and lighting. Materials were selected for their durability, maintainability, low toxicity, recycled content, and local availability. (See Figure 4.91.)

One of the major goals of the project was to achieve zero water runoff, and it has been recognized for its innovative

Figure 4.90 *The Heifer International Headquarters is located on the site of a reclaimed brownfield. Image courtesy Heifer International.*

management of rainwater usage. Rainwater that falls on the parking lot is collected for a reconstructed wetlands adjacent to the building, Runoff from the 30,000-square-foot roof is collected and stored in a 42,000-gallon water tower encased by a fire stair and enclosed behind a glass facade. Water collected from the roof is used to heat the building and flush toilets, and a designated wetland area controls, stores, and reuses surface groundwater. (See Figure 4.92.)

The U.S. Environmental Protection Agency honored the project with a national Phoenix award for brownfield reclamation. The project was also chosen as a Top Ten Green Project for 2007 by the American Institute of Architects

Figure 4.91 *One objective of the building is to provide educational opportunities for visitors. Image courtesy Heifer International.*

Figure 4.92 *At the dedication of the building, visitors showed up to find out more about Heifer International. Image courtesy Heifer International.*

Committee on the Environment. The jury said, "The sustainable features are visible, but not 'in your face.'"

Client: Heifer International, www.heifer.org

Architect: Polk Stanley Rowland Curzon Porter Architects, www.polkstanley.com

Media Contacts:

Heifer International: Ray White or Jennifer Pierce, 800-422-1311; ray.white@heifer.org or jennifer.pierce@heifer.org

Carpenters & Associates: Christine Volkmer or Jean Carpenter

Whitney Water Purification Facility

South-Central Connecticut

Who says that water purification plants have to be ugly? The Whitney Water Purification Facility provides water to south-central Connecticut. The 140,000-square-foot building, which was completed in September 2005, embraces watershed management practices that maintain natural hydrology and manage water runoff while also providing education opportunities for the public. The 360-foot-long building is made of stainless steel and has a sculptural quality to it. It is supposed to resemble an inverted drop of water. The interior facilities include an exhibition lobby, laboratories, a lecture hall, conference spaces, and extensive operational facilities. Total cost of the project was around $46 million. (See Figures 4.93, 4.94, and 4.95.)

The Whitney Facility also features a public park and educational facility, and the water purification occurs beneath the park. In essence, a 30,000-square-foot green roof is over the top of the purification facility. The green roof blends with surrounding wetlands and meadows. (See Figure 4.96.) The entire project sits on a 14-acre site.

The Regional Water Authority (RWA), which funded the project, wanted a state-of-the-art water treatment facility that utilizes an integrated design approach to reflect water treatment processes, is consistent with neighborhood values and aspirations, and protects environmental quality. The RWA is continuing its ongoing source water protection efforts. These include watershed inspections, review of watershed development site plans, construction of stormwater treatment wetlands, water quality monitoring, and spill response.

The RWA is operating the treatment plant in accordance with a management plan prepared in 2005, and this plan is designed to control potential environmental impacts on Lake Whitney and the Mill River. A resolution in 2000 specified that an environmental study team established by RWA be maintained and that a qualified scientist be included as part of the project team.

Treatment

The Lake Whitney plant uses two levels of protection to ensure that high-quality drinking water is available. The Water Treatment Plant was designed and constructed using proven, state-of-the-art technology to treat the water, and major treatment processes include solids removal, filtration, and disinfection. At the watershed level, the source water protection program includes:

- Water quality monitoring
- Reviews of new development
- Periodic inspections of homes, businesses, and industry to prevent pollution
- A 24-hour emergency response program for hazardous materials spills

Figure 4.93 *The Whitney Water Purification Facility is sleek and modern, and is a welcome change from the industrial buildings often associated with treatment facilities. Image courtesy Regional Water Authority.*

Figure 4.94 *The outer shell of the facility is stainless steel. Image courtesy Regional Water Authority.*

Figure 4.95 *The interior facilities include an exhibition lobby, laboratories, a lecture hall, conference spaces, and operational facilities. Image courtesy Regional Water Authority.*

Figure 4.96 *The green roof helps create a parklike setting for the treatment facility. Image courtesy Regional Water Authority.*

One way of protecting water quality in the watershed is by preserving land for open space.

Sustainable Design

This project was designed to demonstrate how sustainable design and watershed management can be integrated in an innovative way. Eighty-eight geothermal wells heat and cool the facility, and other innovative approaches are taken to highlight energy efficiency. Domed skylights allow visitors in the park to see the water treatment facilities below. They also bring daylight to the treatment plant below, and this reduces energy consumption.

The public park is made up of six different sectors that are intended to reflect the six stages of the water treatment in the plant. A zero-off-site stormwater discharge approach is used, and the landscape manages the stormwater drainage system for the facility. A pond to the east of the project serves as a catchment area for detaining stormwater. (See Figure 4.97.) An artificial waterfall was constructed that serves as the means of releasing and aerating water from Lake Whitney to the lower Mill River.

Accolades

The Whitney Facility, designed by Steven Holl Architects, has received a number of accolades over the years. In 2001 it was the only American design to receive the Van Alen Institute Award in the International Projects in Public Architecture Competition. In 2005 the facility was awarded an Honor Award by the New York Chapter of American Institute of Architects (AIA), and in 2007 it was chosen as one of the Top Ten Green projects by the AIA's Committee on the Environment.

Figure 4.97 *The pond on site is used for stormwater detention. Image courtesy Regional Water Authority.*

Client: Regional Water Authority (RWA)
Civil Engineer: CH2M Hill
Civil Engineer: Tighe & Bond
Architect: Steven Holl Architects
Landscape Architect: Michael Van Valkenburgh Associates, Inc.,
Landscape Architects, P.C., New York, New York
ask.whitney@rwater.com
www.whitneydigs.com/

Maplewood Landscaped Rain Gardens

Maplewood, Minnesota

Maplewood is a small city located on the northeast edge of St. Paul (MN), about 10 minutes from the downtown area. In the early 1990s, Maplewood sought a way to improve drainage in the city, and one of the ideas suggested was to use rain gardens. A rain garden is a depression that is planted like a garden, but its primary purpose is to collect rainwater runoff and allow it to infiltrate into the soil.

These are also often called storm gardens because they help control the impact of storm runoff. Rain gardens significantly reduce the amount of stormwater that flows into sewers and drainage ditches, reducing potential erosion and sedimentation problems.

The city implemented a pilot project in 1995, and when that proved successful, it initiated a citywide rain garden initiative. More than 450 boulevard gardens have been installed since the program began, and another 30 have been constructed on city land. By the time you read this the number of rain gardens in the city will be even greater. Some people refer to Maplewood as the "rain garden mecca," and the city seems to take pride in that designation. The goal of the program is to have more than 25% of the homes in a given neighborhood with rain gardens. (See Figures 4.98 and 4.99.)

Figure 4.98 *One example of how rain gardens are being integrated into site design is the Legacy Village Development, a townhouse development set on 20 acres. Image courtesy Jamie Csizmadia.*

Figure 4.99 *The rain gardens are scattered throughout the city. The primary purpose of a rain garden is to soak up stormwater and infiltrate it into the ground. However, creating a beautiful landscape is also beneficial. Image courtesy Jamie Csizmadia.*

Design Process

The five-step process behind the city's rain garden program is fairly straightforward.

Step 1: Sign up for a rain garden. If residents mark "YES" on the project questionnaire to sign up for a rain garden, the city will send out an engineer to evaluate the location in order to determine if it is suitable.

Step 2: City constructs the rain garden. If the site is a good location for a rain garden, the city will begin construction by removing hardscape and creating a depression for the garden. The rain garden should be in a location that naturally collects water, and sand-based soils are preferred. Clay soils are problematic because they do not allow for the water to percolate through the soil. The excavations are not deep—typically no more than 12 to 18 inches—but they are an effective way to catch and hold stormwater runoff.

Step 3: Select a garden design. After the infrastructure for the rain garden is constructed, each resident is given the option to select from a variety of predefined garden designs. The designs have a wet zone in the center of the garden and an upland zone around the edges. There are 10 different gardens to select from:

1. Summer days garden
2. Perennial rainbow garden
3. Cool whites and jazz brights garden
4. Butterfly and friends garden
5. Minnesota prairie garden
6. Easy daylily garden
7. Sunny garden—warm colors
8. Sunny border garden
9. Shady garden
10. Shrub garden

There are three standard rain garden sizes: 12 foot by 24 foot, 10 foot by 20 foot, and 8 foot by 16 foot. The actual layout of each garden is determined by existing site features, such as topography, drainage patterns, trees and vegetation patterns, and road and utility infrastructure. (See Figure 4.100.)

Figure 4.100 *Homeowners can select from a variety of predesigned gardens. This image shows the Summer Days Garden. Image courtesy City of Maplewood.*

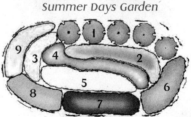

1 Neon Flash Spirea (spirea japonica 'Neon Flash') Height: 3 feet Spread: 3 feet Blooms: May to frost. Burgundy fall foliage

2 Prairie Sunset Heliopsis Heliopsis helianthoides 'Prairie Sunset' Height: 4 feet Spread: 3 feet Blooms: June to August

3 Floristan White Liatris Liatris spicata 'Floristan White' Height: 3 feet Spread: 1.5-2 feet Blooms: June to August

4 Blue Flag Iris Iris versicolor Height: 2 feet Spread: 1.5 feet Blooms: May to June

5 White Swan Coneflower Echinacea purpurea 'White Swan' Height: 2-3 feet Spread: 1.5-2 feet Blooms: June to August

6 Walker's Low Catmint Nepeta x faassenii 'Walker's Low' Height: 2-2.5 feet Spread: 2 feet Blooms: June to September

7 Purple Dome Aster Aster novae-angliae 'Purple Dome' Height: 2 feet Spread: 2 feet Blooms: August to October

8 Little Bluestem Schizachyrium scoparium Height: 3 feet Spread: 1.5 feet Blooms: August to September

9 Goldstrum Rudbeckia Rudbeckia fulgida 'Goldstrum' Height: 2.5 feet Spread: 1.5 feet Blooms: July to September

Summer Days Garden

Figure 4.101 *A series of paths cut through and around the rain gardens, so pedestrians can see the butterflies, birds, and ornamental plantings. Image courtesy Jamie Csizmadia.*

Step 4: Plant the garden. The spring after construction, the city provides plants and hosts a planting day where residents plant their rain gardens. The plants used are typically native or cultivars that can tolerate drought as well as occasional drenching.

Step 5: Maintain your garden. Once the gardens are planted, residents are responsible for maintaining them.

Results

The city has also developed an outreach effort to help citizens understand the benefits of using rain gardens for runoff management. Before installing a project, the city meets with neighborhood residents to talk about the benefits of a rain garden and to address potential concerns. The city has developed a comprehensive educational package that includes a fact sheet that explains everything you ever wanted to know about rain gardens but were afraid to ask.

The city also conducts rain garden construction workshops on a regular basis. For example, it sponsors "Planting Days" and enlists neighborhood volunteers to coordinate and conduct the planting. Maplewood residents who are not on street reconstruction projects are also encouraged to consider installing a rain garden on their property.

The nice thing about Maplewood's rain gardens is that they are affordable and easy to implement. The city estimates that a typical rain garden project costs 75% to 85% of a traditional curb-and-gutter project. It is hard to beat a project that costs less, looks better, and is more environmentally sustainable than the alternative. In addition to enhancing water quality and reducing urban pollution, the gardens also enhance the visual character of neighborhoods and attract a wider variety of birds and butterflies. (See Figure 4.101.)

For homeowners who are concerned about the environment, rain gardens are no-brainers. There is no cost involved for the homeowner, and the end result is a garden that is attractive and sustainable. This is important, because many municipalities around the country that are trying to implement similar programs charge residents a street assessment to cover a percentage of the project cost, and that has limited the development of rain gardens.

The level of maintenance with rain gardens is no more than with any other garden. The gardens are constructed to infiltrate in less than 48 hours after a rain event, so there is no standing water that would be a safety hazard or serve as a breeding ground for mosquitoes. In fact, the plantings typically used in rain gardens frequently attract dragonflies, which eat mosquito larvae.

When paving is dug up to create the depression for the rain garden, the material can be recycled and used as a base aggregate to help with drainage. There will also be significant cost savings associated with reducing the need for conventional storm systems. The city estimates that its rain garden program reduces stormwater runoff by as much as 80% annually.

Funding for the rain garden program came from the city of Maplewood, an EPA grant, and a grant from the Legislative Commission on Minnesota Resources.

Client: City of Maplewood, Minnesota

Chicago City Hall Rooftop Garden

Chicago, Illinois

The city of Chicago utilized a rooftop garden for its City Hall building, an 11-story office building in the downtown area. The City Hall Rooftop Garden is a $1.5 million retrofit project to demonstrate the benefits of green roofs. The city of Chicago Department of Environment initiated the project as part of EPA's Urban Heat Island Initiative.

The City Hall rooftop garden improves air quality, conserves energy, reduces stormwater runoff, and helps lessen the urban heat island effect. The garden's plants reflect heat, provide shade, and help cool the surrounding air through evapotranspiration, which occurs when plants secrete water through pores in their leaves. The water draws heat as it evaporates, cooling the air in the process. Plants also filter the air, which improves air quality by using excess carbon dioxide to produce oxygen. (See Figures 4.102 and 4.103.)

One of the major purposes of the City Hall Green Roof Pilot Project is to provide a green roof demonstration that serves to facilitate research and educational outreach in a Midwestern climate. The rooftop garden mitigates the urban heat island by absorbing less heat from the sun than a tar roof, and the result is that City Hall is cooler in summer and requires less energy for air conditioning. The garden also absorbs and uses rainwater and is able to retain 75% of a 1-inch rainfall, or what is considered to be a typical rainfall.

Unlike rooftop gardens, green roofs typically are not designed to be accessible to the public. One of the primary benefits of taking this approach with the City Hall Green Roof is that the lighter load helps keep construction costs down. Although the rooftop is not accessible to the public, it is visible from dozens of taller buildings in the area, so the final design form was important. The plantings are organized in a sunburst pattern to add a level of visual interest.

Plantings

The 20,300-square-foot City Hall rooftop garden has 20,000 plants of more than 150 varieties including 100 shrubs, 40 vines, and 2 trees. (See Figure 4.104.) The variety of plants include native prairie and woodland grasses and herbs, hardy ornamental perennials and grasses, several species of native and ornamental shrubs, and two varieties of trees. The plants were selected for their hardiness on a roof, where wind and watering are two challenges. The garden is very low maintenance, relying on a blend of compost, mulch, and sponge-like ingredients that retains more water yet weighs considerably less than regular topsoil.

Figure 4.102 *The Rooftop garden at Chicago's City Hall building was installed in an effort to improve air quality, conserve energy, and reduce stormwater runoff. Image courtesy city of Chicago.*

Figure 4.103 *The roof garden is being monitored to determine how well it is meeting the original goals established for the project. Image courtesy city of Chicago.*

Figure 4.104 *The City Hall rooftop garden includes more than 20,000 plants. Image courtesy city of Chicago.*

The rooftop garden design utilizes three types of systems: intensive, "semi-intensive," and extensive. The thickness of the different layers varies, but the types of materials used are basically the same. The layers include a drain layer material, a filter layer, and growing medium. The growing medium consists of a specialized soil mix that is porous and lightweight but able to retain moisture and nutrients. The surface is covered with a biodegradable mesh.

Impacts

Construction began on the rooftop garden in April 2000. The project was completed in the summer of 2001 at a cost of $2.5 million and is being monitored to determine how well the plants are growing and the environmental benefits of the green roof. Test data are being collected from monitoring temperature, rainfall, wind speed, and direction. Monitoring showed that during the first summer the roof garden was in place, the air temperature at the roof was reduced by 15 degrees. If more green roofs were installed around Chicago, the impact would be significant.

Owner: City of Chicago, Dept of Environment
Designers/Manufacturers of Record: Greenroof System:
Roofscapes, Inc.
Roofscapes Contractor: Church Landscape
Landscape Architect: Conservation Design Forum
Architect: McDonough + Partners
Project Engineer: Roy F. Weston, Inc.
General Contractor: Bennett and Brosseau Roofing
http://egov.cityofchicago.org
Conservation Design Forum, Inc., David Yocca, Senior Partner:
Media Relations/Inquiries: (312) 744-5716

Idlewild Park

Queens, New York

Idlewild Park is a 224-acre wetland preserve located on the northwest border of John F. Kennedy International Airport. Approximately 66.1 acres of the site currently are being used to house a garage facility for the Department of Transportation, which was completed in 1996. (See Figure 4.105.)

Idlewild is classified as a "forever wild" site, and it drains approximately 60% of Queens. The park includes freshwater and tidal wetlands, woodland, meadow, grassland dune-scrub habitat, and two meandering tributaries of a local creek. (See Figures 4.106 and 4.107.) It also contains one of the richest salt marshes in southeast Queens. These salt marshes act as a natural filtration system for the groundwater in the area. Contaminants are trapped within the marshes and thus are prevented from entering Jamaica Bay.

Transition

Over the years, New York City's shorelines have been largely dominated by commerce and industry, but efforts are being made to clean up the water's edge and provide access to the public. Idlewild serves as a natural drainage basin for Queens and is linked through tidal action and freshwater runoff to Jamaica Bay. Addressing water quality at Idlewild goes a long way toward cleaning up New York City's waters.

The city is connecting parks to the water by way of its first Water Trail system. The Idlewild Park Preserve launch is an important part of this trail. The master plan for the park creates an experimental research and education center that utilizes trail systems to delineate multiple comparable experimental plots for ecological restoration. The city's Parks Department manages the marsh habitat for the protection of a variety of wading birds, including egrets, ibis, and herons.

Figure 4.105 *Idlewild Park helps manage stormwater runoff from the JFK International Airport. Image courtesy EDAW.*

Figure 4.106 *The site is designated a "forever wild" site, and efforts are being made to protect wetlands, woodlands, and meadows. Image courtesy EDAW.*

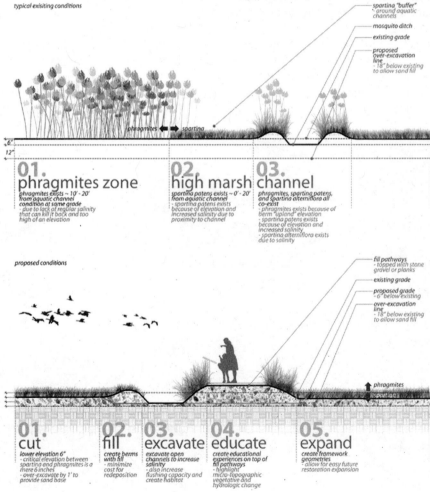

typical exisiting conditions

spartina "buffer"
- around aquatic channels

mosquito ditch

existing grade

proposed over-excavation line
- 18" below existing to allow sand fill

phragmites ←→ spartina

6"
12"

01.
phragmites zone
phragmites exists ~ 10' - 20' from aquatic channel condition at same grade
- due to lack of regular salinity that can kill it back and too high of an elevation

02.
high marsh
spartina patens exists ~ 0' - 20' from aquatic channel
- spartina patens exists because of elevation and increased salinity due to proximity to channel

03.
channel
phragmites, spartina patens, and Spartina alterniflora all co-exist
- phragmites exists because of berm "upland" elevation
- spartina patens exists because of elevation and increased salinity
- spartina alterniflora exists due to salinity

proposed conditions

fill pathways
- topped with stone gravel or planks

existing grade

proposed grade
- 6" below existing

over-excavation line
- 18" below existing to allow sand fill

phragmites
spartina

01.
cut
lower elevation 6"
- critical elevation between spartina and phragmites is a mere 6 inches
- over-excavate by 1' to provide sand base

02.
fill
create berms with fill
- minimize cost for redeposition

03.
excavate
excavate open channels to increase salinity
- also increase flushing capacity and create habitat

04.
educate
create educational experiences on top of fill pathways
- highlight micro-topographic vegetative and hydrologic change

05.
expand
create framework geometries
- allow for easy future restoration expansion

Figure 4.107 *Designs for the freshwater and tidal wetlands focus on maintaining a natural and sustainable environment. Image courtesy EDAW.*

Trails are developed to link restoration projects as well as other parts of the site. These will be part of the New York City Water Trail, which provides information on how to access the waters surrounding the city.

Long Term

Eventually, the idea is to turn all of Idlewild Park into an educational venue for habitat rehabilitation and urban ecology. Several joint projects between the park's Natural Resources Group and the New York City Department of Environmental Protection to address wetland restoration at Idlewild Park have been completed. Future projects will focus on restoring additional salt marshes as part of the excavation of an earthen dike and the replacement of underground culverts.

Client: Eastern Queens Alliance
Landscape Architect: EDAW

Prairie Trail Stormwater Guidelines

Ankeny, Iowa

Prairie Trail is a 1,000-acre new urbanist community in Ankeny, Iowa. The 1,031-acre project will be developed on the site of a former Iowa State University research farm. In 2005, the city selected DRA Properties, LLC to purchase and develop the property, and Urban Design Associates, Wenk Associates, and Nilles Associates were selected to prepare the master plan.

The strength of the plan is that it pays homage to traditional Iowa towns yet incorporates smart-growth principles that include start-of-the-art water resource strategies. (See Figure 4.108.)

Guidelines

The Prairie Trail Stormwater Guidelines are divided into four categories: introduction, development types, best management practices (BMPs) fact sheets, and implementation details. The guidelines emphasize interdisciplinary collaboration among landscape architects, engineers, and architects in preparation of water-sustainable site plans.

Basic Principles

Seven basic design and stormwater quality principles were established for the project.

Principle 1. Consider stormwater quality needs early in the design process. Emphasis is on ensuring that the initial planning phase for a project includes opportunities to integrate stormwater quality facilities into the design.

Principle 2. Take advantage of the entire site when planning stormwater quality treatment. Instead of utilizing conventional methods that focus on getting rid of the water as quickly as possible, a better approach is to spread runoff over a larger portion of the site.

Principle 3. Reduce runoff rates and volumes to more closely match natural conditions. One of the most effective stormwater management approaches is to reduce runoff volumes to the maximum extent practicable to more closely match natural conditions.

Principle 4. Integrate stormwater quality management and flood control. Both stormwater quality treatment and flood control detention goals can be accomplished on a site through a coordinated design approach.

Principle 5. Develop stormwater facilities that enhance the site, community, and environment. The integration of BMPs and associated landforms, walls, landscape, and materials can reflect the standards and patterns of a neighborhood and help to create lively, safe, and pedestrian-oriented districts.

Principle 6. Design sustainable facilities that can be safely maintained. Stormwater quality facilities must be maintained properly and consistently to function effectively and ensure long-term viability. Site planning should include consideration

Figure 4.108 *The stormwater standards for Prairie Trail were developed to provide a framework for addressing water resources. Image courtesy Wenk Associates.*

for access to BMPs by appropriate equipment and for removal of trash, debris, and sediment on a regular basis.

Principle 7. Design and maintain facilities with public safety in mind. Stormwater quality facilities must be designed and maintained in a manner that does not pose health or safety hazards to the public. (See Figure 4.109.)

Stormwater Management

The Stormwater Guidelines were developed to achieve three interrelated objectives: guiding community form and providing public open space and habitat while managing the community's storm runoff in a cost-effective manner. The strategy is to create facilities that are integrated with the landscape and hard surface elements of a site, compatible

with the land use and effective for enhancing stormwater quality and quantity. (See Figure 4.110.)

The stormwater management report recommends a comprehensive stormwater management strategy for peak rate flow management and water quality. Peak rate volumes are accommodated in park and open space areas. Alternative strategies propose reducing the size of stormwater detention basins by reducing runoff volumes and distributing stormwater quality treatment throughout the site.

Stormwater quality treatment approaches were generated for each development type. In some situations, the approaches used in one development type also are applicable in another. The different development types include:

- Light industrial
- Town center
- Commercial

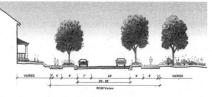

This section illustrates a typical Prairie Trail road with a sidewalk on one side and greenspace on the other.

Precedent images of the street landscape character of surrounding neighborhoods.

Street Character

The typical character of Prairie Trail streets will draw on the character of the most respected streets in Polk County communities. The street patterns will align themselves with the inherent landscape features of the site. Greenways will be natural in character with narrow cartways, uniform tree lines, and with varying naturalistic and ornamental plantings. Neighborhood streets will have sidewalks, at a minimum, on one side of the street with grass verges and tree planting. Other streets might border a park or a preserved vegetation area and have a sidewalk on only one side. Simple landscape elements will define the edges of the street rights-of-way, and will include hedgerows, fences and low stone walls.

Figure 4.109 *The Stormwater Guidelines address both the aesthetics and functionality of streets within the development. Image courtesy Wenk Associates.*

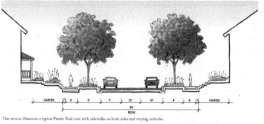

This section illustrates a typical Prairie Trail road with sidewalks on both sides and varying setbacks.

This section illustrates a typical mews with sidewalks on both sides and varying setbacks. The dimensions shown are for illustrative purposes and may vary.

Landscape Character of Prairie Trail Streets

LANDSCAPE PATTERNS

(F) 6

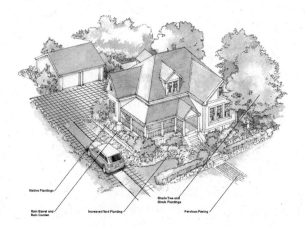

Design With Water: House and Lot

Stormwater runoff from roofs, driveways, and roads carries pollutants such as oil, heavy metals, chemicals, and lawn fertilizers directly to nearby waterways, where they bioaccumulate and seriously harm water quality. To accompany the sustainable practice of planting native and noninvasive species, Prairie Trail residences are to utilize tools and techniques such as rain barrels and rain gardens and to help soil and vegetation capture, neutralize, and manage stormwater runoff. Shade trees help to keep homes up to 20-degrees cooler in the summer time and, coupled with increased yard planting, can help intercept and clean stormwater. Another design technique is to utilize pervious paving materials that aid in percolation, such as individual brick or stone paving units, or pervious concrete.

Despite the varying techniques, the purpose of such ecologically-conscious design is to allow water proper time to soak into the soil where it nourishes plants, can be cleaned, replenishes aquifers, and supports the water systems during dry periods. Onsite stormwater management transforms water from a potential nuisance as polluted and erosive runoff from gutters directly to wetlands and sewers into a resource for the environment and communities. Additionally, proper management techniques will beautify Prairie Trail lots and, in turn, its streetscapes and neighborhoods. Prairie Trail will provide leadership in sustainable and ecological design working with Polk County to develop systems, both natural and manmade, that will help protect and enhance the sensitive watersheds of the communities that are built here.

Figure 4.110 *General guidelines are established for each lot so that homeowners have a better idea how to be efficient with water usage. Image courtesy Wenk Associates.*

Water Ecology of Lots

LANDSCAPE PATTERNS

(F) 27

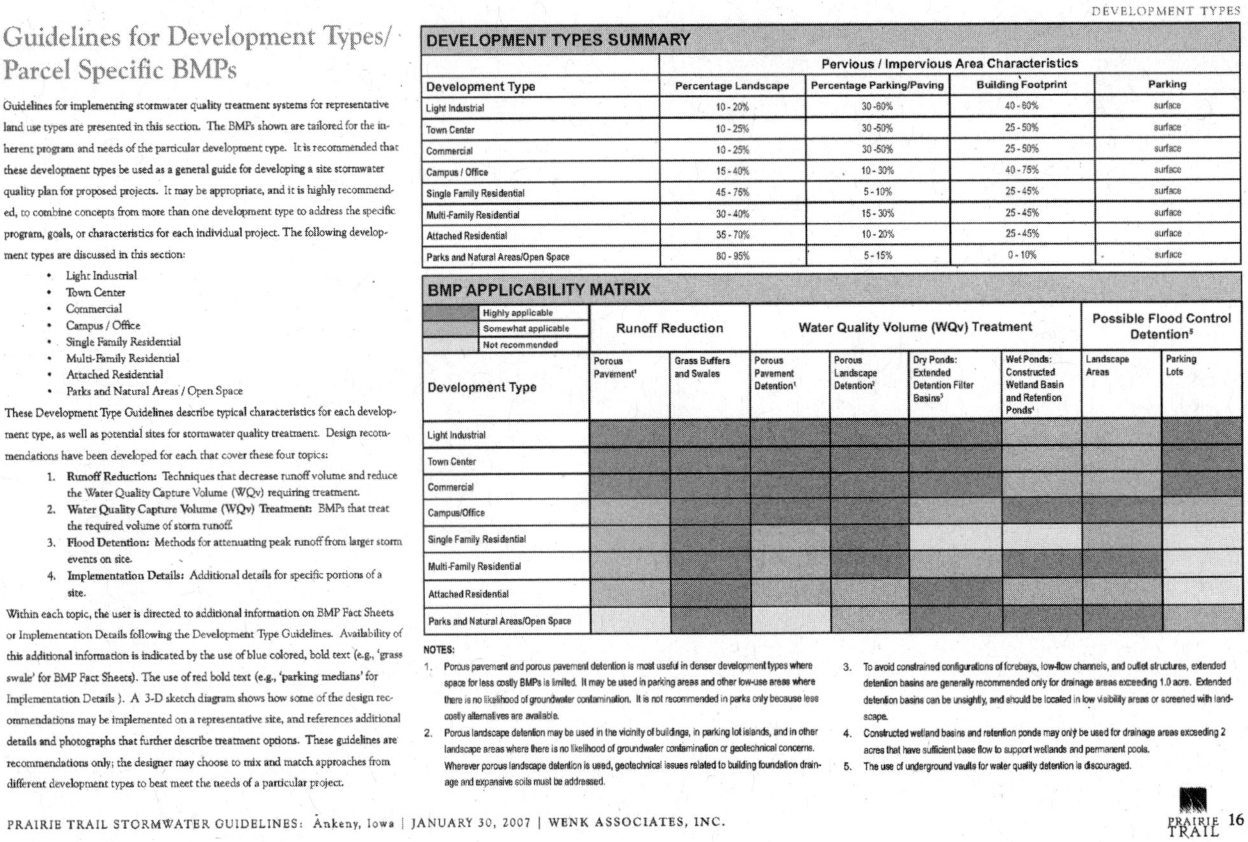

Guidelines for Development Types/ Parcel Specific BMPs

Guidelines for implementing stormwater quality treatment systems for representative land use types are presented in this section. The BMPs shown are tailored for the inherent program and needs of the particular development type. It is recommended that these development types be used as a general guide for developing a site stormwater quality plan for proposed projects. It may be appropriate, and it is highly recommended, to combine concepts from more than one development type to address the specific program, goals, or characteristics for each individual project. The following development types are discussed in this section:

- Light Industrial
- Town Center
- Commercial
- Campus / Office
- Single Family Residential
- Multi-Family Residential
- Attached Residential
- Parks and Natural Areas / Open Space

These Development Type Guidelines describe typical characteristics for each development type, as well as potential sites for stormwater quality treatment. Design recommendations have been developed for each that cover these four topics:

1. **Runoff Reduction:** Techniques that decrease runoff volume and reduce the Water Quality Capture Volume (WQv) requiring treatment.
2. **Water Quality Capture Volume (WQv) Treatment:** BMPs that treat the required volume of storm runoff.
3. **Flood Detention:** Methods for attenuating peak runoff from larger storm events on site.
4. **Implementation Details:** Additional details for specific portions of a site.

Within each topic, the user is directed to additional information on BMP Fact Sheets or Implementation Details following the Development Type Guidelines. Availability of this additional information is indicated by the use of blue colored, bold text (e.g., 'grass swale' for BMP Fact Sheets). The use of red bold text (e.g., 'parking medians' for Implementation Details). A 3-D sketch diagram shows how some of the design recommendations may be implemented on a representative site, and references additional details and photographs that further describe treatment options. These guidelines are recommendations only; the designer may choose to mix and match approaches from different development types to best meet the needs of a particular project.

DEVELOPMENT TYPES SUMMARY

Development Type	Pervious / Impervious Area Characteristics			
	Percentage Landscape	Percentage Parking/Paving	Building Footprint	Parking
Light Industrial	10 - 20%	30 -60%	40 - 60%	surface
Town Center	10 - 25%	30 -50%	25 - 50%	surface
Commercial	10 - 25%	30 -50%	25 - 50%	surface
Campus / Office	15 - 40%	10 - 30%	40 -75%	surface
Single Family Residential	45 - 75%	5 - 10%	25 - 45%	surface
Multi-Family Residential	30 - 40%	15 - 30%	25 - 45%	surface
Attached Residential	35 - 70%	10 - 20%	25 - 45%	surface
Parks and Natural Areas/Open Space	80 - 95%	5 - 15%	0 - 10%	surface

BMP APPLICABILITY MATRIX

	Highly applicable / Somewhat applicable / Not recommended	Runoff Reduction		Water Quality Volume (WQv) Treatment				Possible Flood Control Detention[5]	
Development Type		Porous Pavement[1]	Grass Buffers and Swales	Porous Pavement Detention[1]	Porous Landscape Detention[2]	Dry Ponds: Extended Detention Filter Basins[3]	Wet Ponds: Constructed Wetland Basin and Retention Ponds[4]	Landscape Areas	Parking Lots
Light Industrial									
Town Center									
Commercial									
Campus/Office									
Single Family Residential									
Multi-Family Residential									
Attached Residential									
Parks and Natural Areas/Open Space									

NOTES:

1. Porous pavement and porous pavement detention is most useful in denser development types where space for less costly BMPs is limited. It may be used in parking areas and other low-use areas where there is no likelihood of groundwater contamination. It is not recommended in parks only because less costly alternatives are available.

2. Porous landscape detention may be used in the vicinity of buildings, in parking lot islands, and in other landscape areas where there is no likelihood of groundwater contamination or geotechnical concerns. Wherever porous landscape detention is used, geotechnical issues related to building foundation drainage and expansive soils must be addressed.

3. To avoid constrained configurations of forebays, low-flow channels, and outlet structures, extended detention basins are generally recommended only for drainage areas exceeding 1.0 acre. Extended detention basins can be unsightly, and should be located in low visibility areas or screened with landscape.

4. Constructed wetland basins and retention ponds may only be used for drainage areas exceeding 2 acres that have sufficient base flow to support wetlands and permanent pools.

5. The use of underground vaults for water quality detention is discouraged.

PRAIRIE TRAIL STORMWATER GUIDELINES: Ankeny, Iowa | JANUARY 30, 2007 | WENK ASSOCIATES, INC.

 PRAIRIE TRAIL 16

Figure 4.111 *The James Clarkson Environmental Discovery Center, which opened in 2004, educates users on the importance of environmental protection and restored ecosystems and is dedicated to the exploration and celebration of the natural environment. Image courtesy Wenk Associates.*

- Campus/Office
- Single-family residential
- Multifamily residential
- Attached residential
- Parks and natural areas/open space

In the Town Center, potential stormwater treatment can occur in islands, buffers, and medians at surface parking lots, lawns, plazas, courtyards, and gardens. In residential areas, the focus is on reducing runoff from homes. In the light industrial areas, water treatment occurs in islands and perimeters at surface parking.

The proposed community is organized around an extensive open space system, and stormwater management is integrated into this green infrastructure. There are four landscape types for Prairie Trail: stream and wetlands, neighborhood, commercial, and civic. (See Figure 4.111.)

Client: DRA Properties, LLC

Landscape Architect: Wenk Associates

James Clarkson Environmental Discovery Center

White Lake Township, Michigan

The James Clarkson Environmental Discovery Center is part of a 90-acre site located within Huron-Clinton Metropolitan Authority's 2,215-acre Indian Springs Metropark in Southeast Michigan. The Huron-Clinton Metropark oversees 13 metroparks across a five-county region, including the Indian Springs Metropark. (See Figure 4.112.)

The Discovery Center focuses on the exploration and celebration of the natural environment. The Metropark is situated at the headwaters of the Huron River, and interpreting the area's hydrology is an important part of the planning approach. (See Figures 4.113 and 4.114.)

Initial discussions about developing an environmental education center began in the mid-1970s but the official planning process did not start until 2000. The original goal was to create a facility that would incorporate sustainable building design, maintain the unique ecosystems within the park, and provide educational opportunities. A multidisciplinary team of landscape architects, designers, scientists, engineers, educators, and architects combined forces to develop the center.

The Center

Site construction began in December 2001, and the center opened in 2004. The 20,000-square-foot building was designed using LEED Silver benchmarks, and it includes classrooms, a biology lab, and event and exhibit rooms. A geothermal system is used to heat and cool the building, and a well on-site is used to provide the water needed for the system. Water is pumped from an underground

Figure 4.112 *The James Clarkson Environmental Discovery Center opened in 2004. Photos or Images courtesy: MSI, Ellen Puckett Photography, Justin Maconochie Photography.*

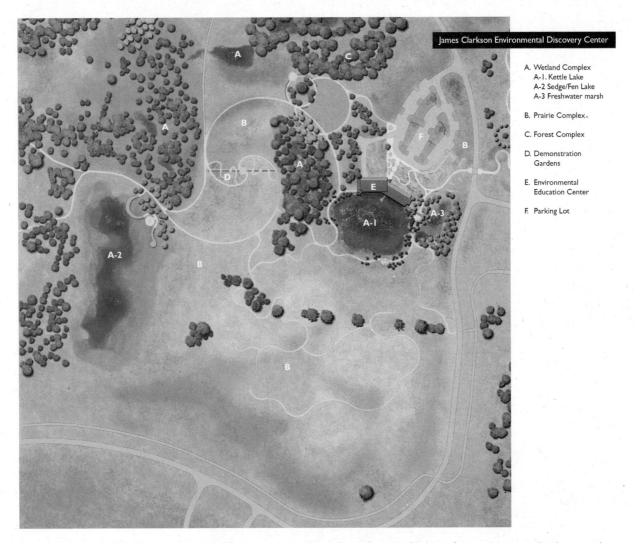

Figure 4.113 *The site is broken down into 14 different ecosystems, including a diversity of habitats from prairies to wetlands to woods. Photos or Images courtesy: MSI, Ellen Puckett Photography, Justin Maconochie Photography.*

James Clarkson Environmental Discovery Center

A. Wetland Complex
A-1. Kettle Lake
A-2 Sedge/Fen Lake
A-3 Freshwater marsh

B. Prairie Complex

C. Forest Complex

D. Demonstration Gardens

E. Environmental Education Center

F. Parking Lot

aquifer and used for temperature control. Once the water is pumped through the building, it returns to the surrounding site, supplying the nearby wetlands and ponds. During summer months the water is piped to an adjacent "spray zone," where it is collected and used for irrigation at an adjacent golf course.

One of the keys to the success of the project is how the building and the site are integrated. A glass facade provides views across to the kettle lake and to the restored prairies and meadows behind, and this helps emphasize the connectivity between interior and exterior spaces. Visitors enter the building at one level, then proceed down a level to the first floor at water level. The journey is completed by going down another level to a point below water level.

The building includes an underwater viewing room where children can be submerged in the middle of a kettle pond via a large acrylic dome that provides a 360-degree window into a natural 1.7-acre pond. The underwater pond was the

Sustainable Practices for Site Planning, Design, and Implementation

Figure 4.114 *Water is an integral part of the site. Located at the headwaters of the Huron River, water usage is demonstrated through the rehabilitation and creation of wetlands, prairies, and forest ecosystems. Photos or Images courtesy: MSI, Ellen Puckett Photography, Justin Maconochie Photography.*

first of its type to be designed and installed for use in wetlands. Tree stumps and boulders salvaged from other parks were used to create the habitats around the underwater classroom. An innovative mechanical system was created to provide the continuous water flow needed by the kettle pond and the children's water sprayground, and all water from these two areas is captured, cleaned, and recycled on-site for other uses.

Site Design

The ecosystems reestablished on the site are reminiscent of Midwestern landscapes. There is more than a 40-foot change in elevation from one side of the site to the other, and the result is a number of different microclimatic conditions that offer an opportunity for different planting design. More than 170 different plant species have been reestablished on the site.

A sedge fen lake was created on the site to provide additional educational opportunities that focus on open water ecosystems. The parking areas on the site utilize bioswales in order to filter stormwater runoff before it enters the surrounding wetlands. Boardwalks through a freshwater marsh (lovingly referred to as the "Muck Pond") allow students to collect samples and study the microorganisms found in the wetlands.

Additional features of the site design include the Council Rings, which are a series of precast stone rings based upon the Jens Jenson model and repeated throughout the Environmental Discovery Center. Each of the 14 restored ecosystems has a Council Ring, which can be used by educators as an outdoor classroom.

A Demonstration Garden provides an opportunity for visitors to learn about the many different native plant species found throughout the park. The different ecosystems include more than 30,000 plants and 40 different varieties of wetland species. Almost 60 acres are seeded with native prairie seeds.

Education Opportunities

One of the goals of the project was to use the site to teach about the wetland, prairie, and forest ecosystems that combine to make this area unique. An educational committee, research scientists, and the Huron-Clinton Metropolitan Authority were all involved in establishing the educational objectives for the Center. The diversity of ecosystems provides a variety of environmental education opportunities.

The Discovery Center received the American Society of Landscape Architects' 2008 Honor Award for excellence in design.

Owner: Huron-Clinton Metropolitan Authority
Landscape Architect: MSI Design
Environmental Consultant: Environtech Consultants, Inc.
Architect: SmithGroup Inc.
Environmental Engineering: Eco-Design & Engineering
Civil Engineer: Johnson & Anderson, Inc.
Education Consultant: Dick Braun, Salley DeRoo and John Covert
Wildlife Habitat Consultant: Dr. Bruce Kingsbury
Geotechnical Engineer: CTI and Associates, Inc.
General Contractor Building: JM Olson Corporation
General Contractor Site: Warren Contractors

Georgia State Water Plan

In 2008, the Georgia legislature approved the new State Water Plan that was intended to help address the state's water crisis and provide a blueprint for future decisions. Critics have expressed great disappointment in the plan, saying it was basically "a plan to make a plan." Joe Cook, executive director and river keeper for the Coosa River Basin Initiative in Rome (GA), called it "a bucketful of promises and tax-dollar-wasting pipe dreams" (Cook, 2008). One problem is that the plan included a number of policy statements but had no teeth since it was not adopted as law.

One of the incentives for developing the State Water Plan was the drought of 2007. Most water experts criticized the Atlanta region for its "total failure of planning" that led to its dependence on Lake Lanier. Atlanta's commissioner of the Department of Watershed Management, Rob Hunter, told a congressional committee in March 2008 that the drought had been terrible, but "it is the management plan implemented by the Corps that has been the real disaster" (Shelton, 2008).

In 2006, the U.S. Army Corps of Engineers accidentally released more than 22 billion gallons of water from Lake Lanier because a gauge was calibrated incorrectly. According to the Georgia Environmental Protection Division, this loss equals the amount of water used by the Atlanta

metropolitan region for 118 days. The water was released over a 52-day period, dropping the lake more than 2 feet during that time. The Corps started investigating only after local residents complained that the lake level appeared to be too low. The incident raised serious questions about the Corps' ability to manage the lake. The situation was not helped when the Corps' response was that it did not notice the problem because its staff was not familiar with the lake (Redmon, 2008).

The Corps uses Lake Lanier in tandem with its other four federal reservoirs on the Chattahoochee River to ensure that enough water is sent downstream for endangered species in Florida and a nuclear power plant in south Alabama (Shelton, Pendered, and Donsky, 2008). Metro Atlanta's water plan is based on getting most of its water out of Lake Lanier, and the city doesn't have any other viable options if that does not happen.

Georgia needs a comprehensive long-range plan that will enable it to meet future water needs. The state has a number of options. It can:

• Continue litigation against Alabama and Florida, and perhaps instigate new lawsuits against Tennessee in an effort to siphon water from the Tennessee River

- Build new reservoirs

- Change existing land use planning approaches

- Develop new strategies for water conservation

- Use a combination of these options

New Reservoirs

The Water Plan calls on the state to conduct a statewide assessment of existing water supplies and to identify "feasible sites for water reservoirs." One problem, though, is that the feasibility study for the reservoirs was supposed to be done before the assessment was completed (Cook, 2008).

The Georgia General Assembly also promoted the concept of building more reservoirs. House Bill 1226 would create a state division for the sole purpose of building new ones and expanding old ones, while Senate Bill 342 would create a funding mechanism for the state to pay up to 40% of the costs, with water consumers paying the rest.

There was also agreement that a comprehensive water assessment be conducted on the Apalachicola-Chattahoochee-Flint River Basin. Some experts estimate that a comprehensive, unbiased study of the basin's water system and how it is used would take two and a half years to complete at a cost of about $1 million.

Farrington, Brendan. "Ga. Official: 3 States Should Do Water Study," Associated Press, July 25, 2008, www.ajc.com/eveningedge/content/news/stories/2008/07/25/river.html?cxntlid=inform_artr.

5.0 CONCLUSION

5.1 AVOIDING PREDICTIONS

One common mistake authors often make when writing the summary of a book is trying to predict the future. I can certainly see that happening, because after spending more than a year researching water resources, I have to admit there are moments when I feel like I know enough about water to make such predictions.

But to be honest, it does not take a Nostradamus to see *the* future issues associated with water resources. Most books about water resources focus on problems such as droughts, water quality issues, conflicts among different users, environmental impacts, climate change, and water wars. We may debate on the details, but the basic issues have been there for years.

In the very first chapter of this book, I wrote that water is the major environmental issue of the 21st century and that all other concerns pale in comparison. Without water, life as we know it would not be possible. That is a given. Water quality is an issue of concern for people in both developing and developed countries worldwide. Water plays a vital role in the proper functioning of Earth's ecosystems. The pollution of water also has a serious impact on all living creatures and can negatively affect the use of water for drinking, household needs, recreation, fishing, transportation, and commerce.

Are we going to run out of water anytime soon? Probably not because typically we have more water available on a given day then we actually use. In the United States, for example, there are 1,400 billion gallons of usable water available every day, and Americans use only 380 billion gallons. The problem, of course, is that we do not always have water where we need it. In reference to the water wars of the Old West, Mark Twain was quoted as saying "Whiskey is for drinking. Water is for fighting." Fortunately, today's water wars in the West typically are settled with lawsuits, not firearms, and lawyers are staying busy. One concern that has been expressed by the U.S. Central Intelligence Agency, Britain's Ministry of Defense, and others is that we may be on the verge of future water wars in many parts of the world. Fortunately, cooperation over water is far more widespread than conflict, at least for now.

5.2 A FOCUS ON SUSTAINABILITY

When researching this book, I was surprised at how much "gloom and doom" was written about water resources. Perhaps it is true that horror stories sell, because so many books paint a drab picture of the future. Perhaps their editors forgot to tell them to not make predictions?

For this book, I wanted to focus on solutions, not problems. Although the issues facing us are massive, I am optimistic that we are moving in the right direction. We seem finally to understand that the goal is to find the right balance between society's needs for economic growth, protection from floods, and affordable power, with environmental concerns such as water quality, the preservation of wetlands, and the protection of threatened or endangered species. We have discovered over the years that groundwater and surface water are fundamentally interconnected and they have to be thought of as one cohesive system.

We seem to have a better understanding of our options. We can continue to pull water from rivers or underground aquifers and build reservoirs, or we can utilize alternative approaches, such as rainfall harvesting, desalination, or other approaches. Water recycling projects are gaining in popularity, and they have helped reduce the demand for freshwater in many parts of the world. Regardless of what happens, water recycling and conservation will be a major part of the long-term water resource management, although water gurus everywhere say that water conservation is not enough.

We are learning that there are better ways to address stormwater runoff than the traditional approaches that collected water and tried to get rid of it as quickly as possible. Cities finally have learned that the answer to stormwater management is not to construct bigger and more expensive concrete channels and piping systems.

As a landscape architect and environmental planner, I like the challenges of complex environmental issues and appreciate the eloquent solutions that many are coming up with to protect and enhance water resources. Why aren't more cities following the lead of Portland's Green Streets program or implementing rain gardens like Maplewood, MN. I love the Oregon Gardens, which takes a "negative" use, such as wastewater treatment, and turns it into an asset. Cutting-edge water management practices can be implemented anywhere. The contrast between the use of natural and constructed wetlands at Richland Creek Wildlife Management Area (TX) and the massive concrete infrastructure of Singapore's Deep Tunnel Sewage System is striking, yet both offer creative ways to improve water quality.

5.3 REVISITING ATLANTA

Since I lived in Atlanta when I wrote this book, it probably makes sense to use the city as an example of the kinds of water resource issues we have to address. Atlanta is between a rock and a hard place when it comes to available water. The city is not located on a major body of water, is at the headwaters of local rivers and streams, and has the smallest watershed of any major city in the United States, so surface water is limited. Because Atlanta sits on bedrock, there is no groundwater available. State law also prohibits

Atlanta from piping in water from outside the 16-county water planning district in which the city is located. In an ideal world, Atlanta would be a small town on the edge of the Chattahoochee River because as far as water availability is concerned, the area cannot accommodate a major city.

Most of Atlanta's water comes from surface water sources, with the Chattahoochee River and Lake Lanier being the biggest supplier. In 2007, when much of the Southeast was in the midst of the most severe drought in more than 100 years, the water level in Lake Lanier dropped significantly and Atlanta was within days of running out of water.

Georgia Governor Sonny Perdue asked President George W. Bush to ease regulations that required the state to send water downstream to Alabama and Florida. When that did not work, hundreds of Georgians gathered with Perdue at the state capital to pray for rain. Amazingly, it actually rained. Well, maybe not so amazingly, since rumor has it that the governor waited to hold his prayer vigil on a day that had a 60% chance of rain.

Atlanta Mayor Shirley Franklin proposed building a desalination plant along the Atlantic coast and pumping the water across the state to Atlanta. Georgia legislators suggested changing the state's northern border so that the Tennessee River would become part of Georgia. On August 14, 2008, Lake Lanier dropped to a level nine feet lower than its level during the droughts of 2007.

5.4 LEGAL BATTLES

A fundamental question has been whether metropolitan Atlanta is entitled to use water from Lake Lanier as its primary source of drinking water. According to Alabama and Florida, the primary purpose of the lake was to provide flood control, hydropower, and navigation. Georgia has argued that it was always the intention that much of the water would be used for metro Atlanta.

On July 17, 2009, U.S. District Judge Paul Magnuson issued a decision saying that metro Atlanta was not authorized to withdraw water from Lake Lanier. The judge gave Georgia, Alabama, and Florida three years to negotiate or water will start being released from Buford Dam, which created Lake Lanier, at 1970s levels. The court ruling was a wake-up call for Atlanta, but other municipalities around the country should also take note. Judge Magnuson stated, "The problems faced in the ACF [Apalachicola-Chattahoochee-Flint] basin will continue to be repeated throughout this country, as the population grows and more undeveloped land is developed" (Gleick, 2009). Many water experts believe that this ruling will be the first of many that shake up how water is managed across the United States.

5.5 ADDRESSING THE PROBLEM

Georgia's current approach to water management has evolved in a piecemeal fashion over several decades. During the 2007 drought, Atlanta started to get serious about its water problems. Irrigation was prohibited, public facilities were asked to lower water use by 20%, restaurants gave customers water only if they asked, hotels put fewer pitchers of water in meeting rooms, and some local hotels began outsourcing their laundry to businesses outside the metropolitan area. Georgia lawmakers strongly supported plans to build a series of new reservoirs around the state, but most of those plans were dropped due to budget constraints and legal issues.

Judge Magnuson's ruling about Lake Lanier requires Atlanta to be more aggressive at addressing its water problems. The city will have to spend millions of dollars on infrastructure and pursue other water-smart options, such as:

- Installing low-flow fixtures
- Developing new treatment facilities
- Changing land use policies
- Institutionalizing rainwater harvesting, gray water recycling, and efficient landscape irrigation

On January 8, 2008, the state approved the Georgia Comprehensive State-wide Water Management Planning Act, which is definitely a step in the right direction. There has been discussion of a moratorium on future growth to allow Atlanta to improve its water infrastructure, but this is unlikely to happen anytime soon because growth increases tax revenue. The city allocated $4.1 billion to overhaul its stormwater system. The result, though, is that Atlanta's water/sewer bills, which are already the highest in the country, will more than triple in the next few years. Unfortunately, the upgrade will not help address the lack of water.

Water reuse in metro Atlanta may be one of the city's best options for a consistently available water supply. Only non-potable reuse and indirect potable reuse are currently being used, but there have been discussions about implementing direct potable reuse and gray water treatment in the near future.

One approach is to return reclaimed water to Lake Lanier and Allatoona Lake for future reuse. Gwinnett and Hall counties have the infrastructure in place to return highly treated wastewater to Lake Lanier, and other facilities are in the works. Indirect potable reuse facilities are being developed in Gwinnett, Cobb, and Clayton counties. Clayton County, located just south of Atlanta, uses a water recycling system that filters treated wastewater through a series of constructed wetlands. The reclaimed water supplies potable water for a local reservoir; leftover solids are used as fertilizer. The state has a number of permit requests from water providers to provide indirect potable reuse.

5.6 THE FUTURE

What does the future hold for Atlanta? By the spring of 2009, water levels in Lake Lanier were much closer to normal, and many of Georgia's other lakes were at or near full capacity. For many, the droughts of 2007 and 2008 have been long forgotten, and Atlanta residents were more concerned about the devastating floods that hit the city in September 2009.

As I write this, it is now 2010. Atlanta has not come up with a quick fix for its water problems, and the clock is ticking on the U.S. District Court's mandate of having an agreement in place in three years. Unfortunately, it seems that if Atlanta is not able to pull water from Lake Lanier, the state's contingency plan, says Governor Perdue, is merely to "conserve and use our water wisely." I knew I should have sent Gov. Perdue a copy of my book. Perhaps he would have come up with a more innovative and sustainable solution for addressing Georgia's water problems. Governor Perdue did form the Georgia Water Contingency Task Force, and on December 11, 2009, the task force submitted their final recommendations that called for "the 3Cs": Conserve, Capture and Control. The task force also outlined options that could be implemented by 2015 and 2020. Until then, it looks like Georgians will have to depend upon the Governor praying for rain again.

Further Reading

Best Management Practice Manuals: available online from various states/localities http://yosemite.epa.gov/R10/WATER.NSF/0/17090627a929f2a488256bdc007d8dee?OpenDocument.

Alabama

Environmental Protection Agency. Water Quality Criteria (2007). http://epa.gov/waterscience/standards/wqslibrary/al/al_4_wqs.pdf.
Environmental Protection Agency. Water Use Classifications for Interstate and Intrastate Waters (2006). www.epa.gov/waterscience/standards/wqslibrary/al/al_4_11wqs.pdf.

Alaska

Environmental Protection Agency. *Alaska Water Quality Criteria Manual for Toxic and Other Deleterious Organic and Inorganic Substances*. May 15, 2003. http://epa.gov/waterscience/standards/wqslibrary/ak/ak_10_toxics_manual.pdf.
Environmental Protection Agency. Criteria Withdrawal. October 29, 2004. www.epa.gov/fedrgstr/EPA-WATER/2004/October/Day-29/w24242.htm.
Environmental Protection Agency. Federal Regulations, 40 CFR 131.36. December 22, 1992. http://epa.gov/ost/standards/rules/ntr.html.
Environmental Protection Agency. Federal Regulations, 40 CFR 131.41. November 16, 2004. www.epa.gov/fedrgstr/EPA-WATER/2004/November/Day-16/w25303.htm.
Environmental Protection Agency. Water Quality Criteria and Standards Plan. June 1998. www.epa.gov/waterscience/criteria.
Environmental Protection Agency. Water Quality Standards. June 26, 2003. http://epa.gov/waterscience/standards/wqslibrary/ak/ak_10_wqs.pdf.

Alabama

Alabama Department of Forestry, *Best Management Practices*. www.forestry.alabama.gov/Publications/BMPs/Foreword.pdf.

Alaska

Alaska Department of Environmental Conservation, *Alaska Storm Water Guide*. www.dec.alaska.gov/water/wnpspc/stormwater/AKSWGuide_Chapter1.pdf.

California

BMP Handbook for San Diego County
California Storm Water Quality Association. *Storm Water BMP Handbooks*. March 2003. www.dot.ca.gov/hq/construc/storm water/manuals.htm.
California Department of Transportation. *California Storm Water BMP Construction Handbook*. March 2003. www.dot.ca.gov/hq/construc/stormwater/CSBMPM_303_Final.pdf.
City of Los Angeles, California. Los Angeles Storm Water Program. www.lastormwater.org.

Connecticut

Connecticut Department of Environmental Protection. 2002 Guidelines for Soil Erosion and Sediment Control 2002. www.ct.gov/dep/lib/dep/water_inland/sesc/sesc_intro_toc.pdf.

Delaware

Delaware Division of Soil and Water Conservation. Delaware Conservation Design for Storm Water Management Guidance Manual: 2000. www.dnrec.state.de.us/dnrec2000/Divisions/Soil/Stormwater/Apps/DesignManualRequest.htm.

Florida

Florida Development Manual: A Guide to Sound Land and Water Management: June 1988. www.dep.state.fl.us/water/nonpoint/docs/nonpoint/erosed_bmp.pdf.
Florida Department of Environmental Protection. Non-Point Source Management Best Management Practices, Public Information, and Environmental Education Resources. October 2009. www.dep.state.fl.us/water/nonpoint/pubs.htm#Best%20Management%20Practices.

Georgia

Atlanta Regional Commission. Georgia Storm Water Management Manual. December 10, 2008 www.atlantaregional.com/html/257.aspx.

Idaho

Idaho Department of Environmental Quality. Catalog of Storm Water BMPs for Idaho Cities and Counties: 2009. www.deq.state.id.us.

Louisiana

Louisiana Nonpoint Source Pollution Unit. State of Louisiana Nonpoint Source Pollution Management Program—Construction: 2009. http://nonpoint.deq.state.la.us/wqa/construction.htm.

Maine

Maine Department of Environmental Protection. Maine Stormwater Best Management Practices Manual: January, 2006. www.maine.gov/dep/blwq/docstand/stormwater/stormwaterbmps/index.htm.

Maryland

Maryland Department of Environment Stormwater Design Manual. 2000. www.mde.state.md.us/Programs/WaterPrograms/SedimentandStormwater/home/index.asp.

Massachusetts

Massachusetts Department of Environmental Protection. Stormwater Handbooks: www.mass.gov/dep/water/laws/policies.htm#storm.

Michigan

Michigan Department of Environmental Quality. Stormwater Best Management Practices. January 2006. www.michigan.gov/documents/MDOT_MS4_Chap_91740_7._09_Drainage_Manual.pdf.

Minnesota

Minnesota Pollution Control Agency. Protecting Water Quality in Urban Areas: A Manual: October 24, 2006. www.pca.state.mn.us/water/pubs/sw-bmpmanual.html.

Minnesota Pollution Control Agency. Stormwater Manual: November 2005. www.pca.state.mn.us/water/stormwater/stormwater-manual.html.

Metropolitan Council. Urban Small Sites Best Management Practice Manual: July 2001. www.metrocouncil.org/environment/watershed/bmp/manual.htm.

Missouri

Missouri Department of Natural Resources. Protecting Water Quality: A Construction Site Water Quality Field Guide: November 1999. www.dnr.mo.gov/env/wpp/wpcp-guide.htm.

Montana

Montana Department of Water Quality—Storm Water Program—BMPs and Erosion Control Plans. www.deq.state.mt.us/wqinfo/index.asp.

New Hampshire

New Hampshire Department of Environmental Services. Storm Water Management and Erosion and Sediment Control for Urban and Developing Areas in New Hampshire. December 2008. http://des.nh.gov/organization/divisions/water/stormwater/manual.htm.

New Jersey

New Jersey Department of Environmental Protection Stormwater BMP Manual: www.state.nj.us/dep/watershedmgt/bmpmanual.htm.

New Jersey Department of Environmental Protection. Revised Manual for New Jersey: BMPs for Control of Nonpoint Source Pollution from Storm Water: www.njstormwater.org/tier_A/bmp_manual.htm.

New York

New York State Department of Environmental Conservation. New York State Stormwater Management Design Manual. April 2008. www.dec.ny.gov/chemical/29072.html.

North Carolina

North Carolina Department of Environment & Natural Resources. BMP & Site Planning Manuals: Stormwater Manuals, Stormwater Factsheets, NPDES Phase II Stormwater Factsheets, and Reports. http://h2o.enr.state.nc.us/su/Manuals_Factsheets.htm.

North Dakota

North Dakota Department of Health. A Guide to Temporary Erosion-Control Measures for Contractors, Designers and Inspectors: www.ndhealth.gov/wq/wastwater/pubs/bmpmanual.pdf.

Ohio

Ohio Environmental Protection Agency. Storm Water Program—. Lists: http://epa.ohio.gov/dsw/storm/index.aspx.

Oregon

Oregon Department of Environmental Quality. Protecting and Improving the Quality of Oregon's Waters. www.oregon.gov/DEQ/WQ/index.shtml.

Pennsylvania

Pennsylvania Department of Environmental Protection—Stormwater Management Program, Best Management Practices (BMP) www.depweb.state.pa.us/watershedmgmt/cwp/view.asp?a=1437&q=529063&watershedmgmtNav=.

South Carolina

South Carolina Department of Health and Environmental Control. NPDES Permit for Discharge to Surface Waters. January, 2009. www.scdhec.gov/environment/water/publicnote/pubs/SCS79PNE.pdf.

South Carolina Department of Health and Environmental Control. NPDES Storm Water Program—Construction Program: 2008. www.scdhec.gov/environment/water/swerfmain.htm.

South Carolina Department of Health and Environmental Control. Water Home Page: www.scdhec.gov/environment/water/.

Tennessee

City of Knoxville Engineering Department, Stormwater Engineering Division. Knoxville BMP Manual: October, 2009. www.ci.knoxville.tn.us/engineering/bmp_manual/.

Tennessee Department of Environment & Conservation. Tennessee Division of Water Pollution Control. www.ci.knoxville.tn.us/engineering/bmp_manual.

Texas

North Central Texas Council of Governments. Regional Storm Water Management Program. www.nctcog.org/envir/SEEclean/stormwater/index.asp.

Texas Water Development Board. Texas Nonpoint Sourcebook— Interactive BMP Selector: www.txnpsbook.org.

Utah

Utah Department of Environmental Quality, Division of Water Quality. UPDES Storm Water Home Page: www.waterquality.utah.gov/UPDES/stormwater.htm.

Virginia

Northern Virginia Planning District Commission & Engineers and Surveyors Institute. Northern Virginia BMP Handbook: A Guide to Planning and Designing BMPs in Northern Virginia: November, 1992. www.novaregion.org/DocumentView .aspx?DID=1679.

Virginia Department of Conservation & Recreation: Virginia Erosion and Sediment Control Handbook. 1992. www.dcr.state.va.us/sw/ e&s-ftp.htm.

Washington

Washington Department of Ecology. Storm Water Management Manual for Western Washington. 2005. www.ecy.wa.gov/ programs/wq/stormwater/manual.html#copies.

King County. Storm Water Design Manual. 2009. www.kingcounty. gov/environment/waterandland/stormwater/documents/ surface-water-design-manual.aspx.

Washington Department of Ecology. Storm Water Management Manual for Eastern Washington. September 2004.

Washington State Department of Transportation, *Engineering Publications Manuals Index*. www.wsdot.wa.gov/publications/ manuals/index.htm.

Wisconsin

Wisconsin Department of Natural Resources. Runoff Management: http://dnr.wi.gov/runof.

Wyoming

Wyoming Department of Environmental Quality. Urban Best Management Practices for Nonpoint Source Pollution. September 1999. http://deq.state.wy.us/wqd/watershed/Downloads/ NPS%20Program/92171.pdf.

EPA Resources

Annotated Bibliography of Source Water Protection Materials (June 2003): www.epa.gov/safewater/sourcewater/pubs/qrg _swpbib_2003.pdf.

Arsenic Treatment Technology Evaluation Handbook for Small Systems (July 2003): www.epa.gov/safewater/arsenic/pdfs/ handbook_arsenic_treatment-tech.pdf.

"Asset Management: A Handbook for Small Water Systems" (September 2003): www.epa.gov/ogwdw/smallsystems/pdfs/ guide_smallsystems_asset_mgmnt.pdf.

"Cases in Water Conservation: How Efficiency Programs Help Water Utilities Save Water and Avoid Costs" (July 2002): www.epa.gov/ watersense/docs/utilityconservation_508.pdf.

"Case Studies of Sustainable Water and Wastewater Pricing" (December 2005): www.epa.gov/safewater/smallsystems/pdfs/ guide_smallsystems_fullcost_pricing_case_studies.pdf.

"Complying with the Revised Drinking Water Standard for Arsenic: Small Entity Compliance Guide" (December 2002): www.epa.gov/ ogwdw000/arsenic/pdfs/ars_final_app_!toc.pdf.

Consolidated Water Rates: Issues and Practices in Single-Tariff Pricing (1999): www.epa.gov/safewater/utilities/stptitle.pdf.

"Emerging Technologies for Conveyance Systems: New Installations and Rehabilitation Methods" (July 2006): www.epa.gov/owm/ mtb/epa-conveyance-report.pdf.

"EPA Water Quality Trading Policy" (January 2003): *Growing Trend Toward More Efficient Water Use: Linking Development, Infrastructure, and Drinking Water Policies* (January 2006): www .epa.gov/waterinfrastructure/toolkit.html.

Guidelines for Water Reuse (September 2004): www.epa.gov/nrmrl/ pubs/625r04108/625r04108.pdf.

"Handbook for Managing Onsite and Clustered (Decentralized) Wastewater Treatment Systems" (December 2005): www.epa. gov/owm/septic/pubs/onsite_handbook_fs.pdf.

"Interactive Sampling CD for Small Systems" (April 2006): www.epa .gov/safewater/smallsystems/samplingcd.html.

"Managing for Excellence: Profiles of Water and Wastewater Utility Management Systems" (August 2005): www.epa.gov/water/ infrastructure/pdf/Utilityprofilesfinal0508.pdf.

"Point-of-Use or Point-of-Entry Treatment Options for Small Drinking Water Systems" (April 2006): www.epa.gov/safewater/ smallsystems/pdfs/guide_smallsystems_pou-poe_june6-2006.pdf.

Principles of Water Rates, Fees, and Charges (2000): www.epa.gov/ waterinfrastructure/pricing/Guides.htm.

Protecting Water Resources with Higher-Density Development (January 2006): www.epa.gov/smartgrowth/water_density.htm.

"Setting Small Drinking Water System Rates for a Sustainable Future" (December 2005): www.epa.gov/water/infrastructure/pdf/ final_ratesetting_guide.pdf.

"A Small System Guide to the Total Coliform Rule: Monitoring Drinking Water Systems to Protect Public Health" (June 2001): www.epa.gov/ogwdw/disinfection/tcr/pdfs/small-tcr.pdf.

"Sources of Financial and Technical Assistance for Small Systems" (July 2002): www.epa.gov/OGWDW/arsenic/pdfs/funding/tfa_ sdws.pdf.

"Small System Partnership Solutions" (September 2002): www.epa. gov/ogwdw000/smallsystems/pdfs/publichealthstudyv1.pdf.

"State and Federal Source Water Assessment and Protection Program Measures—Final Reporting Guidance" (March 2005): www.epa .gov/safewater/sourcewater/pubs/guide_stfedswpguidance final_2005.pdf.

"Strategic Planning: A Handbook for Small Water Systems" (September 2003): www.epa.gov/safewater/smallsystems/pdfs/ guide_smallsystems_stratplan.pdf.

"Taking Stock of Your Water System: A Simple Asset Inventory Guide for Very Small Drinking Water Systems" (October 2004): www .epa.gov/OGWDW/smallsystems/pdfs/final_asset_inventory_for _small_systems.pdf.

"Total Coliform Rule STEP Guide for Non-Community Water Systems" (July 2006): www.epa.gov/safewater/disinfection/tcr/ pdfs/stepguide_tcr_smallsys-3300.pdf.

Using Smart Growth Techniques as Stormwater Best Management Practices (December 2005): www.epa.gov/smartgrowth/pdf/sg_stormwater_BMP.pdf.

Water Conservation Plan Guidelines (August 1998): www.epa.gov/watersense/tips/summ.htm.

Water Quality Trading Assessment Handbook (November 2004): www.epa.gov/owow/watershed/trading/handbook/docs/ch1-national-wqt-handbook-2004.pdf.

"Watershed-based NPDES Permitting Implementation and Technical Guidance" (December 2003): www.epa.gov/water/tribaltraining/resources/npdes.html.

EPA—Policy and Guidance

Draft Implementation Guidance for Ambient Water Quality Criteria for Bacteria (June 11, 2002): www.epa.gov/waterscience/criteria/humanhealth/microbial/.

Designating Attainable Uses for the Nation's Waters, National Symposium 2002: Proceedings and abstracts available for download: www.epa.gov/waterscience/standards/uses/symposium/.

Interim Economic Guidance (April 27, 1995): www.epa.gov/waterscience/standards/policy.htm.

Memorandum of Agreement between EPA, Fish and Wildlife Service, and National Marine Fisheries Service Regarding Enhanced Coordination under the Clean Water Act and Endangered Species Act (February 2001): www.epa.gov/fedrgstr/EPA-SPECIES/1999/January/Day-15/e1029.htm.

National Guidance for Wetlands (July 1990): www.epa.gov/owow/wetlands/regs/quality.html.

Response to Sierra Club Petition (June 25, 2004): www.epa.gov/waterscience/standards/SierraClub.html.

State and Tribal Water Quality Standards—Notice of EPA Approvals (October 7, 1998): www.epa.gov/waterscience/standards/stwqapprv.html.

Strategy for Water Quality Standards & Criteria (August 2003): www.epa.gov/waterscience/standards/strategy/.

Technical Guidance for Developing Total Maximum Daily Loads (1997): www.epa.gov/waterscience/standards/tmdl/.

Water Quality Standards Handbook: Second Edition (August 1994): www.epa.gov/waterscience/standards/handbook.

EPA—Clean Air Act Sections

Clean Water Act, sections related to water quality standards: www.epa.gov/lawsregs/laws/cwa.html.

Section 101(a) Declaration of Goals and Policy: www.epa.gov/lawsregs/laws/cwa.html. http://www.epa.gov/waterscience/standards/rules/101a.htm.

Section 303 Water Quality Standards and Implementation Plans: www.epa.gov/waterscience/standards/rules/303.htm.

Section 401 Permits and Licenses—Certification: www.epa.gov/waterscience/standards/rules/cwa_sec401.pdf.

Section 510 (State Authority): www.epa.gov/waterscience/standards/rules/cwa_sec510.pdf.

References

"5 Water Bills to Watch in 2008." Watercrunch, January 9, 2008.

2007 Iowa State Water Plan Proposal. www.iaenvironment.org/documents/11-27-07FinalStateWaterPlan.pdf.

2007 Tennessee Valley Authority Strategic Plan: www.tva.gov/stratplan.

2007 Texas State Water Plan: www.twdb.state.tx.us/wrpi/swp/swp.htm.

305(b) Reports: www.epa.gov/OWOW/305b.

Alabama Rivers Alliance, "Alabama Water Agenda." January 2007. www.alabamarivers.org.

American Forests: www.americanforests.org.

American Forests. Environmental News Network, 2001. www.americanforest.org/downloads/forestbytes/ForestBytes_Vol_I_Issue_4.txt.

American Rainwater Catchment Systems Association (ARCSA) Web site. www.arcsa.org.

American Rivers: www.americanrivers.org.

American Rivers. "Exploring Dam Removal," www.americanrivers.org/site/DocServer/Exploring_Dam_Removal-A_Decision-Making_Guide.pdf?docID=3641.

American Rivers, "Obtaining Permits to Remove a Dam: Tips for a Successful Permitting Process," February 2002. www.americanrivers.org/site/DocServer/DR_-_Resource_-_Obtaining_Permits_to_Remove_a_Dam.pdf?docID=1602.

American Rivers. "Paying for Dam Removal: A Guide to Selected Funding Sources," www.americanrivers.org/site/DocServer/pdr-color.pdf?docID=727.

Andry, Allain C. IV. "Water Law in North Carolina," April 16, 1996, www.bae.ncsu.edu/programs/extension/publicat/arep/waterlaw.html.

Angelo, Mary Jane, Richard C. Hamann, and Christine A. Klein. "Where Did Our Water Go? Give the Law a Chance." Orlando Sentinel, September 23, 2008, www.orlandosentinel.com/services/newspaper/printedition/tuesday/opinion/orl-angelo2308sep23,0,11538.story.

Army Corps GIS: http://gis.sam.usace.army.mil.

Association of Fish and Wildlife Agencies. "State Wildlife Action Plans, 2007," www.wildlifeactionplans.org.

Associated Press. "Atlanta Asks, 'Will We Run Out of Water?'" Associated Press, October 19, 2007, www.msnbc.msn.com/id/21382688/.

Atlanta Regional Commission: www.atlantaregional.com/.

Battiata, Joseph G. "Choosing the Right BMP—Capital Investment or Long-term Operation and Maintenance Costs—Who Decides?" Roads & Bridges. 5, no. 1 (February 2008). www.roadsbridges.com/Choosing-the-Right-BMP-article8970.

Bay Area Stormwater Management Agencies Association (BASMAA). "Start at the Source," 1999. www.flowstobay.org/documents/business/construction/Start_At_The_Source_Full.pdf.

Beck, Robert E., ed. Water and Water Rights. Charlottesville, VA: The Michie Company, 1991.

Bell, Steve. New Lake Development, Cherokee Shores, Is Environmentally Pleasing." April 24, 2005. www.lakemurraywatch.com/in%20the%20news.html.

Best Management Practices for Coastal Georgia Development (poster): www.georgiaplanning.com/coastal/BMP/default.htm.

Bluestein, Greg. "3 Southern Reservoirs Predicted to Fall," Associated Press, June 20, 2008, http://staugustine.com/stories/062008/state_062008_063.shtml.

Bluestein, Greg. "South Scrambles to Cope with Drought - Water Supply in Atlanta Less than 90 days." Associated Press, October 20, 2007. www.boston.com/news/nation/articles/2007/10/20/south_scrambles_to_cope_with_drought/.

Bonneville Power Administration, HydroAMP Database: https://secure.bpa.gov/hydroAMP/.

Bookman, Jay. "Don't Leave Tri-State Water Woes to a Court Decision," Cox News Service, August 14, 2008.

"Brackish Groundwater Manual for Texas Regional Water Planning Groups" (February 2003), www.twdb.state.tx.us/RWPG/rpgm_rpts/2001483395.pdf.

Brahic, Catherine. "Atlas of Hidden Water May Avert Future Conflict." NewScientist (October 2008), www.newscientist.com/article/dn15030.

Bryan, Hobson. "Interstate Water Disputes." Encyclopedia of Alabama, September 22, 2008, www.encyclopediaofalabama.org/face/Article.jsp?id=h-1498.

California Stormwater Quality Task Force, California Stormwater Best Management Practice Handbook. www.dot.ca.gov/hq/construc/stormwater/stormwater1.htm.

California Stormwater Best Management Practice Handbooks: www.cabmphandbooks.com.

California Watershed Assessment Manual: http://cwam.ucdavis.edu.

Cappiella, Karen, and Lisa Fraley-McNeal. "The Importance of Protecting Vulnerable Streams and Wetlands at the Local Level." Wetlands & Watersheds 6. Office of Wetlands, Oceans and Watersheds, U.S. Environmental Protection Agency, Washington, DC (August 2007).

Cappiella, Karen, Anne Kitchell, and Tom Schueler. "Using Local Watershed Plans to Protect Wetlands." Wetlands & Watersheds 2. Office of Wetlands, Oceans and Watersheds, U.S. Environmental Protection Agency, Washington, DC (June 2006).

Cappiella, Karen, Tom Schueler, and Tiffany Wright. *Urban Watershed Forestry Manual. Part 1: Methods for Increasing Forest Cover in a Watershed.* U.S. Department of Agriculture Forest Service Northeastern Area State and Private Forestry, NA-TP-04-05 (July 2005).

Cappiella, Karen, Tom Schueler, and Tiffany Wright. *Urban Watershed Forestry Manual Part 2: Conserving and Planting Trees at Development Sites.* U.S. Department of Agriculture Forest Service Northeastern Area State and Private Forestry, NA-TP-01-06 (May 2006).

Castle, Anne J. "Water Rights Law—Prior Appropriation" (1999), http://library.findlaw.com/1999/Jan/1/241492.html.

Center for Watershed Protection: www.cwp.org.

Center for Watershed Protection. "Adapting Watershed Tools to Protect Wetlands: Wetlands & Watersheds," Article 3, www.kaws.org/files/kaws/u2/WetlandsArticle3.pdf.

Centers for Disease Control and Prevention. Global Water, Sanitation, & Hygiene. November 23, 2009. www.cdc.gov/healthywater/global/.

Century Commission for a Sustainable Florida. "Second Annual Report to the Governor and the Legislature," January 16, 2008, www.communicationsmgr.com/projects/1349/docs/CCRptJan08.pdf.

Chesapeake Bay Program: www.chesapeakebay.net/overview.htm

Chicago Metropolitan Agency for Planning (CMAP) , www.camp.illinois.gov.

Christie, Jean and Jon Kusler. ASWM model statute to improve protection for isolated wetlands. Association of State Wetland Managers, Inc. 2006. http://www.aswm.org/swp/modelleg.pdf.

City of Olympia, WA. Clearing and Grading Ordinance: www.stormwatercenter.net/Model%20Ordinances/esc_clearing_ordinance.htm.

Clean Water Network. "How Much of Your State's Waters May Not Be Protected by the Clean Water Act," www.cleanwaternetwork.org//issues/scope/factsheets/.

Columbia River Initiative: www.ecy.wa.gov/programs/wr/cwp/crwmp.html

Comer, P., D., Faber-Langendoen, R. Evans, S. Gawler, C. Josse, G. Kittel, S. Menard, M. Pyne, M. Reid, K. Schulz, K. Snow, and J. Teague. 2003. *Ecological Systems of the United States: A Working Classification of U.S. Terrestrial Systems.* NatureServe, Arlington, VA.

Conserve Water Georgia: www.conservewatergeorgia.net/documents/about.html

Cook, Joe. "Ga. Officials Take Wrong Tack on Water." *Atlanta Journal-Constitution*, April 22, 2008.

Copeland, Larry. "Drought Eases, Water Wars Persist." *USA Today*, March 18, 2008, www.usatoday.com/news/nation/environment/2008-03-17-water-wars_N.htm.

Copeland, Larry. "Drought spreading in Southeast." USA Today, updated 2/12/2008. www.usatoday.com/weather/drought/2008-02-11-drought_N.htm.

Dahl, T.E. 2000. "Status and trends of wetlands in conterminous United States 1986 to 1997." U.S. Department of the Interior, Fish and Wildlife Service, Washington, DC, 82 p.

Damron, David. "Orange Leaders End Water War Over Tapping Lakes," *Orlando Sentinel*, August 26, 2008. http://blogs.orlandosentinel.com/news_politics/2008/08/orange-leader-2.html.

Davenport, Bill. "Positives Pervade Through." *Storm Water Solutions* 4, no. 1 (February 2007). www.roadsbridges.com/Positives-Pervade-Through-article7654.

Davis, Vincent W. "Debits & Credits Make Dollars & Sense." *Storm Water Solutions* 5, no. 2 (April 2008).

Day, Mollie. "The Forgotten Forests." Bestofneworleans.com, December 25, 2007, http://bestofneworleans.com/gyrobase/Content?oid=oid%3A39234.

Deen, Thalif. "Climate Change Deepening World Water Crisis." Inter Press Service, March 19, 2008, www.globalpolicy.org/socecon/envronmt/climate/2008/0319deepwater.htm.

Dickey, G. Edward and Leonard Shabman. Making Tough Choices: Hurricane Protection Planning after Katrina and Rita. 2005. www.rff.org/RFF/Documents/RFF-Resources-160-Katrina.pdf

"Drought in America's South-East." *Economist*, October 25, 2007, www.economist.com/world/unitedstates/displaystory.cfm?story_id=10024708.

Drought Monitor: www.drought.unl.edu/dm/monitor.html.

Duke Energy. Shoreline Stabilization Guide: Duke Energy Piedmont Reservoir Shoreline Stabilization and Wetland Horticulture Guide. 2009. www.duke-energy.com/lakes/shoreline-stabilization.asp.

Duffy, Kevin." Lake Lanier's Home Prices Fall with Water Level." *Atlanta Journal-Constitution*, October 8, 2008, www.ajc.com/eveningedge/content/printedition/2008/10/08/lanier.html?cxntlid=inform_sr.

Dunbar, John. "Louisiana Population Rallying after Katrina, Data Shows." *Evansville Courier Press,* December 27, 2007.

EDAW, Inc. "Water Quality Control Plan for the Sorrento Creek Channel Maintenance Project, San Diego, California" (March 2006).

EDAW. *Taking a Longer View: Mapping for Sustainable Resilience.* A Project of the National Consortium to Map Gulf Coast Ecological Constraints (April 2006).

Ellison, Brian A. "Water Projects Writ Large." *Southwest Hydrology*, 7, no. 5 (September/October 2008), www.swhydro.arizona.edu/archive/V7_N5/.

Environmental News Service. Louisiana to Invest $1 Billion in Coastal Protection, Restoration. NEW ORLEANS, Louisiana, August 13, 2008.

Environmental Protection Division. Georgia Department of Natural Resources: www.gaepd.org/.

EPA. Chapter 9 Dam Removal Info web. EPA 841-B-07-002 9-1 July 2007. www.scribd.com/doc/1757544/Environmental-Protection-Agency-Chapter-9-Dam-Removal-Info-web.

EPA. "Compendium of Tools for Watershed Assessment and TMDL Development." EPA Number: 841B97006: May, 1997. www.epa.gov/OWOW/tmdl/comptool.html.

EPA. "Developing a Water Management Plan." www.epa.gov/greeningepa/water/plans.htm.

EPA. "Guidance Specifying Management Measure for Sources of Nonpoint Source Pollution in Coastal Water," 1993. http://www.epa.gov/owow/nps/MMGI/Chapter2/.

EPA. "Handbook for Developing Watershed Plans to Restore and Protect Our Waters," 2008. EPA 841-B-08-002, March 2008. www.epa.gov/nps/watershed_handbook/.

EPA. "Lakes, Reservoirs, and Ponds," Chapter 3 of 2000 National Water Quality Inventory, 2000. www.epa.gov/305b/2000report/chp3.pdf.

EPA. "Municipal Wastewater Management Fact Sheets: Storm Water Best Management Practices," 1996. http://www.epa.gov/owmitnet/sectstm.htm.

EPA. "National Management Measures to Control Nonpoint Source Pollution from Urban Areas," 2005. www.epa.gov/nps/urbanmm.

EPA. National Menu of Stormwater Best Management Practices. http://cfpub.epa.gov/npdes/stormwater/menuofbmps/index.

EPA. "National Water Quality Inventory Report to Congress 305(b)," 2002. www.epa.gov/owow/305b.

EPA. Preliminary Data Summary of Urban Storm Water Best Management Practices, EPA-821-R-99-012, August 1999.

EPA. "Urban Runoff Pollution Prevention and Control Planning," 1993. http://www.epa.gov/nrmrl/pubs/625r93004/625r93004.htm.

EPA. "Using Smart Growth Techniques as Stormwater Best Management Practices." EPA 231-B-05-00. Online at: www.epa.gov/smartgrowth/stormwater.htm. Washington, DC: U.S. Environmental Protection Agency, 2005.

Farm Security and Rural Investment Act of 2002: www.nrcs.usda.gov/programs/farmbill/2002.

Farrington, Brendan. "Ga. official: 3 States Should Do Water Study," Associated Press, July 25, 2008. www.ajc.com/eveningedge/content/news/stories/2008/07/25/river.html?cxntlid=inform_artr.

FEMA. "2003 Federal Disaster Declarations," 2003. www.fema.gov/news/disasters.fema?year=2003.

Filippone, Colleen, and Stanley A. Leake. "Time Scales in the Sustainable Management of Water Resources. Sustainability in an Era of Limits." Southwest Hydrology 4, no. 1 (January/February 2005).

Fischer, R.A., and Fischenich, J.C. 2000. Design Recommendation for Riparian Corridors and Vegetated Buffer Strips, EMRRP Technical Notes Collection, U.S. Army Engineer Research and Development Center, Vicksburg, MS.

Fish Passage Decision Support System: https://ecos.fws.gov/fpdss/index.do 7.

Florida Department of Agriculture and Consumer Services. "Governor Bush Unveils Comprehensive Plan to Restore Lake Okeechobee and Coastal Estuaries," Press Release, October 10, 2005. www.doacs.state.fl.us/press/2005/10102005.html.

Florida Lake Management Society: http://flms.net/index.html.

Freshwater Development Company. Freshwater Florida, www.flemingventures.com/freshwater/semphasis.php.

Friedman, Steve. "Balance on Lake Murray—Storks and Stakeholders." SCANA Insights (Fall 2005). www.sceg.com/NR/rdonlyres/265E1CD2-A6C4-4651-BBF3-103EF5ACBDA5/0/SCANAInsightsFall2005.pdf.

GAO. "Flood Map Modernization: Program Strategy Shows Promise." GAO-04-417. 2001. www.gao.gov/cgi-bin/getrpt?GAO-04-417.

Georgia Comprehensive State-wide Water Management Plan. 2008. www.georgiawatercouncil.org/Files_PDF/water_plan_20080109.pdf.

Georgia Department of Natural Resources. "Water Use in North Georgia Plummets as Citizens Step Up to Conserve," August 11, 2008.

Georgia Department of Natural Resources. Press Release. "Four Major Georgia Lakes Proposed to Be Added to State's Water Quality List," March 29, 2006.

Georgia Lakes Society: http://science.kennesaw.edu/~jdirnber/lake.html.

Georgia Power. Shoreline Management Guidelines, revised 2008, www.georgiapower.com/lakes/pdf/shoreline_management.pdf.

"Georgia's Governor Declares Drought Emergency," www.msnbc.msn.com/id/21393296/.

Georgia Soil and Water Conservation Commission, Manual for Erosion and Sediment Control in Georgia, 5th ed. 2000. Athens, GA. Georgia Soil & Water Conservation Commission. www.georgiaplanning.com/watertoolkit/Documents/WaterProtectionIssues/Chapter6Sec1.pdf.

Georgia Water Coalition. "A Report of the Georgia Water Coalition 2006," www.garivers.org/gawater/pdf%20files/waterreportfinalversion.pdf.

Gilley, Glenn Harlan. "Effective Lake Design for Residential Communities," 2006. www.Dudek.com.

Gilley, John E. "Protecting the Harvest—Bet the Farm on the Right Runoff Control Measures." Storm Water Solutions 4, no. 5 (October 2007).

Glennon, Robert Jerome. Water Follies: Groundwater Pumping and the Fate of America's Fresh Waters. Washington, DC: Island Press, 2002.

Gleick, Peter. "An Eastern Judge Points the Way to Solving Western Water Problems." July 17, 2009. www.circleofblue.org/waternews/2009/world/peter-gleick-an-eastern-judge-points-the-way-to-solving-western-water-problems/.

Go To 2040, www.goto2040.org.

GroundWater Protection Council. Recommended actions to USGS and State Geological Surveys from "Ground Water Report to the Nation," 2007. www.gwpc.org/about_us/grants/epa/2006-2007/attachment%20jm2.pdf.

A Guide to Water Quality at Vacation Beaches. 2009. www.nrdc.org/water/oceans/ttw/titinx.asp.

Gutierrez, David. "U.S. Southwest to Go Dry as Climate Change Spurs Drought," August 26, 2008. www.naturalnews.com/023988.html.

Habitat Conservation Plan: http://endangered.fws.gov/hcp.

Heath, Brad, Paul Overberg, and Haya El Nasser. "Census Shows Katrina's Effects on Populations," USA Today, March 22, 2007. www.usatoday.com/news/nation/census/2007-03-22-new-orleans-census_N.htm.

Henry, Blair. "The Potential Impacts of Global Warming on the Nation's Water Resources," 2000. www.climatehotmap.org/impacts/water.html.

Hesperides Group, LLC. The Water Resources Management for 2050 Plan. Century Commission for a Sustainable Florida. 2007. www.communicationsmgr.com/projects/1349/docs/MeekerPlan.pdf.

Hickory Log Creek Dam: www.hickorylogcreek.com.

Hollis, Paul L. "Southeast Looking at Water Policies." *Farm Press,* September 18, 2002.

Hull, Jonathan Watts. "The War over Water." In *Regional Resource,* published by Atlanta: Council of State Governments, October 2000. www.encyclopediaofalabama.org/face/Article.jsp?id=h-1498.

Natural Resources Defense Council. "In Hot Water: Water Management Strategies to Weather the Effects of Global Warming," 2007. www.nrdc.org/globalWarming/hotwater/contents.asp.

Institute for Wetland Science and Public Policy of the Association of State Wetland Managers. "A Guide for Local Governments: Wetlands and Watershed Management," October 1, 2003. www.aswm.org/propub/pubs/aswm/wetlandswatershed.pdf.

International Political Economy Zone. "Water Wars in the US of A," November 3, 2007. http://ipezone.blogspot.com/2007/11/water-wars-in-us-of.html.

International Stormwater Best Management Practices Database (1999–2008), June 2008, www.bmpdatabase.org.

Interstate Commission on the Potomac River Basin: www.potomacriver.org/cms/.

Iowa State Water Plan: www.iaenvironment.org/documents/11-27-07FinalStateWaterPlan.pdf.

Jacobs, Katharine, Barbara Morehouse. "Why S*&t@!n@bility Is Not a Four-Letter Word." *Southwest Hydrology* 4, no. 1 (January/February 2005).

Jarvie, Jenny. "Gov. to God: Send Rain!" *Los Angeles Times,* November 14, 2007.

Jehl, Douglas. "A New Frontier in Water Wars Emerges in East," *New York Times,* March 3, 2003, http://query.nytimes.com/gst/fullpage.html?res=9900E1D91F3CF930A35750C0A9659C8B63.

Jeremy, Hsu. "Water Woes in the Western US." *Journal of Young Investigators* 12, no. 6, June 2005. www.jyi.org/features/ft.php?id=284.

Johnson, Jeff. "Water Authority Looks Beneath for Drought Protection." *Southwest Hydrology,* 7, no. 5, September/October 2008.

Jones, Jeanine. "History of Large-Scale Western Water Projects." *Southwest Hydrology* 7, no. 5, September/October 2008.

Jordan, Jeffrey L., and Aaron T. Wolf, eds. *Interstate Water Allocation in Alabama, Florida, and Georgia: New Issues, New Methods, New Models.* Gainesville: University Press of Florida, 2006.

Kansas State Water Plan: www.kwo.org/Kansas%20Water%20Plan/Kansas%20Water%20Plan.htm.

Kitchell, Anne, and Tom Schueler, *Unified Stream Assessment: A User's Manual* Center for Watershed Protection, February 2005. www.cwp.org/Store/usrm.htm.

Kneiser, M. J. "Hartwell Lake Hits Official Drought Level 3." Special to the *Independent-Mail,* August 20, 2008, www.independentmail.com/news/2008/aug/20/hartwell-lake-hits-official-drought-level-3/.

Konrad CP, Booth DB, Burges SJ, Montgomery DR. "Partial entrainment of gravel bars during floods." *Water Resources Research* 2002;38(7):9.1-9.16.

Kretsinger, Vicki, and T. N. Narasimhan. "Sustaining Groundwater Resources: California's Shift toward More Effective Groundwater Management." *Southwest Hydrology* 4, no. 1, January/February 2005.

Kundell, James E. "The Southeastern Water World: Where Are We, How Did We Get Here & Where Are We Going?" Progress Energy Water Resources Seminar, Water Allocation Law in Southeastern States, NC State University, April 1, 2008.

Kusler, J.A., 2003. Wetland Assessment for Regulatory Purposes, ASWM, Berne, NY.

LA Department of Wildlife & Fisheries. Integrated Ecosystem Restoration and Hurricane Protection: Louisiana's Comprehensive Master Plan for a Sustainable Coast, 2005. www2.nos.noaa.gov/gomex/coastal_resil/batonr_mar08/03_deshotels.pdf.

Lettenmaier, Dennis P., Andrew W. Wood, Richard N. Palmer, Eric F. Wood, and Eugene Z. Stakhiv. *Water Resources: Implications of Global Warming: A U.S. Regional Perspective.* Amsterdam: Kluwer Academic Publishers, 1999.

Lightsey Ed. "Second Homes," *GeorgiaTrend,* December 2006, www.georgiatrend.com/features-business-industry/200612-second-home.shtml.

Long Island Sound Habitat Restoration Initiative, "Technical Support for Coastal Habitat Restoration," 2003. www.longislandsoundstudy.net/habitat/LIS.Manual.pdf.

Louisiana Department of Natural Resources, Coastal Management Division. "Urban Runoff," http://dnr.louisiana.gov/crm/coastmgt/interagencyaff/nonpoint/urban_bro.asp.

Louisiana State University Ag Center, "Protecting Louisiana's Waters Using Best Management Practices," www.lsuagcenter.com/en/environment/conservation/bmps/Protecting+Louisianas+Waters+Using+Best+Management+Practices.htm.

Lovett, Richard A. "Western U.S. Faces Drought Crisis, Warming Study Says." National Geographic News, January 31, 2008, http://news.nationalgeographic.com/news/2008/01/080131-west-droughts.html.

"Making Smart Growth Happen": www.epa.gov/piedpage/sg_implementation.htm.

Maryland Department of Environment: www.mde.state.md.us/aboutmde/reports/index.asp.

Maryland Department of the Environment. *Accomplishments Report, 2002–2006,* www.mde.state.md.us/assets/document/MDE_Accomplishments_Report02_06.pdf.

Matthews, Olen Paul. "Law, Water," www.waterencyclopedia.com/La-Mi/Law-Water.html. Water Encyclopedia Science and Issues, 2009.

Matthews, Olen Paul. *Water Resources, Geography and Law.* Washington, DC: Association of American Geographers, 1984.

Melcher, Nick. "Introduction to Arizona Water Management and Legal Issues," (2009). www.iwlearn.net/blog/groundwater-learning/archive/2007/04/25/introduction-to-arizona-water-management-and-legal-issues-nick-melcher.

Metropolitan North Georgia Water Planning District: www
.northgeorgiawater.com/html/aboutus.htm.

Metropolitan North Georgia Water District. District-Wide Watershed
Management Plan. 2003. www.northgeorgiawater.com.

Milgrom, Paul, and John Roberts, *Economics, Organization and Management*. Upper Saddle River, NJ: Prentice Hall, 1992, pp. 298–299.

Miller, K., and D. Yates, 2006. Climate Change and Water Resources:
A Primer for Municipal Water Providers. AWWA Research
Foundation and University Corporation for Atmospheric Research.
83p. http://www.awwarf.org/research/topicsandprojects/
execSum/2973.aspx], accessed October 2007.

Mississippi River/Gulf of Mexico Watershed Nutrient Task Force.
Action Plan 2008.

Mississippi River/Gulf of Mexico Watershed Nutrient Task Force. A
Science Strategy to Support Management Decisions Related to
Hypoxia in the Northern Gulf of Mexico and Excess Nutrients in
the Mississippi River Basin, 2004.

Moore, Linda. "From Superfund Site to World-Class Park."
Southwest Hydrology 7, no. 5, September/October 2008.

Moran, Terry, and Katie Hinman. "Water Wars: Quenching Las
Vegas' Thirst." ABC News, April 5, 2007, http://abcnews.go.com/
Nightline/story?id=3012250.

Nasser, Haya El, "How Will the USA cope with Unprecedented
Growth?" *USA Today*, October 27, 2006.

National Drought Policy Commission. *Preparing for Drought in the 21st
Century, Executive Summary,* http://drought.unl.edu/pubs/pfd21/
PreparingforDroughtinthe21stCenturyExecutiveSummary-NDPCpdf.pdf.

National Estuary Program: www.epa.gov/owow/estuaries/nep.html.

National Hydrography Dataset: http://nhd.usgs.gov.

National Research Council. "Heat Advisory - How Global Warming
Causes More Bad Air Days." www.nrdc.org/globalwarming/
heatadvisory/contents.asp.

National Resources Defense Council. "Testing the Waters," 2009.

National Water Program: www.usawaterquality.org/themes/
watershed/default.html.

National Water Quality Inventory: www.epa.gov/owow/305b.

Native Plant Conservation Campaign. Letter to EPA, April 11, 2003.
http://www.plantsocieties.org/PDFs/Iso%20wetlands%20NPCC%
20ltthd%204.03.pdf.

Natural Resources Conservation Service. *National Handbook of
Conservation Practices*: www.nrcs.usda.gov/technical/standards/
nhcp.html.

Natural Resources Conservation Service. 1997 Five-Year National
Resources Inventory. www.nrcs.usda.gov/technical/NRI/1997.

Natural Resources Defense Council. "Bringing Safe Water to the World,"
March 7, 2008. http://ww.nrdc.org/international/safewater.asp.

Natural Resources Defense Council. "In Hot Water: Water
Management Strategies to Weather the Effects of Global
Warming," www.nrdc.org/globalWarming/hotwater/contents.
asp.

Natural Resources Defense Council. "Site Selection for the Survey of
the Nation's Lakes: Technical Fact Sheet," 2007. www.epa.gov/
owow/lakes/lakessurvey/site_selection_factsheet.pdf.

Natural Resources Defense Council. "Watershed Protection and Flood
Prevention," March 26, 2009. www.nrcs.usda.gov/programs/
watershed.

Nature Conservancy: www.nature.org.

Nehrling, Rick. "The Economics of Tourism Should Keep the Lake
Burton Hatchery Open," October 1, 2008. Dawson Times. www
.hometowntimes.com/dawsontimes/news50000/opinion/
the-economics-of-tourism-should-keep-the-lake-burt.shtml.

Nelson, Barry, et al. *In Hot Water:* Nelson, Robin. "Perilously
Low Water Levels in Lake Lanier Reservoir North of Atlanta Is
Threatening the Metro Area's Water Supply," Associated Press,
October 20, 2007.

Nevue Ngan Associates: www.nevuengan.com.

New Georgia Encyclopedia. "Man-Made Lakes," May 14, 2004,
www.georgiaencyclopedia.org/nge/Article.jsp?id=h-1180.

New Georgia Encyclopedia. "Water Cycle in Georgia," www
.georgiaencyclopedia.org/nge/Article.jsp?path=/ScienceMedicine/
EarthSciences/WaterResources&id=h-947.

New Mexico Office of the State Engineer: www.seo.state.nm.us/.

"A New Reservoir for a Growing City in GA—Hickory Log Dam."
Watercrunch, January 8, 2007, http://watercrunch.blogspot
.com/2007/01/new-reservoir-for-growing-city-in-ga.html.

NOAA Fisheries Service. "NOAA Open Rivers Initiative," www.nmfs
.noaa.gov/habitat/restoration/ORI.

Noble, Craig. "Water Officials Warned: Get Used to Drought, Says
New Climate Report." Natural Resource Defense Council, July 10,
2007. www.nrdc.org/media/2007/070710.asp.

North Carolina Lake Management Society: www.nclakemanagement
.org/.

North Georgia Water District. "District-Wide Watershed Management
Plan—Executive Summary," September 2003. www
.northgeorgiawater.com/files/WMP_ExecSum.pdf.

Northeastern Illinois Water Supply/Demand Plan, www.cmap.illinois
.gov/waterplan.

Noss, R. F., E. T. LaRoe III, and J. M. Scott. "Endangered Ecosystems
of the United States: A Preliminary Assessment of Loss and
Degradation," 1995. http://biology.usgs.gov/pubs/ecosys.htm.

Novotney, Michael, and Rebecca Winer. "Municipal Pollution
Prevention/Good Housekeeping Practices," Version 1.0,
September 2008. www.cwp.org/Resource_Library/Center_Docs/
municipal/USRM9.pdf.

O'Driscoll, Patrick. "A Drought for the Ages," *USA Today*, June 8, 2007.

Office of Energy Projects, Federal Energy Regulatory Commission.
"Guidance for Shoreline Management Planning at Hydropower
Projects," April 2001. www.ferc.gov/industries/hydropower/gen-
info/guidelines/smpbook.pdf.

Ohio River Valley Water Sanitation Commission: www.orsanco.org/.

Ortega, Joshua. "Water Wars: Bottling Up the World's Supply
of H2O." Special to the *Seattle Times*, March 21, 2005.
http://seattletimes.nwsource.com/html/opinion/2002213327_
sundaywater20.html.

Otto, Douglas C. Jr. Reservoir Management amidst Epic Droughts
in the Southeast: Balancing Competing Needs and Limited

Resources. Hydrology and Hydraulics Branch, Mobile District, U.S. Army Corps of Engineers.

Panel Discussion. Divvying Up the Apalachicola, Universities Council on Water Resources Annual Conference. (Portland, Ore., July 2004).

"The Parched Country." Economist, October 25, 2007.

Park, Anthony W. Lake Lanier Overview Paper. July 15, 2007. http://anthonywpark.blogspot.com/2007/07/lake-lanier-overview-paper.html.

Parry, Martin L., et al. (eds.), Climate Change 2007: Impacts, Adaptation, and Vulnerability. Contribution of Working Group II to the Third Assessment Report of the Intergovernmental Panel on Climate Change. Cambridge: Cambridge University Press, 2007.

Perlman, David. "Water Managers Told: Plan Now for Crisis," Chronicle Science Editor. February 1, 2008. www.sfgate.com/cgi-bin/article.cgi?f=/c/a/2008/02/01/MNC9UOA3M.dtl.

Perry, Valentine M. "Lake Lanier Water Quality." Proceedings of the 2005 Georgia Water Resources Conference, April 25–27, 2005, University of Georgia, Athens, Georgia.

Pitzer, Gary. "Water Projects Writ Large." Southwest Hydrology 7, no. 5, September/October 2008.

Pitzer, Gary. "Finding a Vision for the Delta." Western Water (March/April 2008). www.watereducation.org/doc.asp?id=1071

Poindexter, Jim. "Lake Murray Engineering Feat Complete 2." SCANA Insights 18, no. 1, Summer 2005.

Portland Bureau of Environmental Services. "A Sustainable Approach to Stormwater Management," 2009. www.portlandonline.com/BES/index.cfm?c=34598.

Powers, Kyna. Aging Infrastructure: Dam Safety. CRS Report for Congress, September 29, 2005. www.policyarchive.org/bitstream/handle/10207/2586/RL33108_20050929.pdf?sequence=1.

"Psst. South Carolina Has a Secret." Watercrunch, February 5, 2007. http://watercrunch.blogspot.com/2008/02/psst-south-carolina-has-secret.html.

Propeck Totty, Teresa A. "Everglades National Park South Florida's great swamp is one of earth's widest rivers," The Cultured Traveler, 2003. http://www.theculturedtraveler.com/Parks/Archives/Everglades.htm.

Puget Sound Action Team. "Low Impact Development: Protecting Our Waters as We Grow," www.psparchives.com/publications/our_work/stormwater/lid/lid_brochure/lid_brochure06_11x17.pdf; EPA Reach File References, 1994. www.epa.gov/waters/doc/refs.html.

Redmon, Jeremy. "$138 Mistake Was Low Blow to Lanier." Atlanta Journal-Constitution, April 20, 2008. www.ajc.com/eveningedge/content/metro/stories/2008/04/20/pulley0420.html?cxntlid=inform_artr.

Reed, Larry, and Loomis, John. "Topping Off Golden Gate Park." Storm Water Solutions. October 2008 Volume: 5 Number. www.estormwater.com/Topping-Off-Golden-Gate-Park-article9699.

Reeves, D. W., et al. "Conservation Tillage in Georgia: Economics and Water Resources." Proceedings 2005 Georgia Water Resources Conference, April 25–27, 2005, University of Georgia, Athens.

Reid, Andy. "Water Managers Look to Keep Some Water Off Limits." South Florida Sun-Sentinel, June 15, 2008. www.orlandosentinel.com/topic/sfl-flpwater0615pnjun15,0,301234.story.

Reimer, Chris. "Here Today, Gone Tomorrow? NGWA Initiatives on Groundwater Sustainability." Southwest Hydrology 4, no. 1, January/February 2005.

Reppen, Deena. "Governor Bush Unveils Comprehensive Plan to Restore Lake Okeechobee and Coastal Estuaries." Florida Department of Environmental Protection, October 10, 2005. http://www.dep.state.fl.us/secretary/news/2005/10/1010_01.htm.

Reyes, David. "O.C.'s Great Park Gets Big Markup." Los Angeles Times, March 5, 2007, http://articles.latimes.com/2007/mar/05/local/me-greatpark5.

Ricks, Markeshia. "Shelby's Amendment Might Tap Tri-state Water Data." Montgomery Advertiser. July10, 2009. http://shelby.senate.gov/public/index.cfm?fuseaction=pressroom.articles&contentrecord_ID=64CF8F6C-802A-23AD-45F5-8101D2310B36&REGION_ID=&ISSUE_ID=&COUNTY_ID=.

Ricks, Markeshia. "Water Wars Could Be Near an End," Montgomery Advertiser, August 20, 2008. www.montgomeryadvertiser.com/apps/pbcs.dll/article?AID=/20080820/NEWS02/808200372/1009.

NatureServe. "Rivers of Life. Critical Watersheds for Protecting Freshwater Biodiversity," 2009. www.natureserve.org/publications/riversOflife.jsp.

Rosgen Stream Classification System: www.epa.gov/watertrain/stream_class/index.htm.

Rowe, Pam, and Tom Schueler. The Smart Watershed Benchmarking Tool. Office of Wetlands, Oceans and Watersheds, EPA, Washington, DC, January 2006.

Ruhl, J. B. "Water Wars, Eastern Style: Divvying Up the Apalachicola-Chattahoochee-Flint River Basin." Journal of Contemporary Water Research & Education, no. 131, June 2005: 47–54. www.ucowr.siu.edu/updates/131/10_ruhl.pdf.

Safe Drinking Water Act and Source Water Protection Programs: www.epa.gov/safewater/protect.html.

Schueler, Tom, and Ken Brown. Urban Subwatershed Restoration Manual. No. 4. Urban Stream Repair Practices Version 1.0, November 2004.

Schueler, Tom, Chris Swann, Tiffany Wright, and Stephanie Sprinkle. Urban Subwatershed Restoration Manual No. 8. Pollution Source Control Practices Version 2.0. Center for Watershed Protection, 2005. www.cwp.org/store/usrm.htm.

Schueler, Tom, David Hirschman, Michael Novotney, and Jennifer Zielinski. Urban Stormwater Retrofit Practices, Version 1.0, Office of Wastewater Management, U.S. Environmental Protection Agency, Washington, DC, July 2007.

Schueler, Tom, Urban Subwatershed Restoration Manual Series. An Integrated Framework to Restore Small Urban Watersheds. Prepared for: Office of Water Management, U.S. Environmental Protection Agency, February 2005, Manual 1, Version 2.0.

Schultz, Jason. "Miccosukees Sue to Restart Construction of Reservoir," Palm Beach Post, July 11, 2008, www.palmbeachpost

.com/localnews/content/west/epaper/2008/07/11/s1b_
everglades lawsuit_0712.html.

Seder, Ron. "Why Must Lake Lanier Suffer So Much?" April 22,
2008, www.cumminghome.com/news30041/opinion1/why-must-
lake-lanier-suffer-so-much.shtml.

Sipes, James L., and Mark Lindhult. *Digital Land*. John Wiley & Sons,
2007.

Southern Environmental Law Center (SELC). "Before the Storm:
Reducing the Damage from Polluted Stormwater Runoff
Recommendations for Albemarle County," 2008. www
.southernenvironment.org/uploads/publications/albemarle_runoff-
july08.pdf.

Southern Environmental Law Center (SELC). "Reducing Runoff
from New Development—Recommendations for the City of
Charlottesville." 2008. www. southernenvironment.org/uploads/
publications/Reducing_Runoff_Print_020508.pdf.

Shapiro, Gideon Fink. "Heifer International Headquarters."
ARCHITECT Magazine, June 1, 2007. www.tampabaywater.org/
watersupply/tbdesalfunfacts.aspx.

Shapiro, N. Site The Stranger Among Us: Urban Runoff, the
Forgotten Local Water Resource. In Proceedings, National
Confernece on Urban Stormwater: Enhancing Programs at the
Local Level. February 17–20, 2003, Chicago, IL. 2003.

Shelton, Stacy, David Pendered, and Paul Donsky. "Ahead of
the Curve: Water Debate Refuses to Dry," *Atlanta Journal-
Constitution*, August 3, 2008. www.ajc.com/eveningedge/
content/business/stories/2008/08/03/curve.html?cxntlid
=inform_artr.

Shelton, Stacy. "Building Walls for Water—Reservoirs Debated
as Response to Drought." *Atlanta Journal-Constitution*,
March 11, 2008. www.ajc.com/eveningedge/content/metro/
stories/2008/03/11/reservoirs0311.html?cxntlid=inform_artr.

Shelton, Stacy. "Can Reservoirs Ease Georgia's Drought?"
Atlanta Journal-Constitution, March 10, 2008. www.ajc.com/
eveningedge/content/metro/stories/2008/03/10/reservoirs_0311.
html?cxntlid=inform_artr.

Shelton, Stacy. "Court Rulings Could Settle Water War." *Atlanta
Journal-Constitution*, August 17, 2008. www.ajc.com/
eveningedge/content/metro/stories/2008/08/17/water_georgia
.html.

Shelton, Stacy. "Funds Dry Up for State Reservoirs," *Atlanta Journal-
Constitution*, August 21, 2008. www.ajc.com/metro/content/
metro/stories/2008/08/21/reservoir_funding_cuts.html.

Shelton, Stacy. "Georgia's Water Crisis: Florida to fight drought
strategy." *Atlanta Journal-Constitution,* July 1, 2008. www.ajc
.com/eveningedge/content/news/stories/2008/05/01/drought
.html?cxntlid=inform_artr.

Shelton, Stacy. "Group: Stop Water Leaks instead of Adding
Reservoirs." *Atlanta Journal-Constitution,* October 22, 2008.
www.wateresources.org/2008/10/23/group-stop-water-leaks-
instead-of-adding-reservoirs.

Shelton, Stacy. "Thirsty Atlanta to Battle Southeast States over
Lake Lanier Water Supply," August 18, 2008. *Atlanta Journal-*

Constitution. www.ajc.com/eveningedge/content/metro/
stories/2008/08/17/water_georgia.ht/.

Shelton, Stacy. "Too Much Lanier Water Was Released, Corps Says."
Atlanta Journal-Constitution, April 16, 2008. www.floridasprings.
info/2008/04/too-much-lanier-water-was-released.html.

Shelton, Stacy. "Water War: Court Rulings Crucial to State."
Atlanta Journal-Constitution, August 17, 2008. www.ajc.com/
eveningedge/content/metro/stories/2008/08/17/water_georgia
.html.

Shelton, Stacy, "Why Lake Allatoona Is Full, Lanier Isn't," *Atlanta
Journal-Constitution,* August 18, 2008. www.ajc.com/
eveningedge/content/metro/stories/2008/08/18/lakes_allatoona_
lanier.html?cxntlid=inform_artr.

Simon, Stephanie. "Out West, Catching Raindrops Can Make You an
Outlaw." *Wall Street Journal,* March 25, 2009. http://online.wsj
.com/article/SB123794222413232887.html.

Singelis, Nikos, Lisa Nisenson, and Martina Frey. "Lots and Lots of
Parking Lots—Tackling Related Planning and Site Design Issues."
Storm Water Solutions 5, no. 2, April 2008.

Sipaila, Jonas, and William McCully. "Ready for a Paradigm Shift? True
Storm Water Management Involves a Change in Design Philosophy
and Methods." *Storm Water Solutions* 4, no. 2, April 2007.

Snitow, Alan, and Deborah Kaufman. "Drinking at the Public
Fountain: The New Corporate Threat to Our Water Supplies."
September 29, 2008. www.globalpolicy.org/socecon/gpg/2008/
0929privatizationwater.htm.

Source Water Protection Programs: www.epa.gov/safewater/protect.
html.

The South Florida Water Management District. "Frequently Asked
Questions about Water Restrictions in South Florida." *South
Florida Sun-Sentinel.* 2009. www.sun-sentinel.com/news/local/
southflorida/sfl-waterrestrictionsnew,0,2725631. .story?coll=sfla-
home-headlines.

"Southeast Drought Update," *Environmental Economics,* February 6,
2008, www.env-econ.net/2008/02/southeast-droug.html.

"Southeast Is Warned of More Water Wars Ahead—South Carolina
Attorney General Worries about Neighboring States." Associated
Press, October 15, 2008, www.msnbc.msn.com/id/27197772/.

Southeast Michigan Council of Governments. *Opportunities for Water
Resource Protection in Local Plans, Ordinances and Programs: A
Workbook for Local Governments,* www.semcog.org.

"Southern Drought Creeping Northward—Extreme Conditions
Spread into Kentucky, Virginias; Water Shortages Loom."
Associated Press, October 17, 2008, www.msnbc.msn.com/
id/27243600.

Southern Power: www.southerncompany.com.

Southern Regional Water Program. *Watershed Management,* http://
srwqis.tamu.edu/program-information/target-themes/watershed-
management.aspx.

Southern Regional Water Program: http://srwqis.tamu.edu/about
.aspx.

St. Johns River, FL: http://sjr.state.fl.us/waterprotectsustain/index
.html.

Starnes, Joe Samuel. "Not on Every Map, but a Desirable Location Anyway." *New York Times*, May 25, 2007. www.nytimes.com/2007/05/25/travel/escapes/25havens.html.

State of Minnesota Stormwater Design Manual. 2005. http://www.pca.state.mn.us/publications/wq-strm9-01.pdf.

Steiner, Frederick, Barbara Faga, James Sipes, and Robert Yaro. "Taking a Longer View: Mapping for Sustainable Resilience." In *Rebuilding Urban Places After Disaster: Lessons from Hurricane Katrina*, by Eugenie Ladner Birch and Susan M. Wachter. Philadelphia, Pennsylvania, University of Pennsylvania Press, 2006.

Steinman, Alan D., Mark Luttenton, and Karl E. Havens. "Sustainability of Surface and Subsurface Water Resources Case Studies from Florida and Michigan, U.S.A." *Water Resources Update*, no. 127, February 2004.

Stormwater Authority Buyer's Guide for Best Management Practices: http://stockpile.stormwaterauthority.org/.

Sustainable Lakes Planning Workbook: A Lake Management Model. Minnesota Lakes Association in cooperation with the University of Minnesota Center for Urban and Regional Affairs, May 2000. www.minnesotawaters.org/resources/Workbook.pdf.

Tavares, Stephanie. "Lawyers Eye Looming Water Wars," *Las Vegas Sun,* March 6, 2009, www.lasvegassun.com/news/2009/mar/06/lawyers-eye-looming-water-wars/.

Tennessee Department of Environment & Conservation—Division of Water Supply. "State Requirements for Building a New Dam in Tennessee," www.tennessee.gov/environment/dws/newdam.shtml.

Tennessee Valley Authority. The Tennessee Valley Clean Marina Guidebook, 2001. www.tva.gov/environment/pdf/cleanmarina.pdf.

Tennessee Valley Authority Environmental Plan: www.tva.com/environment/policy.htm.

Tennessee Valley Authority Land Management Policy: www.tva.gov/river/landandshore/land_policy.htm.

Tennessee Valley Authority Reservoir Operations Study: www.tva.gov/environment/reports/ros_eis/index.htm.

Tennessee Valley Authority Shoreline Management Policy: www.tva.gov/river/landandshore/landuse_shore.htm.

Tennessee Valley Authority. *2008 Environmental Policy,* www.tva.com/environment/pdf/environmental_policy.pdf.

Tennessee Valley Clean Marina Guidebook, www.tva.com/environment/pdf/cleanmarina.pdf.

Texas Tech University Studies. The 2001 Texas Parks and Wildlife for the 21st Century report. 2001. www.tpwd.state.tx.us/publications/nonpwdpubs/media/tpwd_21st_century.pdf.

Texas Water Development Board. "Innovative Water Technologies," www.twdb.state.tx.us/iwt/iwt.html.

Texas Water Development Board. Report 362, *Water Conservation Best Management Practices Guide* (November 2004), www.twdb.state.tx.us/assistance/conservation/Municipal/Water_Audit/documents/WCITFBMPGuide.pdf.

Totty, Teresa A. Propeck. *Everglades National Park South Florida's great swamp is one of earth's widest rivers.* The Cultured Traveler. http://theculturedtraveler.com/Festivals/Archives/Everglades.htm.

"Truth or Fiction? 36 States Will Face Water Shortages." *Water Crunch*, October 30, 2007, http://watercrunch.blogspot.com/2007/10/truth-or-fiction-36-states-will-face.html.

U.S. Army Corps of Engineers. Lake Seminole (Florida) Shoreline Management Plan (November 1995). www.sam.usace.army.mil/op/rec/seminole/Seminole_SMP/seminole_smp.htm.

U.S. Army Corps of Engineers. Permit Application Materials, www.nws.usace.army.mil/PublicMenu/Menu.cfm?sitename=REG&pagename=mainpage_Permit_Applicant_Info.

U.S. Army Corps of Engineers. Systems—Lake Discovery, http://corpslakes.usace.army.mil/goodtime.html.

U.S. Army Corps of Engineers. Wildlife Resources Management Manual. TM 5-633, 1982.

U.S. Bureau of Reclamation: www.usbr.gov.

U.S. Department of Agriculture, Farm Service Agency: www.fsa.usda.gov/pas/default.asp.

U.S. Department of Agriculture, Natural Resources Conservation Service: www.nrcs.usda.gov/about/organization/regions.html#regions.

U.S. Department of Agriculture, Natural Resources Conservation Service. Wildlife Habitat Incentives Program (WHIP): www.nrcs.usda.gov/programs/whip.

U.S. Department of the Interior, Bureau of Reclamation Policy and Program Services. Water for America Initiative Proposed Implementation Plan. Denver, Colorado (July 2008), www.ntis.gov/search/product.aspx?ABBR=PB2008114704.

U.S. Department of Transportation. "Best Management Practices for Erosion and Sediment Control," 1995. http://isddc.dot.gov/.

U.S. Environmental Protection Agency, Office of Water and Office of Research and Development. *Survey of the Nation's Lakes Revision No. 1 Quality Assurance Project Plan.* Washington, DC: Author, August 2007.

U.S. Environmental Protection Agency Office of Water Office of Policy, Economics, and Innovation. "A Retrospective Assessment of the Costs of the Clean Water Act: 1972 to 1997," October 2000. www.epa.gov/waterscience/economics/costs.pdf.

U.S. Environmental Protection Agency. *Survey of the Nation's Lakes. Field Operations Manual.* EPA 841-B-07-004. Washington, DC: Author, 2007. http://science.kennesaw.edu/~jdirnber/lha/resources/draft_lakefield_op_manual.pdf.

U.S. Environmental Protection Agency. "Climate Change—Basic Information," www.epa.gov/climatechange/basicinfo.html.

U.S. Environmental Protection Agency. "Climate Change—Health and Environmental Effects—Water Quality," www.epa.gov/climatechange/effects/water/quality.html.

U.S. Environmental Protection Agency. "Local Drinking Water Information," www.epa.gov/safewater/dwinfo/index.html.

U.S. Environmental Protection Agency. "National Pollutant Discharge Elimination System," http://cfpub.epa.gov/npdes.

U.S. Environmental Protection Agency. "Polluted Runoff (Nonpoint Source Pollution)," www.epa.gov/nps.

U.S. Environmental Protection Agency. "Reducing Stormwater Costs through LID Strategies and Practices," www.epa.gov/owow/nps/lid/costs07/.

U.S. Environmental Protection Agency. "State Wetland Monitoring Programs," www.epa.gov/owow/wetlands/monitor/.

U.S. Environmental Protection Agency. BASINS 4.0, www.epa.gov/ost/basins.

U.S. Environmental Protection Agency. BASINS RF1 and RF3 by HUC: www.horizon-systems.com/nhdplus/tools.

U.S. Environmental Protection Agency. Clean Water State Revolving Fund: www.epa.gov/owm/cwfinance/cwsrf.

U.S. Environmental Protection Agency. Clean Waters Act Section 319: Laws, Regulations, Treaties, www.epa.gov/owow/nps/cwact.html.

U.S. Environmental Protection Agency. Climate Change—Health and Environmental Effects, "Water Resources": www.epa.gov/climatechange/effects/water/.

U.S. Environmental Protection Agency. *Field Operations Manual for Assessing the Hydrologic Permanence and Ecological Condition of Headwater Streams* (October 2006), www.epa.gov/eerd/manual/HISSmanual_full.pdf.

U.S. Environmental Protection Agency. *Getting in Step: A Guide to Effective Outreach in Your Watershed.* EPA 841-B-03-002, December 2003. www.epa.gov/owow/watershed/outreach/documents/getnstep.pdf.

U.S. Environmental Protection Agency. *Handbook for Developing Watershed Plans to Restore and Protect Our Waters.* EPA 841-B-08-002 (March 2008). www.epa.gov/owow/nps/watershed_handbook/.

U.S. Environmental Protection Agency. *Integrated Reporting Guidance*, www.epa.gov/owow/tmdl.

U.S. Environmental Protection Agency. *Manual Constructed Wetlands Treatment of Municipal Wastewaters.* EPA/625/R-99/010 (September 1999). www.epa.gov/nrmrl/pubs/625r99010/625r99010.pdf.

U.S. Environmental Protection Agency. *National Management Measures to Control Nonpoint Source Pollution from Hydromodification.* Chapter 4, "Dams," July, 2007. www.epa.gov/owow/nps/hydromod/index.htm.

U.S. Environmental Protection Agency. *National Management Measures to Control Nonpoint Source Pollution from Urban Areas.* "Management Measure 3: Watershed Protection," EPA-841-B-05-004 (November 2005). www.epa.gov/owow/nps/urbanmm/index.html.

U.S. Environmental Protection Agency. *National Management Measures to Control Nonpoint Source Pollution from Urban Areas*, "Management Measure 4: Site Development," EPA-841-B-05-004 (November 2005). www.epa.gov/owow/nps/urbanmm/index.html.

U.S. Environmental Protection Agency. *National Management Measures to Control Nonpoint Source Pollution from Hydromodification.* Chapter 5, "Streambank and Shoreline Erosion," July 2007. www.epa.gov/owow/nps/hydromod/index.htm.

U.S. Environmental Protection Agency. *National Management Measures to Control Nonpoint Source Pollution from Urban Areas.* "Management Measure 8: Construction Site Erosion, Sediment, and Chemical Control," EPA-841-B-05-004 (November 2005). www.epa.gov/owow/nps/urbanmm/index.html.

U.S. Environmental Protection Agency. *National Management Measures to Control Nonpoint Source Pollution from Hydromodification.* EPA 841-B-07-002 (July 2007). www.epa.gov/owow/nps/hydromod/index.htm.

U.S. Environmental Protection Agency. *National Management Measures to Control Nonpoint Source Pollution from Urban Areas.* "Management Measure 2: Watershed Assessment" EPA-841-B-05-004 (November 2005). www.epa.gov/owow/nps/urbanmm/index.html.

U.S. Environmental Protection Agency. *National Management Measures to Control Nonpoint Source Pollution from Urban Areas.* "Management Measure 5: New Development Runoff Treatment," EPA-841-B-05-004 (November 2005). www.epa.gov/owow/nps/urbanmm/index.html.

U.S. Environmental Protection Agency. *National Management Measures to Control Nonpoint Source Pollution from Urban Areas.* "Management Measure 6: New and Existing On-Site Wastewater Treatment Systems" (July 2007). www.epa.gov/owow/nps/hydromod/index.htm.

U.S. Environmental Protection Agency. *National Management Measures to Control Nonpoint Source Pollution from Urban Areas.* "Management Measure 9: Pollution Prevention," EPA-841-B-05-004 (November 2005). www.epa.gov/owow/nps/urbanmm/index.html.

U.S. Environmental Protection Agency. *Polluted Runoff (Nonpoint Source Pollution),* Tribal Nonpoint Source Program, www.epa.gov/owow/nps/tribal.html.

U.S. Environmental Protection Agency. Section 404 Discharge of Dredged and Fill Material: www.epa.gov/owow/invasive_species/invasives_management/cwa404.html.

U.S. Environmental Protection Agency. *Smart Growth Grants and Other Funding*, www.epa.gov/piedpage/grants/index.htm.

U.S. Environmental Protection Agency. *Smart Growth Implementation Assistance,* www.epa.gov/piedpage/sgia.htm.

U.S. Environmental Protection Agency. State Coastal Zone Management Programs: www.epa.gov/owow/nps/pubs.html.

U.S. Environmental Protection Agency. *Survey of the Nation's Lakes Fact Sheet.* November, 2006. www.epa.gov/owow/lakes/lakessurvey/lakessurveyfactsheet.pdf.

U.S. Environmental Protection Agency. *Survey of the Nation's Lakes: Integrated Quality Assurance Project Plan.* EPA/841-B-07-003 (2006 draft).

U.S. Environmental Protection Agency. Volunteer Monitoring Web site: www.epa.gov/owow/monitoring/volunteer.

U.S. Environmental Protection Agency. *Wadeable Streams Assessment: A Collaborative Survey of the Nation's Streams.* EPA 841-B-06-002 (December 2006). www.epa.gov/owow/streamsurvey.

U.S. Environmental Protection Agency. *Water Quality Trading.* www.epa.gov/owow/watershed/trading.htm.

U.S. Environmental Protection Agency. *Water Quality Trading Evaluation, Final Report* (October 2008). www.epa.gov/evaluate/wqt.pdf.

U.S. Environmental Protection Agency. *Water Quality Trading Toolkit for Permit Writers*. EPA 833-R-07-004 (August 2007). www.epa.gov/owow/watershed/trading/WQTToolkit.html.

U.S. Environmental Protection Agency. Office of Water Office of Policy, Economics, and Innovation. *A Benefits Assessment of Water Pollution Control Programs Since 1972: Part 1, The Benefits of Point Source Controls for Conventional Pollutants in Rivers and Streams* (January 2000). www.epa.gov/waterscience/economics/assessment.pdf.

U.S. Fish & Wildlife Service. National Fish Passage Program: www.fws.gov/fisheries/fwma/fishpassage.

U.S. Fish & Wildlife Services. *National Wetlands Inventory*, http://wetlands.fws.gov.

U.S. Fish & Wildlife Service. Partners for Fish and Wildlife Program: www.fws.gov/partners.

U.S. Forest Service. *A Forest Service's A Soil Bioengineering Guide for Streambank and Lakeshore Stabilization*, FS-683 (October 2002), www.fs.fed.us/publications/soil-bio-guide.

U.S. Geological Survey. "Ground Water," http://pubs.usgs.gov/gip/gw/gw_a.html.

U.S. Geological Survey. National Hydrography Dataset: http://nhd.usgs.gov.

UNESCO. "Aquifers of the World," www.whymap.org/cln_092/nn_1055978/whymap/EN/Downloads/Global__maps/whymap__125__pdf,templateId=raw,property=publicationFile.pdf/whymap_125_pdf.

USGS Washington Water Science Center. *Hydrology: The Study of Water and Water Problems A Challenge for Today and Tomorrow*, http://ga.water.usgs.gov/hydroprimer.html.

University of Georgia College of Agricultural and Environmental Sciences. "Georgia Drought," www.caes.uga.edu/topics/disasters/drought/.

UNFPA (The United Nations Population Fund. Executive Board Documents) Annual Report 2007. http://web.unfpa.org/exbrd/2007/2007_annual.htm.

Vetter, Joseph K. "Are We Running Out of Water?" *Reader's Digest* (May 2008). www.rd.com/your-america-inspiring-people-and-stories/americas-water-shortage-crisis/article55731.html.

Virginia Department of Conservation and Recreation. Annual Report on Cooperative Nonpoint Source Pollution Programs (2005 and 2006). Report Document No. 356. 2006. http://leg2.state.va.us/dls/h&sdocs.nsf/4d54200d7e28716385256ec1004f3130/1df1f8815ec65ef7852570bb006c7268?OpenDocument.

Virginia Department of Forestry. "Rain Gardens, Eco Swales, & Bio Swales." www.dof.virginia.gov/rfb/rain-gardens.shtml.

Walters, Dan. "California's Water War Heating Up," *Sacramento Bee*, March 3, 2008. www.sacbee.com/111/story/754740.html.

Ward, Diane Raines. *Water Wars: Drought, Flood, Folly and the Politics of Thirst*. New York: Riverhead Trade, 2002.

"Water Clears in Southeast's Largest Lake." Environment News Service, November 26, 2007. www.ens-newswire.com/ens/nov2007/2007-11-26-093.asp.

Water Integrity Network, 2009. www.waterintegritynetwork.net/.

Water Management Strategies to Weather the Effects of Global Warming. New York: Natural Resources Defense Council (July 2007). www.nrdc.org/globalWarming/hotwater/hotwater.pdf.

"Water Wars in South Becoming the Norm? Won't Be Long before Atlanta Tries to Build a Pipeline to Savannah River,' S.C. Official Says." Associated Press, October 14, 2008. www.ajc.com/news/content/metro/stories/2008/10/14/water_wars_south.html.

Water Wiki. "Riparian Rights," http://sogweb.sog.unc.edu/Water/index.php/Riparian_rights.

Wenk Associates. Prairie Trail Pattern Book. 2007. http://prairietrailankeny.com/assets/docs/A_Introduction.pdf.

"Western Water Woes Tied to Man-made Warming—Study Says 60 Percent of Changes over 50 Years Were Due to Human Factors." Associated Press, January 31, 2008. www.msnbc.msn.com/id/22935934/.

White, Iain. "Surface water management." *Encyclopedia of Earth*, March 9, 2007, www.eoearth.org/article/Surface_water_management.

Wikipedia contributors. "Drought in the United States," *Wikipedia, The Free Encyclopedia,* http://en.wikipedia.org/w/index.php?title=Drought_in_the_United_States&oldid=325528725.

Wodder, Rebecca. "Damming the Flint Is So Old-School." *Atlanta Journal-Constitution*, August 13, 2008. www.ajc.com/eveningedge/content/opinion/stories/2008/08/13/riversed.html?cxntlid=inform_sr.

Woodhouse, Betsy, "Reclamation Reflects on a Century of Water Projects." *Southwest Hydrology* 7, no. 5, September/October 2008.

Wright, Tiffany, et al. "Direct and Indirect Impacts of Urbanization on Wetland Quality Wetlands & Watersheds," Article 1. Office of Wetlands, Oceans and Watersheds, U.S. Environmental Protection Agency, December 2006.

Zeccola, Joni. "Georgia's Water Crisis: A Weekly Digest." *Atlanta Journal-Constitution*, March 2, 2008. www.ajc.com/eveningedge/content/metro/stories/2008/03/02/droughtpage0302.html?cxntlid=inform_artr.

Zinn, Jeffrey A. Resources, Science, and Industry Division. Coastal Wetlands Planning, Protection, and Restoration Act (CWPPRA): Effects of Hurricanes Katrina and Rita on Implementation. Congressional Research Service Report RS22467. 2007. http://stuff.mit.edu/afs/sipb/contrib/wikileaks-crs/wikileaks-crs-reports/RS22467.pdf.

Index

✳ Environmental Benefits Statement

This book is printed with soy-based inks on presses with VOC levels that are lower than the standard for the printing industry. The paper, Rolland Enviro 100, is manufactured by Cascades Fine Papers Group and is made from 100 percent post-consumer, de-inked fiber, without chlorine. According to the manufacturer, the use of every ton of Rolland Enviro100 Book paper, switched from virgin paper, helps the environment in the following ways:

Mature trees saved	Waterborne waste not created	Waterflow saved	Atmospheric emissions eliminated	Solid wastes reduced	Natural gas saved by using biogas
17	6.9 lbs.	10,196 gals.	2,098 lbs.	1,081 lbs.	2,478 cubic feet